Britain's Guerrilla Army

Britain's Guerrilla Army

Plans for a Secret War 1939–45

Malcolm Atkin

Pen & Sword
MILITARY

An imprint of
Pen & Sword Books Ltd
Yorkshire – Philadelphia

Pen & Sword
MILITARY

First published in Great Britain in 2024 by
PEN & SWORD MILITARY
An imprint of
Pen & Sword Books Ltd
Yorkshire – Philadelphia

Copyright © Malcolm Atkin, 2024

ISBN 978 1 39907 785 9

The right of Malcolm Atkin to be identified as Author of this work has been asserted by him in accordance with the Copyright, Designs and Patents Act 1988.

A CIP catalogue record for this book is available from the British Library

All rights reserved. No part of this book may be reproduced or transmitted in any form or by any means, electronic or mechanical including photocopying, recording or by any information storage and retrieval system, without permission from the Publisher in writing.

Typeset in Chennai, India
by Lapiz Digital Services.

Printed and bound by CPI UK

Pen & Sword Books Ltd incorporates the imprints of Pen & Sword
Archaeology, Atlas, Aviation, Battleground, Discovery, Family History, History, Maritime, Military, Naval, Politics, Social History, Transport, True Crime, Claymore Press, Frontline Books, Praetorian Press, Seaforth Publishing and White Owl

For a complete list of Pen & Sword titles please contact

PEN & SWORD BOOKS LTD
47 Church Street, Barnsley, South Yorkshire, S70 2AS, England
E-mail: enquiries@pen-and-sword.co.uk
Website: www.pen-and-sword.co.uk

Or

PEN AND SWORD BOOKS
1950 Lawrence Rd, Havertown, PA 19083, USA
E-mail: Uspen-and-sword@casematepublishers.com
Website: www.penandswordbooks.com

Contents

List of Illustrations vi
Abbreviations and Acronyms ix
Acknowledgements xii
Preface xiii

Introduction xv
Chapter 1: Attitudes to Ungentlemanly Warfare 1
Chapter 2: Playing the Long Game: the Resistance Organisation
    of Section VII, SIS 9
Chapter 3: The Impact of Dunkirk: Rethinking the Military Options 31
Chapter 4: Home Defence Scheme of Section D 42
Chapter 5: XII Corps Observation Unit 70
Chapter 6: The GHQ Auxiliary Units: Operational Wing 1940–1:
    Resisting the Invader 76
Chapter 7: Auxiliary Units (Operations), 1942–4: A New Purpose 122
Chapter 8: Auxiliary Units (Special Duties Branch), 1940:
    Anti-Invasion Reporting 141
Chapter 9: Auxiliary Units (Special Duties Branch), 1942–4:
    Internal Security and D-Day Planning 160
Chapter 10: GHQ Liaison Regiment (Phantom) 169
Chapter 11: Home Guard Saboteurs, Guerrillas and 'Shock Troops' 175
Conclusions 188

Appendix 1 – Directive 16 195
Appendix 2 – Key Personalities 199
Notes 211
Bibliography 233
Index 237

List of Illustrations

Figures in Text

Fig. 1	Sketch of the 1943 Section VII, SIS secret wireless station at 135 Smedley Street, Matlock.	22
Fig. 2	Known officers of the Home Defence Scheme.	46
Fig. 3	Inventory of Home Defence Scheme Dumps, dated 31 May 1940.	52
Fig. 4	Material simultaneously supplied by SIS to the Home Defence Scheme and the Auxiliary Units in July 1940.	63
Fig. 5	Auxiliary Units Intelligence Officers, 1940.	86
Fig. 6	Auxiliary Units Explosives Dumps (Small). July 1940.	92
Fig. 7	Auxiliary Units Explosives Dumps (Large), July 1940.	92
Fig. 8	Reconstruction and plan of Auxiliary Units Operational Base (based on that at Alfrick, Worcestershire).	99
Fig. 9	Weapons for twelve-man Scout Section, March 1942.	116
Fig. 10	Contemporary tally of Operation Patrols created up to 1 September 1940.	118
Fig. 11	Operational Patrols, Auxiliary Units by density in counties, September 1940 and June 1944.	118
Fig. 12	Contents of 'Aux. Unit Mk II' explosives pack as introduced in December 1942.	123
Fig. 13	List of Auxiliary Units Operational Patrol weapons, August 1942.	126
Fig. 14	Extract from War Establishment for Special Duties Branch, 11 July 1940.	145
Fig. 15	Extract from War Establishment for Auxiliary Units (Signals), February 1941.	154
Fig. 16	Organisational responsibility for Special Duties Branch, June 1944.	156
Fig. 17	Extract from War Establishment Auxiliary Units (Signals), March 1942.	157
Fig. 18	Extract from War Establishment Auxiliary Units (Signals), April 1942, after decision to expand SDB.	157
Fig. 19	Extract from War Establishment Auxiliary Units (Signals), February 1943.	157
Fig. 20	Extract from War Establishment Auxiliary Units (Signals), June 1944.	157

Plates

Plate 1	Sir Stewart Menzies (1890–1968).
Plate 2	Sir Claude Dansey (1876–1947).
Plate 3	Laurence Grand (1898–1975).
Plate 4	Walter Samuel, 2nd Viscount Bearsted (1882–1948).
Plate 5	Jo Holland (1897–1956)
Plate 6	Dr Arthur Straton (1884–1943).
Plate 7	Peter Fleming (1907–71).
Plate 8	General Andrew Thorne (1885–1970).
Plate 9	'Spuggy' Newton of SIS fitting a wireless set into a car.
Plate 10	Sir Colin Gubbins (1896–1976).
Plate 11	Colonel 'Bill' Major (1893–1977).
Plate 12	Maurice Petherick (1894–1985).
Plate 13	Colonel Frank Douglas, last CO of the Auxiliary Units.
Plate 14	John Todd (1899–1980).
Plate 15	David Boyle (1883–1970).
Plate 16	*Stay Where You Are* leaflet.
Plate 17	Shoulder badges of Home Guard, GHQ, XII Corps Observation Unit and Phantom.
Plate 18	HDS Weapons.
Plate 19	Tyesule paraffin incendiary.
Plate 20	Rodgers sheath knife and Fairbairn-Sykes fighting knife.
Plate 21	Colt .32 semi-automatic pistol and Colt .38 'Official Police' revolver.
Plate 22	Welrod bolt-action silenced pistol.
Plate 23	M1918 Browning Automatic Rifle (BAR).
Plate 24	Thompson M1928A1 sub-machine gun.
Plate 25	Mk II and Mk III Sten guns.
Plate 26	Type D Mk V field telephone.
Plate 27	Winchester Model 69 rifle with scope and suppressor.
Plate 28	Type 77 phosphorous grenade.
Plate 29	Page from *Calendar 1937* training manual for the Auxiliary Units.
Plate 30	Auxiliary Units training manual *Countryman's Diary* (1944).
Plate 31	Instructions for making up a half-pound unit charge, from *Countryman's Diary* (1944).
Plate 32	Time Pencils, early and late with L Delay.
Plate 33a	Distribution map of SDB, June 1944.
Plate 34	Murphy B81 portable battery-powered wireless (1939).

Plate 35	TRD set for IN Station (replica).
Plate 36	WS17 Mk II wireless set.
Plate 37	SIS Mk VII 'Paraset' transceiver.
Plate 38	'Keep Mum' poster.
Plate 39	Star Brewery, Eastbourne, Sussex.
Plate 40	Section VII wireless station on Smedley Street, Matlock, Derbyshire.
Plate 41	Some of the original 'Bachelors Hall Gang' who built the TRD wireless.
Plate 42	Home Guard Part II Orders, September 1941.
Plate 43	Home Guard Part II Orders, October 1941.
Plate 44	Stand-down letter to Auxiliary Units, November 1944 and lapel badge.
Plate 45	Tom Wintringham lecturing at Osterley Park Training School.
Plate 46	Home Guard instruction in the use of a remote electrical detonator at Osterley Home Guard Training School in 1940.

Abbreviations and Acronyms

ADGB	Air Defence of Great Britain Command which coordinated the air defence of Britain (fighter aircraft and AA guns) until the formation of Fighter Command in 1936.
Abwehr	German Intelligence Organisation.
ATS	Auxiliary Territorial Service. Women's army organisation.
BEF	British Expeditionary Force (France 1939–40).
BRO	British Resistance Organisation. The erroneous modern designation previously applied to the Auxiliary Units.
CIGS	Chief of the Imperial General Staff.
CSS	Chief of the Secret Service (SIS). Commonly abbreviated as 'C'.
DCO	Director of Combined Operations.
DMI	Directorate of Military Intelligence.
DNI	Directorate of Naval Intelligence.
Electra House	Secret government organisation responsible for conducting psychological warfare. In July 1940 it was merged into the newly-formed Special Operations Executive (SOE).
FANY	First Aid Nursing Yeomanry. Used as a cover for female operatives of SOE.
FSS	Field Security Sections of Military Intelligence Corps. Until July 1940 part of D Division, MI5.
G-2	Irish Intelligence Service.
GHQ	General Headquarters, Home Forces.
HAC	Honourable Artillery Company. Territorial regiment with post-war special forces functions.
HDB	Home Defence Battalions. Unsuccessful attempt in November 1939 to attract retired soldiers for guarding vulnerable points etc within the UK.
HDE	Home Defence Executive. Created on 10 May 1940 under chairmanship of General Ironside, C-in-C Home Forces, to coordinate anti-invasion planning.
HD(S)E	Home Defence (Security) Executive. Created on 28 May 1940 to consider matters of internal security and defence against the 5th Column.

HDM	Home Defence Movement. Small cover organisation of the British Union of Fascists.
HDO	Home Defence Organisation. Alternative name for what is termed here the Home Defence Scheme (HDS).
HDS	Home Defence Scheme. Intelligence and sabotage organisation created in 1940 by Section D of SIS, otherwise known in 1940 as the Regional D Scheme.
HDU	Home Defence Units. RAF/RN coastal wireless monitoring stations as part of the Y Intercept Service.
IRA	Irish Republican Army.
ISIS	Irish Supplementary Intelligence Service.
ISPB	Inter-Services Project Board. Created in April 1940 to coordinate proposals between War Office, Naval and Air Force Intelligence services and SIS for the development of British irregular warfare. Chaired by Col. Jo Holland of MI(R).
LDV	Local Defence Volunteers. Forerunner of the Home Guard.
MI5	Secret Security Service, responsible for counter-espionage operations within the UK. Ceased to be a section of the War Office in 1931 and henceforth its official title became the Security Service, as an interdepartmental intelligence agency. The name MI5 was retained as a popular abbreviation and it took some while for the War Office to realise that the change had been made!
MI6	Popular alternative name of Secret Intelligence Service (SIS). Although it frequently used a War Office address, it was controlled by the Foreign Office rather than Military Intelligence.
MI8	Cover name for the RSS Radio Security Service which used volunteer 'hams' to intercept enemy wireless traffic.
MI(R)	Military Intelligence (Research). War Office counterpart of Section D, SIS.
OB	Operational Base (underground hides of the Operational Patrols, Auxiliary Units).
OP	Observation Post
RDS	Regional D Scheme for Home Defence. Alternative name for the Home Defence Scheme (HDS) of Section D, SIS.
RSLO	Regional Security Liaison Officer (MI5).
RSS	Radio Security Service, responsible for the interception of enemy wireless traffic using detector vans and secret volunteer interceptors.
SAS	Special Air Service.

SCU	Special Communications Unit of SIS. The wireless unit that passed on intelligence to the SLU for onward transmission to the military.
SDB	Special Duties Branch, Auxiliary Units (aka Special Duties Organisation or Special Duties Section).
Section B.26	Joint MI5/ SIS section that allowed SIS to legally operate in the UK. Created in August 1940 under the cover of Section B, MI5.
Section D	Sabotage section of SIS, 1938–40 (aka Section IX of SIS or Statistical Research Department of the War Office).
Section V	Counter-espionage section of SIS.
SIS	Secret Intelligence Service (aka MI6). Controlled by Foreign Office but its existence was not officially acknowledged until 1994!
SLU	Special Liaison Unit of SIS. Responsible for deciphering the intelligence received by the SCU and passing it on to the military.
SOE	Special Operations Executive. Sabotage organisation formed in 1940 on the basis of the amalgamation of Electra House, Section D and MI(R).
TAA	Territorial Army Association.
TNA	The National Archives.
TRD	Duplex wireless set developed for the SDB.
Y Service	Signals Interception Service, with stations run by all three services together with SIS and the Post Office.

Acknowledgements

Much of my early research was inspired by John Warwicker, who broke down the barriers of secrecy around the subject and opened up new avenues of enquiry. Thanks are also due to Stephen Sutton for permission to quote from his unpublished undergraduate thesis of 1995 and for making available documents provided by the Foreign Office SOE Advisor in the late 1990s. The important series of audio interviews that Stephen conducted with Auxiliary Units veterans are now available through the Imperial War Museum audio collection. Personal thanks is also owed to Mick Wilks who pioneered the study of the topic locally, originally as part of the Defence of Britain project in the mid-1990s and latterly as the Defence of Worcestershire project. Together, we enjoyed a number of reunions with some, by now, grand old men. Peter Kindred and the volunteers at the British Resistance Museum at Parham, Suffolk were unfailingly friendly and helpful in opening up their unique archive. The museum itself is well worth a visit and details can be found at http://www.parhamairfieldmuseum.co.uk. The online resource of www.staybehinds.com is also an invaluable resource for details on individual patrols and a particular thanks is owed to Will Ward of Coleshill Auxiliary Research Team (CART) for many discussions regarding the complexities of the Auxiliary Units over the years. A special thanks is owed to the late Peter Attwater for his reminiscences of his time as a resistance wireless operator and for opening up new lines of enquiry, and to Eric Nussen for his memory of nocturnal events in Derbyshire. Many other people have patiently answered queries during the course of compiling the book. It was a great privilege to meet Madeleine Countess Bessborough and Elizabeth Holland – the daughters of Laurence Grand and Jo Holland respectively – who were both able to provide personal insights into these pioneers of irregular warfare. Thanks to Stewart Angell, David Blair, Lucy Bradley, Fred Judge (Military Intelligence Museum, Chicksands) and Sallie Mogford for sharing their information. Thanks also to the sources of the illustrations: Jeff Abendshien, East Sussex County Council Library & Information Service, John Farthing, former Army Medal Office (Droitwich), Imperial War Museum, the Royal Armouries, The National Archives, National Portrait Gallery, Geoffrey Pidgeon, Piers Pottinger, David Sampson, Troendelag Folk Museum (Norway), Getty Images and Corbis. Susanne and Kate Atkin kindly provided additional photography.

This book would not have been possible without the assistance of Lee Richards at ARCRE Document Copying Service (www.arcre.com), allowing a quick and cost-effective remote access to the documents held at The National Archives. Thanks are also owed to Charles Hewitt and the staff of Pen and Sword for seeing the book through the publication process.

As ever, my final thanks go to my wife, Susanne, for her unfailing support and patience during the research of this book, and for compiling the index.

All responsibility for speculation and conclusions remains my own.

Preface

In 2015, the publication of *Fighting Nazi Occupation* forensically unpicked many of the myths that had grown up around the secret plans to oppose a Nazi invasion. The book placed the often misunderstood Auxiliary Units, then erroneously labelled 'the British Resistance Organisation', in its wider strategic context and provided the first detailed account of the actual British resistance network, known by its cover name of Section VII in SIS (MI6), together with a re-assessment of the role of Section D's Home Defence Scheme. Key to the analysis was an application of the British wartime distinction between short-term guerrilla warfare undertaken to support an on-going military campaign and a longer-term resistance conducted outside the accepted rules of war by civilians. *Britain's Guerrilla Army* updates the 2015 publication, refining the arguments and conclusions as originally presented and incorporating the results of subsequent research gathered during work on detailed histories of Section D of SIS and the Military Intelligence (Research) department of the War Office (see Atkin 2017, Atkin 2021 and Atkin 2023). These later publications have also made redundant some of the information on these organisations originally contained in *Fighting Nazi Occupation* and so are omitted in the new work. Such was the wide range of disparate efforts, there was not a single 'guerrilla army' but the different organisations worked towards the single purpose of defeating the enemy, however long that might take and at whatever cost, fulfilling Churchill's rallying cry that Britain would 'never surrender'.

The most significant of the secret organisations were those formed by SIS or which fell under its influence, and although there is now a greater awareness of its work, the details are still shrouded in the official cloak of secrecy that surrounds all aspects of SIS, present and past. Complicating the issue are snippets of evidence relating to more or less unofficial efforts to prepare for guerrilla warfare and resistance, born out of a popular desire to resist at all costs. Much remains that is speculative and stories relating to secret work are frequently uncorroborated, liable to be influenced by previous publications or be subject to 'False Memory Syndrome' and a temptation to embroider any connections to secret war work.

The best-known of the clandestine groups are the GHQ Auxiliary Units, whose profile has been boosted by the romantic mystery of its buried bases as well as the relative ease of recording the memories of men and women who remained in their local areas. There is also now a wealth of documentary evidence that lay unsuspected or was unavailable when modern research began in the late 1980s. A great deal of mythology has accumulated around the Auxiliary Units and the dissection of the popular narrative is not intended to diminish an appreciation of the self-sacrificial courage of the Auxiliary Units' veterans in preparing for invasion, but rather to establish their true role within the secret war effort. Indeed, the study highlights the scale of sacrifice that was expected of the men and women in all the clandestine groups, as well as the beach defenders, Home Guard, Observer Corps and Coastguard Service who would collectively buy time with their lives to enable the army to launch its counter-attack.

Fascinating as the story of clandestine warfare is, it is important to place this within the wider strategic context and so the intelligence efforts of Section D and the Auxiliary Units in 1940 are assessed against the work of the GHQ Reconnaissance Unit (Phantom) which was itself classed as an 'irregular' unit and whose founder, George Hopkinson, made the calculated decision to promote the unit as 'secret' because he believed this would increase the chance of it getting better resources – a lesson learned by other organisations in this story.

Introduction

> We shall fight in the fields and in the streets, we shall fight in the hills; we shall never surrender.
>
> Winston Churchill, 4 June 1940

When Prime Minister Winston Churchill made his famous 'we shall never surrender' speech on 4 June 1940, Britain's Secret Intelligence Service (SIS aka MI6) was already mobilising two civilian organisations to oppose an enemy invasion and, if necessary, continue the fight after occupation. Both organisations were established against official government policy and against the international rules of war. For those few individuals in the military or government who knew of such plans, there was discomfort about the supposed defeatism that preparing for enemy occupation implied and the lack of British 'fair play' in using non-uniformed combatants. The plans did, however, spur the War Office into including a more respectable element of irregular warfare into its wider defence plan, following the initiative of General Thorne in Kent and Sussex, by utilising the new Home Guard as the basis of the GHQ Auxiliary Units. The latter would contribute to the disruption of advancing German troops and their supply lines and hopefully similarly impede their retreat, so securing total annihilation of the invader. The competing approaches of SIS and the War Office crystallised the contemporary conflict over the role of civilians in combat. Supplementing these official initiatives, there is evidence for a raft of more or less unofficial efforts to create local guerrilla or resistance bodies, with hints of involvement by SIS, but steeped in the contemporary fascination with the tales of Lawrence of Arabia and the new best-seller *For Whom The Bell Tolls* by Ernest Hemingway. The plans for irregular warfare in 1940 can consequently appear disjointed and overlapping, although this served the purpose of SIS to obscure the core of its work. The novelty of these new approaches to warfare also meant that terms such as 'guerrilla' or 'irregular' warfare could sometimes be loosely used. Thus General Ironside, the C-in-C Home Forces, described the GHQ Reconnaissance Unit (Phantom) as a 'special irregular unit' because it did not conform to the conventional regimental hierarchy (Chapter 10).

The British government had considered the possibility of war with Germany as soon as Hitler took power in 1933, with a chillingly accurate estimate that Germany would be ready to take the offensive in 1938 or 1939.[1] Not all were convinced by Prime Minister Chamberlain's 'Peace In Our Time' deal at Munich in September 1938, especially Admiral Sinclair, the head of SIS, who had already begun to extend its traditional role of intelligence-gathering abroad into plans for propaganda, political warfare and sabotage, particularly through the new Section D (the 'sabotage service') under Laurence Grand which in May 1940 created the Home Defence Scheme (HDS) for guerrilla warfare in Britain (see Chapter 4). Separately, and known only to a small core of senior staff, SIS had already begun to secretly prepare for the possibility of the occupation of the British Isles. The result was a major shift in the remit of SIS to operate within the

British Isles and its creation in February/March 1940 of a British resistance, concealed within the SIS accountancy branch of Section VII (Chapter 2). Also known vaguely as 'DB's organisation', this would have formed the basis of the British Resistance hidden beneath the cover of the later shorter-term efforts of their colleagues in Section D and the War Office Auxiliary Units. Section VII could be regarded as one of SIS's greatest triumphs of secrecy during the Second World War. Its existence was not revealed until mentioned in a single paragraph in Keith Jeffery's *MI6* in 2010, with the first detailed account in *Fighting Nazi Occupation* (Atkin 2015). The organisation continued in operation until at least 1944, readying for intelligence-gathering, sabotage and the creation of escape lines for fugitives. As a last resort it was positioned to supply intelligence to a government-in-exile and prepare for eventual liberation, either through an implosion of what was considered the fragile Nazi state or by the entry of the USA into the war.

During late 1939 and early 1940 both the top-secret Section D of SIS and the publicly-acknowledged Military Intelligence (Research) department (MI(R)) of the War Office had been evangelical in urging nations under threat of invasion to prepare plans for guerrilla warfare.[2] The remit of the two organisations, often partners but sometimes rivals, was for Section D to secretly organise civilian saboteurs whilst MI(R) focused on a more respectable military approach, in consultation with the national governments. A clear distinction was made between plans for short-term guerrilla warfare in support of a field army, attacking the supply lines of the enemy forces in the rear or on its flanks, and a structurally separate longer-term resistance to follow any occupation. It was stressed that there should be minimal contact between the two. Even so, few took the possibility of the invasion of Britain seriously until the speed of the *blitzkrieg* across the Low Countries and France caused a wave of panic across the British establishment. Thus, even though Section D and MI(R) had both studied the measures for guerrilla warfare that Poland and Czechoslovakia had put in place before the invasion of their countries, no plans for guerrilla warfare to support a military defence plan began to be considered until the retreat from France in May 1940 (Chapter 3). During the evacuation from Dunkirk it was Section D that took the initiative in immediately creating the civilian HDS, as a new guerrilla force distinct from the existing deep-cover Section VII resistance. This was a layered compartmentalisation that had just been promoted in Norway but, when threatened with disbandment following opposition from the War Office, there grew a confusion as to whether the HDS would become more of a resistance force, ready to replace the Auxiliary Units in action once the latter were wiped out. This risked competing with Section VII and there was consequently some relief in SIS when the HDS was shut down, officially passing all responsibility for guerrilla warfare during an invasion campaign to the military.

The War Office had quickly realised it risked losing the initiative to what it saw as the threat of a private army under SIS control and, following an individual initiative by General Thorne in XII Corps to form a local military alternative (Chapter 5), hurriedly introduced wider plans to bring guerrilla warfare in the potential coastal invasion zones under military control through the Auxiliary Units (Chapter 6), whilst other Army Corps may well have pursued similar, less well-documented, local initiatives. War Office frustration led to a concerted effort to pour scorn upon the efforts of Laurence Grand and Section D, but delays in fully mobilising the Auxiliary Units meant that it was the HDS that would have provided the main guerrilla organisation to oppose a

Nazi invasion if it had occurred in the summer of 1940, whilst Section VII laid down the foundation for a longer-term resistance. These official bodies were all secret but the well-publicised popular appetite for guerrilla warfare meant that the Nazis would have been well aware in broad terms of the likely threat that they would face from irregular warfare. These included the Home Guard guerrillas trained by Tom Wintringham at the Osterley Park Home Guard Training School, whose lessons were quickly disseminated in local training schools across the country (Chapter 11). By the end of September 1940 Osterley Park had trained more guerrillas than the Auxiliary Units and, along with their secret role of industrial saboteurs, was a role of the Home Guard far from the comedic bumbling image of the late 1960s/70s TV series *Dad's Army*. As the strength of conventional forces improved towards the end of 1940, not for the last time in the Second World War the General Staff sought to dispense with irregular warfare with proposals for the disbanding of the Auxiliary Units. Meanwhile the responsibility of planning for the unthinkable possibility of a country under enemy occupation remained in the hands of the unavowed SIS.

Although the influence of SIS is pervasive, its policy of not revealing details of staff or operations (past or present) and the equal reluctance of its veterans to break their silence has had a major impact on the focus of historical studies, distorting the overall strategic picture. Both during and after the war not-disinterested detractors could focus on a small number of errors by the HDS but any challenge to this perspective was not encouraged by SIS. It may be supposed that SIS shared the view of a CIA analyst in 1969 on the Second World War *Lucy* spy ring:

> The profession of intelligence may owe some duty to Clio [the mythological muse of history], but it cannot be said to be the general one of cleansing all confusions and deliberate disinformation from the public record about intelligence matters.[3]

Many of the records of the SIS operations were destroyed in a purge during the invasion scares of 1940 or post-war in an era of long-running official paranoia over the existence of the wartime secret services. The surviving files of Section D were first passed to SOE in whose hands there were similarly purges towards the end of the war. The files passed back to SIS in 1946 and almost immediately afterwards a small fire in the former Baker Street HQ of SOE was used as an excuse to explain the destruction of further intelligence records. The small fire mainly damaged some FANY files but it served as a useful excuse to avoid disclosure of records of officers who had a connection to SIS. Later, in 1949 another weeding of documents reputedly resulted in the destruction of 100 tons of material![4] A detailed history of Section D was compiled in late 1943 by Anthony Samuel, then in SOE but a former Section D officer and son of Viscount Bearsted; it was notably reticent about the HDS that had been led by his father.[5] Early post-war published accounts of the work of SIS operations in Britain, confined to knowledge only of Section D, were mainly provided as a preface to histories of SOE, and relied heavily on Colin Gubbins (former head of the Auxiliary Units and SOE) as a source. Gubbins (Plate 10) had a deep-rooted resentment of Section D and so not surprisingly tended to be dismissive and even scathing. Mackenzie mentioned the HDS only briefly in his otherwise comprehensive summary of the work of Section D in the first official history of SOE.[6] Following the tone set later by Lampe, again advised by Gubbins, Foot wrote off Section

D's attempts to create stay-behind units during the fraught months of 1940 as incompetent.[7] Thereafter almost any embarrassment was likely to be blamed on Section D. David Stafford's opinion was that the work 'became a fiasco: too many of its organisers were arrested as German agents while preparing ammunition dumps and expanding badger sets as underground HQs'.[8] Stafford here conflated HDS experience with early Auxiliary Units disasters where underground hides and buried radio sets were discovered. The sheer scale of the HDS and its influence on the Auxiliary Units, which Gubbins had been reluctant to acknowledge, was not appreciated. As further sources have been made public or have been re-discovered in obscure government files within The National Archives, other historians have been more charitable about the work of Section D overall. In 2004 Davies suggested that there had been a 'systematic undervaluation' of the achievements of Section D.[9]

The history of the GHQ Auxiliary Units is now more accessible. Contrary to early assumptions it is well-documented in The National Archives, bolstered by the oral history of its veterans and given impetus by the romantic mystique of its surviving hidden operational bases. A well-entrenched mythology has, however, created an imbalance in the perception of their significance. The long-assumed wall of silence on their activities that seemed to prove their significance was neither immediate nor complete. In November 1944 the War Office requested the submission of a detailed report by 15 January 1945 to set out 'a complete historical record, and to facilitate the formation of a similar organisation should it be needed in the future'.[10] A draft of this had already been prepared by the Training Officer, Nigel Oxenden, with an intended title of *Auxiliary Units, History and Final Teaching* but was apparently never completed.[11] Some of its less-complimentary conclusions have been studiously avoided in more modern accounts. There was an official press release in 1945 on the work of the Auxiliary Units followed by newspaper reports which were driven by a nationalist need to find a British equivalent to compete with the now famous European resistance movements. Reuters circulated the story internationally that 'Britain had secret army'. A brief account was even published in the service newspaper *Sunday SEAC* on 15 April 1945, describing 'an elaborately organised maquis'.[12] *The Times* obtained a copy of the stand-down letter to the Special Duties Branch (SDB) and an account was published on 12 April 1945 under the heading 'Britain's Secret "Underground" – Invasion Spy Force Stood Down'. It went on to explain the 'home underground' force had wireless sets, messengers, code clerks and 'about 300 specially picked officers of the Army Special Duties Branch to guide their work'. On 14 June, the *Western Morning News* ran another story on the 'British Maquis', describing the work of both the Operational Patrols and the SDB. The comparison was flawed in that the French *Maquis* fulfilled the concept of MI(R) that a popular army of the interior should rise up prior to external liberation, rather than be formed at the outset of enemy occupation. Such terminology provided a basis for later myth. An imaginative account of plans for an underground war was contained in E.H. Cookridge (Edward Spiro) *Secrets of the British Secret Service* (1948) conflating the work of several organisations under the broad heading of 'British Secret Service'. Cookridge describes a 'highly efficient and most secret organisation of "British Maquis"' including 'the very cream of the country's man and woman power'. Some details are hazy versions of known facts but others are pure journalistic invention, written in the knowledge that they were unlikely to be officially disputed. A more informed article in *The Spectator* by Peter Fleming on the XII Corps Observation Unit was published in 1952, and a rather prosaic summary of the role of the Auxiliary Units by Collier was included in the 1957 volume of the *Official History of the Second World War* dealing with Home Defence. Here, with no sense of mystery, it was recorded 'Auxiliary Units were trained to work in the rear of an invader, harrying his advancing columns and cutting them off from supplies of water, food and petrol'. Collier continued: 'Thus an enemy who landed would find himself opposed, not only by a Field Army supported by substantial bomber and fighter forces and backed by the Home Guard, but also by patrols emerging from hidden centres to check his advance and strike at his communications.'[13] It should, therefore, be no surprise to see a broader discussion of the Auxiliary Units in Fleming's 1957 *Invasion 1940*.[14] It was, however, David Lampe's pioneering publication of *The Last Ditch* in 1968 that really brought the Auxiliary Units to public attention and associated them with the label 'British Resistance'. Not yet appreciating how biased Colin Gubbins was as a source, the book was accepted almost without question by historians and was avidly read by veterans. This then became part of their memory when they began to tell their stories decades later. *The Last Ditch* introduced a flawed mythology that has been hard to dispel. The next generation of researchers, one of the earliest being the Hailsham History Group whose work was published in 1986, focused on local studies based on veterans' accounts at a time when information on a national framework was still sketchy. The Hailsham study conflated the work of Section D with the Auxiliary Units and termed them 'Special Groups' who would take military action to support the mobile reserve of the field army. This, like Arthur Ward's *A Nation Alone* (1989), carefully avoided the 'Resistance' tag, but as interest grew so did the attraction of a simple marketable label. By 1996, with as yet no knowledge of the existence of Section VII, the assumption that the Auxiliary Units was the 'British Resistance' had taken firm hold. The British Resistance Organisation Museum at Parham, Suffolk, dedicated to the Auxiliary Units, opened in 1997. The Auxiliary Units were now considered 'on a par with the famous French Resistance'.[15] In this atmosphere, the failure at the time to find any official documents naming the Auxiliary Units as the 'British Resistance Organisation' was only seen as evidence of a security blanket that in itself proved their importance. Warwicker explained in 2022 how the confusion had arisen: 'if in doubt about any secret discoveries, we were to contact a certain individual with a Whitehall telephone number. When contact was established with him, he asserted, with some emphasis: "I have one hundred and fifty thousand WW2 organisations to declassify, and I can't even find the British Resistance Organisation!" Of course, he could not, simply because we had given him the wrong name!'.[16] In fact, some documents regarding the Auxiliary Units had been released into the public domain as early as the mid-1970s.

If British efforts to oppose Nazi invasion could only be contextualised within a vision of European resistance movements, continuing the wartime Anglocentric view of the conflict, there grew a nationalistic assumption that Britain must have been the pioneers in this field – ignoring planning in Poland, Norway, Hungary, Romania and elsewhere.[17] Despite the accumulation of evidence to the contrary, and reservations expressed by Warwicker in 2008 and Ward in 2013 about the readiness to attach a 'resistance' label, without an alternative model there was a reluctance to abandon the media appeal of a 'British Resistance Organisation'; this has obscured the real purpose and significance of the Operational Patrols of the Auxiliary Units as a uniformed commando force supporting an active military campaign.[18] Interpretation of the Auxiliary Units' role also suffered from an initial reliance on a 'bottom-up' perspective from the surviving local veterans, who were to be left to their own devices once having 'gone to ground', and whose opinions were influenced by their Intelligence Officers who sometimes had their own vision of official policy and were also concerned to boost the morale of the volunteers. There was also an element in building the mythology to redress the 'guilt' that many veterans remembered about not being able to explain their secret wartime role to neighbours. Most obviously, in an era where visions of the Home Guard were distorted by the popular TV series *Dad's Army*, there was a natural inclination to over-emphasise the distinction between the Auxiliary Units and the regular Home Guard, even to the point of claiming they would fight as 'civilians'. As early as 1957, Peter Fleming (himself a pioneer of the XII Corps Observation Unit) had written a warning on the use of oral history in *Invasion 1940*.

> Yet legend plays a large part in their memories of that tense and strangely exhilarating summer, and their experiences, like those of early childhood, are sharply rather than accurately etched upon their minds. The stories they tell of the period have become better, but not more veracious, with the passage of time. Rumours are remembered as facts, and – particularly since anti-invasion precautions continued in force for several years after the Germans had renounced their project – the sequence of events is blurred.[19]

If true in 1957, this reliance on oral history was much more problematic in the 1990s when veterans first began to tell their stories, their memories now influenced by the accumulated mythology. Former Intelligence Officer Stuart Edmundson offered a warning in 1998: 'many glamourised stories have come out on the media, told by the warriors themselves. Membership of A. U. was the big event of their young lives.'[20] When Arthur Ward began collecting accounts in the mid-1990s the term most used by the veterans was 'Scout Sections' – a good description of their role in relationship to the regular army.[21] Steadily they adopted the popular mythology and became a 'resistance'. Thus, when the Special Duties Workshop Officer Ken Ward wrote in 2000 he admitted he had 'done some reading' since his earlier interviews and incorporated what are now known to be wholly inaccurate statements from Foot 1984 and Wilkinson and Astley 1993 into his first-hand account.[22]

A major concern in 1940 was to improve the quality of immediate intelligence on the location and scale of any enemy landings. Existing organisations such as the Coastguard Service and Observer Corps, using telephone systems, were quickly incorporated and it also became the role that provided at least a nominal legitimacy for Section VII to operate within Britain. The new HDS and Auxiliary Units also included civilian intelligence networks that, it was optimistically hoped, would pass on information to the regular forces during an active military campaign (Chapters 4 and 8). Created in a rush, their networks in 1940 were, however, built around a more static vision of warfare than a rapid *blitzkrieg*, using the traditional methodology of couriers and 'dead-letter drops', rather than modern wireless communication. Romantic as such schemes might seem now, they bore no comparison to the ability of the new army GHQ Reconnaissance

Unit and a proper appreciation of the role of the HDS and SDB can only come by direct comparison (Chapter 10). These intelligence networks remain the least well-known of the clandestine operations in Britain. Those involved tended to be in the older age range which meant that its members had largely passed away before it was seen as acceptable to tell one's story. They also had a secret that they were perhaps unwilling to make known to their neighbours – that one of their key roles was as part of the highly sensitive internal security monitoring of their neighbours and locally-stationed troops during the Second World War. Although referred to in only one official document, this may well be the most significant wartime contribution of the Auxiliary Units (Chapter 9).

It may never be possible to unravel the full story of the clandestine activities in Britain during the war, thanks to the enduring pride in their secrecy of the wartime SIS. One can do no better than repeat the broad conclusion as regards the organisation of British Intelligence as reached by the Gestapo in 1940:

> Nobody can truthfully say the service is organised in such and such a way, is located here or there, or employs this or that person who does this or that task. If any details about the British Intelligence Service are ever made known or published by the English, one can be sure that only those authorities and officers whose existence cannot be hidden in the long term will be highlighted.[23]

The following study focusses on the philosophy behind the various initiatives and their place within the wider context of the defence of Britain. Developments were greatly affected by the personalities of those involved and, as a consequence, thumbnail biographies of the key figures have been provided (see Appendix 2). The story is, by necessity, highly speculative in places, based as it is on surviving snippets of evidence. There remain significant gaps, confusions and conflicts of evidence as one might expect in trying to reconstruct the narrative of a successful secret intelligence operation. Some pieces of evidence simply do not fit the jigsaw and it is only possible to broadly suggest who might be responsible for their activities and to try to 'join up the dots' along the path of least resistance. It is hoped that this book might help stimulate a continuing re-assessment of existing information and the testing of any future evidence that might be released into the public domain by the intelligence agencies. Sadly, the opportunity to ask questions of those directly involved in this secret war has now almost completely passed.

Chapter 1

Attitudes to Ungentlemanly Warfare

> The preparations which are being made all over England to arm the civilian population for guerrilla warfare are contrary to the rules of international law. German official quarters warn the misled British public and remind them of the fate of the Polish francs-tireurs and gangs of murderers. Civilians who take up arms against German soldiers are, under international law, no better than murderers, whether they be priests or bank clerks. British people you will do well to heed our warning!
>
> German radio broadcast, 16 May 1940[1]

Modern society is used to wars waged by paramilitaries without formal uniform or identifiable badges of rank, but this was *not* the case in 1940, although the battle landscape was to quickly change during the course of the war. It is therefore important to consider the wider context of what was considered acceptable behaviour in warfare and how this informed the controversy over the role of civilians in combat that took place in Britain in 1940.

For centuries the armies of Europe marched into battle in ordered lines, announcing their presence by the beat of the drum and wearing brightly-coloured uniforms so that all would know for whom they fought, but in the early nineteenth century the French had to face the irregular Spanish *guerrilleros* who fought their 'little war' against Napoleon. Later the French had their own irregulars in the form of the *francs-tireurs* ('free-shooters') who took on the might of the Prussian army during the war of 1870–1 and had a lasting effect on the psyche of the German soldiers in both the First and Second World Wars. At the end of the nineteenth century the British were finally obliged to abandon their red coats for khaki, just in time to protect themselves against the Boers in drab grey and brown civilian clothing, who had the unsporting habit of shooting them from long range whilst sheltering behind rocks and trees. The term *francs-tireurs* remained widely used when defining the illegal status of guerrilla fighters.

The rights of citizens to defend their own country and the legality of the *francs-tireurs* was hotly debated during the discussions leading to the 1907 Hague Convention. Whilst large states contended that lawful combatant status should only be given to members of recognised armed forces, smaller countries wanted to protect the right of a general population to defend itself against an invader. Article 1 of the Hague Convention eventually provided four criteria for lawful combatant status:

1. to be commanded by a person responsible for their subordinates
2. to have a distinct emblem that was recognisable at a distance

3. to carry arms openly
4. to conduct their operations according to the laws and customs of war

In a concession to the smaller states, Article 2 also protected the concept of the *levée en masse* for populations who spontaneously took up arms but carried them openly and obeyed the laws of war, but this was open to wide interpretation.

The consequences were to be seen at the start of the First World War. The atrocities committed by the German army in Belgium were excused as being a consequence of the activities of *francs-tireurs*. In actuality, the threat was more imaginary than real but it showed the impact that such forces had caused to the army in 1870–1. Vivid accounts of mass executions of civilians and rape and arson used as reprisals became burned into the consciousness of the Allies. The British government was determined to maintain the concept of lawful combatants and persistently resisted the efforts of the First World War Volunteer Training Corps – the Home Guard of its day – to be seen as a combat force. Only reluctantly were they allowed to bear arms but great stress was placed on the need to wear a clearly distinctive armband which had the status of a legal document, worn even when uniforms were allowed. Officially they were regarded as an organisation that merely *trained* men for possible active service and they would not be recognised as a combative force under martial law until Britain was actually invaded. Ironically, much of the syllabus of the VTC was in training for guerrilla warfare – at the same time as the British army was walking upright across no man's land into hails of machine-gun fire. In language that the Auxiliary Units or students at the Home Guard Training School at Osterley Park would have recognised in 1940, the VTC Regulations of 1916 called upon its units 'to constantly harass, annoy, and tire out the enemy, and to impede his progress, till a sufficient force can be assembled to smash him'.[2] By the end of the war the VTC formally became Volunteer battalions of their county regiments as part of the Volunteer Force and neat military order was restored.

After the First World War, British troops served alongside White Russian partisans in 1919–20 and had to face the unseen threat of the IRA in Ireland during 1919–21. In Ireland the British government experienced at first hand the tactics of sabotage and terror and in doing so, army officers such as Colin Gubbins and Jo Holland developed a grudging respect for the IRA leader, Michael Collins. War in the twentieth century was becoming less 'civilised' and 'gentlemanly'. The Spanish Civil War of 1936–9 brought new threats to the accepted conventions. Both sides committed atrocities on civilian populations and the summary execution of prisoners was well known. For the International Brigades, the chances of any man being taken prisoner by the Nationalists was slim and the experience of the British Battalion was to have a profound impact on the development of the Home Guard in 1940. The veterans of the Spanish Civil War who taught at the Osterley Park Training School would provide an introduction in Britain to a new ruthlessness in warfare, but already, during 1938, Orde Wingate was putting the principles of irregular warfare into practice. As an Intelligence Officer in Palestine, Wingate created the 'Special Night Squads' of British and Jewish Haganah volunteers. They ambushed Arab saboteurs and raided border villages, criticised by friend and foe alike for their brutal tactics.

In the Second World War, Prime Minister Winston Churchill famously exhorted the paramilitary SOE to 'set Europe ablaze' and encouraged foreign civilian resistance. But well before the outbreak of war, in April 1938, Admiral Sinclair, head of the Secret Intelligence Service (SIS), had created Section D under a Royal Engineer officer, Laurence Grand, as 'the sabotage service' to explore the potential of a no-holds-barred approach to irregular warfare against Germany, operating from neutral countries and using civilians. The 'D Scheme' of Section D had been reluctantly approved by the government in March 1939 and was uncompromising in its methodology (see below, p.44). Section D went to war immediately, attacking German economic interests from Scandinavia to the Balkans.[3] Meanwhile the War Office, through its small research department MI(R), focused on a more respectable approach to guerrilla warfare using military units although even here the Chief of the Imperial General Staff was reluctant to have regular (as opposed to reserve or territorial) officers seen to be involved.[4] This was not an issue confined to the British: in 1940 the Norwegian General Staff were equally resistant to the suggestions of MI(R) to organise guerrilla warfare behind enemy lines.[5] A reluctance to engage with the principles of clandestine warfare was evident in early British efforts to operate out of uniform. When the MI(R) mission left for Poland in August 1939 in 'mufti', one officer insisted on wearing his Brigade of Guards tie and the NCOs were issued with identical brand new sports jackets, neatly-pressed flannel trousers and trilby hats. The Naval Intelligence mission to Romania in March 1940 was similarly discovered by the *Abwehr* because the supposed tourists to Braila – 'writers' and 'artists' according to their passports (suspiciously all issued on the same day in Alexandria) but actually Royal Navy officers – were again wearing identical sports jackets and flannels while the naval ratings masquerading as civilian barge crews were still called upon every morning to muster and perform RN physical exercise drill on deck, in full view of Galatz harbour.[6] It is not surprising that Hugh Dalton in July 1940, when battling for the creation of SOE out of War Office control, declared that clandestine warfare was 'no more suitable for soldiers than fouling in football or throwing when bowling at cricket'.[7]

Although it turned a 'blind eye' to the activities of Section D abroad, the British government still maintained the legal definition of the *francs-tireurs* as terrorists and strenuously resisted various schemes to officially arm its own civilians. It had an ambivalent attitude to the unofficial US campaign to provide weapons to 'Defend British Homes' because it fundamentally believed that defence should be organised strategically and be in the hands of the military.[8] Thus, despite popular admiration for the Continental resistance forces, the victorious Allied nations at the Nuremburg Trials took a conservative line about what constituted being a 'lawful combatant', and the partisans of Yugoslavia and Greece, despite being allies and supported by British military missions, were declared *francs-tireurs*. The court agreed that they were legally entitled to have been executed – which the Nazis had done in their thousands – but the Nazis were, however, found guilty of doing so in a summary fashion without any form of judicial process.

> We are obliged to hold that such guerrillas were *francs-tireurs* who, upon capture, could be subjected to the death penalty. Consequently, no criminal responsibility attaches to the defendant List because of the execution of captured partisans ...[9]

Such legal concerns were to have a great impact upon the government's plans for opposing any enemy invasion in 1940 but although the War Office might have been unwilling to be associated with the creation of civilian *francs-tireurs*, there were many in society that were less squeamish.

The Auxiliary Units patrols and others reputedly carried death lists of suspected collaborators, or simply people that might have known of their existence, who they were ordered to execute after invasion. Who might have authorised such a programme is unclear and has been greatly exaggerated post-war for dramatic effect, but both SIS and Auxiliary Units Intelligence Officers could take an uncompromising stance, even promoting the mutilation of their victims to act as a warning to others. Were there memories here of the tactics used by the IRA against British intelligence operations in Ireland during 1920?[10] A large section of the general public also had no legalistic qualms about taking up arms in an era of total war. For them, Ernest Hemingway's book *For Whom The Bell Tolls*, which was first published in 1940 and focused on the fate of a guerrilla band in the Spanish Civil War, became a romantic inspiration, following on from T.E. Lawrence's classic First World War autobiography *Seven Pillars of Wisdom*, posthumously published in 1935. The concept of guerrilla warfare was attractive to many sections of the Home Guard and books on guerrilla tactics and the manufacture of improvised explosive devices became instant best sellers in 1940 and 1941. Tom Wintringham's *New Ways of War* and Yank Levy's *Guerrilla Warfare* both included explicit details of how to make improvised explosives and booby-trap devices that would cause outrage in the twenty-first century. Captain Cronk's pamphlet, *Explosives for the Home Guard* (1943), even explained how to dismantle service grenades in order to make alternative weapons. The preface stated somewhat optimistically, if not irresponsibly, 'I hope it will assist to dispel the prevalent idea that the handling of explosives is a dangerous business'. In June of the previous year, Charles Pearce, a corporal in Halesowen Home Guard, had been killed in an explosion in his garden shed. He had been attempting to remove explosives from a shell case, probably to make improvised grenades. *The Manual of Guerrilla Tactics* was published by Bernards in a convenient size suitable for one's back pocket and sold for just one shilling. It included a special section on the 'preparation and use of explosives' in a style highly reminiscent of the official manuals issued to the Auxiliary Units. The War Office, determined to control the intrusion of civilians onto the battlefield, must have looked upon such publications with horror but its patience was finally tested beyond the limit by Tom Wintringham's enthusiastic 'We make a mortar for 38/6d' published in *Picture Post*, July 1941. This article described how to make what amounted to a medieval cannon, firing a First World War-era jam-tin bomb, and demanded careful coordination between the length of fuse on the mortar and that on the bomb. The promised second part of the article on how to fire the mortar was never published and one suspects that the War Office desperately tried to persuade the magazine to withdraw it on grounds of public safety!

The War Office faced a particular problem of how to deal with women who wanted to become involved in the fighting. These calls were led in Parliament by Edith Summerskill, who eventually founded the Women's Home Defence Corps as what amounted to an illegal private army. Popular support for this was mixed. In popular culture, films such as *Mrs Grant Goes To The Door* (MOI, August 1940) and *Went the Day Well* (Ealing, December 1942) showed women taking up arms alongside the men to promote the mood of a nation united in a common cause. But a patriarchal society struggled to balance encouraging involvement in the war effort whilst avoiding accepting a direct combat role. John Langdon-Davies, another left-wing champion of the Home Guard, supported calls for a Women's Home Guard Auxiliary but drew the line at them being involved in the fighting and adopted a patronising tone:

> I think the average Home Guard has joined it because he wants to protect his hearth and home; and feel a bit annoyed if the hearth and home insisted upon coming along with him and doing some of the protecting.[11]

Individual Home Guard units soon began to unofficially recruit women into first aid and communications roles. Eventually the War Office had to give way and in 1943 official recognition was given to what were officially called 'Nominated Women' in the Home Guard – more commonly (and confusingly) called the 'Home Guard Auxiliaries'. They were only supposed to take on a non-combative role, although individual commanders might go further. The Commanding Officer of the Air Transport Auxiliary at White Waltham, Kent, in 1943–4 told his Home Guard Women's Shooting Team that their role, if attacked by a parachute raid, was to climb onto the roof of the aircraft hangars and shoot the paratroopers as they descended.[12] The official War Office guidance on guerrilla warfare in 1942 similarly struggled. Here, the contribution of women was described as invaluable but consideration of a combat role was avoided. Instead, women were said to be most usefully directed to work such as agents, messengers, guides and first aid as well as 'looking after the wants of men with guerrilla forces, acting as cooks and so on'. It also went on to note that the 'exercise of feminine charms on occupying troops will always be worthwhile'.[13] Within the scope of the present study, the SIS (including Section D) had a long history of employing female officers and SDB also had women serving as agents, couriers, wireless operators and possibly as 'honey traps'. Only the ATS operators at the SDB IN Stations and the Section VII wireless operators were known to be issued with guns and then it was only for personal protection. There are, however, uncorroborated hints of female saboteurs in Section VII.

Despite the worsening situation during 1940, great suspicion remained regarding the moral and practical consequences of embarking on a programme of guerrilla warfare. Few in authority agreed with the rousing devil-may-care attitude of Colonel J.C. Wedgwood, MP for Newcastle-under-Lyme, who on 7 May 1940 had cheerfully expressed the view in Parliament that civilians should be armed.

> They ought to be taught that they should not leave it to the regular forces to do the fighting but that they must fight themselves . . . We should use them like *francs-tireurs*. They would no doubt be shot if they were taken, but they would be able to harass any small invading forces and not wait until some regular troops came to help.

Wedgwood, who had a distinguished war record from the First World War, was roundly criticised for being irresponsible in openly endorsing a suicidal terrorism.[14] How would Parliament have reacted if they had known that this was exactly what Section D of SIS had been trying to engineer across Europe since March 1939 as the 'D Scheme' and which it would shortly introduce into Britain as the 'Regional D Scheme' or 'Home Defence Scheme'? (See Chapter 4.)

Following Wedgwood's speech, the Home Office felt obliged to issue a press release, published in *The Times* on 11 May, to advise civilians what they should, or should not, do in the event of invasion: do not take pot-shots at the enemy, and leave the fighting to the army. Parliament, from the very start of the war in September 1939, had repeatedly expressed concern about the definition of the *francs-tireurs* and a firm government policy against arming civilians was published in *Official Instructions to Civilians* on 18 June 1940 (the day after the decision to form the Auxiliary Units), partially drafted by the deputy head of MI(R), Lionel Kenyon. In late July fifteen million of the leaflet *Stay Where You Are* (Plate 16) were distributed. This maintained the public would only 'get in the way' if they tried to join the fighting. The advice was amplified on 30 July 1940 as part of the debate on the Emergency Powers (Defence) Bill, when Lord Atkin stated that it would be a mistake

> if members of the public were encouraged to believe that, without belonging to the Home Guard, they could seize their shotguns and shoot down the first parachutist that they saw. They would then be *francs-tireurs*, and would be so treated, I have no doubt, by the enemy, and would bring themselves and their families into danger.[15]

Such parliamentary concern over the definition of *francs-tireurs* had, no doubt, been spurred by the furious Nazi reaction to the foundation of the Local Defence Volunteers (LDV), later to become the Home Guard: 'The British Government is committing the worst crime of all. Evidently it permits open preparation for the formation of murder bands.'[16] The British government moved quickly to legalise the formation of the new defence force by passing, on 17 May, The Defence (Local Defence Volunteers) Regulations, 1940. This was explicit that the Local Defence Volunteers were members of the armed forces of the Crown and subject to military law as soldiers, legally distinct from the rest of the general populace.[17] Throughout this story a firm distinction was made between the military, uniformed, Home Guard/Auxiliary Units and the civilian *francs-tireurs* of SIS (Plate 17). Nonetheless, some county lords lieutenant who had continuing doubts as to the legal status of the Home Guard were still later described as 'obstructionist' in failing to provide support for their mobilisation.[18] If they reacted in this way to the Home Guard, how would such men react to the idea of a secret civilian guerrilla and resistance movement being created within their counties? It was not surprising that Section D of SIS faced direct opposition from some in regional government as they proceeded with the mobilisation of the HDS – and this was without knowing that SIS was planning to burn crops and poison both wells and their enemies.

Such concerns extended to the then Commander-in-Chief, Home Forces (General Ironside) and the Secretary of War, Anthony Eden. Eden wrote a memorandum to the War Cabinet on 8 July 1940:

> It is the view of the Commander-in-Chief, Home Forces, with which I am in agreement, that actual fighting should be restricted to the military and Local Defence Volunteers, and that no civilian who is not a member of these forces should be authorised to use lethal weapons. Only if this principle is accepted would it be possible to ensure control of military activities by the military authorities.

> I therefore ask the War Cabinet to decide that active defence plans are to be based solely on the military and Local Defence Volunteers; that no civilian who is not a member of these forces should be authorised to use lethal weapons . . .[19]

This statement was, not least, a fierce rebuttal of the brief support that General Ismay and Colonel Hollis of the Chiefs of Staff Committee had expressed for an unofficial proposal of 19 June from Captain Davies of MI(R) to create a new civilian resistance organisation (see below, p.66). In the Cabinet meeting of 8 July, Churchill now gave support to Ironside and Eden in their objections to civilian warfare, despite having recently confirmed approval to recruit civilian saboteurs for the HDS of Section D. Churchill repeated the official policy at the 19 July War Cabinet: 'the Government could not countenance active armed resistance by any but those enrolled in the armed forces of the Crown or in the Home Guard'.[20] A clearly-conflicted Churchill later sought to backtrack on this official stance and maintain the principle of the *levée en masse* as permitted by the Hague Convention *in extremis* by claiming (23 August) that his previous statements in the War Cabinet had not meant to prevent civilians from spontaneously taking up arms or to punish them for doing so as 'the citizen retained his natural right to fight in defence of his family and his home. This might well result in civilians joining in the fight in support of the military.'[21] The role of the HDS was also refined over the course of June/July 1940 to make clear that its civilians were not to become involved in fighting during the military anti-invasion campaign. Instead, as with Section VII, it would only operate after enemy occupation when SIS would officially take the lead in any resistance. Such debates were to have a fundamental impact on the organisation of the Operational Patrols of the Auxiliary Units as a military body and more than just a nominal part of the Home Guard.

One particular aspect of warfare that appears particularly disturbing in the twenty-first century but which did not raise so much concern in the 1930s/1940s, was the role of children in combat. Teenagers could be found fighting in the guerrilla organisations of many countries. During the Spanish Civil War George Orwell reported that the POUM militia included children as young as 11. He complained about their stamina as much as anything else:

> At the beginning it was almost impossible to keep our position properly guarded at night. The wretched children of my section could only be roused by dragging them out of their dug-outs feet foremost, and as soon as your back was turned they left their posts and slipped into shelter; or they would even, in spite of the frightful cold, lean up against the wall of the trench and fall fast asleep.[22]

In the Second World War, military service for some teenagers was simply a matter of survival. Many members of the Jewish youth movement *Hashomer Hatzair* fought in the Warsaw Ghetto Uprising of 1943. Young boys similarly served with the partisans of the Soviet Union, Poland and Yugoslavia. In Germany, there was a Hitler Youth Panzer Division and boys as young as 12 were eventually drafted into military service. In Britain, Boy Scouts regularly served as non-combatant ARP or Home Guard messengers but in 1942 the age of enlistment into the Home Guard was lowered to 16 years. The official War Office guide to guerrilla warfare in 1942 stressed that children 'should not be neglected' as messengers so it is not surprising that there are instances of SIS and the Auxiliary Units planning to use boys and girls as young as 14 behind enemy lines as couriers.[23] Perhaps most disturbing of all, 14-year-old Worcester Grammar School boys were reportedly being trained in guerrilla warfare, including tactics that approach the idea of suicide bombing (see below, p.28). Guerrilla warfare and 'resistance' were indeed the most brutal and uncompromising forms of warfare.

Chapter 2

Playing the Long Game: the Resistance Organisation of Section VII, SIS

> The last thing these English know is how to practice fair play. They're very bad at accepting their defeats.
>
> Adolf Hitler, 9 February 1942[1]

The resistance organisation now known as Section VII, although the least documented or understood, was probably the most significant of Britain's secret plans for clandestine warfare. Its task was to collect intelligence and conduct sabotage after any occupation but, in line with policy urged on occupied countries in 1940, not to expose themselves unnecessarily during the invasion but rather to serve as the cadre for the recruitment of a guerrilla army that would participate in an eventual liberation of the country. Thankfully it was never put to the test. The Secret Intelligence Service had been formed in 1909 although its existence would not be formally acknowledged until 1994. Its HQ was at 54 Broadway, under its cover of the 'Minimax Fire Extinguisher Company', an address known to London taxi drivers and German agents alike as the home of Britain's secret intelligence service! The traditional role of the SIS was in covertly gathering intelligence across the world but it was forbidden to operate in Britain, where intelligence was the responsibility of MI5. The head of SIS from 1923, Admiral Sinclair (known as 'C'), did, however, have a broader vision for the organisation in what he foresaw as the probable war with Nazi Germany. This would take SIS into the realms of political warfare, subversion and sabotage.

Clandestine warfare was seen as distasteful and 'un-British', with British forces largely having been its victims. Lord Hankey, the Minister without Portfolio and government adviser on security, had commented in his March 1940 review of SIS: 'At first sight the natural instinct of any humane person is to recoil from this undesirable business as something he would rather know nothing about.'[2] Although from March 1939 the government began to actively encourage civilian resistance bodies abroad through Section D of SIS (in neutral countries thought likely to be occupied by the Nazis as well as in Germany and Italy), well aware they were encouraging *francs-tireurs*, it was more reticent about using this tactic within Britain; nonetheless, in spring 1940 Sinclair's successor, Stewart Menzies (Plate 1), created the cadre of a civilian resistance organisation for Britain itself, something that many in government and the War Office would have regarded as defeatist if they had been aware of its existence.

In line with the SIS policy that it preached abroad of strict compartmentalism between short-term guerrilla and longer-term resistance organisations, the plan for British resistance was not put under the 'sabotage service' of Section D but was given a completely separate organisation, reporting directly to 'C'. Section D, which was waging a disruptive war against Nazi interests allied with foreign socialist and Jewish groups, was now mistrusted almost as much within SIS as beyond its secretive walls but the new resistance organisation would also have its own sabotage function. It was secret even within SIS itself, given cover within the accountancy division of Section VII and otherwise known only vaguely as 'DB's organisation' (David Boyle) with a sabotage wing known as 'X branch'. Section VII was officially responsible for SIS finance and accounting but its wartime operations have long been considered as a mystery, described as a 'persistent puzzle' and vaguely responsible for 'economic intelligence'.[3] The secrecy of the Section VII organisation was jealously guarded, especially as, when formed, SIS had no official remit to operate within the British Isles. A flavour of the attitude of SIS to outside scrutiny can be gauged from the results of General Marshall-Cornwall's review of the poor relations between SOE and SIS in 1942. He spent six months in each organisation but was frustrated that in his time in SOE he felt he had learned everything about the organisation – but absolutely nothing about SIS! Marshall-Cornwall had to ruefully admire how Claude Dansey, the Machiavellian Assistant Chief of the Secret Service (ACSS) who was in charge of intelligence operations, kept everything compartmentalised to the point that only Dansey 'knew anything about his agents, who remained very much his own'.[4] Dansey was a hidden force behind the British resistance.

Any running of agents in Britain by SIS was particularly sensitive following disputes with MI5 and Special Branch in the late 1920s to 1931 over the operation of the SIS 'Casuals' within the UK. At one point their chief agent, Maxwell Knight, was placed under surveillance by Special Branch who, he was discretely informed, would make his life, and that of his agents, a complete misery unless he stopped operations![5] This network was finally transferred to MI5 as M Section in October 1931.[6] Thereafter, SIS theoretically had no responsibility for domestic operations but it is no coincidence that one of the strongest supporters of Section D in 1940 was Desmond Morton, at the time Churchill's personal assistant and intelligence advisor but formerly the head of the SIS 'Casuals'. The justification for the creation of the two SIS organisations, Section VII and the Home Defence Scheme (HDS) of Section D (Chapter 4), was that they were designed to operate after the British government and army had ceased to have any control in the UK which would then have the status of an occupied country and so fall within the purview of SIS. This was 'disaster planning' by Menzies that the government and War Office could barely bring themselves to contemplate but, as the opening quote to this chapter indicates, was ruthlessness appreciated by Hitler.

If defeated militarily, there would eventually have been a formal surrender of all army formations, including the Operational Branch of the Auxiliary Units. Lord Ismay, Churchill's Chief of Staff, later pointed out the distinction in service tradition between a naval commander who was expected to go down with his ship and an army commander whose final duty was to avoid fruitless sacrifice of his men by capitulation.[7] It may be presumed that, by then, the Royal Family had been spirited out of the country to avoid them becoming a figurehead and that Churchill had gone down fighting. It can also be assumed that most of the Home Guard in the combat areas would have been destroyed in the first days of invasion. Their orders were to stand and fight to the last round and man to buy time for the regular army to regroup, and they had already been declared *franc-tireur* terrorists by Hitler. The hidden guerrillas of the Auxiliary Units would have continued to disrupt the enemy supply lines for a few days more. Some elements of the civilian Home Defence Scheme sabotage teams (see Chapter 4) and ad hoc groups of Home Guard guerrillas (see Chapter 12), trained to operate without reliance on military supplies, could possibly have continued to provide what might have seemed an increasingly futile resistance to delay surrender but such efforts would have little coordination.

If successful, the Nazis may have been considering the possibility of occupied and unoccupied zones in the UK (similar to what was agreed in France), at least as a temporary measure, which would have the advantages of limiting the resources required to occupy the whole country and therefore allow attention to return more quickly to Hitler's primary long-term objective of destroying the Soviet Union.[8] Significantly, the initial invasion plan of Operation Sealion looked no further than the campaign in southern England, hoping that this would be enough to ensure British surrender. Even the total occupation of the British Isles would not necessarily mark the end of British resistance. The empire was still intact and there were plans to establish a government in exile in Canada or the West Indies, supported by a free Royal Navy. The hope was that if the struggle could be continued in some form, then either the Nazi state overstretched by its conquests would implode from internal dissent, supported by resistance forces across Europe, or the USA would eventually be drawn into a war against Nazi Germany and Britain could be liberated. An internal intelligence network capable of communication between any occupied and unoccupied zones as well as with a government in exile, ready to sow the seeds of a future armed revolt, was a necessary element in such long-term planning. This 'unthinkable' possibility was the context for the creation of the cadre of a last ditch, and ultra-secret, resistance organisation created in the depths of SIS. The establishment of the Section VII resistance was only publicly identified in 2010 within the official history of SIS by Jeffery, and then only in a single paragraph without being able to cite the source.[9] Jeffery identified the Section VII network as being initially organised by a senior triumvirate consisting of Valentine Vivian (Deputy Chief of SIS and head of Section V, Counter-Espionage), Richard Gambier-Parry (head of Section VIII, Communications) and David Boyle (head of Section N, interception of diplomatic mail and the personal assistant to CSS). This has remained the most secret (and therefore almost by definition the most successful) of the plans to oppose Nazi occupation. It was so secret that contemporaries avoided referring to it by name, only as 'DB's organisation', if indeed it was ever given a formal name. Its operatives may never have known for whom precisely they worked other than vaguely for 'British Intelligence'. Certainly the one surviving wireless operator who has recounted his story (Peter Attwater in Derbyshire) was never told for whom he was working.[10]

Stewart Menzies (Plate 1) had succeeded Admiral Sinclair in November 1939. He allowed much of the day-to-day running of SIS, and especially its agent networks, to fall under the control of his *de facto* deputy, Claude Dansey, a ruthless master-spy (Plate 2). The genesis of the ultra-secret Section VII network bears all his hallmarks, although Dansey's name is never mentioned in connection with the operation. From the early 1930s, Dansey had run a totally unofficial network of agents in Europe known as 'Claude's private ventures'.[11] In 1936 he set up the Z Organisation which in wartime was designed to take over from the normal SIS network based upon passport control officers which, it was assumed, would be quickly destroyed after war broke out. To aid the deception, Dansey and Sinclair concocted a story that the former had been dismissed in disgrace from the service for embezzlement, intended to lead to the assumption that the Z Organisation had also been wound up. Instead, Dansey was installed in a suite of offices on the eighth floor of Bush House in London (from where Section D was organising clandestine broadcasts into Europe), where he managed what was, in effect, a shadow SIS. Dansey maintained this top-secret office throughout the war. A parallel may lie in the official disbanding of Section D in August 1940 to obscure the continuing presence of Section VII as a deep-cover organisation, expanded with elements of Section D's HDS that were otherwise supposed to have been incorporated into the Auxiliary Units, and also shielded by the existence of the more vulnerable Special Duties Branch of the Auxiliary Units. It was Dansey that had first suggested to Admiral Sinclair, in 1937, the need for a sabotage unit attached to SIS although he then became appalled with the wide brief and latitude given to Section D (which, ironically, Dansey described as 'mafia-like') under Laurence Grand.[12]

Valentine Vivian (Deputy Chief of SIS) was well-qualified to help establish the new intelligence network in Britain. In the late 1920s, he had been responsible for overseeing the SIS agent network of 'Casuals' in Britain. In August 1932 he founded an SIS spy network in Eire, setting a precedent for Section VII by having instructions to report only to Admiral Sinclair and not to mention the matter to anyone else inside or outside SIS, unless they were directly involved.[13] As with the later Section VII organisation, most documents connected with the Irish intelligence operation were destroyed. Initially the work consisted of collecting information on public opinion in Ireland using a loose network of sympathetic local contacts. On 27 November 1939, however, there was a meeting to discuss a proposal by the Director of Naval Intelligence (DNI) that SIS should expand their operation in Eire by establishing a clandestine coast-watching service. Initially, neither SIS nor MI5 were happy with the proposal – not least because it might interfere with their existing good relations with the Irish Intelligence Service (G-2), with whom they had formally cooperated since the Anglo-Irish Agreement of 1938. Vivian expressed concern that the new plan could only work with wireless communications and would require over 1,000 agents, with great risks of being detected in a not entirely sympathetic environment. Clandestine radio networks were still at an early stage; the technology was primitive and many agents were deeply suspicious of wireless, fearing that it limited mobility and made them more vulnerable to capture. Despite the enthusiasm of the DNI, the Royal Navy were unable to guarantee the provision of a fast naval response should any German ship or submarine be spotted, and without this, the effort would have been pointless.

A compromise was reached that Vivian would 'extend his existing organisation in a very small way'.[14] In December 1939 he established three or four 'head agents' who then built up a network of agents strung out along the Irish coast, some with wireless sets.[15] They reported to Captain Charles Collinson in Dublin, who used the traditional, if unenterprising, cover of the passport control officer. A hidden wireless set to control the network was installed in the house of the Air Attaché in Dublin and operated by SIS. The brief of the agents was expanded from watching for signs of German naval activity along the coast to monitoring anyone thought to be acting against the British war effort. Here were the twin functions of spying on enemy activity and on local populations that were to be at the core of Section VII and the SIS-inspired/managed SDB (see Chapter 9). By November 1941, SIS had agents in every county of the Republic and had infiltrated the police service and government, although equally, as Vivian had feared, the Irish G-2 had also penetrated the network.[16] G-2 was reported to have been passed one of the British wireless sets by an informant within the coast watchers but in this friendliest of relationships between spies and counter-spies, SIS also began supplying wireless sets to the official Eire coast-watching service.[17] With such experience behind him, Vivian was an obvious choice to become one of the triumvirate that created the Section VII network in England.

The second member of the triumvirate was Richard Gambier-Parry, formerly of Philco, who was recruited to SIS in 1938 (at the same time as Laurence Grand) to oversee the innovative idea of clandestine wireless networks. He was the mastermind of SIS communications strategy during the Second World War and was involved in what was probably the most extreme plan ever conceived for a 'stay-behind' unit. In 1941 he was wireless consultant for an extraordinary plan devised by Naval Intelligence on Gibraltar. The idea of Operation Tracer was, as the island was being overrun by the enemy, to seal a team inside an observation post hidden deep within 'The Rock', and for them to continue broadcasting information on enemy shipping movements back to the Admiralty in London. The men expected to be sealed in for about a year although plans had been made for a stay as long as seven years. The wireless equipment used the standard SIS combination of Mk III long-range transmitter and an HRO receiver as supplied to XII Corps Observation Unit (see Chapter 5). Trials began in January 1942 during which the wireless communications remained undetected by the Radio Security Service. By August the Operation Tracer team was ready and plans were being drawn up to extend the scheme to Malta and elsewhere but the plan was cancelled in the following year.[18]

The operational head of the British Resistance was David Boyle (Plate 15). He was a lifelong intelligence agent implicated in kidnapping, operations against the IRA with the notorious Auxiliary Division, and trusted with the last-minute attempt to contact sympathetic German generals. He had demonstrated ruthlessness and an ability for delicate missions together with an unshakeable regard for secrecy. He was now the personal assistant to Menzies and therefore provided a direct conduit to the highest authority in SIS. In early 1941 it is not surprising that he was the man chosen to act as minder and guide to William J. Donovan (the future head of OSS) who had been sent by Roosevelt as an unofficial emissary to gauge the determination of Britain to resist invasion. If Gambier-Parry was the wireless expert and Vivian brought his expertise in creating agent networks, then Boyle was the hard-bitten operations manager of the agents.

Exactly when Vivian, Gambier-Parry and Boyle began to establish their ultra-secret network in the UK is unclear. There is a logic in suggesting that Vivian began to consider a British coast-watching service immediately after expanding his network in Eire during February 1940. There is also a tantalising reference in Guy Liddell's diary to a security leak involving, on 8 March, the discovery of a Foreign Office code book labelled Plan Y (Y being a code designation of SIS HQ). Was this connected? If so, then there was also a wireless station in Berkshire at this time.

> A Mr BURGOYNE, when visiting the Manor Club, Bracknell, Berks, saw an F.O. cypher and de-cypher book on a shelf under the bar. It had a message on the fly-sheet 'open on receipt of Y plan' and contained a loose sheet of F.O. paper showing issue of cypher 147 on 19.3.39. The book is now in the possession of the manager.[19]

A cell at the Star Brewery, Eastbourne, Sussex, was created by the end of March 1940, based around a number of senior brewery staff who made weekly transmissions from a wireless transceiver contained within a 'briefcase' and hidden in a secret compartment at the top of the brewery water tower (Plate 39).[20]

In its initial phase of operation the Eastbourne cell was equipped for sabotage operations as well as intelligence-gathering but was later confined to intelligence work. Significantly, the cell was not included in the 1944 map of the War Office SDB network.[21] This early cell may be connected to others in Sussex previously assumed to be SDB. William Neil Allin, landlord of The Lamb Inn, Wartling, Sussex, was approached by the head of the network from Eastbourne, who was described as having a wireless set upstairs in the place he worked. The description and brewery connection suggests he was referring to the Eastbourne Section VII cell. Allin was in contact with another wireless station located in Sidney Dinnis's Parkwood Farm, Upper Dicker, where lectures were also held with twenty or thirty others whose identities he did not know. Allin thereby concluded that agents 'must have been dotted about all over the area'.[22] Dinnis moved to Park Farm, Wilmington in 1943 and again his wireless set was located within the farmhouse, with the aerial running up the inside of the chimney. Allin had other contacts in Bodle Street, Normans Bay and with wireless operator Edwin Trangmar Wadman at Priesthawes House near Stone Cross. Wadman's wireless was in a 'dug-out' in the garden, its entrance concealed by an earth covered hatch leading down, via a wooden ladder, to a 10ft x 5ft chamber constructed of wood. There was a table and chair in the chamber and an emergency exit tunnel ran under the garden wall to a field. Unfortunately security was compromised by Edwin's three dogs who would follow him to the hide and patiently wait outside for him to reappear.[23] Allin explained: 'The idea was we would carry on with our work as if nothing was happening and then if there was any information we could go to our next contact and inform them.' He went on: 'A good excuse to get to Bodle Street was to take the horse to the Blacksmiths and then they wouldn't suspect anything.' Allin used dead-letter drops: 'We had secret places where we could leave a message ... and this reduced the risk of exposure.' He also explained the 'fellow from down the coast could quite easily come in and have a pint of beer and give me the wink and the message could be left somewhere else. He was a "looker" on the coast.'[24]

Reflecting the nature of Section VII as a cadre prior to expansion following occupation, the organisation in Sussex appears to have been scattered rather than either the later Matlock Section VII cell or the local SDB network: 'There was just a single person in each place, not a group. We had no secret hiding place. Their idea was that we would carry on working as normal.' Like others, Allin experienced the difficulties in not appearing to be contributing to the war effort: 'Being a Publican I had the local Home Guard always trying to get me to join in the Home Guard and they put forward my name as a recruit; but I was sworn to secrecy and couldn't tell them what I was doing. They put my name in several times but it was always turned down ... I got rather unpopular with some of the Home Guard chaps.'[25] Dr Hector Hogg in Westham, Sussex, is believed to have been 'head agent' for the Pevensey area. As with the Eastbourne cell, he eventually had a portable wireless set concealed in a briefcase, which could be connected to a permanent aerial strung up around his back garden.[26] These 'briefcase' sets, outside the inventory of the SDB are presumed to be 1941 or later Parasets (Plate 37) which could replace the bulky HRO receiver/Mk III transmitter combination or the more portable Mk V suitcase set, all using Morse code rather than the voice telephony of the SDB TRD sets.

The network spread during the spring and early summer of 1940. In late May/early June, an intelligence cell was formed in Matlock, Derbyshire (see below), which was, in 1941, in contact with other cells formed in Manchester, Nottingham and Birmingham. Together with the other wireless stations identified by Jeffery as part of the initial trial in Norfolk, Suffolk, Sussex, Somerset, Cornwall and Devon, it indicates that the organisation operated nationally and therefore on a different basis to the SDB which was designed to report only on a coastal invasion. The network was tested by an exercise held with the SIS mobile communications units (SCUs) as Plan 333 sometime in, or before, July 1940 (see below, p.19). The organisation was then said to have extended to at least twenty-eight 'head agents' equipped with wireless sets but its full scale prior to its assumed disbandment in 1944/45 is not known.[27] At this stage of the war it was not apparent how vulnerable the wireless operators would be to capture, otherwise the head agent would not have shared the role of wireless operator. With the typical over-confidence of the period, in April 1940 Guy Liddell of MI5 recorded the opinion of the head of SIS on the latest wireless: 'Stewart [Menzies] believes that they are extremely difficult to pick up and doubts very much whether any monitoring system however widespread will be effective against them.'[28]

Prior to the introduction of the 'briefcase' sets, the type of wireless used by the early Section VII can only be guessed at but former SCU member, Geoffrey Pidgeon, identified the SIS communications HQ at Whaddon as 'providing the early wireless sets for the "Hidden Army" of trained wireless operators to be left behind in the event of the Germans invading and occupying the British Isles'.[29] The set used a Morse system, more technically-demanding for operators than that of the later SDB set, with a range that could reach unoccupied territory in the UK, a vessel off the coast or, if necessary, neutral countries in Europe for passage to a government-in-exile in Canada. The level of required training is an indicator that the network was fundamentally different to that of the more basic SDB (see Chapter 8). The wireless sets were also portable, giving a much greater chance of survival long term than the fixed TRD sets of the SDB. Peter Attwater's description of the first set at Matlock is that it was portable, used Morse, and looked as though it was built by a radio ham, which suggests the 1939 Mk II with its exposed components; both this and the 1940 Mk III (which Peter did not use at Matlock) were based upon a traditional 6V6 crystal circuit with a 6L6 Doubler circuit and an 807 amplifier output.[30] The descriptions from Eastbourne and Westham are for a wireless that would fit into a 'briefcase'; the comparatively lightweight Mk VII Paraset (a mainstay of Continental SIS networks and a back-up set for the SCUs), introduced in 1941, would fit into an attaché case or small suitcase (Plate 37). The Paraset had a normal range of c.500 miles but over 1,400 miles in the right atmospheric conditions; transmissions might be received by wireless sets hidden in neutral ships (a common method), submarines or via stations in neutral countries. The Matlock station later used a variant of the No.22 set, which normally had a range of only c.35 miles but which were known to have been upgraded by SIS, communicating with a local control centre.

Recruitment of the Section VII 'stay-behind' agents created a precedent for the recruitment of men and women for the later Home Defence Scheme and Auxiliary Units

Special Duties Branch. They were primarily 'people who, by nature of their occupation, could remain in enemy-controlled territory and continue their normal occupations without arousing undue suspicion' and included 'doctors, dentists, chemists, and small shopkeepers'. The head agents needed a reasonable excuse 'either to move around in the course of their professional duties or to receive many visits from other people'.[31] Another advantage of using such volunteers was that, in the main, they were likely to be middle-aged and not liable for call-up, which would have put the network at risk. Older recruits were also less likely to be deported to Germany by the Nazis. A number were local doctors like Dr Hogg from Westham. On the Isle of Wight, two GPs (Dr Straton and Dr Drummond) played a prominent role (see below). Dr Thomas Russell Stevens, a surgeon at Dorchester County Hospital and a pre-war radio ham, after the war showed radio equipment in his house to a former auxilier – with which 'he had contacted people from all around the world'. If a wartime set, it suggests a long-range SIS wireless. He was also reported to have fitted aerials into the thatched roofs of long thatched barns across Dorset – a duty not associated with SDB outstation operators.[32]

There were also teenage recruits, too young for call-up. Peter Attwater in Matlock (see below) was recruited from being an ARP Messenger; he was advised by his controller to go into hiding if invasion occurred, to avoid him being commandeered by the British army. Another teenager, Kenneth Masters Hay (then aged 17), was recruited in Montrose, Scotland in mid-August 1940.[33] Interested in electronics at school, a friend of his father had a 'Ham' wireless set and Ken listened in on broadcasts emanating out of Norway and, if tropospheric conditions were right, from the USA. This man introduced Hay to Mr Cramb, a local watchmaker/jeweller, and four other people 'whom he was told he could trust'. One was bearded and in his 40s, with a Scottish west-coast accent while two others had distinctive English accents. The fourth never revealed his name nor spoke to Ken and always stayed in the background in Mr Cramb's shop. Ken collected messages in an envelope from the shop and then used various dead-letter drops within Montrose and Hillside (just north of Montrose) in the vicinity of Rosemount House – a wartime accommodation for officers from RAF Montrose. This suggests that either there was a timetable to use different drops or the messages were being directed towards different contacts. The common links between the Matlock and Montrose accounts are the use of teenagers and the use of a shop as contact point – somewhere couriers could visit without attracting attention. This anecdote dates before the SDB was given authority to extend into the Montrose area in March 1942, but it is not clear if this expansion was ever implemented and the Jones Map of 1944 (Plate 33) does not show an SDB station in Montrose.[34] It is therefore most likely to represent a Section VII cell. SIS officer Viscount Bearsted would later recruit similar people for the HDS and SDB, which has added to the confusion as to the relationship between the organisations, and 'key men' continued as a term into the Auxiliary Units.

The Section VII network was primarily designed to operate in a period of settled enemy occupation and its role during an actual invasion was to be limited. The overall British strategy for resistance in 1939–41 throughout Europe (albeit tested to the limit by Section D) was to discourage violence and instead to collect intelligence and build-up supplies to eventually support an external liberation army or a dissident rising within the German army. Section VII was therefore to remain largely 'quiescent' during an actual invasion. The strain that this policy might cause is clearly seen in the dealings of MI(R) and SOE with occupied Poland in this period where they tried to discourage sabotage.[35] During the Cold War, this was again the policy promoted by Britain in North Germany, where local resistance groups were instructed to lay low during any invasion and early occupation phases and only begin to operate (supplying intelligence, recruiting fighters and conducting sabotage operations) during the third phase of 'every-day/routine occupation'.[36]

Nonetheless, after Dunkirk Section VII was drawn into the need to provide initial intelligence to GHQ on the scope of any initial German landings. Key to its success as a network that could transmit intelligence prior to any collapse of British forces was its partnership with the mobile signal units of the newly-created Special Communications Units (SCUs) of SIS. This assistance also helped legitimise the activities of SIS in Britain. During the campaign in France, SIS had deployed two mobile wireless units to transmit intelligence received from Bletchley Park to the BEF HQ via the SIS communications centre at Whaddon. After Dunkirk, Gambier-Parry planned to deploy similar mobile wireless units across military commands in Britain as well as the HQ of the GHQ Reconnaissance Unit, otherwise known as Phantom (see Chapter 10). The organisation consisted of two highly compartmentalised elements: a Special Communications Unit (SCU) would handle the wireless traffic from Whaddon and deliver it to the adjacent Special Liaison Unit (SLU), where the message would be decoded and passed by the unit to a designated intelligence officer in the military command, but otherwise the SCU/SLU would have minimal contact with the neighbouring army organisation. The operation was initially on a small scale, with mobile units ready to deploy from Whaddon and from St James's Park in London, conveniently adjacent to the Battle Section HQ of Phantom. The SCUs/SLUs were formally created on 5 June 1940 and expanded rapidly thereafter with a growing fleet of Packard saloon cars fitted with wireless, wireless trucks and even a bus. They were then based at each regional army command, the Admiralty and Fighter Command and subsequently deployed across all theatres of operation abroad. Each SCU used the standard SIS Mk III transmitter/HRO receiver combination, with an Mk V or later the Mk VII (Paraset) set as back-up (Plate 37).[37] They also had cypher machines, mobile telephone exchange and a number of regular army No.19 and No.24 wireless sets.

Although their core role was in transmitting the most secret intelligence, the ability of the SCUs to provide mobile nationwide communications that would not be subject to enemy interruption of telephone lines had begun to attract other interest, if not envy. The Chiefs of Staff Committee had already raised, on 27 May, the need to have an emergency communications system in case an enemy invasion disrupted the telephone system. The SCUs could provide a ready-made answer but SIS was not about to relinquish control to the army. In discussions of 31 May 1940 between Stewart Menzies (Chief of SIS) and Anthony Eden (Secretary of State for War), refereed by Lord Hankey, the latter asked Eden to emphasise to the War Office that the SIS system was 'apparatus of a very special character' using specialist personnel and 'specialist material' (ie from secret sources). In other words, the message to the army was 'hands off'! However, in order to encourage cooperation, Hankey told Menzies that the payback would be that Gambier-Parry 'will be able to get what he wants' and that he would be given as free a hand as possible in the organisation.[38] To avoid any dispute over the matter, Eden and Hankey agreed that there was no need to refer the raising of the SCUs to the Chiefs of Staff Committee, no doubt only increasing the paranoia of the chiefs of staff towards the ambitions of SIS (in 1941 the Director of Signals at the War Office, Major General Rawson, was to describe the SCUs as the 'private army' of SIS).[39]

Gambier-Parry took full advantage of this agreement and the formal establishment of the SCU/SLU which followed on 5 June led to an immediate increase in resources and a formal allocation of frequencies to the organisation.[40] Gambier-Parry also realised that the SCUs offered an efficient means of receiving and disseminating intelligence in Britain from the Section VII network; if necessary, they could provide an integrated, and flexible, mechanism for the immediate transmission of battlefield intelligence that the HDS or later SDB could never achieve – but this had to be balanced against the risk to the long-term security of the resistance network. A Section VII agent could transmit to a regional centre or directly to the SIS communications centre at Whaddon which would filter the information to hide its source and speedily send it on to army Regional Commands via either an SCU or Phantom. By contrast, the more hastily-created HDS in 1940 relied on traditional 'runners' while the SDB from 1941 to 1944 had a laborious system of agents and cut-out couriers using 'dead-drops' and reporting to a brittle wireless network of short-range OUT and IN Stations, before the intelligence could be finally passed to an Intelligence Officer at a military command.

Having been attacked in the late 1920s–1930s for establishing a spy network in Britain outside its official charter and with antagonism from the War Office because of Laurence Grand's HDS, SIS felt it wise to create a mechanism that would give Section VII a more official, albeit still secret, status. An understanding was reached with MI5 that provided a new legal basis for SIS operations within the UK. SIS already had an urgent need to 'legitimise' the work of recruiting agents to work abroad through the trawling of incoming refugees at reception centres, and this was extended to include the work of Section VII.[41] The negotiations were undertaken by Valentine Vivian whose Section V had the prime responsibility for liaising with MI5. On 2 July – the very day that the War Office circulated the War Establishment of the Auxiliary Units – Vivian wrote to Guy Liddell, the head of Section B of MI5, to explain his objectives, including (original numbering retained):

- d. Provision for the collection of military information in areas in this country, or Ireland, which may be occupied by the enemy;
- e. The provision of internal communications to be placed at the disposal of the military and other authorities in the event of invasion of this country and the breakdown of regular communications;
- f. The recruitment of agents for certain special activities (of which you are aware), both in this country and abroad;

The methodology for achieving such objectives was to be:

- e. The employment of British subjects of some standing (their identity will, of course, be known to your Regional Officers) as 'agents places' in areas in this country likely to be invaded by the enemy;

    f. The establishment of concealed wireless stations in various parts of the country;
    g. The recruitment and placing of agents for the special tasks of which you are aware;[42]

The offer of 'internal communications' borrowed the phraseology used by Hankey in regard to the communications capability of the SCUs. This all provided legitimacy for Section VII but any role in delivering intelligence on the initial movements of the enemy to military commands had to be delicately balanced to avoid risking discovery of their hidden wireless sets. This was enough for the War Office, desperate for such information, to agree to give Gambier-Parry a free hand, at a time when SIS was officially supposed to be handing over its interests in the UK to the Auxiliary Units. The effectiveness of the system was demonstrated in a joint SCU/Section VII exercise, Plan 333, sometime in July; it was described as having produced 'good signalling' and the SCUs were able to decipher 76 per cent of the messages sent by the agents.[43] In August 1940 the SCUs held further exercises with the army which successfully demonstrated their ability to continue to deliver intelligence even if the Regional Commands were obliged to relocate frequently, a flexibility that was impossible with the later SDB wireless network.

Probably with the results of Plan 333 in hand, the proposal to formally recognise the agent network was discussed on 18 July 1940 when Vivian met with his counterpart in MI5, Guy Liddell, and the Director of MI5, Jasper Harker: 'They [SIS] are also engaged in operations here in the event of a German landing.'[44] This was at a time whilst the HDS was still functioning independently of the War Office Auxiliary Units, but the discussion was only formalised *after* the official dispersal of the HDS. Consequently, this brief reference indicates the point at which MI5 and SIS discussed the continuation of Section VII as a long-term intelligence/resistance organisation outside War Office control. The next day, on 19 July, Lord Swinton as head of the Home Defence (Security) Executive and now ministerial head of MI5, was given 'operational control' of SIS activities in Britain and Eire.[45]

The discussions were formalised on 1 August 1940 under the cover of improving relations between the counter-espionage functions of SIS and Section B of MI5. A new liaison section was created, to be known as B.26, and based within MI5, which would 'interlock the functions of MI5 and MI6'.[46] SIS did not officially exist and so if necessary a limited number of named SIS officers were able to identify themselves to the authorities as being from B.26 of MI5, including the ability to 'arm ourselves with your permission with your office stationery'. This device was purely for the benefit of SIS and as a consequence there is no further mention of the arrangement in the Guy Liddell diaries even though he was overall head of Section B, or in the official history of MI5.[47] For its part, SIS was determined to keep its operations totally secret.

On 28 April 1941 Felix Cowgill, Vivian's former deputy and now his successor as head of Section V, told Comyns Carr of MI5 that ' I do not think it necessary under present circumstances to place on record in your section or in any other MI5 section a list of agents whom we [SIS] are employing in this country. The keeping of such records is always a danger even though the most stringent rules are made for their safe custody.'[48] Such care contrasts with the publication of names of the members of Operational

Patrols of the Auxiliary Units in Home Guard enrolment forms or Part II Orders (Plates 42 and 43). Cowgill had specific responsibilities under the August agreement for liaising with MI5 over the SIS 'special agents' in the UK but was notoriously reluctant to share any information and this secretive attitude over the scope of B.26 may well have extended to colleagues within SIS. Kim Philby often acted as a more amenable link between Cowgill and MI5 but he has made no mention of any knowledge of the British spy network. Is this a measure of Cowgill's recognition of the sensitivity of the network? One pertinent feature of the agreement allowed SIS coordinating officers from B.26 to deal directly with Chief Constables over any problems with their local agents, and it is no coincidence that the identity passes for the SDB agents and officers were signed by the local Chief Constable to avoid them being arrested as spies.

Section B.26 was merely the liaison body for UK operations rather than being the actual organising body for agents, which provided an important added level of security. Thus, on 10 October Liddell wrote to Vivian confirming that he had arranged introductions to MI5 Regional Officers 'for DB and various members of his organisation', which he noted 'is now I gather a going concern'.[49] DB is identified elsewhere in Guy Liddell's diary as being David Boyle, a member of the triumvirate who supervised the pilot mobilisation of Section VII, and a man implicated in the purging of Laurence Grand in September. This is the confirmation that David Boyle, operating at the highest level of SIS, was then given the task of running a small network of UK agents for the rest of the war.[50]

Immediately after the war, SIS acknowledged the existence of around 200 'Key Men' of Section VII. As a deep-cover organisation it was preferable to formally recruit only a cadre of head agents until a wider establishment was needed after any occupation, but by then a considerable number of cells had been formed and SIS may have been unwilling to reveal the total number in the organisation, if indeed, through its reluctance to compile membership rolls, the HQ ever knew the total on the ground. One of the reasons given after the war for the refusal to award the Defence Medal to members of SDB (here described as the Special Duties Organisation) was that:

> It is said that there was a Secret Service organisation in the United Kingdom of about 200 civilian members. They were to go to ground in case of invasion. It is not proposed to claim that these should be eligible for the Defence Medal. They seem to fall into much the same category as the Special Duties Organisation.[51]

The qualifying period for issue of the Defence Medal in the UK was three years, therefore, for the members of this secret SIS organisation to be even mentioned in connection with this award suggests that their mobilisation was at least for that length of time. Details of operations and activities of Section VII remain sparse although in general terms what SIS admitted to the Honours Committee suggests it covered some functions of the Auxiliary Units Special Duties Branch, although organised for a longer-term and wider operation.

The most detailed account of a Section VII cell comes from Peter Attwater, who operated with the Matlock wireless station between 1940 and 1943.[52] In late May/June 1940, aged just 14 years, he was recruited by a local journalist, Frank Ford, who was also an ARP organiser and knew the teenager from his work as an ARP Messenger as being someone with a good memory and artistic skills. It is not known when Ford himself had been recruited and therefore the date of the earliest SIS operations in Matlock. Peter was also an Air Cadet and so had some basic military understanding, including weapons handling. He was then introduced to his training officer, Captain William Lawrence, who wore the badge of the Royal Warwickshire Regiment but who had been commissioned into the Royal Artillery after long service as a senior NCO. Lawrence was attached to a mysterious military intelligence establishment at Matlock Hydro with the seemingly-innocuous role of billeting officer and quartermaster. This base predated the establishment there of the Intelligence Corps School in January 1941. Lawrence became the Adjutant and Quartermaster of the new school but only formally transferred to the Intelligence Corps in April 1941. As a reliable ex-NCO with long experience in training and administration, it seems likely that Lawrence had been seconded to SIS to help manage the network, using his work at Matlock Hydro as a cover. In particular, his official role as billeting officer provided an excuse to regularly visit civilian homes and provided cover for his intelligence activities.

Attwater was introduced to two female recruits and signed the Official Secrets Act; all of them were warned to avoid having their photographs taken, and were given code names (which bears a similarity to the system known to have been used in another clandestine operation in Birmingham). Miss Swann and Mrs Keyes were 'Lilian' and 'Agnes', recruited as the first wireless operators. Peter, code name 'Jim', was originally a courier (later a wireless operator). This meeting was recorded by an unknown second lieutenant who had just returned from Dunkirk, suggesting a date in early June. The cell operated what was called a 'Zero Station' (pre-dating the use of the term by the SDB but indicating their joint heritage) hidden at the rear of Mr Joe Toplis's tailor's shop at Burton House, 135 Smedley Street, Matlock (Plate 40 and Fig. 1). Mr Toplis was the 'keeper' of the cell, code-named 'Harry'. The shop was only about 100 yards from the Military Intelligence School at the Hydro, but Peter's resistance cell were warned that if the army had to evacuate the town the Hydro would be blown up, along with any other large building that might be useful to the enemy. They would then be on their own apart from the disembodied messages coming out of the wireless set from 'Control'. The wireless was hidden in an alcove behind racks of uniforms; a revolver and grenade, with its pin stapled to the table so that it could be quickly withdrawn with one hand, was always kept beside the set. An adjacent window provided an emergency exit for operator and wireless but the grenade might slow down pursuers or if necessary destroy the set. This SIS transceiver was later replaced by a No. 22 set, first introduced to service in 1942; it was a low powered, short-range, portable set with a range of c.35 miles (although modified by SIS to increase its range), which suggests that by then the wireless station was acting in similar fashion to an SDB OUT Station, reporting to an unknown control station. All the Matlock operators ever heard from this was the brief response to their coded test messages: 'Received, Control Out'. Peter eventually became a wireless operator, sending out test messages nightly at 10pm. Each message had to include a 'safety' word and Peter remembers that one of these was 'duck'. As an additional security measure, frequencies were changed daily between odd and even frequencies (a security technique missing in accounts of the SDB).

Attwater was originally trained as a courier and observer, learning how to travel silently at night and to accurately identify enemy weaponry. His nocturnal activities

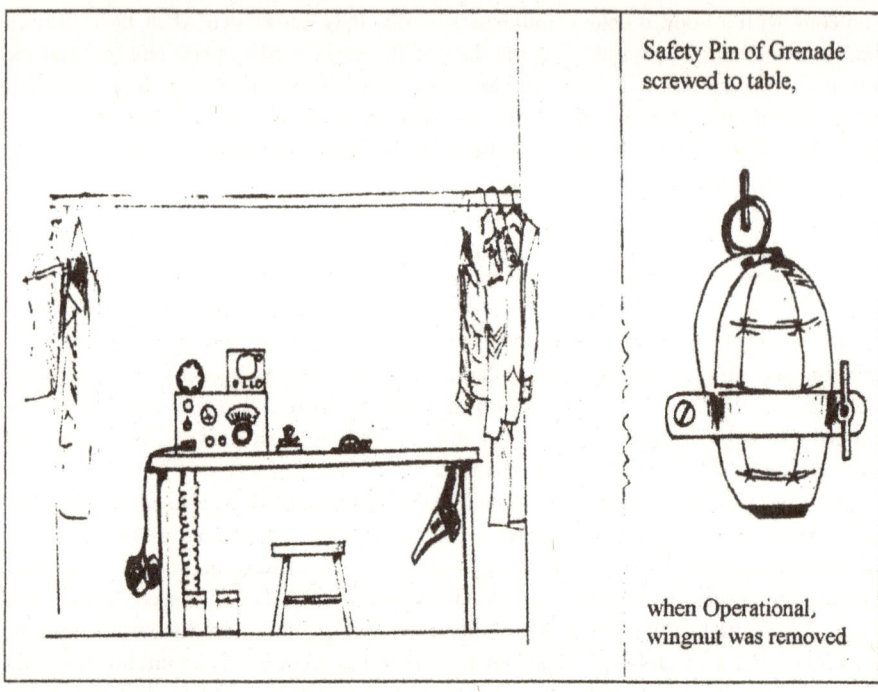

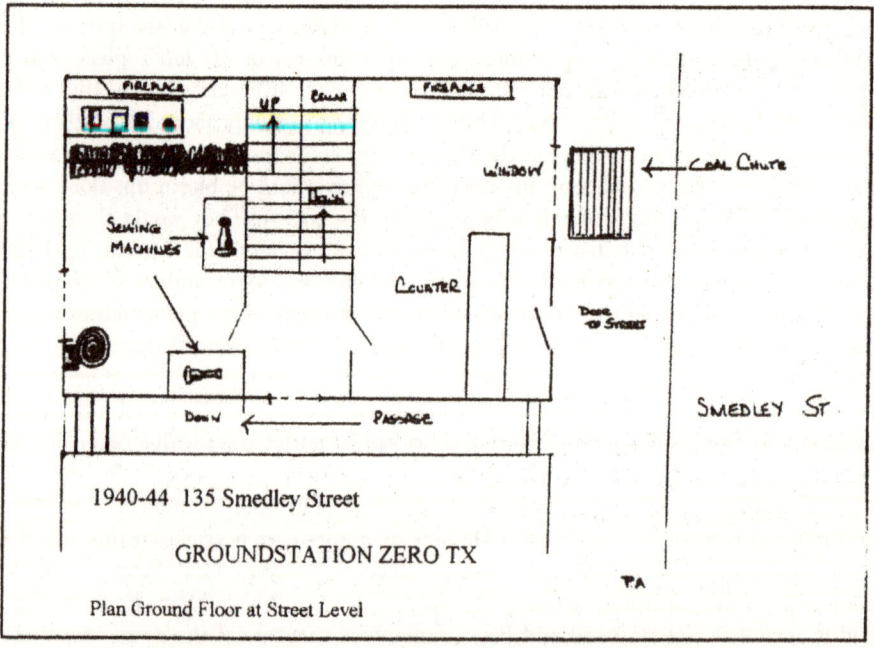

Fig. 1 Sketch of the 1943 Section VII, SIS secret wireless station at 135 Smedley Street, Matlock. Wireless behind clothes rack at rear of shop. (*Peter Attwater*)

were carried out under cover of his ARP Messenger duties so his parents were never aware of his real responsibilities; he had to familiarise himself with the layout of the town, and be able to move through people's back gardens whilst knowing the location of any crunchy gravel paths or noisy dogs. He also had to make plans on where to cross the River Derwent, including shuffling silently across a water pipe. One specific task was to identify abandoned stables where any fugitives after occupation could be hidden and passed along an escape route. It therefore appears that Section VII was preparing escape lines as a precedent for the work of MI9 across Europe. On occasion he was given test exercises, although it seems possible that some were more real than Peter was led to believe at the time, including accurately estimating the numbers of people attending meetings and events, and included keeping a watch on a local pacifist meeting – exactly the sort of assistance that MI5 might have been looking for in its agreement with SIS. Peter visited Captain Lawrence's offices at the Hydro where he had to familiarise himself with life-size prints of German armoured vehicles in order to be able to accurately identify them; the Winter Gardens (part of the Hydro) also had a large collection of German uniforms and equipment, including dummies of German paratroopers hanging from the ceiling.

Some of Peter's training was carried out at the Intelligence School by uniformed men other than Lawrence. They explained that they were acting under orders from the 'men in suits', a typical way of referring to SIS. Peter knew the other two wireless operators and his instructor, but no others in the network. Then, in early 1941 Peter was sent to a meeting in Birmingham attended by six other young men who came from Birmingham, Manchester and Nottingham and who would become his contacts after any enemy occupation. It was considered a real possibility that Britain might be divided, like France, into 'occupied' and 'unoccupied' zones and it would only be then that the traditional system of runners or couriers relied upon by HDS and the SDB in 1940 would be viable, passing messages from district to district and zone to zone. The meeting was managed by a huge imposing man who, like Lawrence, seems suspiciously like an ex-NCO type; Peter described him as a strict disciplinarian and 'the most frightening man I have ever seen'. Peter was convinced, however, that the smartly-dressed civilian instructors at this meeting were those 'men in suits' from SIS, and the training included the issue of their safety codes to prove their identity if they ever had to meet in the future. On meeting, they were to follow the traditional British habit of discussing the weather: each of the seven men had a key word they would use, which together spelt out the word BRITISH, thus Blizzard, Rain, Ice, Thunder, (More) Ice, Snow, Hail; Peter was to introduce himself by working the words 'more ice' into conversation. The couriers were warned that the pattern of invasion might be one of initial landings on the south-east coast but to expect a second wave coming up the Bristol Channel and the Germans establishing a general headquarters at Bridgnorth, Shropshire, before striking deeper into the Midlands. It was clear that this scenario would then bring the Midlands spy network into the front line. Despite his huge responsibilities, Peter did not remember feeling worried or afraid about his secret activities, but rather accepting it as something that had to be done at a time when everyone was doing their bit in one way or another. Peter continued to act as a wireless operator until December 1943 when he was called up into the army. It is hardly surprising that he was posted to the Royal Signals and for a period was also attached to the Intelligence Corps.

Curiously, Peter also remembers attending a presentation in mid-1941 at the Hydro by Colonel Gubbins (then in SOE) and Sefton Delmer (Political Warfare Executive) on the relative merits of sabotage and black propaganda. Delmer thought that sabotage would be counter-productive due to the brutal response by the Nazis. Peter remembers this well because Delmer said 'I'll spell that for you in capital letters – BRUTAL'. He also attended what was clearly an SIS briefing where one of the 'men in suits' described the security situation in the USA and in occupied Europe. Why a local cell member was invited to attend such high-powered meetings is a mystery. It does, however, have some parallel in the conferences held in Sussex (see above) and the treatment of Eric Deverill in Annesley (who was reputedly later commissioned into Military Intelligence). It may be that Peter was being groomed for a future wider role.

Section VII was also to have an internal security role (which would later become the driving force behind the Auxiliary Units SDB), a condition of MI5 acquiescence to the operations of SIS within the UK. The unedited text of the Guy Liddell MI5 Diary includes two intriguing references to the operation of Boyle's network. In March 1942 Liddell records how 'The extra assistance that he [Gambier-Parry] was proposing to get to deal with the Met. problem [suspected German transmitters in Croydon and Blackpool sending meteorological reports to the enemy] would come from DB's various agents dotted about the country.'[53] They were not merely waiting in readiness for any invasion but were also being used on counter-espionage duties. It seems that the intention was to use the Section VII wireless sets to supplement the direction-finding vans of the Radio Security Service (RSS) and the latter's volunteer wireless interceptors, and possibly also to use the agents for surveillance work. David Boyle was involved throughout 1941–4 in discussions with MI5 on the progress of the surveillance and infiltration of pro-Fascist groups, suggesting that Peter Attwater's experience in Matlock was not an isolated incident but that Section VII was playing an active part in this vital work.[54]

On 7 April 1943 there was an air raid on Newport in the centre of the Isle of Wight by Fw 190 fighter-bombers. On 12 April Liddell, following a meeting with the Head of SIS recorded that 'one of DB's people', the 59-year-old Dr Arthur Straton (Plate 6), had been killed and his house on Medina Avenue destroyed during the raid. The unfortunate doctor had been on a night call and had only returned to his surgery to write up his notes when the house was hit by a bomb. Straton's maid, Cissy Draper, was also killed but his wife survived. Straton was a former captain in the RAMC and then a consulting surgeon at both the prison and the County Hospital at Ryde, in addition to having a private practice. His only son, 21-year-old Robert, had been killed at Dunkirk. Robert had only been commissioned in March and one wonders if this sad loss influenced his father's decision to join Section VII. This well-known and highly-respected doctor was also a Fire Guard but unknown to the local community, Straton was the Section VII cell's wireless operator; according to Liddell in his house 'Somewhere in the ruins are important papers and a wireless transmitter'. In accordance with the agreement establishing B.26, SIS asked MI5 to dispatch an officer to investigate the scene and recover the wireless set, as well as interview another network member – Dr Drummond, also a surgeon and GP from the west side of the island in Yarmouth, as well as a Police Surgeon and a medical officer to the local Home Guard. Local doctors do appear to have been particular targets for recruitment to these secret intelligence organisations due to their ease of movement across the locality. Neither men are known to be members of the SDB cell on the Isle of Wight, which was an especially sensitive location.[55] Plans were afoot to make it the terminal for the fuel pipeline that would serve the future invasion beaches but there had already been arrests on the island for suspected spying. Reports that the first person on the scene of the air raid was a suspected Nazi sympathiser and a contact of the double-agent 'Snow' created concern that the network had been betrayed to the enemy.[56]

The very fact that every effort was made not to give a name to the organisation in official records is a signal of its extreme secrecy, and it seemed quite acceptable to be recruited to unnamed bodies that were only vaguely described as being part of 'military intelligence'[57] with no other proof being offered. The case of Peter Attwater in Derbyshire has already been discussed; Albert Toon in Birmingham, Grammar School boys in Worcester are mentioned below, as well as a possible Section VII/SDB observer, Emma ——— , in Sussex (see below, p.165). Similarly, when Edmundson was recruiting for the HDS or early Auxiliary Units (and it is possible he was himself unsure of the distinction) he explained: 'These early recruits were told nothing about being in a special unit of the Home Guard – or indeed about being in any formal organisation – and their names were never committed to paper.'[58]

Sabotage: X Branch
Section VII also had a separate sabotage wing. Peter Attwater's network had arms and explosives dumps hidden in the hills around Matlock (at the Masson Cavern and in local quarries) but he was never given details.[59] The sabotage wing may have been that known to Albert Toon from Birmingham as 'X branch' (see below). David Boyle was certainly no stranger to violent tactics, having played a leading role in the brutal secret war with the IRA in 1920-1, and Vivian referred in a deliberately vague fashion to 'special activities' and 'special tasks' in his agreement with MI5 over Section VII. There may not, however, have been a unified structure to the sabotage operations and an arms-length methodology had earlier been favoured by Dansey as a means of protecting SIS intelligence operations. Consequently, a number of accounts of recruitment for sabotage operations do not fit either regular army or Auxiliary Units operations but rather suggest the now-indistinct fingerprint of the intelligence services. In many respects they answer the criticisms of Wilkinson over the direction of the Auxiliary Units (see below, p.97). Some sabotage cells survived into 1944 as a copy of the *Countryman's Diary 1939* (published June 1944) was found in an arms cache discovered at the bottom of a garden in a south-east suburb of Birmingham.[60] This may or may not be the same as a report of a cache including Sten guns and grenades found in a sandpit used by a riding stable at Solihull Lodge in the 1960s.

When Section D was formed as the 'sabotage service' of SIS in 1938 (see Chapter 4), the whole concept of a section to directly organise and undertake disruption and sabotage caused great unease within the rest of SIS. The task was fundamentally at odds with the primary role of SIS in quietly collecting and assessing intelligence. Bickham Sweet-Escott, an officer in Section D and later SOE, put it thus:

> The man who is interested in obtaining intelligence must have peace and quiet, and the agents he employs must never, if possible, be found out. But the man who has to carry out operations will produce loud noises if he is successful, and it is only too likely that some of the men he uses will not escape.[61]

There was also a political aspect with long-time SIS and Section D officer Major Monty Chidson believing that the attempts to ferment armed resistance groups in Europe risked leading to anarchy.[62] Nonetheless, the Eastbourne cell, at least, was initially equipped to undertake sabotage as well as intelligence-gathering. The sabotage function of Section VII is likely to have increased from 1940 when it absorbed HDS sabotage cells that lay beyond the coastal Auxiliary Units; some of these can now be identified by references to a wireless set. In the West Riding of Yorkshire Irene Lockley and her father (a butcher and Home Guardsman) were part of a group 'who met underground and trained to kill, maim and cause as much damage to the enemy as possible' including making Molotov cocktails and derailing trains. This is the language of the HDS but her group met in a quarry where a trap door led into an underground chamber containing a radio and where she learned Morse code.[63]

New cells continued to be formed. In 1941 Attwater recalled meeting a young contact from Nottinghamshire and it is tempting to connect this with a story from Annesley. Lieutenant Colonel John Chaworth-Musters, former Lord Lieutenant and latterly CO of 150th South Notts Hussars Field Regiment (RA), was elder brother to former Section D officer James Chaworth-Musters (then working in Britain in the SOE Scandinavian section). In 1941 he retired from active service in the Middle East to his home at Annesley Hall, Nottinghamshire.[64] Quite possibly on the suggestion of his brother (who rejoined SIS in 1943) John formed a network of at least two cells, with one based in the wooded estate of Annesley. This cell of six men was under 18-year-old mining engineer Eric Deverill who, despite his youth, may have had wider responsibilities, together with three miners (Jack Attwood, Jack Kirk and Charles Bramley), the estate gamekeeper (Frank Saint) and a local poacher (Kelly Cooper). At first meeting in a building at Home Farm, a hide was later constructed on a densely-wooded ridge within the Annesley estate and explosives laid ready in two railway tunnels, the local telephone exchange and electricity sub-station. The cell included Deverill's later wife, Joan (they married in 1943), who had also signed the Official Secrets Act and may have been a wireless operator. There was another cell at Moor Green.

After the war Eric's son recalled his father having two identity cards identifying him as 'Captain Eric Deverill, Military Intelligence MI7'. MI7 was the largely civilian Press and Propaganda section of the War Office Directorate of Military Intelligence but in June 1940 its responsibilities had been transferred to the Ministry of Information. Press organisations were frequently used as convenient cover by SIS but, although the exact date of the ID cards is not known, an 18 to 22-year-old captain might raise questions. It might suggest Deverill had a wider role than the leader of a single cell, even receiving some form of payment, and perhaps Colonel Chaworth-Musters wanted a traditional military chain of command. A use of the officially-disbanded 'MI7' might have been used as a cover code for a Section VII operation in the same way as B.26 of MI5. Another curiosity in the story is that Eric Deverill reportedly described Colonel Chaworth-Musters as head of '202 Division', implying a relationship with the Auxiliary

Units whose Operational Patrols from September 1942 were designated 201, 202, 203 Reserve Battalions, Home Guard. There is no evidence that the Auxiliary Units were organised in Nottinghamshire and this may have been a later war device, at a time when the existence of the Auxiliary Units was becoming more widely known, to conceal the involvement of SIS in case their operations were also discovered.[65]

Some cells used a working membership of the Home Guard as a cover for extra-curricular guerrilla activities. About 30 miles north of Matlock is the small village of Mellor, near Stockport. Some years ago a rusty Thompson M1A1 sub-machine gun was recovered from a well in the garden of the Old Vicarage. It was discovered after the property owners were told the story of a teenager, Eric Nussen, one night helping a group of men hide an arms cache there during the war. The material was placed on a ledge half way down the well but the Thompson had evidently slipped off and escaped recovery at the end of the war. Subsequent excavation revealed 300 rounds of live .45ACP ammunition as well as ammunition for a .455 revolver. Auxiliary Units and Home Guard were only issued with the early Thompson M1928A1. The Home Guard Thompsons were withdrawn as early as March 1942, followed by the Auxiliary Units from September whereas the Thompson M1A1 was only introduced to British service in 1943. The Mellor Thompson was hidden in 1943 as part of a secret arms cache organised by a local corporal in the Home Guard, Peter Adshead. He had approached the teenager, who was an underage member of his Home Guard platoon (aged just 15), to ask if there was a hiding place for some material on his parents' isolated property. Having discreetly shown Adshead the location of a well in the garden, Eric was ordered to open the slab covering the steps leading down to the well, then to meet the corporal at a farm gate at 3am one morning. From there Adshead led a party of around 10 heavily-laden men to the well entrance and was then told to make himself scarce. The incident was never mentioned again.[66] This clandestine unit had clearly been issued with the latest weaponry, of a type not used by the Home Guard or Auxiliary Units (who are not, in any case, known to have operated in this area). However, the site is only c.30 miles from the known SIS resistance cell at Matlock, Derbyshire which is known to have had a number of arms caches in the surrounding area.

In Birmingham, Home Guard Albert Toon was recruited by an unnamed lieutenant from a mysterious organisation calling itself 'X Branch'. He was told to keep a low profile within his Home Guard unit, although the various training courses that he was sent on would have qualified him as a weapons instructor; one such course was at the isolated Western Command Altcar Training Area on Merseyside, ostensibly a Lewis-gun course, but where he was taught how to make and use home-made explosives. He was also trained in Morse code (implying the use of a wireless set).[67] Toon was also trained in the use of the clockwork timing mechanisms that had been developed by Section D.[68] Trainees on his Altcar course included officers and other ranks from both the regular army and Home Guard; all were treated equally and addressed simply as students by the instructors. Given the mix of students, the likelihood is that these men were being trained to operate after both regular and Home Guard forces had collapsed and the country had been occupied. The instruction for Toon upon invasion was to report to a local school where, and only then, he would be given further orders and be told where his explosives dumps were hidden, at which point it is presumed that he would be given instructions on the method of his wireless communication. He was told that he would be working alone and needed to practice silent movement at night. Toon did not directly provide a date for these activities but he did tell how he was trained to link up Type 73 'Thermos' grenades (introduced in November 1940) in order to create huge demolition charges.[69] Toon's code name was 'Charlie' and is therefore reminiscent of the series of aliases given to the SIS intelligence cell at Matlock which also connected to units in Birmingham and Nottingham.

Another possible story of 'X Branch', albeit with a more rogue feel, comes from south of Birmingham in Worcester. Although uncorroborated, the account has a number of unique details not to be expected if simply a re-telling of Auxiliary Units history. A 14-year-old pupil at Worcester Grammar School recounted being recruited, along with half a dozen older boys from the school OTC, by three unnamed officers from 'X Branch' and given intensive training, three nights a week, in guerrilla warfare by two mature NCOs (a sergeant and corporal), described as 'particularly hard characters' who wore no insignia on their battledress. An officer also made monthly visits. In common with other known SIS operatives, they were given false Christian names as code names. When at school they were ordered not to associate with each other and were told to explain their nocturnal activities as being Home Guard messengers. The boys were introduced to a hide on Gorse Hill, on the east side of Worcester, whose existence, although now destroyed and built-over, has been independently verified. Although having an entrance shaft on the Auxiliary Units pattern, it comprised only a single room built of railway sleepers. There were bunks but only a bucket for toilet needs. The regular appearance of the two NCOs over two years suggests the latter were based at the 23rd Infantry Training Centre at Norton Barracks, Worcester, where both the boys and the local Auxiliary Units were trained and where the maverick SIS officer John Todd, Intelligence Officer for both the Auxiliary Units Operational Branch and SDB (Plate 14), had an office.

Like the Auxiliary Units, the boys are reported as having Smith and Wesson revolvers, P17 rifles, Sten guns, a .22 rifle with telescopic sights and 'silencer', and Fairbairn-Sykes knives. The boys also apparently received a Vickers heavy machine gun and later a Bren gun; they also received instruction on captured German weapons. There was a harder edge to their training that has not been reported elsewhere: they were taught to operate singly or in pairs, including acting as suicide bombers – having been told that their life expectancy was likely to be only 72 hours after going into action. One technique was to approach a German guard-post pleading hunger and begging for bread. Having been given a chunk to tear it in half and put one part into a pocket – on the excuse that this was 'for my brother' – they would then pull out a grenade. For this task they were taught such German phrases as 'Ich habe hunger. Haben sie Früsuck'. This story, and the existence of a series of Auxiliary Units-type Operational Bases ringing Worcester but unknown to any of the Auxiliary Units veterans interviewed in the late 1990s (see below, p.75), suggests there was a complex of guerrilla organisations around Worcester whose story has yet to be fully understood although it seems very likely that the ruthless John Todd may have been the common denominator, running an SIS operation as well as his Auxiliary Units duties. The Gorse Hill cell was stood down in 1942 with the words from one of the 'X Branch' NCOs 'That's it lads, it's finished'.[70]

In the twenty-first century such training of boy soldiers seems abhorrent but it was not so unusual in the 1940s, especially in resistance groups. Anthony Butler, like Attwater, was also a young ARP Messenger in Surrey aged 16 in 1940, who told his future wife in the late 1940s that he had been recruited to an unknown organisation, signed the Official Secrets Act and been trained with dum-dum bullets. He had later been unable to join the forces due to a burst eardrum and such uncorroborated stories risk being dismissed as a post-war justification for a perceived lack of involvement in the war effort, but on this occasion his wartime souvenirs included a Mk1 Pull Switch![71]

There are other stories of individual saboteurs and assassins that are, by their nature, difficult to corroborate. From Bristol, a Post Office communications worker revealed on his deathbed that the revolver he had kept beside his bed throughout the war was to have been used to assassinate his supervisor following any invasion – because the supervisor knew the location of secret telephone lines. From the Black Country region a man claimed he was trained how to assassinate using poison from a hidden hypodermic needle (in the manner enthusiastically proposed in the discussion over the Davies plan of June 1940, see below, p.68). The story was not beyond what was being planned at the time. In February 1940 Hugh Pollard, small arms specialist in Section D, made a discreet enquiry to the Home Office forensic scientist and leading expert on the use of poisons in murder, Gerald Roche Lynch, over a 'toxicological matter'. Roche Lynch was so concerned that he demanded 'the fullest credentials from those who were instructing him'.[72] In June 1940 Lord Hankey (Minister without Portfolio, Churchill's security advisor and champion of Section D) had enthusiastically suggested the use of an 'undetectable poison for assassination on the Irish model' (see below, p.68).

In the Midlands therefore, there are a number of accounts of operations run by 'X Branch' where saboteurs were told to work singly or in pairs. Linking Matlock and Birmingham there are aliases based on false personal names. The agent from the Matlock cell was instructed by a mature former NCO who became an officer and had an ambiguous relationship to Military Intelligence. He met one of the organisers in Birmingham who also showed all the signs of being an ex-NCO. The teenage guerrillas in Worcester were also trained by tough, mature NCOs. The evidence is circumstantial but there are enough similarities to suggest they may have belonged to the same organisation. Did SIS recruit ex-army NCOs to organise their sabotage or 'dirty tricks' wing after the demise of Section D in a return to the loose practice favoured by Dansey (see Chapter 2)?

The Auxiliary Units SDB was not as efficient an intelligence-gathering body as Section VII or Phantom. However, in the Machiavellian world of Boyle and Dansey's SIS, its likely rapid discovery by German intelligence upon invasion might potentially divert attention from the existence of the deep-cover Section VII resistance, which would have operated at only a minimum level during the actual invasion. To continue to protect its interests, the SDB remained under discreet SIS control at least during 1941. A precedent for such a coldly-calculating strategy was the creation of Dansey's Z Organisation in Europe in anticipation that the traditional network of agents posing as 'passport control officers' was likely to be quickly broken. The summary dismissal of

Laurence Grand in September 1940 – the figurehead of the HDS and a name already known to German Intelligence – also helped in this process by implying that SIS had ceased any responsibility for a secret intelligence network within Britain.

Here, therefore, is tantalising evidence for a long-term intelligence and sabotage organisation operating in the UK throughout the war by SIS as the cadre of Britain's resistance organisation, ready to expand when the time was ripe. It escaped both the attention of Nazi and Soviet spies during the Second World War and later historians during the Cold War. Is it, indeed, one of the last, best-kept secrets of the Second World War?

Chapter 3

The Impact of Dunkirk: Rethinking the Military Options

The carefully-laid contingency plans for a long-term British Resistance were well underway by June 1940 but the more rushed plans for guerrilla warfare from that time can only be understood by appreciating the wider panic following the retreat through France and the Dunkirk evacuation, combined with a rising public mood to fight in whatever way they could. Until April 1940 and the successful German invasion of Norway, the War Office had regarded invasion as 'an unlikely contingency'.[1] The Chiefs of Staff held a meeting on 7 May to discuss the new dangers but remained confident that the Low Countries and France still provided a buffer to the narrow Straits of Dover with, if necessary, the English Channel as a secure defence against seaborne invasion. In just a few days Holland had been overrun and airborne assault was seen as the new threat, able to land behind beach defenders and disrupt reinforcements. The defence planners now had to consider the possibility of both airborne and seaborne landings as well as the potential for an invasion via Ireland. They also feared a collapse of morale from aerial bombing and the consequences of political division. One immediate response to the worsening situation was the formation of the Local Defence Volunteers (LDV) on 14 May. This nationwide organisation of 'Parashots' could at least provide an early warning system against the realisation that parachute landings could occur anywhere in the country; not all of them were to be armed and their role was initially not to engage the enemy but to simply report such landings to the authorities.

The speed with which France was overrun shocked British and German generals alike. On 20 May the first Panzer units reached the English Channel and on 22 May the Chiefs of Staff recognised that invasion on the south coast had become a very real threat. On that day, John Dolphin of Section D presented his ideas for what became the Home Defence Scheme to Laurence Grand, who began an immediate mobilisation (see Chapter 4). The Chiefs of Staff were pessimistic; a report to the War Cabinet on 25 May concluded 'should the enemy succeed in establishing a force, with its vehicles, firmly ashore – the army in the United Kingdom, which is very short of equipment, has not got the offensive power to drive it out'.[2] It is no coincidence that this was the day that Captain Peter Fleming of MI(R) was instructed by the Directorate of Military Intelligence (DMI) to begin thinking of ways to use the LDV to redress the weakness in conventional forces by engaging in guerrilla operations behind enemy lines (Plate 7 and Appendix 2).

On 26 May the evacuation of the British Expeditionary Force (BEF) began from Dunkirk. Almost 340,000 men were rescued from the beaches from 27 May to 4 June but the army lost almost all its heavy equipment, leaving Britain defended by eighty obsolete tanks. Section D of SIS immediately switched from supplying arms caches and training for nascent resistance organisations in France and the Low Countries to distributing similar supplies across Britain for the new Home Defence Scheme (HDS). These fast-moving events brought about a wide range of emotions from steely resolution to what future second-in-command of the Auxiliary Units, Major Peter Wilkinson, described as a 'numbing incredulity'.[3] The widespread enthusiasm to join the LDV showed a determination to resist by whatever means but there were still those in government prepared to consider a peace settlement. Lord Halifax and Neville Chamberlain led a concerted campaign to convince the War Cabinet that a negotiated peace was the only option. By 28 May it seemed as if the peace party had the upper hand but the new Prime Minister, Winston Churchill, outmanoeuvred Halifax by calling a meeting of the Outer Cabinet where he had a better chance of swaying opinion. Here he delivered one of his most important speeches, passionately declaring 'If this long island story of ours is to end at last, let it end only when each one of us lies choking in his own blood upon the ground'. Having convinced the Outer Cabinet to agree to fight on whatever the cost, the Inner War Cabinet felt obliged to fall in line and Halifax's peace plan was defeated. At this point, the whole course of the war and the future of Europe was on a knife-edge. Churchill had won this crucial debate but Halifax and Chamberlain would both act as brakes on the development of Britain's 'illegal' plans for civilian resistance.

Fortunately, despite the disaster of the fall of France, the Royal Navy was still intact and the technology of the time made large-scale amphibious landings difficult. The Germans were intending to tow the main invasion army across the Channel in flat-bottomed barges which would have proved a nightmare for the soldiers. They also still relied heavily on horses for general transport and, in particular, to drag heavy equipment ashore – consequently planning to land over 11,000 horses under fire in the first two waves.[4] Hitler was also expecting that the British government would recognise their hopeless condition and seek terms of surrender, which would allow him to turn with minimum effort towards his main enemy – communist Russia. Only with hindsight was it known that Hitler did not formally begin preparations for invasion until the issue of Directive 16 on 16 July (see Appendix 1) and by the end of that month his military planners were already having serious doubts about its practicality. At the time, intelligence on German plans was mixed and invasion seemed imminent. On 4 June Churchill delivered his famous 'We shall fight on the beaches' speech and within a week General Thorne, the new commander of XII Corps responsible for the most likely invasion area, had created his 'Observation Unit' as a prototype military guerrilla force (see Chapter 5). The Germans entered Paris on 14 June and on 17 June the Cabinet agreed in outline to the creation of the Auxiliary Units as a legal, military, alternative to the HDS although it took until 2 July for their War Establishment to be approved and they could begin mobilising. France finally surrendered on 22 June; a further 144,000 British troops were evacuated through other French ports from 15-25 June. The USA looked on closely, unwilling to provide support until they were certain that Britain would stand and fight, rather than similarly sue for peace.

On 19 June the Chiefs of Staff formally warned the War Cabinet that the threat of invasion seemed imminent but it was not until 25 June, as the last British troops escaped from France, that General Ironside, Commander-in-Chief, Home Forces, presented to the Chiefs of Staff his plan for the defence of Britain, known as Operational Instruction No.3. The basic idea was for a 'coastal crust' of defences, manned mainly by sacrificial second-line troops, to delay the enemy advance for as long as possible. A series of static 'Stop Lines' behind the coast would then provide a defence in depth and hinder free movement of any enemy that might penetrate inland and, in the words of General Ironside, 'rip the guts out of the country'.

The main front-line infantry and armour would be held back behind the last line of defence on the GHQ Line, protecting London and the industrial heartland and ready to mount a counter-attack once the principal focus of the enemy attack became clear. These 'Leopard' brigades were not expected to be deployed until the third day of landings, when they could concentrate against an enemy that was expected to be low on supplies.[5] In the meantime the LDV would harry the enemy advance as best they could, focused on blocking 'nodal points' and obliging the enemy to use up its limited supplies of fuel and ammunition in their destruction. The LDV were not expected to survive more than a few hours but their orders from GHQ were to 'defend their post to the last man, since every minute gained may be of vital importance'.[6] It was with good reason that West Cornwall LDV described themselves as a 'suicide squad'.[7] On the invasion front line in south-east England, Home Guardsman Bert Northwood agreed: 'Our lads . . . expected to die and accepted that fact: they wouldn't have run away.'[8] For their part, the German General Staff likened the prospect of facing a defence in depth as putting their troops through a 'sausage machine'.[9]

The counter-invasion plan coldly relied on a huge level of sacrifice by 'expendable' manpower in order to exhaust the enemy before the front-line troops mounted their counter-attacks. Ironside was trying to make the best use of very limited resources but his plan met with immediate dismay amongst the General Staff, not least because the plan seemed to accept that a large percentage of southern and eastern England might fall, albeit temporarily, under enemy occupation. The concept of static defence lines also brought back uncomfortable memories of First World War trench warfare and the spectre of a long-drawn-out siege on British soil, leaving large slices of the country under much longer-term occupation, a possibility that was brought home to the Cabinet when they were obliged to consider the role of the British police under occupation. On 26 June the Vice-Chiefs of Staff expressed considerable opposition to the 'coastal crust' concept with comments that the main counter-attack might only be offered when nearly half the country had been overrun. Indeed, they described the plan as suicidal.[10] In the background, the HDS of Section D was already rushing to distribute arms dumps and mobilising civilians nationwide to cause general mayhem across any occupied area (see Chapter 4), and XII Corps in Kent and Sussex was putting in place its local plans for military guerrilla warfare (see Chapter 5). Unknown to all, Section VII of SIS had quietly put into place a scheme for long-term resistance and intelligence-gathering (see Chapter 2). The Auxiliary Units were at this stage little more than a twinkle in the eye of GHQ (see Chapter 6).

As the first wave of invasion was expected to suffer 50 per cent casualties and to land with supplies for only four days' operation and fuel for 100 miles, the priority was to cut the enemy supply lines and supplement the Home Guard in bogging down its advance for as long as possible.[11] The absence of War Office forward planning for guerrilla warfare in Britain, followed by initial indecisiveness of planning for the Auxiliary Units, is ironic given the supposed expertise of British officers through MI(R) who had tried to advise foreign governments across Europe on such matters. It is, however, in keeping with the wider indecision in the War Office and government surrounding the creation of the LDV.[12] Section D and MI(R) had both been briefed in May 1939 on the plans by Poland for guerrilla warfare in advance of invasion and the MI(R) Polish Mission of August 1939 had been intended, somewhat arrogantly, to provide advice to the Polish General Staff on how to organise the new units. Unaided, by the time of the German invasion of Poland in September 1939, 800 guerrilla fighters had been trained and equipped (with some explosives and devices from Section D), organised in what finally became, from August 1940, a model for the Auxiliary Units. The Polish guerrillas had formed patrols of three to seven men, organised in groups of seven to twenty-five patrols. Based in underground hides, they were to let the invasion pass over them and then carry out pre-determined sabotage. There were also larger partisan bands of fifteen men, tasked with raiding across the Polish/Slovakian border and behind German lines. Ignoring such precedent in Poland and Czechoslovakia and in a continuance of the arrogant nationalism of the military command of the time (which saw Peter Wilkinson feverishly reading Gubbins' recent pamphlets on the journey to Poland in August 1939 so that he could appear as an 'expert' to the Poles), there was an assumption post-war that Britain must have been the first country to prepare in advance for the eventuality of invasion by creating a guerrilla network to assist conventional forces. Instead, the HDS and Auxiliary Units were the product of last-minute desperation and were considered as more or less suicidal short-term expedients within the broader strategic defence plan. Only the XII Corps Observation Unit, created after 8 June on a personal initiative by the Corps Commander, General Thorne, was fully integrated into the battle strategy.

Into this charged atmosphere came a myriad of rushed proposals for irregular warfare to supplement the regular forces. Captain Walker, Royal Marines, wrote a paper on the subject on 23 May and forwarded it to Lord Hankey on 31 May.[13] Under the heading 'Preparations of the nation for total war within this country' he proposed that 'Every citizen of this Country must now be prepared to take an active part in fighting an invader . . . There are many men and women who will be prepared to give their lives in order to deny success to the enemy; as were the people of Spain, Poland and Finland.' Ignoring the legal status of such combatants, he went on 'It is submitted that in all our villages and towns men and women must be organised and armed to deal with enemy mobile parties of motor-cyclists and tanks, or troops in lorries'. Significantly, Walker notes 'The organisation of our civilian population must be linked up with the military defence measures but, it is considered, should not be a Service organisation. There must be no unnecessary delays in organising, due to service routine or the necessity for Committee decisions.' Breaking ranks with War Office and DMI policy, he proposed a civilian Chief of Defence responsible only to the Prime Minister. One wonders who he had been talking to as he makes the point 'The Spaniard knew how to deal with individual tanks. We have many men with experience of the Spanish War.'[14] Is this a veiled reference to Tom Wintringham whose profile was beginning to rise through newspaper articles, lecture tours and the lobbying of Parliament? Walker went on to recommend that throughout the country there should be bands of 'do-or-die volunteers equipped with dynamite and petrol bombs'. He explained 'These volunteers to be secretly enlisted and organised as speedily as possible'. Given that Walker was a serving officer and addressed his paper as being from Admiralty Arch one wonders what his commanding officer thought of this departure from the normal chain of command and his suggestion of a non-military control of such forces – but both Grand and Wintringham would no doubt have approved| Hankey's reply on 3 June, coming after the ISPB meeting on 27 May (see below), was diplomatic and non-committal: 'The whole of this question has been taken in hand'. The Home Defence Scheme of SIS had, in fact, just mobilised.

From Parliament came the unofficial 'Guerrilla Warfare Committee' led by the MP for Ormskirk, Commander Stephen King-Hall, RN. On 2 July, unaware of the existing HDS and the approval of the War Establishment of the Auxiliary Units on that very day, the committee produced a report wanting more emphasis on 'Totalitarian Guerrilla Warfare' and better coordination of irregular warfare with an official Guerrilla Warfare Committee that would include civilian representatives as well as the fighting services.[15] On 9 July Hankey wrote to King-Hall to congratulate him on his 'quite admirable' report and repeated the assurance given to Walker that plans for a coordinator of such activity was in hand. Indeed, Hugh Dalton, Minister for Economic Warfare, had just seized the initiative from the War Office and SIS to create the new Special Operations Executive (SOE).[16]

Characteristically, Winston Churchill was attracted to any novel means of resistance and particularly to the concept of 'storm troops' as employed on a large scale by the Germans in the First World War. Thus, when the Cabinet agreed on 17 June to the formation of the Auxiliary Units, based around the new LDV, it was in terms of 'sections of Storm Troopers on a full-time basis, as part of the LDVs'.[17] On 19 June Churchill asked on the further progress of 'storm troops' but these were not the small sabotage teams that were to characterise the Auxiliary Units. Instead he wanted 20,000 men 'ready to spring at the throat of any small landing or descents' armed with the latest equipment including Thompsons and with motorcycles and armoured cars. Rather than the large units that Churchill had in mind, Ironside replied by saying there should be a number of smaller specialist units including tank-hunting platoons (which were being formed in each battalion of the Home Guard as well as in the regular army), the Independent Companies and 'Special Irregular Units (Wingate's, Hopkinson's and Americans)'.[18] The 'Hopkinson's' were the Phantom unit (see Chapter 10) and the 'Americans' were the 1st American (Motorised) Squadron of the Home Guard (see Chapter 11). Wingate's potential contribution is discussed below.

Orde Wingate, later to achieve fame as founder of the Chindits in Burma, was in May 1940 a captain in Anti-Aircraft Command. He proposed a version of the Special Night Squads that he had raised in Palestine. Ironside was dubious about the idea but on 2 June suggested that Wingate might raise an 'Ironside' unit, comprising a lightly-armoured mobile column out of volunteers from his Anti-Aircraft Brigade. Wingate immediately raised 150 men and 10 officers for training in guerrilla warfare. By then Wingate had demonstrated his famous knack of irritating his superior officers and his plans foundered. Lord Ismay concluded 'I wonder if there has ever been a man who went so far out of his way to be intolerable to the very people who wished to help him'.[19] Wingate persisted with his ideas for British Special Night Squads but GHQ demanded to know 'full and exact details of the proposed establishment' and nothing came of it. He did give a lecture on guerrilla warfare at Tom Wintringham's Osterley Park Training School where the meeting between fiercely fundamentalist Christian

Wingate and Marxist Wintringham must have been interesting. The likely paranoia of MI5 over this contact with Wintringham's suspected plans to raise a 'red army' can only have been increased when forty-three former members of Wingate's Special Night Squads in Palestine, members of the Jewish Haganah, were arrested for illegal possession of weapons which it was feared might be used in the future against the British establishment.[20]

Through his increasing public profile in the media and his lobbying of both government and sympathetic military figures, Tom Wintringham (Plate 45 and Appendix 2) had a huge influence in the period following Dunkirk by creating a popular mood that demanded a more aggressive role for the LDV and its expansion into a 'people's army'. He went beyond the private reports of Walker and King-Hall that could be contained by Hankey. On 15 June the first of Wintringham's rousing articles on civilian resistance was published in Edward Hulton's *Picture Post*. Hulton was, at the time, working with Section D. Wintringham outlined the principles of effective road blocks, destruction of petrol stocks, demolition of bridges, creation of village fortresses and how to successfully ambush tanks. At this stage, however, the term guerrilla had not entered his vocabulary (a term he did not use until the opening of the Osterley Park Home Guard Training School in July). Instead, his focus was on encouraging mass action. For the government, although they took advantage of his practical advice and the positive mood that his articles engendered, he represented the dangerous possibility of a descent into anarchy. He announced 'I am trying to do what I advise everyone to do – get on with the job of defence against invasion, without waiting for official approval'.[21] On the next day he sent a 'Plan of Action' to the government via the radical Liberal MP Tom Horabin, calling for Churchill to broadcast an appeal for a citizen army and to promise 100 million hand grenades within a fortnight together with two million rifles and 50,000 Thompson sub-machine guns from the USA as soon as possible.[22] Wintringham, in pragmatic mood, did suggest that Horabin, before circulating the Plan, might prefer to delete his suggestion that the King renounce the title of Emperor and that India should immediately be given its independence!

There was a fear that enemy invasion would be assisted by local collaborators (the 'fifth column'). The speed of the Nazi advance through the Low Countries and France was widely blamed on local sympathisers who were believed to have provided intelligence to the German armed forces, committed acts of sabotage and subversion and then formed the core of a puppet government. The Chiefs of Staff saw this as a key element of Nazi invasion planning and 'a very dangerous and important part in any operation the enemy may undertake against this country'.[23] Fears were fuelled by scare stories of deliberate breaches of the blackout, flashing light signals to German bombers, crops cut to leave arrows pointing at military installations and other activities. It was well known that the German intelligence services had been involved in economic espionage in Britain prior to the outbreak of war but the agents had been withdrawn along with the German embassy staff in 1939. Subsequent fresh agents were sent in 'blind' or to contacts that, unknown to the *Abwehr*, were either wireless operators that had been 'turned' by MI5 or had never existed in the first place. As a consequence, the Germans were deprived of up-to-date intelligence and were unable to engage with the small groups of Nazi sympathisers in the country. Equally worrying was the fear of how far British Intelligence, the military and government had been infiltrated by

Soviet agents, with MI5 believing, with subsequent justification, that, prior to June 1941, any information collected by idealistic communists could be passed straight to the Nazis.

The threat of fifth-column activity had been greatly lessened by the effective infiltration of communist and pro-fascist groups by MI5, including extensive secret copying of mail and their work as agent-provocateurs to draw any likely recruits out of the shadows. One of their agents was the person in charge of the secret headquarters of the British Union of Fascists (BUF)![24] They also had access to the discussions of the Central Committee of the Communist Party of Great Britain (CPGB). Nonetheless, although their official bodies were neutralised, the recognition that there was indeed a significant body of potential pro-Nazi sympathisers remained a worry in 1940. As well as the 8,700 members of the BUF, there were 20,000 members of the CPGB to consider, with their newspaper, *The Daily Worker*, having a much wider circulation of 90,000. The confused attitude of the British Communist Party to the war in 1940 was replicated across Europe and it is arguable how far its members would have supported an active resistance in an occupied Britain during 1940. In France, their Communist Party retained an ambivalence towards the war until just before the invasion of Russia. Only then did it launch the National Front whose members soon gained a reputation as one of the best-organised of the various resistance groups. In 1940-1 during the era of the Hitler-Stalin Non-Aggression Pact, the BUF and CPGB were seen as two edges of the same sword. An added complication was the spectre of renewed activity by the IRA. This was the context for the interest of MI5 in the potential for internal security offered both by Section VII and the Special Duties Branch of the Auxiliary Units. Given the wide range of potential threats and what they considered to be the unwillingness of MI5 to share their intelligence, in early May the Chiefs of Staff Committee had wanted to ensure that people known to belong to subversive organisations could be contained; by the end of June some army commands were already compiling arrest lists which may be the origin of the assassination lists reputedly handed (officially or not) to the Auxiliary Units (see below, p.101). [25]

The work of MI5 together with SIS Section VII, the Special Duties Branch of the Auxiliary Units and the Field Security Sections of Military Intelligence were a vital part of the network of covert spying on local communities that contained the growth of any significant organisation of collaborators. This was an integral part of the complex network of secret activities that helped thwart the invasion threat and it is no coincidence that the mechanism by which SIS established its resistance network in Britain was as a partnership with the counter-espionage section of MI5. As the invasion threat receded, the SDB of the Auxiliary Units took on a further internal security role, which General Franklyn, then C-in- C Home Forces, eventually described as the most important contribution of the Auxiliary Units – to guard against loose talk in the run-up to D-Day.

ISPB Meeting 27 May 1940

The Inter-Services Project Board (ISPB) was a not very effective advisory body created in early May 1940 to try to coordinate plans for Europe-wide sabotage. It was, however, subordinate to the Chiefs of Staff with little power in its own right. The ISPB had a floating membership, usually with representatives of the Air and Naval intelligence services, Section D (represented by Laurence Grand) and MI(R) (represented by Jo Holland, who was also chairman). The Joint Intelligence Committee on 21 May requested that Holland, together with the Air Ministry and Admiralty representatives on the ISPB, produce a paper for the Prime Minister on the likely German strategy against Britain.[26] Consequently, the ISPB meeting of 27 May, originally intended to focus on the need for irregular warfare in France and Belgium, was quickly tasked with considering contingency plans for Britain following any invasion. As a result, the meeting had a notably wider attendance than usual. There was Captain Peter Fleming, well-known author and adventurer, recruited to MI(R) in August 1939 whilst a reserve officer in the Grenadier Guards, to research the potential of assisting and developing Chinese guerrilla warfare against the Japanese. He had headed the No.10 Mission to Namsos in Norway and had just been tasked with researching ways of using the growing LDV as a guerrilla force behind enemy lines. Also present was Captain John Dolphin, a Section D research engineer who had, on 22 May, proposed the idea of the Home Defence Scheme (HDS).[27] Dolphin was an expert on sabotage methodology who had also provided counter-espionage advice to MI5 as to potential German sabotage targets in London.

Jo Holland had prepared a briefing paper prior to the meeting which opened with the surmise 'that we are entering a phase of "total war" and in consequence the civil population of all classes should be asked to make the same sacrifices as the fighting forces'. This comment had been aimed particularly at populations on the Continent with a view to organising sabotage in advance of further enemy occupation in line with the 'D Scheme' of March 1939 (see below, p.44), but the scope was to expand dramatically at the meeting towards the organisation of guerrilla warfare within Britain.[28] An analysis of previous German offensives particularly identified the need to disrupt lines of supply and a settled consolidation of the enemy forces:

> When a part of the country had been overrun, and at a time when the strain on a loose line of communication must have been great, and the strain on operating personnel in advanced elements must have been greater, little was done either to deny the enemy essential supplies, or to ensure that the invader had no rest.[29]

Grand pre-empted the debate with his announcement of the creation of the Home Defence Scheme (see below, Chapter 4). This was said to be 'already partially organised' in Britain.[30] Under Viscount Bearsted, the HDS would provide a short-term civilian guerrilla force in line with the layered approach to resistance advocated abroad by SIS. His guerrilla campaign would support regular forces, protected to a degree by its covert nature within the community, but to avoid risk it was critical that there be no contact with the deep-cover resistance organisation of Section VII. This entry of civilians onto the battlefield caused consternation among the representatives of the War Office and echoed the nervousness of the French and Norwegian authorities on organising irregular guerrilla activities. The meeting was obliged to accept this *fait accompli*, which Grand could argue was applicable as a contingency against the collapse of organised military resistance and enemy occupation at which point, under existing convention, SIS would assume control of action. On the outbreak of war the DMI had accepted Holland's analysis: 'it is for Section D when action must be subterranean, i.e. in countries which are in effective enemy occupation, and it is for us, when the action is a matter of military missions, whether regular or irregular'.[31] This was repeated in the evidence of the DMI to the Hankey Inquiry into SIS in March 1940, where Hankey concluded that it was for MI(R) to organise sabotage in arenas where regular British forces were directly involved whilst Section D would undertake operations in areas under enemy occupation.[32] Applying this principle, the ISPB meeting tried to restore the balance by agreeing that until that event, present guerrilla activities in England should be controlled 'on a military basis'. That this had to be discussed at all is a pointer to the tensions between the War Office and SIS. Here was an attempt to rein in the expanding ambitions of Section D by a War Office worried that a civilian private army, acting outside its control, was being created. At the same time there were proposals to expand the SIS Special Communications Units (SCUs) into what was later termed by the Director of Signals at the War Office as an SIS 'private army'.[33] It was instead assumed by Holland that any guerrilla warfare in Britain should be based around an expansion of the recently-formed Independent Companies (early commandos) originally formed for the Norwegian campaign on the instigation of MI(R) and still referred to in the ISPB meeting as 'the MI(R)s', rather than create a new underground guerrilla movement. The Independent Companies had been rushed into action in Norway with little specialist training and served there primarily as light infantry.[34] Five companies were still in Scotland after their deployment to Norway had been cancelled. The meeting eventually agreed: 'The regular defences require supplementing with guerrilla-type troops who will allow themselves to be overrun and who thereafter will be responsible for hitting the enemy in the comparatively soft spots behind zones of concentrated attack.'[35] The concept was therefore firmly focused on Holland's vision of a deployment of regular troops to undertake work behind enemy lines (as implemented after D-Day by the SAS) and this focus on formed military units rather than civilian saboteurs was continued into the later Auxiliary Units.

With the HDS already mobilising, it was, however, agreed that SIS should organise a specialised civilian sabotage programme preceding any occupation and in support of the Independent Companies. 'The Secret Intelligence Service must be prepared similarly to organise and execute action of a technical sabotage kind requiring special equipment.'[36] Although Holland might have been thinking of a very targeted programme of specialist sabotage by Section D agents, Grand instead interpreted the conclusions of the ISPB meeting as an authority to continue to mobilise the HDS as a nationwide civilian guerrilla movement, as a natural extension of the work he had been engaged on abroad since March 1939 and continuing the work currently underway supplying arms dumps in France and the Low Countries. The ISPB discussion was not about creating a resistance movement in an area under firm control of the enemy (as we think of later Second World War resistance movements in occupied Europe). What was under discussion here was short-term guerrilla action on the flanks and rear of an enemy as part of the overall military strategy. Within days of the ISPB meeting, Fleming had moved to Scotland as an instructor at Lochailort and MI(R) influence on events floundered. Instead, it was General Andrew Thorne, commanding XII Corps in Kent and Sussex, who independently from MI(R) established his regional 'Observation Unit' of army guerrilla patrols (see Chapter 5), basing his concept on a visit to a Prussian estate in 1934 where he had learned of the local 'stay behind' units of peasants.[37] Fleming credited Thorne as being the first senior officer to see the potential if 'the enemy in his bridgeheads were harassed by light forces left behind for the purpose' and attacking lines of communications and concentration areas.[38]

Respecting government and War Office policy, the ISPB stopped just short of recommending the organisation of civilian armed resistance in Britain, although Section D had been authorised to encourage this abroad, but did state:

> The whole population, whether in formed or loose formations, or whether as individuals, must be instructed in the sort of contribution they can make to assist the services, and must be encouraged to make their contribution, should the need arise, with the same ruthlessness we may expect from the enemy, whether he is provoked or not.[39]

As the encouragement of civilian subversion was already part of the role of Section D, Grand felt able to interpret this recommendation of the ISPB as further support for his mobilisation of the HDS. Overall, there was plenty of leeway in the decisions to convince Grand that he had a free hand. If the War Office felt that they had brought Grand under control, they were to be swiftly disabused. The history of Section D as compiled by SOE in 1941 (written by Viscount Bearsted's son Anthony, who had also served in Section D) and clearly based on Grand's papers, consequently runs contrary to later accusations that the HDS was set up without authorisation. The SOE report claims that the new HDS was specifically discussed at the ISPB meeting and a clear strategy agreed. In this version of events it was agreed thus:

> At a meeting of the Inter-Services Projects Board held on May 27th it was agreed that a force should be formed, to act in close co-operation with the military authorities, to deal with the enemy in the case of invasion or occupation of parts of England. This force was to be divided into two main sub-sections, – the MIRs [Independent Companies] who would wage guerrilla warfare, and selected D officers who would be attached for special duty to the twelve Regional Civil Commissioners. Under this plan a D officer would work under the Regional Commissioner until the area passed under martial law, when he would serve under the military commander.[40]

The ISPB meeting did not discuss any need for guerrilla units in Britain to have their own two-way wireless system, despite the existing use of wireless in SIS's Eire and Section VII networks, the rushed supply of sets to resistance groups in the Low Countries and recommendations in Gubbins' 1939 manual *The Art of Guerrilla Warfare*. Nonetheless, SIS would shortly install wireless sets in the hides of the XII Corps Observation Unit. This was an element of clandestine operations over which SIS wished to maintain control but the failure to consider this aspect at the meeting may have been a realisation of the likely lack of time for training before invasion. Instead the meeting looked towards what became known as the BEETLE communication system, using broadcasts over existing commercial wireless receivers. The Minutes of the ISPB meeting note 'some form of coordination . . . is necessary. Orders can be received by any wireless set owner. The issue of orders will almost certainly only be possible by the Military Command.'[41]

The idea of BEETLE was that information and instructions could be broadcast from government offices and army commands onto ordinary domestic wireless sets, using regional transmitters, thus allowing a simultaneous transmission of orders without having to go through normal signals channels and avoided the problem of normal telephone communications being cut. Murphy wireless sets (Plate 34) became the standard issue to military commands, with instructions not to use them for any other purpose (there being an obvious temptation to use them for recreational purposes!). The system operated on specific long-band wavelengths to broadcast messages and could include coded operational instructions sent from Army Commands to local HQs. The first priority for deployment in 1940 was for the battalions based on the potential invasion beaches but this was extended in July 1941 to anti-tank islands or other units not in a normal wireless group who were at risk of cuts to their normal communications, and included units of the Home Guard. The Special Duties Branch of the Auxiliary Units was, however, only incorporated into the system in 1943 as a reflection of its limited role in anti-invasion planning.

Even if a two-way wireless network seemed impractical at the time, there was a recognition of the need for maximising the potential to obtain intelligence on the movements of an invader and stated that 'Some form of "watcher" organisation linked with a command centre on the lines of ADGB control is required'. The Air Defence of Great Britain (ADGB) coordinated anti-aircraft units, Fighter Command and the Observer Corps.[42] There was already the Observer Corps to serve the RAF and the Admiralty had just taken over and were expanding the coast watchers of the Coastguard Service. What was missing was a more landward service. The meeting goes into no further details and was either being extremely circumspect, or ignorant, as regards the plans already underway in Section VII of SIS, although it is perhaps significant that the term 'watcher' service was already widely used in SIS. This discussion may, however, have set Grand's train of thought in motion for an expansion of his sabotage plans for the HDS into an intelligence-gathering role, which would in turn eventually lead to the Special Duties Branch of the Auxiliary Units, so finally giving the War Office a direct stake in this process.

Chapter 4

Home Defence Scheme of Section D

> At our most forlorn moment when our army was pouring back from Dunkirk through gates we could never have shut against an invading enemy, Colonel Grand conceived the plan of organising throughout Great Britain a closely-coordinated sabotage and intelligence network among the civilian population who would be left behind in any territories which the German armies might temporarily be able to occupy.
>
> Section D Closing Report, 27 August 1940[1]

In April 1938 Admiral Sinclair, in readying SIS for war, had extended the traditional focus on quietly collecting intelligence into creating a dedicated sabotage service in the new Section D (aka, Section IX, the 'Sabotage Service' or the 'Statistical Research Department of the War Office'), reporting directly to the Chief of SIS. Section D was under Laurence Grand, previously a Royal Engineer major in the War Office, and it would operate worldwide outside the normal conventions of warfare. (The background to the creation of Section D has been detailed in *D for Destruction: forerunner of SOE* and need not be repeated here.)[2] This was a radical departure for SIS, as it was preparing to go on the offensive in a 'no-holds barred' approach which caused consternation in Whitehall. Section D was 'To investigate every possibility of attacking potential enemies by means other than the operations of military forces'.[3]

Grand (Plate 3) had been commissioned into the Royal Engineers in 1917 and after attending the School of Military Engineering at Chatham he was posted to the Western Front in October 1918. He then served briefly in North Russia during 1919 before service with the Queen Victoria's Own Madras Sappers in Iraq and the Iraq Levies in Kurdistan. There then followed a series of staff appointments at the War Office, where he became Deputy Assistant Director of Mechanisation. Almost inevitably with anyone at the time who served near the Middle East and was subsequently involved with irregular warfare, a myth has grown up that he served with Lawrence of Arabia but this was patently untrue. His main existing claim to fame, or infamy, was that whilst in Kurdistan he had doctored ammunition that he knew would be stolen by the rebels so that their rifles would blow up in their faces. His fellow officers regarded this as ungentlemanly behaviour but it brought him to the attention of the then head of the Military Section of SIS, Stewart Menzies (later head of SIS). Grand was a free thinker, not something that sat easily within the corridors of power in either the War Office or SIS HQ. Kim Philby, one-time Section D officer, described him thus: 'his mind was certainly not clipped. It ranged free and handsome over the whole field of his awesome responsibilities, never shrinking from an idea, however big or wild.'[4] Such men tend to inspire and infuriate in equal measure. Grand certainly inspired great loyalty amongst his staff but he also made many dangerous enemies across the government and military – particularly Colin Gubbins, future head of the Auxiliary Units and SOE. Many of the early post-war accounts of Section D depended on the opinions of Gubbins whose animosity to Grand and SIS was influenced by the frustration of having to rely on Section D both in his work in MI(R) and in the early days of the Auxiliary Units, and his later enforced retirement by Menzies on the pension of his substantive rank of colonel (while Grand and Jo Holland of MI(R) both became major generals). Nonetheless, the Press Attaché in Belgrade, S.L. Childs, concluded a glowing appreciation of the work of Section D in Hungary by saying 'I know of no one who could have taken his place and done what he has done. He has broken some eggs but the omelettes were produced.'[5] Grand went on to play a major role in the success of the Burma campaign by organising a complex bridge-building programme – proving he was more organised and efficient than his detractors had claimed.

Grand's first question to Sinclair, was 'Is anything banned?' to which Sinclair replied: 'Nothing at all'. Sinclair also made it clear that the task would not be popular: 'Don't have any illusions. Everything you do is going to be disliked by a lot of people in Whitehall – some in this building. The more you succeed, the more they will dislike you and what you are trying to do.' This was prophetic and had consequences for Grand's plans for a guerrilla organisation in Britain.[6] By May 1940 Section D was involved in operations from Scandinavia to the Balkans and into the Middle East, bringing it into conflict with the Foreign Office and War Office alike who were suspicious of Grand's dynamism and forthright manner, as well as his embrace of political subversion, bribery and sabotage. Such 'ungentlemanly' tactics were too close for comfort to the tactics recently used against them by the IRA and in Palestine. One of the detractors was the then Director of Military Intelligence, General Pownall. In Pownall's opinion, Grand was 'gifted, enthusiastic and persuasive, but I do not regard him as being well-balanced or reliable'.[7] In 1940 Pownall became Inspector General of the Home Guard and was similarly opposed to the efforts of Tom Wintringham to promote Home Guard guerrilla activity. The view of the establishment may be summarised in the conclusion by Lord Hankey in his March 1940 report on SIS. 'At first sight the natural instinct of any humane person is to recoil from this undesirable business as something he would rather know nothing about.'[8] Walter Stirling, head of Section D operations in Albania, cheerfully commented that Section D had 'no scruples, few morals and was without shame'.[9] In November 1939, Claude Dansey, with unintended irony given his own reputation, declared Section D to be 'mafia-like'.[10] Commander Langley, head of the Technical Section, also recognised unease within official circles. 'A Cabinet minister might ask himself what business the Secret Service had in running some sort of secret war. The SIS were supposed to concentrate on getting useful information, not be mixed up with a lot of piratical ruffians.'[11]

The history of Section D, compiled by SOE in 1941, concluded with some sympathy and feeling: 'D Section was not only unwelcome, but considered unnecessary by all the older established Government agencies'.[12] Section D was tolerated whilst it confined its work abroad but in late May 1940 came the uncomfortable realisation that it was mobilising in Britain! Grand did not make friends in the War Office by stepping on the toes of GHQ by first proposing 'Detection Lines' to provide outer perimeter defences around key points to deter fifth-column surprise attacks.[13] Then in June 1940 he suggested a reorganisation of UK defence into small all-arms 'Brigade group' areas. At the same time he proposed a new 'Ministry of Progress' to improve efficiency of the implementation of government decisions.[14] There were few sections of government that by now he had not antagonised! William Mackenzie, the first official SOE historian, concluded:

> D section and all its works were a nuisance to the Foreign Office, the Secret Intelligence Service, and the War Office alike. . . . There were therefore many people who were anxious to make a case against D section for not achieving what no one could have achieved in the conditions of the time . . . on the whole there are few departments which did much better in 1939–40.[15]

The basis of Section D's European-wide remit was the 'D Scheme', presented on 20 March by Grand to the army in the shape of the CIGS (Lord Gort), DDMI (General Frederick Beaumont-Nesbitt) and DMO (General Henry Pownall). In view of the sensitivity of the proposals, another meeting was held on 23 March with the Foreign Secretary (Lord Halifax) and Colonial Secretary (Lord Cadogan), as well as the CIGS and Admiral Sinclair (CSS). The idea was to ferment widespread revolt against the Nazis and to create cadres of resistance in presently neutral countries liable to be overrun. The nervousness of government over this new form of irregular warfare was clear. Grand had not spared them details of the brutal methodology that would be employed: 'Where possible they would endeavour to execute members of the Gestapo with as much show as possible, in order to produce in the minds of the local inhabitants that the guerrillas were more to be feared than the occupying secret police.'[16] This would become part of the tactics taught to the Auxiliary Units in 1940 by some of Grand's former staff. The government approved the scheme – but wanted to know as little as possible about it. Lord Halifax said that 'he agreed in principle with the scheme, which he now intended to forget'.[17] A campaign of sabotage against German interests in the Balkans began immediately. In May 1940 Section D were engaged in a last-ditch effort to provide supplies and training to potential resistance fighters in France, Belgium and Holland. Grand took this work as immediate authority to begin to build a network of civilian stay-behind cells in Britain, to be activated prior to any threat of invasion, known as the 'Regional D Scheme' or the 'Home Defence Scheme' (HDS). The code for the HDS was D/Y indicating a top-level link to the HQ of SIS.[18] (In pre-war SIS, the code 'Y' was used to identify staff at headquarters.) The HDS is poorly documented, and it is noticeable that, while the history of Section D by SOE in 1941 contains detailed staffing and structural information on foreign operations, there is no such information for the HDS. Many of its former officers and agents were still in place as part of Section VII or the Auxiliary Units and its details were too sensitive to commit to paper, even in an internal document.

The HDS was completely separate from the Section VII resistance, following the principle of compartmentalisation recommended by Section D in Norway where immediately before its invasion on 9 April 1940 Gerald Holdsworth was instructed by Grand to create two organisations:

1. short-term sabotage before the Germans fully occupied the country
2. longer-term organisation to operate in occupied territory.

Holdsworth was told to keep the two organisations separate on security grounds. There was the implication that the organisation responsible for immediate sabotage would be exposed and destroyed but if so, this would not compromise the longer-term resistance body.[19] Just over a month later, SIS mobilised on similar principles in Britain with the HDS providing short-term and medium-term guerrilla warfare while the military campaign was still in progress or there was no settled occupation, and Section VII a distinct longer-term resistance in case the country was fully occupied. But as the War Office pressed for the absorption of the HDS and Grand countered with plans for a longer-term role, by the end of July Dansey and Boyle may have decided the risk to Section VII was too great and did not opposed its disbandment. The Auxiliary Units took over the role of the HDS in some coastal areas as the short-term guerrilla organisation whilst other cells were absorbed into the national Section VII which then continued for most of the war.

It was Captain John Dolphin (D/XE), a targeting officer at the Section D research base at Aston House, who on 22 May 1940 had suggested to Grand the idea of extending the existing 'D Scheme' into the 'Regional D Scheme' for a British guerrilla organisation. His memo, entitled 'Pessimism', argued that the previous disasters in the war had been caused by undue optimism. 'It would therefore appear wise to take the most pessimistic view about invasion of this country and prepare for successful invasion by the Germans, even though successful invasion may only be a very remote possibility.' It is ironic that both Section D and MI(R) had been urging foreign governments to establish plans for guerrilla warfare in advance of invasion but Britain's plans, other than the independently-organised Section VII resistance, turned out to be equally last-minute. Dolphin proposed firstly recruiting 'everybody's reliable friends plus their friends reliable friends thus forming a basically sound body of men to operate particularly in the event of a successful invasion'. He called for weapons dumps to be distributed for the sabotage of enemy aircraft, bridges, communications and petrol supplies. The dumps would contain weapons suitable for use by the general public or for British troops that had been disarmed, without having to rely on official replenishment.[20] Grand seized enthusiastically on the idea, using the March 1939 approval of the D Scheme as his authority and took immediate steps to put it into operation as a *fait accompli* before seeking more specific official approval. By the ISPB meeting on 27 May (see above, pp.37–41), Grand claimed its Home Defence Scheme (HDS) in Britain was 'already partially organised', with contact made with regional army commanders and the civil regional commissioners. Entries in the later Nominal Roll of the Auxiliary Units suggests some men were recruited as early as 24 May.[21] Within each region, the plan was to 'organise a chain of individuals not liable to be called up for military service who would carry out acts of sabotage, and by judicial whispering he would encourage the general public unconsciously to train their minds to attacking the enemy by unarmed methods'.[22] A surviving plan for the distribution of weapons dumps to guerrilla cells, prepared to continue if necessary into a period of occupation and spread over as wide an area as possible, dates to 31 May (Fig. 3). On 1 June Grand produced a briefing document for the thirty SIS officers who would operate the scheme on a national basis.[23] (By comparison, the early coastal Auxiliary Units had less than half this number of coordinating Intelligence Officers.) To ensure the mobilisation would proceed as quickly as possible, Grand had significantly shifted the focus of Section D towards operations in Britain. He drew in his closest associates from the existing sections of Section D, including the head of planning, Walter Wren and his assistant Robert Fraser, together with the former head of the propaganda section, Douglas Saunders (Fig. 2). The coordinator was Walter Samuel, 2nd Viscount Bearsted (Plate 4 and Appendix 2), assisted by his friends and fellow bankers Major the Honourable Lionel Montagu (Royal Marines) and Captain Christopher Holland-Martin (General List). George Hill organised the logistics (including compiling inventories for the arms dumps) whilst similarly organising weapons dumps and training saboteurs in France and Belgium.[24] Bearsted, a Director of Royal Dutch Shell, had been recruited to SIS in 1938 by his friend Stewart Menzies and then was co-opted to Section D in 1939, re-commissioned as a lieutenant in September 1939 on the 'Special List' of the Territorial Army Reserve, and by March 1940 he was an acting colonel. Bearsted's original task was to organise possible work in China but was then involved in Section D's efforts to establish intelligence networks in Scandinavia and was also in the propaganda section D/Q. It is possible D/Q also extended its operation to preparing for clandestine broadcasting and propaganda material in Britain in the event of occupation through the section's former head, Douglas Saunders, now organising the HDS along the south coast. This was clearly considered a priority area with Rupert St George Riley and Robert Fraser in Kent and Sussex, and probably Anthony Ashley-Cooper (Lord Ashley) in Dorset. Other officers included Gerard Holdsworth (just back from Sweden) in East Anglia and Francis Ogilvy (whose planned deployment to the Balkans was suddenly cancelled) in Scotland.

Fig. 2 Known organising officers of the Home Defence Scheme.
* = those who transferred into the Auxiliary Units

HQ	Viscount Bearsted *	
	Major the Hon. Lionel Montagu *	
	Captain W.E. Hope	
	Walter Wren	
	George Hill	
	Christopher Holland-Martin *	
Regional Officers	Robert Fraser *	Kent and Sussex
	Gerard Holdsworth	East Anglia
	Kenneth Johnson *	
	Eric Maschwitz	East Yorkshire
	Francis Ogilvy	Scotland
	Rupert St George Riley *	Kent
	Douglas Saunders *	South Coast / Isle of Wight
	John Todd *	Wales and South Midlands
	? Lord Tony Ashley *	Kent

Grand explained that, under current plans, the main opposition to invasion would be provided by the regular forces and by the 'MIR Guerrilla section', an optimistic reference to an expansion of the Independent Companies, recently deployed in Norway.

The official contact of the Section D officers would be the regional civil commissioner (who, it was said, had been asked to assist in any way, although it was unlikely that they would be given any details). The regional military commanders had also been sent written requests to provide facilities to the Section D officers. A car would be provided for each of the twelve regions; the contents would include a wireless and other specified contents including a box of cigars or cigarettes and 'Plenty of chocolate'! In June 1940 SIS was beginning to install both hidden wireless sets and mobile wireless stations in its fleet of Packard saloons and many people 'in the know' must have looked upon these with both interest and envy. SIS wireless engineers 'Spuggy' Newton, Bob Hornby and Wilf Lilburn had all been recruited from Gambier-Parry's old firm of Philco where they had worked on the design of two-way radios in cars; Lilburn had installed wireless in cars for the Glasgow police. The wireless sets would allow the scattered officers to maintain contact with their HQ or for final instructions following invasion but there is no mention of wireless being used by the rest of the HDS operatives, meaning that any coordination after invasion would be difficult. In Sussex, HDS Intelligence Officer Robert Fraser was known by his agents to have had a wireless transmitter in his car, before his operation was transferred to the SDB.[25] This was the spur for Gubbins' failed attempt to install the same system in the cars of the later SDB Intelligence Officers (see below, Chapter 8).

The HDS officers were expected to supply their own driver – who had to be 'ready for anything' – and were issued with a copy of the Section D sabotage manual *Home Hints* (then being distributed to foreign resistance groups) and a revolver. The cars were supplied with coupons for 81 gallons and the expectation was that the regional commissioners would be able to supply more. Each regional officer would be given £100 expenses with each area holding a further £5,000. The document does, however, make clear that the only paid staff would be the drivers, suggesting that many HDS officers were still part of the unpaid 'territorial' network of officers with private incomes that Section D had been recruiting from before the war. Such officers were soon to be given regular army commissions to provide a legal authority for their activities.

In his inimitable way, Grand sought a formal retroactive approval and funding for the scheme on 2 June. A further set of notes dated 4 June clearly identifies this as a work in progress, explaining some of the inconsistencies in the surviving documentation.[26] Later in June Menzies had a meeting with the Foreign Secretary where it was noted 'D's great ideas. Doesn't seek advice before putting out schemes . . . schemes not weighed sufficiently . . . but C can't control him.'[27] It is tempting to suggest that the meeting was referring to the HDS. It must be presumed that Grand did, in the end, get his approval as at the time, facing the prospect of immediate invasion, there was, as yet, no alternative – but it proved to be the final nail in the coffin of his SIS career.

In a matter of just days, Grand laid the basis of a nationwide civilian guerrilla and intelligence organisation that could hopefully survive into the first stages of occupation or longer, but which would remain separate from Section VII. He began distributing arms dumps over as wide an area as possible (Fig. 3), hoping that they would seed future resistance. Grand and his team were a whirlwind of activity and it was the speed of the initiative as much as anything else that led to criticism. Speed of action did not necessarily go down well with the War Office and comparison may be made with similar complaints made by the War Office over the instant creation of the LDV.[28] According to Mackenzie's official history of SOE, 'D Section with its usual energy speedily created a network of local representatives, operating in deepest secrecy'.[29] On the Isle of Wight Samuel Watson, a local auctioneer and executive officer of the local War Agriculture Committee, was asked to attend a meeting with the Chief Constable who introduced an unnamed man in civilian clothes and then withdrew. This was Douglas Saunders, who was now a regional officer of the HDS. Consistent with his expertise in propaganda, Saunders drew Watson into both a sense of jeopardy and a belief that he was party to the most secret intelligence by falsely telling him that they had the plans for invasion from a spy in the German War Office that included landings on the Isle of Wight. This may have been a reasonable supposition but, of course, if Saunders' claim of the source had been true then this would have been a most serious breach of security. This anecdote is a warning that not everything the intelligence officers of the HDS or Auxiliary Units told their men may have been true! Saunders asked Watson to organise a set of people distributed across the island but who lived no more than three miles apart. They were to be known only to Watson and not to each other. Each of these would then recruit four or five other men in their locality. Saunders would then instruct Watson in sabotage methodology and the latter would then pass this knowledge on to the others. One of the recruits, Leonard Mew (the managing director of a brewery), maintained he was recruited on 31 May 1940 – just four days after the ISPB meeting. This network later became the basis of the Auxiliary Units organisation in the Island.[30] Saunders remained as Auxiliary Units Intelligence Officer for Hampshire and the Isle of Wight after the incorporation of Section D into SOE but was still funded by SIS, suggesting he may have continued to be involved in their work on clandestine broadcasting within Britain. He was dismissed from SOE at the end of September and left the Auxiliary Units shortly afterwards, to return to propaganda work in the War Office. There may have been a similar pattern in Worcestershire where Thurstan Holland-Martin was suspected by his colleagues in the Auxiliary Units of having had a wider role than his eventual position as patrol sergeant of the Overbury Patrol. His brother, Christopher, was one of the national organisers of the HDS (and subsequently the Special Duties Branch of the Auxiliary Units). It seems likely that Thurstan had been involved in setting up an HDS network in the county with the Section D regional officer John Todd before it was absorbed into the Auxiliary Units.

This new initiative produced apoplexy in some sections of the War Office, spurring them to action of their own and is the context for the post-war opinion of Major Peter Wilkinson from the Auxiliary Units: 'As for Section D, one of Gubbins' early tasks had been to take over Grand's civilian stay-behind organisation, hastily and unofficially set up earlier and providing a source of embarrassment to all concerned.'[31] Not surprisingly, Grand presents an opposite view of events. He claimed he had War Office approval through his interpretation of the discussion at the ISPB meeting and through the earlier government approval of the D Scheme. Indeed, General Ironside is likely to have been referring to the HDS when he summarised anti-invasion preparations to the War Cabinet on 10 June, including 'Special bodies of men were being appointed in the various districts adjoining the coasts, who would know the country intimately, and who were mobile'. At this stage Ironside was desperate for any assistance and the Director of Military Intelligence also appears to have not raised objections (see below, p.59). But soon there was criticism.[32] After the Chief Regional Commissioner (Neville Chamberlain) raised objections to this civilian army of *francs-tireurs*, Grand went directly to Churchill for permission to proceed. He wrote on 14 June:

> I therefore asked permission in principle and for facilities to contact the Regional Commissioners. This was refused by the Chief Commissioner on the grounds that the distribution of arms and explosives would be dangerous. The danger of invasion, however, seemed to me so great that I appealed to the P.M. (as M. of Defence) and he gave permission to go ahead.[33]

The system of Regional Commissioners to control twelve civil defence regions and ensure that the civil defence plans of Government Departments and local authorities were properly co-ordinated had been established in August 1938, but they only took up their posts a year later. If communications should break down with central government the Regional Commissioners and their staff (which included a liaison officer from MI5) would then coordinate civil defence and maintain law and order until a national government could be restored. Until put to the test of invasion, however, their role was 'diplomatic rather than executive', having 'minimum interference with the existing organisation'.[34] As a formality, Section D of SIS was supposed to consult with the Regional Commissioners in establishing their Home Defence Scheme but as the names of the Commissioners and their staffs were public knowledge, SIS would not have risked sharing any operational details, although the Commissioners were expected to act as bankers for the Section D officers. Some, at least, of the Regional Commissioners shared the concerns of Chamberlain. The Commissioner for East Anglia, William Spens (former Secretary of the Foreign Trade department of the Foreign Office and now Vice Chancellor of Cambridge University), on 21 June expressed concern to General Ironside over the people 'staying put' in case of an invasion. He had it on his conscience that 'we were arranging sabotage behind the lines if the Germans succeeded in landing'.[35] As the War Cabinet had only agreed to create the Auxiliary Units on 17 June and their recruiting in East Anglia did not begin until the very end of June, Spens is probably referring to a contact with a Section D regional officer. Major Peter Wilkinson later had a similarly awkward meeting with Spens when the latter threatened to arrest any member of the Auxiliary Units acting 'illegally', whether before or after German occupation.[36] Spens returned to the subject once again in 1941 when he raised with General Alan Brooke (Viscount Alanbrooke) the 'undesirability of non-combatants joining in the shooting'.[37]

On 3 June, Menzies briefed the first meeting of the intermittent Secret Service Committee 'on the part which the SIS might play in the event of an invasion of Great Britain' but, not surprisingly, no further details were committed to writing.[38] The HDS was certainly rushed but it should be remembered that invasion was expected in a matter of days and that behind the scattergun contingency efforts of distributing arms dumps almost randomly across the country there was also a more considered mobilisation of recruits, divided into low-level mass action and sabotage by trained volunteers. Grand's plan for the HDS was:

a. to make as many persons as possible in areas liable to invasion into conscious obstructionists.
b. to have a nucleus of trained persons who, in the event of invasion, will remain behind and direct further obstruction under the direction of the military where such acts could aid military operations.[39]

Grand therefore at least notionally preserved the agreement made at the ISPB meeting that the work should theoretically be under military control but any liaison would rely on the uncertain continued operation of his regional officers in their wireless cars.

Recruitment

The thirty 'D officers', nominally attached to the twelve Regional Civil Commissioners for '*Special Duties*', divided up the regions into sub-areas and within these recruited a number of reliable and discreet individuals as 'Key Men'. These would then recruit their own cell members. In an effort to retain security, Grand suggested that each cell might be self-contained units of a family or of estate workers (a methodology continued by the Auxiliary Units). He recorded the process of recruiting the HDS agents:

> Recruiting went well. The qualifications were courage, intelligence, and discretion, and the bait was a certainty of execution if caught. The results were the finest body of men that have ever been collected. All classes and trades were represented, bankers and poachers, clergymen and burglars, farmers and lawyers, policemen and shopkeepers, every sort and kind of trade and interest, and the whole representing a cross section of the England that would never submit to being ruled by an invader.[40]

By the third week of July Grand claimed to have recruited 200 'Key Men' with an unknown number of associated cell members.[41] They were not the fit young spies of James Bond mythology but rather middle-aged citizens well-established in business or trades within their local communities, not least so that they would not be liable for call-up to the services and who could move around occupied areas without attracting suspicion. Volunteers were warned to avoid anything that might affect their future service in HDS, which meant that they risked being accused of not assisting the war effort. Both men and women were recruited, although it is likely that the women joined the intelligence network rather than as saboteurs.

The HDS was intended to operate from within the community and in his 'Preliminary Notes on Regional D Scheme' of 4 June, Grand stressed that the Regional Commissioners had to prevent any general civilian evacuation from threatened areas so that the stay-behind units could hide within the general populace. (This ethos of sabotage teams remaining with the community would also be the initial methodology of the Auxiliary Units, until abandoned in August 1940.) If, however, there was a general evacuation of the civilian population then Grand suggested that, as a last act, licenced victuallers could be given a supply of 'knock-out drops' (probably actually laxatives) to doctor supplies of alcohol with which to 'immobilise, hamper or embarrass' enemy troops. Meanwhile the HDS would create a force of what were termed 'narks' hiding by day and operating by night, using weapons in hidden dumps (a precursor of the Operational Bases of the XII Corps Observation Unit and the Auxiliary Units Operational Patrols from mid-August 1940). It is a characteristic that the volunteers never knew precisely for whom they were working and a principle of decentralisation blurred the relationship of the HDS to a range of other more or less unofficial guerrilla bodies (see below, p.178). Grand explained:

> 'D' officers should select a suitable region-wide organisation, take the chief officers of it into their confidence, and allow them to plant the idea in the heads of their subordinates without betraying the fact that there is any official organisation behind the scheme. . . . Suggest that no doubt the bloody Government, which is always years behind the times, has never thought of anything of the kind but we, the citizens of . . . shire, will bloody well show them! Let each man according to his trade suggest a simple form of obstruction which he personally will do and which he recommends others to do. Take care, though, that the officials taken into confidence are reliable and are capable of 'acting up' sufficiently to plant the idea without arousing suspicion. 'D' officers in civilian clothes, if suitably introduced, might help here.[42]

The regional officer for the East Riding of Yorkshire was 39-year-old Eric Maschwitz, another former member of the Section D propaganda unit. In May 1940, he was sent on a brief demolitions course at Aston House. Maschwitz had no previous military experience but, in just 24 hours, he found himself commissioned as a second lieutenant and expected to go to Calais with a demolition party, although the operation was cancelled at the last minute and he was sent back in civilian clothes to establish a regional HQ for the HDS in Beverley. There were no written instructions and he was responsible only to the Regional Commissioner.

> He would recommend us to the Chief Constable who, without knowing exactly what we were up to, would provide us with a list of local citizens likely to prove daring and also as close as oysters. We had a secret telephone number to ring if in trouble and a garage in Yorkshire packed to the roof with various dangerous devices. For a long hot month, we toured the hills and dales and seaside resorts with samples of our 'wares' (time bombs and Molotov Cocktails), a couple of commercial travellers trying to 'interest' prospective customers in the prospect of death and danger.[43]

Maschwitz recruited a sizeable list of volunteers 'who had buried in their gardens, under hayricks and manure heaps, the wherewithal with which to cause the invader quite a lot of trouble'.[44] Many such arms dumps were never recovered. In Kent, the use of an empty chest tomb in Rainham churchyard as a supply dump by an un-named organisation, likely to be either the HDS or Section VII, was known to both the vicar and churchwarden, although no evidence now remains. The ivy-covered tomb was protected from views from the road, with extensive woodland behind. Rainham was on the main anticipated route of an invader from the coast through Chatham to London and a likely place from which to mount an ambush.[45]

It is not known how many men and women were eventually recruited to the HDS but one of Grand's last acts was to appoint eighty specialist saboteurs trained in explosives. The scale of the mobilisation was clearly much larger than the later Auxiliary Units knew about or chose to acknowledge post-war and may have formed a significant element within the early Auxiliary Units in coastal areas. Grand later claimed 'Some 30 Officers of this Section went to work at high pressure and completed this organisation and distributed in several thousand secret dumps throughout the country a vast quantity of incendiary materials'.[46] As well as the immediate distribution of local dumps managed by the volunteers, a number of regional dumps were established under military guard.[47] By the end of May alone, 800–1,000 individual dumps had been distributed, based on extrapolation from the 31 May inventory (Fig. 3). It was suggested that the arms dumps should be hidden in galvanised rubbish bins, buried and turfed over. The material was delivered in cardboard boxes called 'Auxiliary Units', the name harking back to the much-feared 'Auxiliary Division' assassination squads of British intelligence that operated in Dublin in 1920; SIS officer David Boyle, a key figure in the wartime plans for British resistance (Plate 15 and Appendix 2), had been a prominent member.[48] The name was then inherited by the GHQ Auxiliary Units, although Colin Gubbins never publicly acknowledged this ancestry. The contents of the dumps suggest that cells of six operatives were envisaged, each armed with a pistol and c.80 rounds of ammunition. The scale of ammunition supply compares well with the handful of rounds later provided to the Auxiliary Units. HDS was clearly planning for longer-term operations. In late July, as Grand tried to rationalise a dual working arrangement with the Auxiliary Units, a final 300 incendiary arms dumps were distributed, alongside the explosives dumps also being distributed by Section D to the new Auxiliary Units.

Fig. 3 Inventory of Home Defence Scheme Dumps, dated 31 May 1940.
(From 'D Organisation for Home Defence', 1 June 1940, with thanks to Stephen Sutton)

Per crate	Item	Total distributed
25	Flare, Type M, fitted with 1ft of Bickford	2,000
30	Match-headed Tyesules (paraffin)	24,000
1 dozen	Battery Pills	800 dozen
2 dozen	Capsules	1,600 dozen
2	Pint bottles of Sulphuric Acid	800
2	Small Hooded Torches	1,600
4	additional batteries for torches	3,200
1	spare bulb for torch	800
6	rubber truncheons	4,800
6	sheathed knives	1,800
1	Crowbar	1,000
1	each machine-gun rattles	800
1	packing case opener	1,000
6	pistols with 500 rounds	

Sabotage

No advice on specific targets was provided to the HDS officers but in March 1940 Grand had shared information with the Finns on irregular warfare and he clearly borrowed some of their ideas on tactics.[49] The 1 June briefing outlined how 'Broadly speaking, this section will not have objectives to destroy, but a policy of obstruction to the enemy'. They were to interfere with ease of movement and supplies rather than trying to sabotage infrastructure which might be required in any counter-attack.[50] The 31 May inventory and 1 June briefing make it clear that the main weapons were incendiary in nature as it was thought there might be little time before invasion in which to train large numbers of civilians in the use of explosives. Personal arms were basic. Rather than use regulation army revolvers, members of the HDS were issued with unattributable Colt revolvers on the basis that the government could not then be held directly responsible for their actions. For this reason, pre-war SIS had a special section that bought up handguns from around the world and this was continued by the small arms section of Section D. Although Section D had already distributed a small number of Thompson sub-machine guns to the Norwegian resistance, supplies from the USA were still limited and the HDS was reduced to using decoy 'machine gun rattles' (Plate 18). Grand explained 'I allotted one or more officers to each area and directed them to contact and recruit suitable persons, lay down concealed stores of food, arms and devices to make a frame-work that would remain in place if, and when, the Germans occupied the area'.[51] Section D had been producing incendiary devices since late 1939 and the HDS dumps (Fig. 3) contained both the Large and the easily-concealed fountain pen-sized Medium Magnesium Incendiary bombs as well as the Tyesule paraffin bomb. All were later supplied to the Auxiliary Units. The Tyesule comprised a 5in-long by 1.25in diameter gelatine capsule filled with 2oz of paraffin, with one half coated in the chemical used to make match heads (Plate 19). As well as being incendiary devices in their own right they could be tied around magnesium flares (Flares, type M) to increase their effectiveness. Other incendiary materials were designed to be easily concealed in the home from enemy searches, anticipating that the saboteurs would potentially be operating during enemy occupation and would be working from home. Materials for Molotov cocktails were distributed as widely as possible, including pint bottles of sulphuric acid 'labelled so as to appear to be innocent'; and a supply of chemical time-delay capsules invented by Section D, which Grand suggested be labelled as 'dog medicine' or similar. The gelatine capsules (later known as Capsule H) were filled with a mixture of potassium chlorate and sugar which acted as a crude time delay to a petrol bomb where a small quantity of sulphuric acid had been added to the petrol/tar mix.[52] The device was placed on the target and two of the capsules were added to the bottle. The acid would expose the chemical in about two hours and a violent ignition would follow. Placed so that the fire would quickly get out of control, such crude incendiary devices could have a more powerful impact than explosives, cause additional confusion, and could be used to create effective diversions. They also had the advantage of being easily supplemented from everyday domestic items. The battery pills were a failed attempt to destroy vehicle batteries by adding tablets of platinic chloride but issue was discontinued in July 1940.

Some of the ideas for opportunistic sabotage were very basic and required little or no training – nothing more than what was being proposed in the *Picture Post* by Tom Wintringham, 'e.g. putting a pick through a petrol tank, slashing tyres, piles of stone on the road, felling trees, etc.' The incendiaries could, however, be used to destroy fuel or supply dumps, lorry convoys or, borrowing from the Finns, used to burn crops in a programme of 'scorched earth' (as Section D was already planning in Europe). Explosives were requisitioned for a later distribution to more specialist cells. John Dolphin had already carried out a survey for MI5 on likely fifth-column targets and counter-measures and it may be presumed that this list served to highlight future key targets for the HDS. Expecting that the enemy would take over airfields or create their own temporary landing strips, enemy aircraft were a priority target. Units based near airfields or flat ground potentially useful as landing sites were to be given special instruction and supplies, including explosives and MI(R) L delays (Plate 32). Hence 'they will also, in special cases, be instructed in the use of certain aeroplane-destroying devices in case of Enemy landings in their areas'.

Although the distribution of explosives to the HDS was limited, it was the discovery of a number of explosives dumps in the south-east during June that became notorious within the War Office and proved the death knell for the HDS. This was a last ditch effort to distribute as much material beyond the existing networks as possible in the hope of seeding future resistance units (as Section D was doing in Norway at the time). One post-war account even claims that selected personnel from London gun dealers were called secretly to the War Office in Whitehall, given keys to lorries full of Bren guns (which seems unlikely given the national shortage at the time), grenades and ammunition, and told to 'take the bloody stuff and bury it — we don't want records and we don't want to be able to be forced to tell where it is — and use it for resistance in the invasion'.[53] MI5 petulantly reported that the HDS had left 'dumps of explosives all over East Anglia and the southern counties', but the caches had been spread nationwide.[54] In Hornsea, Yorkshire, a man was approached during May–June 1940 by a 'mystery man' in civilian clothing, was given a box of explosives and was asked to form a resistance organisation if the Germans invaded. The box was buried in the garden and was re-discovered in 1968.[55] Similarly, in North Wales, Welsh slate worker Jeffrey Watkins recalled:

> I worked in the slate mines in Snowdonia and I was asked to go to Chester where I and some other lads were met by a posh chap with shiny shoes and a lovely suit to sign the Official Secrets Act. I was asked if I could handle explosives and when I said yes I was told to go away with a map. I was to mark on it where explosives could be stored in secret places. If the invasion happened, we were to disappear into the bowels of the earth and wait for orders. These were never needed but I can assure you that we were ready.[56]

Similarly from Scotland, Captain Eustace Maxwell, an early Auxiliary Units Intelligence Officer, also relates a tale of a peer delivering midnight supplies to an old woman in a village, knocking loud enough on her door to risk waking the neighbours and so arouse their curiosity.[57] Bickham Sweet-Escott, former member of Section D and later SOE, also wrote how 'One of our emissaries arrived, complete with black hat and striped trousers, in a remote Scottish village, and on asking the postmaster if he would accept a parcel of stores, was promptly handed over to the police'.[58] Some SIS officers clearly found it difficult to shed their stockbroker image! The operation was clearly more extensive (and therefore more successful) than Peter Wilkinson, second in command of the Auxiliary Units, chose to report:

> In early June 1940, army units re-forming in the south of England after their evacuation from Dunkirk reported the presence of mysterious civilians

behaving suspiciously in their divisional areas. These were members of Section D who had been given the task of recruiting an underground organisation to carry out subversion and resistance behind the German lines in the event of an invasion . . .

The appearance of these strangers in their city clothes, sinister black limousines and general air of mystery caused alarm amongst the local inhabitants and infuriated subordinate military commanders since they refused to explain their presence or discuss their business except to say that it was 'most secret'.[59]

The reference to limousines travelling the country delivering arms dumps might seem unusual but in 1940 SIS bought up the entire stock of Packard saloon cars from the UK distributor for conversion to wireless cars.[60] Many of the senior SIS officers, having just left careers in the city, were wealthy enough to purchase their own! The 1941 History of Section D points out that the more plutocratic officers loaned their cars to the Section, gaining only moral reward.[61] Pinstripe city suits apart, eccentricity in dress seems to have been a feature of the SIS. John Todd, later Auxiliary Units IO for South Wales, Herefordshire and Worcestershire and a former stockbroker, tended to wear tweed fishing gear including a deerstalker hat festooned with fishing flies, which might pass for an attempt at camouflage in rural England (although his large black polished Pontiac car rather stood out), but he carried on wearing the same outfit in South Africa when he commanded the SOE East Africa mission in 1941–2. Todd was, however, an eccentric in more ways than one. His later tests for prospective auxiliers was to a) drop a stick of plastic explosive at their feet and judge their reaction and b) entertain a group of them in a public house and only choose the last one who had to visit the lavatory (a strong bladder being a useful consideration whilst out on patrol).

Passive resistance

The second part of the 'obstructionist' strategy of the HDS would involve Section D officers covertly working in the community to broaden the range of civilians willing to oppose occupation by passive resistance – 'turning conversations' to the subject of resistance: 'by judicial whispering he would encourage the general public unconsciously to turn their minds to the problem of dealing with the Enemy by unarmed methods'.[62] This might have spurred some of the more unofficial efforts to organise resistance groups (see Chapter 11) but it also included such simple tactics as misdirecting enemy troops and has been misinterpreted at times to suggest that Britain was training people to act as double-agent collaborators. After such initial suggestions, the action might develop without any official coordination. Such non-combative tactics might include encouraging underground newspapers (as suggested by stories of secret printing presses in Kent) or even establishing secret radio stations, so maintaining a control of the narrative against inevitable Nazi propaganda. Such work would explain the transfer to the HDS of propaganda specialist Douglas Saunders, formerly Chief Executive of the J. Walter Thompson Advertising Agency and now head of the Propaganda Section (D/Q). Saunders had been a founder of the *Britanova* press agency as a front for distributing Section D and Electra House propaganda across Europe.[63] The J.W. Thompson agency had also worked with Section D to build secret studio and recording facilities at Bush House to facilitate their broadcasts from Continental radio stations and the Propaganda Section, now under Leslie Sheridan, may then have worked with Saunders, attempting to extend the concept of clandestine radio stations into Britain. Alex Peterson, a Cirencester schoolteacher, was recruited to D/Q under SOE in December 1940 but this may have been a re-appointment from an earlier appointment with Section D. Peterson had been tasked with operating a one-man clandestine radio station from the loft of a country house near Cirencester, writing his own news stories which would be broadcast via a nearby army transmitting station. He describes it as 'quite the maddest thing I ever got involved in' and was under no illusions as to the chance of success, believing it might only last 12 hours.[64] Peterson later headed the SOE propaganda operations in India. A key resource for resistance groups abroad proved to be the ability to listen in to broadcasts from the BBC using, if necessary, simple home-made 'cat's whisker' receivers that needed no external power and were easily concealed (including being made and used by Allied prisoners of war).

Taken together, these non-combative tactics were aimed to build resilience in the civilian population so that they would not allow the occupying forces to relax, provide intelligence to resistance groups (as they had to the IRA in Ireland), and prepare for a general revolt at the time of liberation by an external army or (something seriously considered in 1940) by a revolt of the German army. Some idea of what such a 'whispering campaign' of unarmed resistance might involve comes from the Channel Islands which were the only part of the British Isles to be occupied by the Nazis. The size of the Channel Islands meant that any military resistance was impractical and discouraged by the civil government for fear of reprisals. Indeed, the official instruction from the British government upon occupation was for 'passive cooperation'. Instead, at least in the initial stages of occupation there was resistance in the form of shunning the troops or making them wait to be served in shops. Anti-Nazi graffiti appeared on walls even though painting the V sign on a wall was denounced by the civil authorities as causing unnecessary aggravation to the Nazis and it risked the death penalty. A number of underground newspapers were produced in small numbers but were then more widely circulated from hand to hand; listening to the BBC became an act of rebellion. Some residents went further and assisted the slave labourers on the islands to hide and escape. In general, political events are shaped by small groups of activists and Grand saw one task of the HDS as being to identify, encourage and develop those anti-fascist activists to the point that the hold of the occupying forces would become untenable.

Intelligence gathering

In line with the discussions of the May ISPB meeting and befitting the origin of the HDS in SIS, Grand stressed another purpose of the organisation would be to feed intelligence from temporarily occupied areas back to the British army. On 4 June he maintained 'The communications side of our work to be stressed equally with the "obstruction" side'.[65] This role was not well documented but appears to have been the specific responsibility of the original coordinator of HDS, Viscount Bearsted. The SOE history of Section D declared that this operation had been transferred 'en bloc' to the Auxiliary Units implying that by then it existed as a distinct section of the HDS (see Chapter 8).[66]

Although the regional officers may have had wireless sets in their cars, the methodology for the intelligence network relied on the traditional technique of runners from each cell who would pass on information to its neighbour and thence through the front line as a 'grape vine telegraph', a method best suited to settled conditions after occupation rather than reacting swiftly to the new conditions of *blitzkrieg*.[67] More realistically, during the actual invasion agents might be able to pass on intelligence to the local HDS sabotage cells or directly to the Independent Companies or commando units who were anticipated to be infiltrated through the enemy lines, as an extension to the guiding role of the Home Guard and similar to what was later envisaged in the Auxiliary Units. This crude communication system would clearly have been difficult to maintain as a reliable source of information during an active invasion campaign and has an air of desperation about it, although it was inherited by the SDB of the Auxiliary Units (albeit this had no link with the Operational Branch). Nonetheless, the optimistic intention of HDS overall was to become: 'a closely coordinated sabotage and intelligence network among the civilian population who would be left behind in any territory which the German armies might temporarily be able to occupy'.[68]

'Standfast Club'

Captain John Dolphin sought to extend the scope of the organisation that he had originally proposed on 22 May in 'Pessimism' and on 1 July, possibly a result of the continuing confusion of the LDV's role, wrote to Grand with the suggestion of expanding the Home Defence Scheme to include the 'Standfast Club'. His extended plan would comprise citizens prepared to stay in their homes in the event of invasion. Grade A would be given weapons and instructions on how to make defences. Grade B were people prepared to undertake sniping and minor sabotage. Grade C were those who were prepared to stay in their homes under any circumstances, their value being they would not clog the roads with refugees while their presence would also ensure that the civilians of Grades A and B (as well as the operatives of HDS) would not stand out in an empty landscape. Dolphin's ideas were merging in a confused fashion with the existing LDV. Like them, his 'Standfast Club' would be clearly identified with badges or armlets and Dolphin hoped that the movement would snowball into very large numbers.[69] There is no evidence that this suggestion was taken any further. If so, it would only have reinforced fears that SIS were attempting a takeover bid of Home Forces.

Opposition to the HDS

The Home Defence Scheme was, potentially, a fearsome (not to say illegal under international law) addition to the defence plan in the immediate aftermath of Dunkirk and unlike anything the Germans had faced since their invasion of Poland in 1939. Yet it was a development that did not meet with universal approval in Britain. One Dorset LDV officer, A. Gordon MacLeod, had been approached by an officer, possibly Major the Lord Anthony Ashley, who is suspected to have been a regional officer of the HDS at the time this was transitioning into the Auxiliary Units in Dorset, when he then became its Intelligence Officer.[70] MacLeod took the unusual step on 3 July of writing directly to the Prime Minister to complain.

> Sir,
> Since it seems unlikely that the matter is within your knowledge, I must respectfully beg to direct your attention to the fact that L.D.V. officers in this and presumably other areas have been approached by persons stated to represent the War Office, with a view to the organisation of a system of sabotage which could be brought into operation within the enemy lines in the event of his establishing a foothold in this country.
>
> For the carrying out of this sabotage it is proposed that caches of explosives and the like shall be established at certain secret points, these to be utilised for *franc-tireur* operations by selected members of the LDV, who would remain behind in the occupied area for this purpose.
>
> Quite apart from its questionable aspect under International Law, in view of the brutal retaliatory measures which action of the kind has already evoked from the enemy, in occupied territory both in this war and in that of 1914–18, and the certainty that it will similarly bring death and untold suffering to innocent non-combatant members of the community if embarked upon in this country, I cannot think that the ill-considered proposal has been made with your knowledge or approval.[71]

The letter excited a furious denial of any responsibility by the War Office for civilian sabotage operations. In a letter of 30 July General Paget, the Chief of Staff of the new C-in-C, Home Forces, General Alan Brooke, instead blamed SIS for the activities in Dorset and distanced the new military Auxiliary Units from the concept of organising civilian sabotage in an 'occupied' area. He wrote:

> Mr MacLeod's misapprehension may, on the other hand, be due to the fact that there was until recently an organisation working under the SIS, of whose activities he may have heard, which was charged with the task of organising sabotage and obstruction by civilians who, in the event of invasion, would remain behind and operate locally. Special stores for this purpose were issued to selected individuals.[72]

Such comments show the gulf between what the CIGS and the Foreign Secretary had first agreed to implement in Europe in March 1939 and the more 'gentlemanly' tactics that were considered acceptable for use within Britain.

It was not until 22 June that Major General Macdougall (Deputy CIGS) discovered the existence of the HDS and immediately raised concerns over its role vis-à-vis the new Auxiliary Units with Major General 'Pug' Ismay, Secretary to the Chiefs of Staff Committee. With the superiority complex typical of the War Office at the time, Macdougall naturally assumed that the new War Office Auxiliary Units should take the lead role (whilst admitting he was not really sure of the remit of Bearsted's operation) – but nevertheless suggested that SIS might fund the Auxiliary Units.

> My Dear Pug,
>
> Regarding the question of paramilitary activities in this country in the event of the enemy gaining a footing, the CIGS has decided that an organisation is to be set up under Brigadier Gubbins to undertake this task. The organisation will be directly under the Commander-in-Chief, Home Forces.

I now find that Lord Bearsted works under 'D' Section, and has also been charged with a similar role.

There is thus obviously great danger not only of over-lapping but more important, of considerable confusion arising as both organisations will be working in the same areas and also seeking recruits among the same personnel.

I feel that, in a matter of this nature, it is most important that there should be proper military control from the outset, as obviously these auxiliary units, whether uniformed or not; must be prepared to co-operate with and possibly even work under the local military Commander.... That being the case, I consider that Bearsted, with whatever staff he has collected, should definitely be placed under Gubbins and work under his orders. Whatever organisation Bearsted got going could easily be absorbed if it is suitable. The only other alternative would be to close down Bearsted's show, but I think this would be a pity and there is probably no necessity for such a step....

In view of the above, I hope you will agree that only one organisation is, not only required, but advisable and that this must be under military authority and accountable for their progress and actions to a military Commander. I would be very grateful if you could get this recognised and the necessary instructions passed to Bearsted.

A small amount of money will be required to start with, say £1,000 a month. I believe Lord Bearsted draws his funds from SIS and it would appear to be the easiest way if Gubbins could be authorised to do the same.

Yours

Ian[73]

Ismay, who the next day had to admit 'We here are not, of course, fully in the picture about all that has been done and is being done to organise civil resistance', took this up with the Director of Military Intelligence, Major General Beaumont-Nesbitt, who had been aware of the HDS since the ISPB meeting of 27 May and in his reply was relaxed about the co-existence of the two bodies, believing that Gubbins and Bearsted had worked out a 'modus operandi' of working together, as their concepts were very different.[74] With only a few days into the creation of the Auxiliary Units, Beaumont-Nesbitt may also have realised that the War Office were in a poor bargaining position, despite his wider goal of taking over Section D in its entirety. Similarly, as late as 5 July, the Director of Combined Operations accepted Section D as being responsible for the 'Organisation of civil resistance and sabotage in the UK'.[75] But such a concept was an anathema to the Chiefs of Staff who seized upon the Auxiliary Units as a legal, military, alternative. In this conflict, there may also have been simply frustration that the dynamism of Laurence Grand had not been matched by a similar progress to activate the Auxiliary Units since their Cabinet authorisation of 17 June and it was also just the latest in a series of complaints over irregular operations being carried out without the knowledge of the Chiefs of Staff.[76] Menzies had earlier explained to the Hankey Inquiry 'that from the earliest days S.S. [Secret Service] had, for vital reasons of secrecy, deliberately been kept aloof from regular Government Committees such as the Committee of Imperial Defence and the Chiefs of Staffs organisation'.[77] For his part, the CIGS had earlier approved the European-wide 'Scheme D' on the specific understanding that information was not to be shared with the Chiefs of Staff Committee.

Grand's ideas were exciting opposition from all quarters. The Chiefs of Staff made the reasonable point that there would be particular problems if the army was expected to fight an anti-invasion campaign on the same ground as another, civilian, army acting outside its control and outside of international conventions. This argument was part of the difficulty of established bodies in coming to terms with a new form of paramilitary warfare. Wilkinson claimed Colin Gubbins, the later CO of the Auxiliary Units, was aghast at what he saw as the amateurishness and extravagance of some of the wilder projects of Section D when he began to work alongside them in MI(R), but at the same time he grudgingly admitted he found the risk-taking attitude of the young ex-businessmen refreshing in contrast to the ponderous hierarchy of the War Office.[78] For the government there was the fear of a mass arming of civilians as *francs-tireurs*. For SIS, and especially Dansey who had an intense dislike and suspicion of Grand, the later plans to extend operations into a period of occupation also risked damaging their careful build-up of the Section VII resistance organisation in a wave of uncontrolled sabotage and subsequent reprisals. The War Office seized on several embarrassing incidents where HDS arms dumps were discovered to promote a military alternative in the Auxiliary Units and as part of a wider campaign to take over Section D. SIS had no inclination to reveal details of the actual scale of HDS operations and only limited publicly-accessible accounts survive to provide a more balanced account. Nonetheless, the fact that the organisation is known to have spread rapidly across England and into Scotland, with only a small number of recorded breaches of security, suggest that the HDS had a greater level of success than has previously been considered.

The difficulties in dealing with Section D, combined with a degree of lust over their resources, stimulated a quickly-moving consensus in the War Office and SIS that the various initiatives for conducting irregular warfare across Europe needed to be better coordinated and be given a higher priority in government by being placed under ministerial control. The ISPB had failed because its members were not sufficiently senior and did not have decision-making powers. Although the principle might be agreed, the sticking point was, unsurprisingly, which ministry would control any new coordinating body. Naturally the War Office, with the same arrogance that it had shown in dealing with its foreign allies, believed that any new form of warfare should be automatically under their control, whilst SIS believed that any clandestine operations fell within the realm of the Secret Service. At the time, no one realised that Hugh Dalton at the Ministry of Economic Warfare was also flexing his muscles to take direct control of any new venture. The War Office made determined efforts to take over Section D. On 3 June 1940 DMI proposed that Section D should come under control of a new Directorate of the War Office under a senior officer also responsible for commandos, the irregular warfare school and all plans for sabotage in occupied countries. On 6 June MI(R) commented that commando units, the propaganda organisations of the Ministries of Information and Economic Warfare, and the sabotage service of SIS 'should be co-ordinated and the co-ordinating authority should be the General Staff as it is a matter of strategy'. Whilst committees argued over organisation, and as yet with no active competition on the ground, the HDS still went its own way recruiting and distributing arms dumps in anticipation of imminent invasion. On 17 June the CIGS and C-in-C Home Forces finally proposed an alternative to the War Cabinet by creating the Auxiliary Units - but their War Establishment would not be agreed until 2 July. Meanwhile the HDS continued to grow, maintaining that its civilian basis was not in competition with the military Auxiliary Units. Yet another proposal for Section D to come under the DMI was rejected on 1 July by a meeting of Lord Halifax (Foreign Secretary), Sir Alexander Cadogan (Foreign Office), Gladwyn Jebb (Foreign Office), Lord Lloyd (Secretary of State for the Colonies), Lord Hankey, Hugh Dalton (Minister of Economic Warfare), General Beaumont-Nesbitt (Director of Military Intelligence), Sir Stewart Menzies (CSS), and Desmond Morton (Security Adviser to the Prime Minister). Significantly the opposition to the proposal was led by Dalton who borrowed ideas on methodology from Grand and held that 'war from within' was better led by civilians rather than by soldiers. Not surprisingly, this conclusion was dismissed by MI(R) as being amateurish.[79] The attacks on Section D continued at the Chiefs of Staff Committee meeting on 8 July where there were complaints that there was 'no effective control of the operations of "D" who might well be brought under the control of the Joint Intelligence Sub-Committee'.[80] On the same day the Commander-in-Chief, Home Forces, General Ironside, and the Secretary of War, Anthony Eden, presented a firm rebuttal of the principle of civilian combatants and, by implication, the HDS:

> It is the view of the Commander-in-Chief, Home Forces, with which I am in agreement, that actual fighting should be restricted to the military and Local Defence Volunteers, and that no civilian who is not a member of these forces should be authorised to use lethal weapons. Only if this principle is accepted would it be possible to ensure control of military activities by the military authorities.[81]

But the War Office was over-confident in its claim on irregular warfare, and was to be disappointed. Dalton manoeuvred to take the Ministerial coordinating role over the existing work of Section D, MI(R) and Electra House that all agreed was necessary.[82] He then went further to begin to absorb the above establishments within a new independent organisation under his direct control. Menzies had become increasingly concerned over the risk of embarrassment to the wider responsibilities of SIS by Section D's sabotage operations abroad and offered little resistance, but the War Office was particularly irritated by the emergence of the new organisation. Holland, forever the champion of uniformed irregular warfare, commented in the MI(R) War Diary for 22 July: 'It looks a little as though the Army has missed the bus, so to speak, and has allowed paramilitary activities to be carried on outside its jurisdiction.'[83] SOE were focused on Europe-wide operations where the government attitude to civilian *francs-tireurs* had always been more cavalier, but as far as Britain was concerned Churchill was persuaded by Ironside and Eden to reverse his earlier support for the HDS and so at the end of July it was finally decided to absorb the HDS within the Auxiliary Units. The decision was made on the grounds that 'the risk of reprisals incurred by allowing civilians to engage in sabotage activities was too great'.[84] Section D was caught in something of an administrative limbo until 16 August when it was formally transferred to SOE, but in the meantime, at the end of July, the HDS was finally officially transferred to the Auxiliary Units in those areas where the latter operated.

The post-war assumption has been that the HDS was a chaotic and short-lived aberration, quickly absorbed by the more organised Auxiliary Units. According to Mackenzie's official history of SOE, the HDS 'had to be dissolved, and there were many complications, humorous and otherwise'.[85] Following this simplistic statement, and constrained by the limited information available at the time, David Lampe rejected any idea that there may have been any significant contribution of the HDS to the new Auxiliary Units:

> A few of the men who had been in Section D's resistance set-up were asked to join the Auxiliary Units organisation, but most were politely thanked for what they had been prepared to do for the nation and told simply that their organisation no longer existed.[86]

This dismissive attitude was followed by most later writers and originally it may have been promoted in order to obscure the continuing contribution of SIS in the story. Gubbins had become deeply resentful of his reliance on Section D whilst in MI(R), and its continuing influence was unwelcome. In truth, GHQ could not afford to dismiss so easily the expertise of Section D and its civilian agents and saboteurs during the dangerous summer of 1940. The Auxiliary Units were, after all, not formally mobilised until 2 July or fully trained and armed until September. Nigel Oxenden, originally Intelligence Officer for Norfolk and then the Training Officer for the Auxiliary Units from 1941–4, provided a more informed contemporary opinion. He acknowledged in the draft official history of Auxiliary Units, that

> most I/Os [Auxiliary Units Intelligence Officers] were assisted by introductions to one or two men who had already been chosen by MI5 [*sic* – actually MI6] . . . These were generally outstanding individuals, who eventually became group commanders. Meanwhile their local knowledge made them invaluable in finding the right recruits.[87]

Thus some HDS 'Key Men' morphed into being Group Commanders of the Auxiliary Units, although they all kept their previous work (or any continuing contact with SIS) a closely-guarded secret. Even Oxenden does not, however, acknowledge that a significant number of the original Auxiliary Units Intelligence Officers were themselves former HDS officers (Fig. 2). During July, despite the complaints from the War Office over their behaviour, there was an overlap when HDS continued to be supplied and to operate as before, driven by necessity and by a short-lived policy of joint working. At this stage, the methodology of the Auxiliary Units was still muddled. It was almost entirely reliant on Section D for demolition materials and did not begin to receive weapons or systematic training until later in August. Section D supplied the Auxiliary Units with *c.*30 demonstration demolition sets, 400 small weapons dumps and 10 large weapons dumps. It also supplied the first training manual to the Auxiliary Units – 200 copies of its *Brown Book* on the use of explosives which seems likely to have formed the basis of Wilkinson's *Calendar 1937* (Plate 29).[88] Section D also organised some of the first training for Auxiliary Units Intelligence Officers, including the Scottish CO, Eustace Maxwell, at Aston House.[89] The difference in concept between the Auxiliary Units and HDS can clearly be seen in Fig. 4: the Auxiliary Units were heavily supplied with explosives whilst the HDS at this stage was supplied exclusively with incendiary devices that were easier to replace and to conceal under occupation. What became an infamous distribution of explosives took place in a very narrow band of time in June 1940, but is reflected in the later provision of crimping tools and detonators in the July inventory.

Fig. 4 Material simultaneously supplied by SIS to the Home Defence Scheme and the Auxiliary Units in July 1940. (*TNA HS 8/214*)

	Home Defence	Auxiliary Units
Time fuzes	4,060	46,380
Safety fuze (ft)		14,016
Safety fuze, lengths match ended	1,810	
Detonating fuze (ft)		27,000
Instantaneous fuze		4,950
Detonators		27,020
Blasting Gelignite (lbs)		5,600
High Explosive (lbs)		5,246
Medium – Large Incendiary Bombs	450	5,270
Medium Incendiary Bombs	1,610	5,450
Tyesules (paraffin incendiaries)	29,479	10,124
Petrol Paraffin Mixture (gallons)	400	
Capsules for Petrol Bomb	63,540	
Acid for Petrol Bomb (quarts)	206	
Magnets		2,336
Fog Signals		1,560
Crimping Tools	42	540
Tape (15-yd reels)		1,538
Vaseline (tubes)		950
Fuzes (boxes) [Detonators]	1,540	1,571
Striker Boards	1,668	
A.W. Bombs		1,200
Pressure Switches		50

Grand fought back against the attempts of the War Office to absorb the HDS. As an appeasement, he first made every effort to stress that the HDS would fall under military control during the phase of an active military campaign, although without wireless any form of strategic control after invasion would have been difficult (as the Auxiliary Units were to find). By the end of July, however, a clear policy decision was made for Britain (but not abroad), that the risk of allowing civilians to engage in sabotage was too great and therefore that the HDS should be absorbed within the Auxiliary Units, organised around the legally-constituted Home Guard.[90] Consequently, Grand shifted towards a clearer division of function which would place the HDS outside the remit of the War Office but would risk bringing it into greater competition with Section VII. Based on the earlier model of a dual-level resistance organisation in Norway, Grand tried to change focus from the counter-invasion phase into a phase of longer-term resistance. Now he proposed a phase of quiet intelligence-gathering during the immediate invasion period 'for the purpose of obtaining information for our own forces' (this later becoming the rationale for the SDB) but leaving sabotage to the Auxiliary Units who were now mobilising. At the time the Auxiliary Units were only anticipated to survive a matter of days but after the collapse of the military defence, the HDS would then carry out 'resistance projects of all sorts'. This is a rare contemporary use of the term 'resistance'.[91] Grand even seconded a number of his officers to the Auxiliary Units in an attempt to demonstrate cooperation and secure a degree of integration of the two schemes. Six such officers have now been potentially identified (Fig. 2 and see below, pp.85 and 146).

> At the same time I detailed officers to my D.M. group to work with a second organisation of special units allotted by the War Office for the same type of work. In this way we had two organisations available and one would be brought into action when, as was inevitable, the other was discovered and broken up. The D organisation was the one that was to remain quiescent at the outset.[92]

Grand's proposal received no support from SIS, who saw it as a risk to the security of Section VII and much of the HDS in coastal areas was absorbed within the Auxiliary Units (with the intelligence wing transferred as an intact unit). One clue to this comes from the significant number of auxiliers whose date of joining, according to the Nominal Roll compiled from 1942, actually pre-dates the creation of the Auxiliary Units.[93] In the inland areas, its networks quietly morphed into being part of Section VII where some cells were eventually equipped with wireless sets.

The existing HDS volunteers were probably ignorant of such policy shifts. A characteristic of recruitment was that many were not told the identity or affiliation of the recruiting officer as the HDS continued to independently recruit and supply their saboteurs. In South Wales and the South Midlands, Intelligence Officer John Todd (alias 'Tommy Atkins') was one of the Section D regional officers from HDS attached to the new Auxiliary Units by Laurence Grand. The hybrid nature of the HDS compared to the strictly divided Auxiliary Units meant that he began the tradition in this area of having a single Intelligence Officer control both Operational Patrols and the Special Duties Branch. The SDB did not officially begin operating in South Wales until after March 1942 but George Vater from Monmouthshire was recruited by Todd before August 1940 as a Key Man for the HDS and continued this role into the SDB.[94] He was given the names of eight other people who formed his cell by Todd. Observations were made by day, and each night Vater had to collect messages from half a dozen dead-letter drops in the local area. Each message had to contain the safety word 'precisely'. The cell had a local HQ (a derelict barn) where the agents would rendezvous after invasion to receive orders (cf. similar instructions given to Section VII's Albert Toon in Birmingham, see above, p.27).[95] Vater also remembers being driven by Todd to a meeting at Hannington Hall, close to Coleshill and, at the time, the HQ of the SDB. This would have been prior to Todd joining SOE in July 1941. At some point Reverend Sluman of Llantillio Croesenny became the wireless operator, who was expected to be contactable 24 hours a day. Vater was told to expect 14 days of activity after invasion – their likely life expectancy. Vater's HDS cell was a hybrid of intelligence-reporting and operational activity. They went out on stalking exercises, had an emergency HQ, and Vater was issued with a .22 sniper rifle and a sealed envelope believed to contain a 'hit list' of potential assassination targets. In truth the rifle was a poor tool for long-range assassination (see below, p.131) and even at short range could not easily guarantee a silent kill. George Vater's rifle was given to him by a 'Mr Graham'. Todd was unhappy about this but accepted the situation as being from a more senior officer. 'Mr Graham' was actually an alias used by Laurence Grand.[96]

In Herefordshire, Geoffrey Morgan-Jones recalled being contacted by telephone 'about the time of the Dunkirk evacuation' by someone asking if he was willing 'to do something to help his country'. A meeting was arranged where he met John Todd and local man Alex Beck. This would also pre-date the creation of the Auxiliary Units and suggests that the men were initially recruited into another HDS cell by Todd, which then morphed into Adam Patrol of the Herefordshire Auxiliary Units. Other patrol members were recruited but at this time there was no Operational Base.[97] Alex Beck, a former Flight Commander in the RAF, who joined the LDV in May 1940, became patrol leader but his view of action after invasion was that each member would act independently, so they all kept individual supplies of equipment, and again this was very much in the spirit of the HDS. In Worcestershire the spy cell at Upton was linked directly to the Operational Patrol HQ at Wolverton Hall where there was already an SIS interest. Other shadowy intelligence and guerrilla units operated in Worcestershire and the Midlands during the war and it is possible that in 1940–1 John Todd, largely invisible in surviving Auxiliary Units documents, was still working to an SIS agenda that was only partially absorbed by the Auxiliary Units.

In Devon, Stuart Edmundson established the early Auxiliary Units village cell system but his account of the organisation at this stage is redolent of the earlier HDS and its frantic distribution of its arms dumps and it is possible he was originally recruiting for the HDS. The later Nominal Roll of the Auxiliary Units for Devon indeed lists several men as joining as early as 24 May, well before the creation of the Auxiliary Units and presumably originally part of the HDS.[98] It may be no coincidence that Laurence Grand had family property in the south-west. Edmundson recruited teams of a leader and two men who were expected to operate discreetly from home as civilians. 'These early recruits were told nothing about being in a special unit of the Home Guard – or indeed about being in any formal organisation – and their names were never committed to paper.' Each team was given a cardboard box containing a sabotage kit, initially delivered to Edmundson's garden. 'His wife, who had been let in on the secret, rushed frantically around, trying to find new hiding places in the neighbourhood'.[99] In such areas it seems the members and methodology of the HDS simply morphed into the early Auxiliary Units.

As resources from the HDS were gradually handed over during the summer of 1940 in the areas where the Auxiliary Units were now operating, its existing arms dumps were, wherever possible, transferred, although some were lost forever. Nonetheless, Section D's base at Aston House remained the main supply base for the Auxiliary Units for the rest of the war, continuing this role after being absorbed by SOE.[100] 'Aux Packs' were assembled at Aston House and packed for distribution across the country; in February 1941 there was an order for 1,000 cases of stores for the Auxiliary Units. A storeman at Aston later recorded loading Auxiliary Units 'Dumps' into large A12 ammunition crates during the winter of 1942/3: the heavy and unwieldy metal A12 crate was 25.2in x 17.3in x 8.5in, originally used to pack six charges for the now-obsolete 8in Livens gas projector.[101]

Thus, in the darkest days after Dunkirk it was Section D of SIS who had mobilised quickly to form a nationwide civilian guerrilla force and encourage wider resistance, whilst the military Auxiliary Units were still being formed and equipped around the coast. In even more secrecy, SIS also continued its plans for a deep-cover resistance intelligence and sabotage network in Section VII. Despite being formally sidelined in terms of plans to respond to an invasion of Britain, Section D continued its more or less independent existence within SIS until 16 August when it was agreed that it would fall within the new SOE. Even then, Grand still served as the deputy to the new head of sabotage operations, Sir Frank Nelson (aged 58), who also transferred from SIS. Section D remained a semi-autonomous body until it was finally fully absorbed into the new SOE after 18 September, when Grand was brusquely dismissed by Hugh Dalton. A note was appended to the letter of dismissal by a civil servant in the Ministry of Economic Warfare to say 'a word of thanks would not have come amiss'.[102] With parallels in the false narrative created over the role of Section D in the Auxiliary Units' history by some early Auxiliary Units commentators who went on to serve with SOE, there were claims of a wholesale purge of Section D staff although in reality the new SOE relied heavily on former Section D staff in the early years.

By August 1940, the concept of a civilian guerrilla organisation to actively fight during the invasion itself, as represented by the HDS, appeared to have been completely abandoned in favour of a military option controlled by GHQ (see Chapter 6). Laurence Grand, the *bête noir* of the Chiefs of Staff Committee and elements within SIS, had been neutralised and, with a sigh of relief from all concerned, was posted to India. But deep in the shadows, beyond the control, or even knowledge, of GHQ there still existed the Section VII resistance organisation.

Postscript: The Davies Plan – Scheme D reborn

In a rearguard action to reject the policy against using civilians as combatants, on 17 June (the day the Cabinet approved the concept of the Auxiliary Units, see Chapter 6) 'Tommy' Davies of MI(R) submitted an unofficial and radical plan for a civilian resistance which briefly excited some interest before being quashed by the C-in-C Home Forces and the War Cabinet. Knowing that he could not promote the idea himself, Jo Holland may have allowed Davies to circulate his plan, as a Machiavellian means of reviving the Scheme D but without any suggestion of SIS initiative and under more acceptable military control. It is even possible that Grand might have seen this as a means of countering opposition to his HDS. Davies had been used before by Holland as a back-door conduit to argue the case for 'shadow missions' with the Foreign Office.[103] Now Davies raised his plan for a British resistance with Lieutenant Colonel Arthur Cornwall-Jones, Assistant Secretary to the War Cabinet, and on 17 June, having seen the papers relating to the formation of the Auxiliary Units that were presented to the Cabinet, wrote:

> I am afraid that you will never forgive me for bothering you again but this is even more actual than my last plan. It may seem unconstitutional and unorthodox but it is the only possible way of getting one step ahead of the Boche. I know from documents you have already discussed this matter and that certain steps have been taken but it is all too incomplete. There is such

a strong feeling in the country that an effective and reassuring organisation is necessary.[104]

The plan for the Auxiliary Units was indeed a pale reflection of the endorsement of Scheme D for the rest of Europe by the War Office and Foreign Office in March 1939.

Members of the Chiefs of Staff Committee and the new Ministry of Defence excitedly discussed his proposal, momentarily forgetting the official policy against involving civilians and their complaints against the almost identical HDS. Davies countered concern over the risk of reprisals by saying that if any guerrilla units were formed to operate behind enemy lines then the Germans were likely to take reprisals on the civilian population whether it was involved or not. He believed that the acceptable rules of warfare had already been changed, and that the country wanted some concrete application of the principles that Churchill had proclaimed in his 'Fight on the Beaches' speech of 4 June. He called for the civilian population to 'resist by all practical means in their power whatever the cost', going on to say 'There is no-one who may not be called to give their life for their country', and calling on the civilian population to 'place themselves unreservedly in the hands of the military authorities'.[105] Here was the cornerstone of Holland's belief in the conduct of guerrilla warfare but extended to incorporate civilians in the manner of the HDS and Dolphin's 'Standfast Club' from the Section D stable.

Repeating MI(R)'s long-standing research, in *Need for Organisation of Civil Resistance* Davies highlighted the nuisance value of guerrilla tactics in India, Ireland and Palestine and the vulnerability of modern warfare to the interruption of lines of communication. As MI(R) had proposed for France, he suggested a Civil Resistance Section of the army Area Commands to organise destruction of stores likely to be of use to the enemy at the time of an enemy landing and demolition of infrastructure (bridges, railways, roads, power stations etc) in the event of occupation. Personnel to be enrolled for civil resistance would include selected ARP and police for demolition work, an intelligence service drawn from schoolmasters, priests, women and Boy Scouts, and guerrillas from local inhabitants and serving soldiers. Davies called for 'constant organised civilian opposition to the invader in the back areas and even in the fighting zone' and believed that the vulnerability of the German lines of supply had not been sufficiently tested in previous campaigns. The War Office firmly rejected any resistance role for the Auxiliary Units but Davies declared that after the occupation 'of any locality, or even of the whole country, some form of secret resistance organisation would be essential, which would both tie up large numbers of enemy troops and also preserve the morale of the population'. He was also prepared to raise the unthinkable necessity to consider options 'if the possibility of the government and armed forces leaving for a Dominion were considered', one of the clearest statements of the possibility of a defeat of British forces and an evacuation of government.[106]

On 18 June Cornwall-Jones submitted Davies' proposal to General 'Pug' Ismay, Churchill's Chief of Staff and a member of the Chiefs of Staff Committee, who in turn forwarded it to Colonel L.C. Hollis (Secretary of the Chiefs of Staff Committee) and Victor Cavendish-Bentinck (chairman of the Joint Intelligence Committee). Despite clearly running contrary to official policy, there was a rush of initial enthusiasm. Hollis on 22 June declared the proposal of Davies to be 'forceful and logical' but had to admit doubts on how it could be implemented.[107] Hollis forwarded the Davies scheme to Lord Hankey, Churchill's security advisor, who also made enthusiastic suggestions, clearly borrowed from what he knew of the existing SIS plans. He suggested a resistance organisation that had learned lessons from experience in Ireland with

I. Intelligence
II. Sabotage
III. Assassination

There was an interesting handwritten addition regarding an intelligence network able to pass information through enemy lines: 'SIS must run this' (as it would do in the Auxiliary Units during 1940). In his note Hankey described in effect the Section D intelligence network of the HDS and their railway sabotage operations in the Balkans. He saw the core of saboteurs as previously-trained LDV who had been able to merge back into the civilian population after the tide of battle had passed over them. Civilians in 'subjugated areas' could then 'keep the enemy continually on the jump as we were in Ireland'. The methodology of LDV hiding their weapons and fighting on as civilians from within the community, with a school that could train instructors who would then 'spread the gospel to local instructors', was soon to be expounded by Wintringham at Osterley Park.[108] Hankey was also enthusiastic about 'Assassination on the Irish model' suggesting the use of an undetectable poison.[109] Cavendish-Bentinck had doubts but, caught up in the mood, he also proposed that schools for spies and saboteurs should be established in likely areas for invasion.[110]

On 23 June General Ismay, who had only the day before received the letter of complaint over the HDS from Major General Macdougall (Deputy CIGS) but was perhaps now surprised by such apparent enthusiasm for a departure from official policy, then forwarded the plan to General Henry Pownall, now Inspector-General of the Home Guard, and Sir Samuel Findlater-Stewart (Chairman of the Home Defence Executive). Ismay, however, had to admit with a comment directed at SIS operations: 'We here are not, of course, fully in the picture about all that has been done and is being done to organise civil resistance'. Ismay also emphasised 'the fundamental question of whether the civil un-uniformed population is to be encouraged to fight [underlined in original]'.[111] Pownall and Findlater-Stewart took up such hints, with Pownall saying that this went beyond his responsibility and Findlater-Stewart querying the availability of resources, pointing out that there were not yet sufficient arms for the new LDV, never mind any new venture.[112] The idea was finally quashed on 8 July when the Commander-in-Chief, Home Forces, General Ironside, and the Secretary of War, Anthony Eden wrote their memorandum to the War Cabinet rejecting the concept of civilian combatants and signalling the end of the HDS (see above, p.6).[113]

Perhaps not surprisingly, Davies, chafing at what he saw as a lack of 'drive and direction' by the War Office and no doubt now agreeing with Dalton's belief that the War Office were not suited to managing irregular warfare, joined SOE on 23 September as personal assistant to Frank Nelson, with the remit of advising on SOE's resources of staff and supplies.[114] In autumn 1941 he became Director of Research and Supply, and held that post until the end of his SOE career. The whole sequence of correspondence is extraordinary given that SIS had begun mobilising its civilian resistance of the HDS in late May, the Cabinet agreement for the creation of the Auxiliary Units on 17 June and the widespread opposition of other sections of the General Staff and Cabinet to the very principle of the participation of civilians in warfare. There appears to have been a brief infectious enthusiasm amongst those corresponding on the topic, followed quickly by rather restrained and polite rebuttals, but the episode is another example of the confusion that surrounded the plans for Britain's defence in 1940.

Chapter 5

XII Corps Observation Unit

As Laurence Grand moved ahead with the Home Defence Scheme, within days of the 27 May ISPB meeting MI(R)'s plans to create a guerrilla movement based around the LDV had faltered, with Peter Fleming (Plate 7) moved to Scotland as an instructor at the Lochailort guerrilla warfare school to provide urgently-needed training for the Independent Companies. Instead, it was General Andrew Thorne, commanding XII Corps in Kent and Sussex, who independently established his 'Observation Unit' of army guerrilla patrols. Fleming credited Thorne as being the first senior officer to see the potential if 'the enemy in his bridgeheads were harassed by light forces left behind for the purpose' and then attacking lines of communications and concentration areas.[1]

Thorne had become a Major General in October 1938 and a year later took command of 48th (South Midlands) Division. In May 1940 he was fighting along a 26-mile front as part of the British rearguard to Dunkirk before being evacuated on 1 June. A week later, Thorne (now a Lieutenant General) took command of XII Corps in the key areas of Kent, Sussex and parts of Hampshire and Surrey; despite being on the front line of any invasion threat they suffered from very weak resources. He desperately needed to find ways of strengthening his regular forces with whatever resources were at hand and to use them to disrupt the seemingly unstoppable flow of the German *blitzkrieg*. Thorne (Plate 8 and Appendix 2) could not wait for the War Office to sort out its plans for irregular warfare and created his own local solution. Not for nothing was the biography of General Andrew 'Bulgy' Thorne entitled *Forgotten General*; few people now know his name or his contribution to the war effort. Thorne was a forward-looking regular officer who had commanded a battalion of the Grenadier Guards in the First World War and in 1932 became Military Attaché in Berlin, seeing the rise of the Nazis to power at first hand. His reports on the German army were well-informed and in particular he was able to predict its increasing mechanisation as well as plans for long-range rockets. Thorne had a particular concern for army education; he wanted officer cadets to undergo normal recruit training before going to Sandhurst and for senior NCOs to be given more responsibility. He supported many of the ideas (if not the politics) of Tom Wintringham who he first met on the publication of the latter's *How To Reform The Army*; they subsequently developed a shared interest in guerrilla warfare and corresponded throughout the war. Thorne would have found little to criticise in Wintringham's call in March 1940 to encourage initiative in NCOs and private soldiers, the necessity to be able to fight in small groups and the importance of infiltration as a tactic. 'And for the development of these tactics, a new spirit and discipline in the army, a release of the initiative and independent energy of the men who are our soldiers.'[2] Thorne sent a number of his officers to observe the Osterley Park training course and also took a personal interest in the army career of Hugh Slater, another instructor at Osterley Park. After Slater was commissioned (much against the wishes of MI5), Thorne had him transferred to Scottish Command and appointed as an Instructor at the Company Commander's Training School.

The concept of XII Corps Observation Unit was to slow down the enemy advance towards the GHQ 'stop-line', attacking their supply lines from the rear, in order to give more time for a major counter-attack to be launched and to cut off the crucial German supply lines to the sea. This was not a purely defensive strategy: Thorne's new guerrilla units, based on twenty army battalion 'Battle Patrols' might also disrupt any enemy retreat and so enable its complete annihilation. The decisive Thorne put his plans into place immediately after completing the first survey of his command, and XII Corps Observation Unit was operational in its most basic form within a matter of days. Unlike Gubbins in the later Auxiliary Units, Thorne had the advantage of direct authority as Corps Commander to immediately implement his ideas. He is reputed to have got his inspiration from a visit to an East Prussian estate in 1934, where the staff had been traditionally trained in this role against the possibility of invasion from the East and it is hard to escape the conclusion that he came to XII Corps with the idea already formed in his mind.[3] He then asked the War Office for a specialist officer to lead the unit and Peter Fleming was the obvious choice; it finally gave Fleming a mechanism with which to implement the ideas for the LDV that he had been considering over the previous couple of weeks.

Fleming acknowledged that the original idea came from Thorne, but he developed it into a form that was to become recognisable as a pilot for the later Auxiliary Units. One crucial new element was a request for a detachment of Lovat Scouts to be brought in as a regular army scout section and the core of a training unit. The Lovat Scouts were one of the earliest of Britain's 'special forces'. Originally raised in 1900, they were recruited from hardy Scottish ghillies (gamekeepers) and were experts in camouflage, sniping and stalking. In 1916 the Lovat Scouts (Sharpshooters) were formed to provide nine 'Observation Groups' for the Western Front, each consisting of one officer and twenty-one other ranks; they specifically recruited older men, including the redoubtable 62-year-old Lieutenant Macpherson. Their principal task, usually working in pairs, was patrolling and reconnaissance through no man's land in order to collect intelligence. It is no coincidence that the name given to Thorne's new unit was 'Observation Unit'; Fleming had recently been involved in discussions during mid-April 1940 between DMI, MI(R) and the Lovat Scouts as to the role of the latter in the new Independent Companies. MI(R) had first proposed a 'Composite Battalion' comprising the 5th Battalion, Scots Guards and 400 men of the Lovat Scouts, which would then be subdivided into ten companies who would act as independent commando units in Norway. Colonel Melville, CO of the Lovat Scouts, was opposed to the idea as it would risk the end of the regiment's independent existence. The idea was abandoned when it was discovered that the 5th Battalion Scots Guards had already been disbanded but, instead, it was suggested that the Lovat Scouts would act as an independent commando unit – a proposal also overtaken by events but which indicates the special skills of the regiment. Fleming had a personal connection to the Lovat Scouts as his brother Richard was its Training Officer; he had just returned from a specialist course in sniping and observation. Peter Fleming badly wanted to incorporate the Lovat Scouts into the new Observation Unit but securing their participation was to be no mean task and was a tribute to Fleming's well-known reputation as a talented and determined 'scrounger'. Since his discussions with Colonel Melville in April, the regiment had been dispatched to garrison the remote Faroe Islands, 200 miles north of Scotland, where they were under great pressures due to shortage of personnel and persistent illness. Fleming persuaded the War Office, through Thorne, to agree to a detachment of Lovat Scouts under his brother to be recalled from the Faroes, resulting in a rather irritable entry in the Lovat Scouts War Diary for 19 June 1940.

> A cable came from the War Office to dispatch by the first available ship Captain R.E. Fleming, 1 Sergeant and 13 Other Ranks to report to XII Corps at Tunbridge Wells for special duty under GHQ Home Forces. The Other Ranks to be stalkers and good shots. This can be done once or twice, but will be impossible to comply with often.[4]

The attempt to get the Lovat Scouts back from the Faroe Islands is a clear indication of the importance attached to the XII Corps Observation Unit by the War Office. The regiment, however, tried to find a means of circumventing the order. On 20 June the movement order for Richard Fleming and his men was cancelled when the Commanding Officer of the Lovat Scouts' depot in Edinburgh sent a cable to say that as an alternative he had sent twelve men from the Home Detail to XII Corps. Had they managed to outflank the attack on their Faroes garrison? Peter was still desperate to involve his brother and maintained the pressure on the War Office. On 30 June the regiment received another cable from the War Office ordering Captain Fleming to report to XII Corps as soon as possible, and this time there was no way out. Fleming and his batman eventually left the Faroes for Tunbridge Wells on 2 July. Such was the importance of the Lovat Scouts detachment, that on 7 August 1940 orders to transfer the Lovat Scouts personnel away from XII Corps were cancelled.[5] Richard Fleming's service with the Observation Unit only lasted four months and he returned to the Faroes on 11 November. Nonetheless, on 13 November another small detachment of Lovat Scouts left for services in an 'Observation Group', presumably referring to XII Corps.[6] Eventually the Lovat Scouts contingent was reduced to just two NCO training instructors in the Scout Section. Although he had already left the Lovat Scouts, Major Simon Fraser, the Lord Lovat, visited the XII Corps Observation Unit along with other dignitaries interested in this novel approach to warfare.[7] In June he had become the first Chief Instructor at the Lochailort Commando Training School, where Mike Calvert had been his demolitions instructor, and then joined the new Combined Operations HQ.

The original methodology of Thorne did not include the use of hides but Peter Fleming, influenced by a report by Jo Holland of 7 June 1940 (see below, p.89), believed the absence of such 'bolt holes' would limit the operational life of the cells, and introduced the idea of fixed hides, some of which were made from enlarged badger setts. General Thorne visited one and was delighted: descending a rope ladder he found some Lovat Scouts and half a dozen Home Guard sitting on barrels of explosives.[8] The hides were constructed by 172 Tunnelling Company, Royal Engineers, and two-man sapper teams from 262 Field Company, Royal Engineers. Other labour was drawn from XII Corps troops. The hides were then carefully camouflaged by the Lovat Scouts. The most spectacular hide was dug into the bottom of what was known as The Airship Hole, in King's Wood above The Garth, Bilting in Kent; it was a large oval hole about 30m long, 10m wide and 5m deep and originally dug as a mooring sub-station for British airships during the First World War. The gondola of the airship would nestle into the pit to give protection against the wind. Fleming reasoned that the last place the Germans would look for a hide was in the bottom of an existing hole. It became a command centre and redoubt, with food, water and sleeping accommodation for around 120 people.

The hides were linked to observation posts by cable-connected field telephones (Plate 26), but Fleming arranged with SIS for some of the hides to be linked by wireless. Initially two mysterious men wearing RAF uniform were attached to the unit, equipped with portable wireless sets. For fixed communications SIS provided one of their top wireless engineers 'Spuggy' Newton (Plate 9), lately back from France having built and delivered the first of SIS's mobile communication units, installed in a Dodge armoured car. Newton then installed wireless sets inside a number of the underground hides constructed within Ashdown Forest, pre-dating the installation of the Auxiliary Units' pilot network in the same area by around three months.[9] The fact that the wireless had to be installed by a specialist from Section VIII of SIS suggests they were using the standard SIS combination of HRO National Receiver and Mk III long-range transmitter that Newton had installed in embassies and secret radio stations all over Europe, and was now building into the Packard cars and trucks of the SIS Special Communications Units. The long-range wireless sets could report directly to Corps HQ, rather than having to use the type of IN/OUT Station relay system as used by the later, less powerful, SDB system of the Auxiliary Units. The other key recruit to the Unit was Captain Mike Calvert, a Royal Engineers officer, an expert in explosives who would go on to command a Chindit column and then the SAS. He was brought down in mid-July from the Commando Training School at Lochailort where he was a Demolitions Instructor. Like many others, he was shocked by the reality of the preparations for invasion: 'I had been caught up, along with everyone else, by the invasion fever, but this official recognition that desperate measures might soon be needed brought home, as nothing else had, the full gravity of our situation in 1940.'[10]

At the strategic core of the XII Corps Observation Unit were the regular army Battle Patrols and the Lovat Scouts training unit. The Battle Patrols were formed in each battalion of XII Corps and would act independently as guerrilla units, attacking the rear and flanks of the enemy. Most of the twenty Patrols were divided into two sections of six men each. They had hidden hides and, crucially, their wireless sets meant they could be directed more strategically. From February 1941 Henry Hall, a former student at the Lochailort Commando School, commanded the Battle Patrol of the 4th Battalion, Dorset Regiment, This was more substantial with three NCOs and thirty other ranks (probably to be divided into three sub-units of ten men each under an NCO). They were trained in close-quarters combat and demolition skills with orders to go to ground upon invasion and create as much havoc as possible. In the meantime they would test the security of HQs, ammunition dumps and communication systems and act as the 'enemy' in brigade exercises. Hall went on to assist the Auxiliary Units Intelligence Officer in Kent. One NCO who served with the Battle Patrols was Tom 'Chalkie' White. He was recruited by Peter Fleming into a patrol of the West Surrey Regiment with seven other NCOs from the reserve depot. One thing that struck him was that Fleming insisted they all be treated as equals and call each other by their

Christian names – a tricky line for an officer to follow whilst retaining both his authority and their respect. Fleming acknowledged that he did not naturally have the common touch with his men but made great efforts to talk and listen to them, taking their advice on choice of weaponry and encouraging them to use their initiative.

These Battle Patrols went on to provide the inspiration for the Scout Sections of the Auxiliary Units (see Chapter 6) and potentially to other army initiatives elsewhere (see below, p.75). They were soon supported by the LDV/Home Guard patrols recruited by Peter Fleming: he was armed with a letter of authority from the general commanding Tunbridge Wells Home Guard to choose whatever men he needed 'which may necessitate their going with Captain Fleming or his subordinates in the event of an emergency'.[11] Fleming established a training centre in a farm, The Garth at Bilting; his HQ was in a hut where the officers dined on top of a crate of explosives, using other crates of explosives as chairs. There they entertained curious generals and even the Prime Minister.[12] Fleming later described their respective roles: 'This was a nucleus to which in time we precariously linked a network of picked sub-units of the Home Guard, who would in theory—after fighting like lions in their normal role—withdraw to well-stocked hide-outs in the woods when their localities were overrun by the Germans.'[13] It is curious that the LDV patrols were only expected to go to ground after having defended their allotted posts with their battalion. How many would have survived to join the Observation Unit is therefore debatable. Fleming was not hopeful about their success: 'The whole scheme in its early stages was typical of the happy-go-lucky improvisation of those dangerous days, and though we gradually built it up into something fairly solid I doubt if we should have been more than a minor and probably short-lived nuisance to the invaders.'[14] He warned that their life expectancy would then be just 48 hours.[15] Fleming was joined by Mike Calvert from Lochailort in July. Together, Fleming and Calvert demonstrated the potential of the guerrillas by infiltrating General Montgomery's 3rd Division HQ. Calvert mined bridges and railway lines, filled the basements of country houses liable to be used as German HQs with explosives ready to be detonated and over-enthusiastically booby-trapped Brighton West Pier. Unfortunately, an inquisitive seagull set off one of the charges, producing a spectacular chain reaction which destroyed part of the structure.[16]

The XII Corps Observation Unit was a tighter structure, more directly integrated with the regular forces, than that which developed in the Auxiliary Units. Thorne had a battle plan that made guerrilla warfare an integral part of the Corps strategy, made possible by being directly administered at Corps level and having wireless communications. The separately-organised Auxiliary Units struggled to find a mechanism that achieved the same ends. Peter Fleming had a huge admiration for Thorne's common-sense approach to irregular warfare but was more scathing about what he later saw as the romanticism of Gubbins and his staff who sought an increasing range of booby traps and devices. This from the man who tried to re-introduce the longbow to the British army via the Observation Units! 'We had not been there very long before I procured, at the taxpayers' expense, two large bows and a supply of arrows and told the Lovat Scouts to learn how to use them'. They found that a detonator and short length of fuse taped to an arrow made an effective distraction device when fired over the top of an enemy post.[17]

In November 1940, as part of the exodus of Auxiliary Units staff including Gubbins and Wilkinson, Fleming moved on to SOE and Calvert to the Mission 104 Training School in Australia. XII Corps Observation Unit was then absorbed into the Auxiliary Units under Intelligence Officer Norman Field but it still retained the original title until August 1943. Why did Thorne surrender authority for his innovation to an outside body? It may be that he too shared the wider opinion that the main risk of invasion had now passed and had more confidence in the improved conventional strength of his Corps. General Montgomery succeeded Thorne as commanding officer of XII Corps on 25 April 1941 and Thorne became General Officer Commanding, Scottish Command. Although this was technically a promotion, few could understand why he had been moved to what was considered to be a backwater. There were suspicions that Montgomery (then commanding V Corps) might have engineered the move to increase his own profile, but Thorne was too much of a gentleman ever to make public comment on the matter. In the vast area of Scottish Command, with scattered resources, he saw a renewed advantage in the Auxiliary Units and supported their extension across Scotland, with Hugh Slater now instructing his company commanders in the techniques of guerrilla warfare.

Thorne's initiative is now well known, largely because of the autobiographies of Fleming and Calvert and the subsequent history of XII Corps Observation Unit with the Auxiliary Units. There are, however, tantalizing hints that other army districts may have been inspired by Thorne to plan something similar. A sergeant in the Leicestershire Regiment, Samuel Hall of Ellistown, garrisoned locally for training, was ordered to form what he described post-war as an 'underground resistance group' base in the caves of Charnwood Forest, with a 'contact point' at Mount St Bernard's Abbey. As an exercise they placed plastic explosives (which suggests SIS cooperation if prior to 1941) under the suspension footbridge alongside the Trent bridge in Nottingham. In Worcester, the 23rd Infantry Training Centre at Norton Barracks, home to two Corps Training Companies, was clearly a focus for local guerrilla training for the Auxiliary Units and possibly SIS, led by NCO instructors (see above, p.75). The discovery of a number of hidden Operational Base-type structures in the outskirts of Worcester, forming a ring around the anti-tank island whereby any besieging forces could be attacked in the rear and also at Droitwich, some constructed by local builders and all unknown to the Auxiliary Units veterans, suggests the possibility that army 'battle patrols' based around the infantry instructors were also preparing to 'go to ground' themselves.[18] Some men of the Phantom squadrons were also unofficially preparing to fight on as guerrillas in civilian clothes (see below, p.173). Were such initiatives replicated elsewhere?

Chapter 6

The GHQ Auxiliary Units: Operational Wing 1940–1: Resisting the Invader

> In July it was decided by the authorities that the risk of reprisals incurred by allowing civilians to engage in sabotage activities was too great. It was therefore decided that M.I.R. and D Section home activities should be united and called G.H.Q. Auxiliary Units (under Colonel Gubbins) and the members would be selected from Home Guard Units.
>
> Section D, Early History to September 1940[1]

The Germans entered Paris on 14 June 1940. This focused the need to prepare for possible invasion and a desperate General Ironside had already (10 June) discreetly reported on the development of the HDS (see above, p.48). There was, however, growing disquiet by some in the War Office over the insertion of SIS into the invasion landscape and by the government on its use of civilians in combat. The response was for the Cabinet to agree on 17 June to the formation of the military Auxiliary Units, based around the new Local Defence Volunteers (LDV), recording: 'Steps were also being taken to organise sections of Storm Troopers on a full-time basis, as part of the LDVs. Tough and determined characters would be selected.'[2]

Ten days had passed since the ISPB meeting of 27 May which announced the arrival of the HDS but neither the Cabinet nor War Office had any clear idea of how a more legal alternative would operate. The clear link made at the outset between the Auxiliary Units and the LDV (the Home Guard from 22 July) created an enduring tension as they were to be explicitly a structural part of the LDV/Home Guard but at the same time operationally secret. Their existence became something of an 'open secret', protected mainly by the contemporary readiness to avoid gossip over any evidently 'hush hush' work of one's neighbours.

Unlike the HDS or Section VII, the Auxiliary Units were not a national organisation but were first established in the vulnerable coastal counties of the south-west, and on the south and east coasts of England as the most likely invasion areas, plus the anomalous inland counties of Herefordshire and Worcestershire (to help protect the Midlands from attack up the Severn Valley or from Ireland). Never envisioned as the 'last ditch' defence of modern romance, the Auxiliary Units were part of the multi-faceted military strategy, alongside the Home Guard, to delay the enemy advance from the beaches and prepare for a counter-attack. With the enemy weakened by the sacrifice of the beach defenders, the Home Guard were to provide a frontal check by blocking communication hubs ('nodal points') and harrying the enemy advance, obliging it to use up its limited supplies of fuel and ammunition. The Auxiliary Units, working more covertly behind enemy lines, were initially expected to guide in army commando units but increasingly focused on its own interruption of lines of communications and destruction of supply dumps. An assessment of 1941 concluded that the Germans might suffer 50 per cent casualties on the beaches and land with just four day's supplies and fuel for only 100 miles. Any delay caused by the Home Guard and Auxiliary Units might therefore be crucial. The Home Guard might count their life expectancy in hours after confronting the enemy but the Auxiliary Units, by going to ground, could hopefully survive their initial attacks on pre-determined primary targets to attack more opportunistic targets over the next couple of weeks – by which time the battle would either have been won or lost by the field army.

The philosophy of the Auxiliary Units had its origin in a complementary unit to Section D, based in the War Office: Military Intelligence (Research) began as a small working group, GS(R), of the War Office which, unlike Section D, was publicly acknowledged and subject to Treasury scrutiny. Tasked with exploring tactical innovations, from December 1938 GS(R) came under Jo Holland (Plate 5 and Appendix 2) who initiated a short-term project to developing a military application of irregular warfare that would complement the civilian, agent-led, work already being developed in Section D by near-contemporary and fellow Royal Engineer, Laurence Grand.[3] Holland had served in the First World War in Salonica with the Royal Engineers and Royal Flying Corps (the idea that he served with Lawrence of Arabia is, as with Laurence Grand, a persistent myth) and in 1921 had been wounded by the IRA under mysterious circumstances (see Appendix 2).[4] He was now a Major in the Staff Duties department of the War Office but a foreign posting had to be postponed due to illness. Instead, with the British Army having long been at the receiving end of guerrilla warfare, he was invited to research its potential military value. Having undertaken a desk-top study of all available literature, in June 1939 Holland wrote a paper for the War Office on *An Investigation of the Possibilities of Guerrilla Activities*. This stressed Holland's core belief that irregular warfare had to be coordinated and used as a tactic to support conventional warfare. If so 'it should, in favourable circumstances, cause such a diversion of enemy strength as eventually to present decisive opportunities to the main forces of his opponent. It is therefore an auxiliary method of war of which we have not yet sufficiently exploited the possibilities.'[5] This was a principle at the heart of the later Auxiliary Units. GS(R) reported to the Deputy Chief of the Imperial General Staff but Holland worked closely with Laurence Grand and together they devised the 'D Scheme' in March 1939, not least because this would provide a mechanism whereby GS(R) could expand staffing on the basis of secret SIS funding. GS(R) then became D/M Branch but this apparent surrendering of authority to Section D caused dismay in the War Office. D/M was consequently formally chartered as MI1(R) in June 1939 and finally simply as MI(R), under the Directorate of Military Intelligence (DMI). It remained small and the time of its dispersal in October 1940 was still only one lieutenant colonel, four majors, nine captains and six clerks.[6] Holland never saw it as an operational body and was resentful when drawn into such, but MI(R) did have considerable advisory influence in the development of War Office policy. Grand and Holland had very different personalities but they became good friends, working well together until the separation of their offices on the outbreak of war led to their partnership drifting apart. The distinction in their approaches, particularly relevant for the evolution of plans for guerrilla warfare in Britain, was described by Holland's secretary, Joan Bright Astley, who witnessed the sometimes mutual bewilderment of the Section D spies and military personnel of MI(R) working alongside each other:

> Grand's Section D deeds would be done by undercover men, spies and saboteurs, who, if caught, would be neither acknowledged nor defended by their government. Holland's MI(R) plans would be subject to proper strategic and tactical requirements and carried out by men in the uniform of the established Armed Services for whom the normal conventions of war would operate.[7]

Here was the essential difference between the civilian Home Defence Scheme (HDS) of Section D and the later Auxiliary Units: Holland worked in a department that was not secret *per se* and relied on cooperation with foreign general staffs. He believed that irregular warfare should be built into existing military structures and strategy rather than creating any separate organisation. In his evidence to the Hankey report on SIS in March 1940, the Director of Military Intelligence explained the difference between Section D and MI(R):

> It had however now been arranged in principle that MIR, which consisted of ten officers, should devote itself primarily to plans and research and that actual sabotage in enemy countries should be undertaken by the SIS. If, however, there was a possibility of our own troops acting in conjunction with the local Government, then the actual work of sabotage should more properly be entrusted to MIR.[8]

The agreed division of responsibility was for MI(R) to organise sabotage in arenas where regular British forces were directly involved whilst Section D undertook operations in areas under enemy occupation or in neutral countries.[9] The Auxiliary Units were consequently designed to operate under the control of GHQ whilst there was still military resistance to an invader. If, however, Britain had been occupied, then responsibility for civilian intelligence and sabotage would pass to SIS through Section VII (and Grand's awkward attempt in late July at creating a middle stage with the HDS).

According to Major Peter Wilkinson (the original second in command of the Auxiliary Units), General Ironside had 'read the riot act' after being told by his (not unbiased) subordinates about the 'chaotic' distributions of arms dumps by Section D to its civilian agents who were unknown to GHQ – and demanded that all such activities should now be under military control.[10] This bluster dovetailed into a wider concern of the War Office to bring all irregular warfare under its control – a battle it ultimately lost in the machinations that led to the creation of SOE. Despite its history in researching guerrilla warfare, the record of MI(R) in going beyond theory into practical operations had not been good and it had particularly struggled when expected to operate out of uniform. Nonetheless, Jo Holland was tasked with offering the outline of a more respectable and legal military alternative to the HDS. The Auxiliary Units were explicitly a formal part of the LDV/Home Guard and a legal, uniformed, unit of the 'Armed Forces of the Crown' under the control of GHQ, designed to support regular army commando units. They also provided a structured solution for the increasing calls for the Home Guard to engage in guerrilla warfare (see Chapter 11). Part of the modern confusion over status is because, like the Home Guard, they would only be fully mobilised upon invasion and until then, were an army-in-waiting able to go about their normal business much like members of the peacetime Territorial Army (now The Army Reserve). The idea that they were intended as a 'civilian' resistance movement is a modern romance, most obvious in the fact that they are overwhelmingly photographed in uniform including, by 1944, regular army webbing that emphasised their status. Although the War Office was clear on what they were not going to be, quickly finding an effective methodology in the face of imminent invasion proved difficult. This was despite MI(R) having been briefed by Polish Intelligence on their scheme for guerrilla warfare in May 1939 and having then spent over a year of confidently, if not arrogantly, offering its services as 'advisors' on guerrilla warfare to foreign general staffs.

The concept of Holland, followed initially by Gubbins, was to use selected members of the LDV as support to the new Independent Companies (commandos) as they covertly moved through a locality into enemy territory. Having been briefed by Holland, on 17 June the Chief of the Imperial General Staff (General Sir John Dill) and C-in-C Home Forces (General Ironside) won the approval in principle of Churchill and the War Cabinet for the formation of the Auxiliary Units. Holland did not seek operational control of the Auxiliary Units for MI(R) and the latter had no direct involvement in the development of the Auxiliary Units after Holland's briefing, beyond transferring some staff and subsequently making available its explosives stores. Nonetheless, by 22 July and fighting for organisational survival against the threat of the new SOE, Jo Holland was opportunistically listing Auxiliary Units in 'Duties and Activities of MIR' as one of the projects MI(R) set in motion 'through an inter-change of personnel and ideas'.[11]

Acting Brigadier Colin Gubbins, formerly of MI(R) and imbued with its philosophy, was immediately appointed as the first Commanding Officer (Plate 10). Gubbins, like Grand and Holland, was also working as a staff officer in the War Office before being recruited to MI(R) in April 1939, bringing particular skills in linguistics, recruitment and training. In MI(R) he wrote two seminal manuals, *The Art of Guerrilla Warfare* (with Holland) and *The Partisan Leader's Handbook*, which were essentially compilations of existing thinking as gathered together by Holland's desk-top study.[12] These, together with his subsequent leadership of the Independent Companies in the Norwegian campaign (despite them never being employed in their anticipated role as guerrilla troops), established his credentials to lead the new Auxiliary Units organisation. He was also already known to General Ironside, having been his *aide de camp* in Archangel in 1919. There was another incentive in Holland's suggestion of Gubbins for the posting. Gubbins had caused political embarrassment in MI(R) before leaving to command the Independent Companies and he returned from the Norwegian campaign on 13 June with a mixed reputation and the rank of Acting Brigadier as temporary CO of the 24th (Guards) Brigade. There was now no suitable place for him within MI(R) and on 17 June the former CO (William Fraser) resumed command of the Brigade. The opportunity to recommend him for command of the new Auxiliary Units, with the possibility of retaining his rank, was therefore timely. The MI(R) diary entry for 17 June noted that Gubbins was to command the Auxiliary Units and on 19 June the Chiefs of Staff Committee discretely noted that Gubbins had been transferred from CO of the Independent Companies to 'other duties connected with home defence'.[13] Gubbins later maintained that the name 'Auxiliary Units' was conceived as giving no indication of their role and appeared uninteresting.[14] There were, indeed, a number of auxiliary bodies designed to support regular services (e.g. Auxiliary Fire Service, Auxiliary Territorial Service, Auxiliary Coastguard) but it was particularly a term that Holland had used in his June 1939 report describing an 'auxiliary method of war', which the Chiefs of Staff repeated on 3 June 1940 when they decided that subversive and irregular activities should be an 'auxiliary' to winning of the war (as part of its unsuccessful attempt to control what eventually became SOE).[15] It would not, however, have escaped the War Office that the 'Auxiliary Division' was a paramilitary unit of the Royal Irish Constabulary under the control of SIS, formed in December 1920 from former British army officers to carry out counter-insurgency operations against the IRA. This became notorious for reprisals against civilians. The term 'Auxiliary Units' was also being used currently for the boxes of stores being supplied to the HDS. The SIS connection was certainly not something that Gubbins would have later liked to admit; he had a long-standing antipathy towards SIS after it had thwarted his ambitions whilst in MI(R) and its treatment of him post-war.

As with the recent formation of the LDV, Churchill and the Cabinet had little idea how the Auxiliary Units would actually operate. The MI(R) War Diary implied that the Auxiliary Units had, from the start, been created to use 'Much the same methods as Captain Fleming is using in Kent with his little headquarters' but this entry was only written in November 1940, with the benefit of hindsight.[16] Driven by a rushed timescale, Gubbins struggled to find a methodology that could be immediately implemented, but went through three iterations before mid-August, differing pragmatically from the ideal he had expressed in *The Art of Guerrilla Warfare*. He was not helped by what Wilkinson recalled as the 'slight muddle' in thinking 'because nobody could quite make up their minds whether we were trying to set up something for immediate action against the Germans in the event of an invasion. Or, whether we were trying also to set up a nucleus of an English secret . . . a British Secret Army'. Wilkinson believed that 'If it was the former, which I think was probably the idea of the War Office and probably GHQ Home Forces, then security was not a paramount consideration'. It was beyond the remit of the War Office to prepare for resistance following an enemy occupation but Wilkinson, who had worked closely with Section D, was more inclined towards a more 'long-term' organisation, on the lines of the HDS, where 'obviously one had to deal with an entirely different sort of clandestine technique'. He believed 'Gubbins, I think, was about half way in between' and followed the GHQ desire for a short-term, uniformed body, in continuance of the MI(R) strategy.[17] From the outset, therefore, there was a clear rejection of the Auxiliary Units as a civilian 'resistance' organisation and in 1997 Wilkinson noted 'any suggestion that Auxiliary Units could have provided a framework for long term underground resistance is, in my opinion, absurd'.[18]

The recovery of the initiative from SIS may have been one of the drivers in creating the Auxiliary Units but their assistance could not easily be rejected. The scale of influence of SIS in the establishment of the Auxiliary Units is something that Gubbins would never care to admit. Throughout 1940 the intelligence wing (see Chapter 8) was still essentially that of Bearsted's HDS, with Bearsted himself in command, still assisted by his friends, the Honourable Lionel Montagu and Captain Christopher Holland-Martin. Four of the five known early SDB regional Intelligence Officers came from Section D and three of the early Intelligence Officers of the Operational Branch (with John Todd doubling in both roles – see Fig. 5). The early Auxiliary Units sabotage teams relied heavily on Section D for supplies and by 25 August the latter's Technical Section at Aston House had supplied 7,200lb of plastic explosives, 7,470lb of gelignite, 4,000 SIP grenades, 36,020 detonators and 67,400 time pencils to the HQ of the Auxiliary Units. It also provided 200 copies of its *Brown Book* manual on the use of explosives as what became the first training manual supplied to the Auxiliary Units.[19] Section D organised some of the first training for Auxiliary Units Intelligence Officers at Aston House, and some of the HDS, already trained in making home-made explosives, became local commanders of the Auxiliary Units – although none ever subsequently spoke of their service with SIS.[20] Some of the most brutal methodology of the early Auxiliary Units also had an origin in Section D (see below, p.102). Nigel Oxenden, Intelligence Officer for Norfolk during 1940 and later the Training Officer and official historian of the Auxiliary Units, acknowledged:

> most IOs [Auxiliary Units Intelligence Officers] were assisted by introductions to one or two men who had already been chosen by MI5 [*sic* – Section D] . . . These were generally outstanding individuals, who eventually became group commanders. Meanwhile their local knowledge made them invaluable in finding the right recruits.[21]

Gubbins was driven by the imperative to get something up and running in what was anticipated to be a short window of opportunity before invasion but had no clear idea of what this might entail, initially rejecting the existing blueprint of the Polish guerrilla teams as presented to him in May–June 1939. It is clear his ultimate goal was still derived from his experience in MI(R) and in the Norwegian campaign, to deploy new versions of the Independent Companies, assisted by covert Home Guards – rather than the small sabotage units into which the Auxiliary Units ultimately evolved. Wilkinson later maintained that Gubbins 'had little confidence in sabotage and subversion as such; in fact a somewhat old-fashioned sense of propriety' but believed Gubbins accepted the post out of loyalty to Holland.[22] His approach was, indeed, in line with strategy of MI(R) in the use of uniformed troops and is reflected in Gubbins' efforts to put both the Auxiliary Units and later the SOE on a more military basis.

Modern accounts have stressed the separation of the Operational Patrols of Auxiliary Units from the Home Guard, based on the late 1990s perspective of the local volunteers who were the main source of information before the scale of official documentation was realised. Whilst recognising that the Home Guard had a formal organisational responsibility for the Operational Patrols, it was maintained that the auxiliers' uniform was merely a part of their cover story. There was too ready an acceptance of the veterans' desire to draw a clear distinction between their work and the Home Guard at a time when TV's *Dad's Army* had seriously distorted the reputation of the latter. But even during the war some auxiliers were irritated by the regular army Scout Sections referring to them dismissively as 'our Home Guards'; they became very protective of their special status. Some Worcestershire veterans never even volunteered the information that they were already members of the LDV before being recruited into the Auxiliary Units; this only became apparent when it was possible to study their Home Guard enrolment forms. Yet the War Office from the start clearly regarded the Auxiliary Units as an integral part of the Home Guard, albeit operationally managed as GHQ troops (a parallel being the status of independent infantry brigades). The War Cabinet on 17 June were therefore clear that the new 'storm troopers' would be 'part of the L.D.V's'.[23]

The inherent link between Auxiliary Units and the Home Guard was repeatedly stressed, hence the progress report provided to Churchill on 8 August described the 'Auxiliary Units of the Home Guard' which were organised 'within the framework of the Home Guard organisation'.[24] Consequently, in September some local Home Guard commanders still believed they should have direct control of the new Auxiliary Units patrols. Until late May 1941 local Territorial Army Associations (TAAs), which were responsible for the administration of the Home Guard within their counties, could be found holding the supplies of clothing, arms, ammunition and equipment for Auxiliary Units. Only from late May 1941 was the responsibility for holding supplies formally transferred to the local HQs of the Auxiliary Units.[25] The basic relationship was set out in a letter of 20 January 1941 from the Director General of the Home Guard to the TAAs regarding 'the control of Auxiliary Units of Home Guard known as "Scout Patrols" or "Observation Units"'. The men were to be formally enrolled into the Home Guard, with their enrolment form 'endorsed to show membership of Auxiliary Units'. It is ironic that this instruction was to be securely kept in a locked safe whilst the names and patrol structure could be found published in Part II Orders (Plates 42 and 43).[26] The operational links increased later in the war when the patrols were tasked as reconnaissance units of the Home Guard (see Chapter 7). Consequently, a letter of 11 May 1944 from the CO of the Banff Home Guard in Scotland called for greater liaison at all levels between the Auxiliary Units and the Home Guard but also refers back to a previous instruction of around May 1943 which indicated that, by then, knowledge of the scope and purpose of the Units was known within the Home Guard, in some areas at least, down to the level of Company Commander.[27]

The security arrangements were a source of tension throughout the history of the Auxiliary Units. Gubbins recognised this in his circular letter to LDV commanders on 5 July 1940, explaining 'It must be stressed that it is desirable to keep as secret as possible the existence of this organisation. The present situation obviously necessitates speed at the expense of security, but at the same time it is most important that, whatever else be known generally, the names of the operatives, the existence of dumps of stores, their location, etc., should be kept as secret as possible.'[28] Even so, in his report of 26 July, Gubbins recognised that the organisation and operations of the Auxiliary Units had to be planned in the closest co-operation with the local army Commander and with Home Guard Area Commanders and, other than the location of the supply dumps, seemed relatively unconcerned about security. The calculation was that they would not survive long enough to make this a concern:

> in order to ensure the necessary degree of secrecy, the sites of the dumps of special stores for these units are not disclosed except to the local leader, and the units are given the general title of 'Observation Units' to mask their real role. Secrecy beyond this degree would merely handicap efficiency.[29]

Gubbins' second-in-command, Peter Wilkinson, with some exasperation, soon believed that 'By the middle of August security was finally thrown to the winds . . . With its increased numbers the character of the organisation changed and it became virtually a guerrilla branch of the Home Guard.'[30] The rush to establish some sort of presence on the ground in consultation with the LDV commanders had compromised security from the outset. Both Gubbins and Wilkinson then came to see secrecy as a means of boosting the reputation of the organisation and improving the supply situation; security continued to be somewhat illusory.

For four years the auxiliers openly wore Home Guard uniforms but did not participate in regular parades or activities. They were seen around the locality with weapons that were out of the ordinary and latterly wore distinctive insignia. It was not unusual for David Patrol, sited to cover the Throckmorton airfield in Worcestershire, to be marching in one direction on a Sunday morning after an exercise, and to pass the local Home Guard marching in the opposite direction. In many respects the Auxiliary Units were hiding 'in plain sight', their main defence being an acceptance by the rest of their local community that they should not be inquisitive at a time when gossip could be regarded as a criminal offence. The volunteers were ordered to be modest, pretend that their job was dull and uninteresting, and never to be mysterious. If asked what they were doing they were not to say 'something secret' but to give a matter-of-fact response – fighting patrol, scout patrol, observer, runner etc.[31] This was difficult to maintain. Auxiliers soon began to travel to Coleshill for training courses by train, dressed as privates in the Home Guard but openly toting large American revolvers. Later came a new distinction as they were given the privilege of army webbing belts and gaiters rather than the leather equipment of the rest of the Home Guard.[32] Drinking in the same pub as the regular Home Guard cannot have helped security. John Boaz from Samson Patrol remembered them drinking in The Plough at Broadheath, Worcester, after one night exercise. They were plastered in mud, with blackened uniform buttons and rubber boots but there met the neat and tidy local Home Guard who had just returned from Sunday Church Parade. The auxiliers rebuffed questions as to what they were doing but the curious Malvern Home Guard later tried to track their local patrol to their hide and a friendly game of hide and seek ensued.[33] In order to make them less conspicuous, auxiliers travelling to a patrol competition at Syderstone, Norfolk, were specifically ordered to travel there wearing battledress with polished brassware.[34] In April 1942 Beatrice Temple, ATS Senior Commander of the Auxiliary Units, discovered that even her bank manager in Lewes knew about the Patrol Leaders' courses at Coleshill House.[35] Nonetheless, veterans have frequently stressed what they believed to be the top secret nature of the organisation, not least as a means of self-justification to counter any possible criticism from their neighbours over a perceived lack of involvement in the war effort.

Unavailable to early researchers, and possibly unknown to the auxiliers themselves, Home Guard enrolment forms for auxiliers and surviving Home Guard Part II Orders have now revealed that movement to and from the Auxiliary Units patrols, together with promotions, could be openly recorded at a local level and posted on battalion noticeboards from mid-1941 onwards (Plates 42 and 43).[36] Their enrolment forms even included the full addresses of patrol members. The Worcestershire Home Guard Part II Orders show that administration for the patrols was initially handled at as low a level as Company HQ with their names and ranks incorporated into general Company and Battalion orders. This continued even after responsibility passed to the regional TAAs in late 1942. Similarly, on 3 November 1943 it was confirmed that transfers from Banffshire Home Guard should be recorded on Part II Orders as to

'201 (GHQ Reserve) Btn'.³⁷ Despite a confident assertion in 2008 that the commissions given to the Group Commanders from 1941 were not recorded on either regular Army or Home Guard lists this has proved to be another myth.³⁸ The names of the Group and Area Commanders of XII Corps Observation Unit were published in the 1941 Home Guard List for South East Command (John Graves and Alfred Beatty, Group Commanders; and Area Commanders John Foreman, Sir Thomas Neame and Henry Sabbage).³⁹ The promotions of Lieutenant Edmund Van Moppes, Lieutenant Roger Smith, and Captain Lewis Van Moppes, who were the Group Commanders in Worcestershire, are recorded on both their Home Guard enrolment forms and on Part II Orders (Plate 43). It was only from 18 October 1941, in an attempt to restrict access to information at lower levels of the Home Guard, that Auxiliary Units were to be shown 'for administrative purposes' on the strength of the Home Guard Battalion, rather than Company, HQ.⁴⁰ Yet Auxiliary Units HQ in October 1942 was still trying to stop Auxiliary Units patrols being identified locally in the promotion of officers. Home Guard Battalion COs continued to have a key role to play in the administration of the Auxiliary Units as from 30 March 1942 the War Office instructed Battalion COs to include members of Auxiliary Units on their battalion strength for the purpose of assessing capitation grants. The money would then be paid directly by the Battalion CO to the local Intelligence Officer of the Auxiliary Units.⁴¹ Whether the patrol members actually visited HQ to see posted Orders is, of course, a different matter. Their Intelligence Officers may have cultivated an aura of secrecy which coloured post-war accounts, but the auxiliers would have been shocked to know how far knowledge of their existence had been officially shared. Subsequently, the new shoulder flashes introduced in late 1942/early 1943 only served to make them more distinctive and members could be easily identified. Such examples clearly illustrate the problems of the military nature of the Operational Branch, Auxiliary Units, and their reliance on the Home Guard.

The first HQ of the Auxiliary Units was at 7 Whitehall Place in London, where Gubbins gathered together his small staff. Major Peter Wilkinson, Gubbins' colleague from the 1939 Polish mission, took charge of organisation, planning and liaison with SIS. He also compiled the first in-house training manual (*Calendar 1937*), replacing the earlier *Brown Book* provided by Section D. Despite the urgency of the situation, Wilkinson only took up his post from 25 June. Alongside him was Major Bill Beyts, formerly of the Rajpuntna Rifles. At the start of the Second World War Beyts was a staff officer in the India Office before becoming a training officer with the 1st London ('Black Cat') Division then back to the War Office in the Middle East section and finally Operations and Training Officer for the Auxiliary Units. Captain the Honourable Michael Henderson (16th Lancers and latterly a staff officer at GHQ) was the Quartermaster. There was also Algernon 'Monty' Rodulfo of the Royal Tank Regiment, who had served as Gubbins' intelligence officer during the Norwegian campaign. After these key appointments the Auxiliary Units officially came into being on 2 July 1940 when the War Office circulated a notice of the War Establishment of the Operational Branch. The formal establishment of the HQ, Special Duties Branch (SDB) followed on 11 July 1940, with the cryptic comment that the organisation had already commenced activities but was now 'attached to' the HQ of Auxiliary Units, a discrete reference to the intelligence wing of the HDS.⁴² As with the

HDS, local organisation would be undertaken by a number of Intelligence Officers and the first eight met in Whitehall on 13 July. Others quickly followed, with promotions to acting captain for those not already at that rank (Fig. 5). The posting allowed a high degree of independence, especially from those distant from London. Peter Forbes, Intelligence Officer in the Scottish Borders, remembered: 'I loved it, it was the best time of my life. It was unusual in the army to be given a General's car and promoted to Captain and to be three or four hundred miles away from one's bosses, whom one probably saw once or twice a year.'[43] Norman Field, Intelligence Officer in Kent from November 1940 to summer 1941, also cherished the initial independence. He maintained that during 1941 he never received any order or request from the local army command and believed that operations would be entirely down to the individual patrol: 'Nothing seemed gained by the Army knowing where they were'.[44] One consequence of such independence was that Mike Calvert's scheme to mine the roads leading from the sea to the North Downs was unknown to GHQ – potentially causing great confusion for the counter-attack planned by the field army. Such freedom would soon be curtailed.

Three of the fifteen Operational Branch Intelligence Officers appointed in 1940 came from MI(R). Andrew Croft became the Intelligence Officer in East Anglia, Hamish Torrance in Northumberland and Scotland, and Peter Fleming with XII Corps Observation Unit (then absorbed into the Auxiliary Units). Matching this, John Todd, Douglas Saunders and possibly The Lord Anthony Ashley came from the Home Defence Scheme of Section D. At least 20 per cent had been personal friends of Wilkinson from his Cambridge days. Some had earned their reputation in the retreat through France such as John Gwynne who had become known as a fiercely determined artillery officer. Others were friends or family of Gubbins. The average age was 35–40 years old: these were older men in military terms who could be spared for front-line service and later there was to be a clear policy of only retaining IOs over 38 years old and of 'B' medical grade or lower. If not young commando officers, the older men were confident, self-assured individuals who, in the main, had already proved their ability to lead men in civilian life without being too rigid in military thinking. As a consequence, they were exactly what the intelligence services were looking for, and most of them were later recruited into SOE, the Intelligence Corps or, in the case of 30-year-old Ian Fenwick, into the SAS.

The oldest was Douglas Saunders, aged 46. He had served in the Bedfordshire Regiment during the First World War but had resigned his commission in 1921 and then became Chief Executive of the J. Walter Thompson Advertising Agency. The latter put its whole organisation at the disposal of Section D and Saunders became head of the propaganda branch (D/Q) before becoming a regional officer of the Home Defence Scheme. In May 1940 he was establishing an HDS network on the Isle of Wight but smoothly transferred with it to the Auxiliary Units and then worked as an Intelligence Officer for the Auxiliary Units in Hampshire, based at 4th Division HQ. Officially he was still a member of Section D and when this transferred to SOE he remained on the SIS payroll. He was dismissed from SOE a few days after the similar removal of Laurence Grand, without any mention of his role in the Auxiliary Units. His dismissal was part of a tranche of officers centred on Saunders' old propaganda section. Saunders continued as an Auxiliary Units Intelligence Officer until March 1941 when he transferred to a propaganda department of the War Office.

Fig. 5. Auxiliary Units (Operational) Intelligence Officers, 1940 * = at initial meeting of 13 July

Name	Age 1940	Previous service	Rank	Area	Later service
Douglas Saunders	46	(Section D, SIS)	Major	Hampshire and Isle of Wight	Propaganda Dept., War Office
*Stuart Edmundson	45	Territorial Royal Engineers	Temporary Captain, 16 July 1940	Devon and Cornwall	SOE
Nigel Oxenden	45	Royal Northumberland Fusiliers	Temporary Captain, 24 July 1940	Norfolk	Remained with Aux Units
Guy Atkinson	43	Royal Fusiliers (formerly Coldstream Guards) MIR	Promoted Captain, 3 July 1940	North Yorkshire	RAOC / Royal Fusiliers
John Todd	41	General List (Section D, SIS)	Temporary Captain, 22 July 1940	Monmouthshire, Herefordshire and Worcestershire	SOE
W. W. Harston	41	Dorset Regiment	Lieutenant September – November 1940 Captain, Nov 1940		
*Lord Ashley	40	Major, General List, Territorial Reserve. (Possibly Section D, SIS.	Gazetted Captain, Intelligence Corps, 22 July 1940	Dorset	Intelligence Corps to Royal Tank Regiment
*Donald Hamilton –Hill	39	Queens Own Cameron Highlanders / MIL(b)	Acting Captain	Lincolnshire	SOE
*John Gwynne	35	Royal Artillery	Acting Captain	Sussex	SOE
*Peter Fleming	33	Grenadier Guards / MIR	Captain	Kent	SOE
*Andrew Croft	32	Essex Regt / MIR / Independent Companies	Captain	East Anglia	SOE
Ian Fenwick	30	King's Royal Rifle Corps	Lieutenant (Special Emp.) 30 June 1940; Acting Captain, 11 Dec 1940	Somerset	SAS
*Alan John Crick	27	Foreign Office General List (comm. 20/4/40)	Temporary Captain 2 Oct 1940 (Int. Corps)	Somerset	Intelligence Corps
Eustace Maxwell	27	Argyll and Sutherland Highlanders	Temporary Captain 27 July 1940	Angus, Fife	Argyll and Sutherland Highlanders
*Hamish Torrance	24	Highland Light Infantry / MIR / Independent Companies	Captain	Forth, Berwick and Northumberland	SOE

Nigel Oxenden, aged 45, had seen service in the First World War with the Welsh Regiment and the Machine Gun Corps. He was recalled from the reserves in November 1938 and was commissioned into the Royal Northumberland Fusiliers. A year later he was promoted to Acting Captain and seconded to 341 Machine Gun Training Centre based on Alderney until the evacuation of the Channel Islands in June. Oxenden was, at least temporarily, out of a job with his age making future employment unlikely. He was, however, a cousin of Gubbins and whilst staying with relatives in Sussex asked one of Colin's sisters to mention to her brother that he was looking for a post. Oxenden joined the Auxiliary Units a few weeks later on 13 July, as Intelligence Officer for Norfolk. He later became Training Officer and the official historian of the Auxiliary Units.

Another of the oldest, Stuart Edmundson, was also in the first wave of Auxiliary Units IOs. Edmundson had special skills in demolition and engineering which were an obvious attraction. He had worked pre-war for a fertilizer company in Devon which gave him a knowledge of the ingredients in improvised explosives. He joined the Territorial Army and in August 1937 was commissioned as a Second Lieutenant in the Devon & Cornwall (Fortress) Engineers TA at Plymouth. Promoted Lieutenant in January 1940 in the Royal Engineers, as part of the latter's national training plan, he set up a production line of Molotov cocktails for the LDV at Fort Austin, Plymouth and travelled the region to instruct the LDV on their use. There is some evidence he may also have been recruiting for the HDS, or was at least influenced by its methodology (see above, p.65), before being recruited to the Auxiliary Units on 13 July. He received his promotion to Temporary Captain on 16 July 1940. Fort Austin then became the regional HQ of the Auxiliary Units although initially the local corps commander was not informed and as a consequence he surrounded the base with armed troops after reports of explosions inside. Edmundson left the Auxiliary Units in November 1943 and continued his engineering research first with SOE at Station XII and then in the Far East with Force 136 and the School of Army Ordnance South East Asia.

The Yorkshire Intelligence Officer was 43-year-old Captain Guy Atkinson. Born in 1897, he had joined the Bedfordshire Yeomanry straight from school in 1915 and was then commissioned into the Coldstream Guards and won the Military Cross on the Western Front in 1918. Like Gubbins and Holland he served in North Russia in 1919. In 1926 he was seconded as a Lieutenant into the Colonial Office where he was promoted captain in 1929. He retired from the Coldstream Guards in October 1931 but it is not known how long he remained with the Foreign and Colonial Office or what his job with them entailed. Atkinson was recalled from the reserves into the Royal Fusiliers in August 1939 and served with Gubbins in MI(R). He was promoted back to his old rank as Captain on 3 July 1940. Atkinson finally retired from the army in 1956 as a Major and died in 1964.

John Todd (Plate 14) was aged 41 at the time he joined the Auxiliary Units. He had served in the Honourable Artillery Company during the latter part of the First World War and then became a successful London stockbroker. His City career may, however, have hidden a more secret occupation; on 31 May 1940 he was suddenly gazetted as a Second Lieutenant on the General List – 'without pay and allowances' – a classic indicator of an SIS officer. Indeed, he was commissioned and listed in the same batch as other known SIS officers. It seems likely that Todd became a regional officer for the HDS and was then seconded to the Auxiliary Units as one of Grand's officers from his 'D.M group' (see above, p.64) while already recruiting men for the HDS. He was recruiting saboteurs in Herefordshire in June and recruited the first Auxiliary Units patrol in Worcestershire during late July 1940.[45] It was only on 26 July that a report of HQ Auxiliary Units noted that an intelligence officer had been dispatched to South Wales and was expected to organise fifty weapons dumps there by 4 August, but there is no mention of any authorised activity in Herefordshire or Worcestershire.[46] Neither are these counties mentioned in the August Progress Report of the Auxiliary Units, and throughout their lifespan the organisation in the counties for which he was initially responsible remained a sparsely-documented oddity. Worcestershire had been surveyed as early as 1938 for the eventuality of a move of government offices into the county following invasion – the 'Yellow Move'. If the capital became untenable then 'Black Move' would bring the Prime Minister, Cabinet and Royal Family to Worcestershire, along with emergency communication HQs of the three services, making the county of great strategic importance. Bank of England staff would have been evacuated to Overbury Court while the BBC had a shadow broadcasting centre at Wood Norton. Combined with the potential risk of invasion up the Severn estuary to threaten the southern approaches of Birmingham, it would therefore have been an obvious area in which to create early HDS and Section VII networks and a decision could, likewise, have been made to extend the coastal distribution of Auxiliary Units into these areas based upon Todd's earlier work.

Todd left the Auxiliary Units in July 1941 with a promotion to Lieutenant Colonel to lead the SOE Mission in East Africa. It was only from this point, having finally left SIS, that he was badged as a member of the Intelligence Corps. Curiously, in late 1944 he returned to his old haunts in Monmouthshire and it was he who presented George Vater with his stand-down letter of thanks from Colonel Douglas. In true Todd fashion he then burnt the letter in front of George![47] The HQ records of the Auxiliary Units are notably blank when it comes to any direct reference to John Todd. Nonetheless, he was well-remembered by Willie Wilmott, an ATS secretary at Coleshill. Wilmott was secretary to the CO of the Auxiliary Units, 'Bill' Major, and was living at Coleshill House. Rather than a hub of clandestine warfare, she remembered it as an idyllic setting where she would spend the mornings sunbathing and being brought cups of tea by the NCOs. Eventually Wilmott became bored and when, in the summer of 1941, the 'IO from Cardiff' announced he was leaving, she asked to go with him as his secretary – although she had no idea as to his posting. After first being threatened with disciplinary action for daring to communicate directly with a superior officer she was allowed to go, and found herself in the offices of SOE in Baker Street where Todd was preparing the East Africa Mission.

Old Etonian Anthony Ashley-Cooper (Lord Ashley), heir to the Earl of Shaftesbury, was aged 40 when he is suspected of first becoming an Intelligence Officer for the HDS in Dorset (where lay his family estates) before discretely transferring his organisation to the Auxiliary Units (see above, p.57). He was one of the original Intelligence Officers who attended the first meeting on 13 July. He had been commissioned into the Royal

Wiltshire Yeomanry in 1925 but in January 1940 he transferred to being a major on the General List of the Yeomanry. This possibly marks his recruitment into SIS and thereafter there is the typical lack of detail in the careers of former SIS officers, including records of his time with the Auxiliary Units, before transferring to the Royal Armoured Corps in December 1941.

Gubbins was limited by existing resource and time constraints. He later identified two stages in the development of the Auxiliary Units during 1940. From its War Establishment on 2 July until 15 August Gubbins saw the approach as one of rapid improvisation at a time when invasion was considered imminent and the distribution of 'whatever stores were available pending the sanction and delivery of others'. The priority at this stage was the distribution of explosives and incendiaries but not personal weapons for protection (Fig. 6). Gubbins' initial phase has been subdivided in the present book.

Phase 1a Advisory model

Gubbins initially rejected the use of concealed hides on the Polish model for his LDV volunteers and as also recommended in a report by Holland of 7 June 1940. Holland's report was a perceptive vision of special forces units operating as an integral element of military strategy which even predicted the use of newly-invented helicopters to support insurgents. The report outlined the basic principles which informed the first iteration of the Auxiliary Units and that into which they would soon evolve. Firstly there was an essential need for 'An organisation on the ground to provide guides and local information'.[48] Thus, a primary task of the early Auxiliary Units would be to assist proposed units of the Independent Companies (the 'MI(R)s') which, like the Polish guerrillas and the Battle Patrols of XII Observation Unit, were envisaged as operating from behind enemy lines in concealed hides, constructed before any withdrawal and ready to support any counter-attack. These commandos would 'disrupt enemy L of C [Lines of Communication], destroy dumps and disorganise HQ, its methods being to travel fast, . . . remain concealed . . . avoid organised opposition as much as practicable . . . attack the weak points in the enemy's organisation, make the sites untenable as long as possible and then, in most cases, depart'.[49] Such troops would operate in conjunction with the regular forces, simultaneously attacking the enemy front with their principal targets being railways, roads, supply dumps and headquarters. The concept quickly devolved through lack of resources into the later hidden patrols of the Auxiliary Units. Crucially, Holland believed successful operations would depend on effective portable wireless communications although in 1940 the limit of imagination was for a set transported in a 'perambulator'. Unfortunately it was never possible to widely provide wireless communications to the Operational Patrols of the Auxiliary Units.

In this initial stage, Gubbins was heavily influenced by his experience with the Independent Companies and which he ultimately wanted to replicate either as regular army units of GHQ or, if that proved impossible, build up from his Home Guard patrols. But in July 1940, Gubbins probably judged that there was not time to establish a system on the Polish/Jo Holland model before invasion and the first iteration of the Auxiliary Units was minimalist. After the war, Gubbins explained 'Time was [of] the essence . . . at the shortest we had six weeks before a full scale invasion could be launched; if we were lucky we might have until October.'⁵⁰ Gubbins therefore saw the role of Auxiliary Units HQ and its Intelligence Officers primarily as an advisory and supply body to local LDV commanders, who would be encouraged to form small units of their own which would guide Independent Company commando units through their area and extend the poorly-defined harrying function of the LDV into sabotage, but without a suggestion of their own hidden 'hides'. This was all consistent with the long-standing advisory principle of MI(R) and fulfilled the belief expounded at the ISPB meeting in May 1940, that 'irregular warfare should be controlled by, and undertaken in conjunction with, the actions of regular forces'.⁵¹ Later in 1940 John Langdon-Davies made an open appeal for such Home Guards guides using very similar terms (see below, p.184). Officers were first sent out on reconnaissance missions to establish the location, in army bases, of the main regional arms dumps and to make contact with local LDV commanders and landowners who would become local 'dump owners', and suggest suitable recruits. The Quartermaster, Captain Michael T. Henderson, was dispatched in late June into Essex and Suffolk and established dumps at Warley Barracks, Brentwood and the Cavalry Barracks in Colchester before reporting back on 30 June.⁵²

The Auxiliary Units were formally constituted by their War Establishment of 2 July and three days later Gubbins sent out a letter to LDV Area Commanders to advise them of the existence of the new organisation. He explained that the intention was for small teams which would 'take action against the flanks and rear of such forces as may obtain a temporary footing in this country . . . The personnel will consist of existing LDV volunteers and others who will be enrolled therein for the purpose.' Significantly, the operational responsibility for these teams 'will be decided between the local military commander and the LDV commander' rather than being, at this stage, an independent body. The Auxiliary Units Intelligence Officer would merely act as an adviser 'in the closest touch with the military commander and the LDV commander so as to assist in every possible way [with] the selection, training and organisation of these sub-units, and the provision and storage of equipment'. The teams quickly began to be supplied, via Section D, with sufficient quantities of explosives to mount small sabotage attacks but without personal weapons: the only expectation was for them to carry out as much disruption as possible before they were annihilated (Figs 6 and 7). Speed was everything, with Gubbins warning LDV commanders that 'The present situation obviously necessitates speed at the expense of security, but at the same time it is important that, whatever else be known generally, the names of the operatives, the existence of dumps of stores, their location, etc should be kept as secret as possible'.⁵³

This purely advisory model did not survive much more than a fortnight but the circular letter of 5 July was to cause some problems later with local Home Guard commanders who would use it to claim that the later Operational Patrols should come directly under their command. In September 1940 there were difficulties in the Portsmouth area where retired Brigadier General Bryan Curling, CO of the local Home Guard, believed that it had been agreed that the Auxiliary Units patrols should be under the command of his platoon commanders and not the Auxiliary Units

Intelligence Officer (Douglas Saunders). Curling had already made plans for guerrilla units of his own and believed that the Auxiliary Units should be regarded merely as 'specialists' of his own command.[54]

Phase 1b Village Cells

It was quickly realised that the still-developing LDV, despite enthusiasm for the task, were not capable of managing these guerrilla teams. By 13 July, and the first meeting of the Intelligence Officers, the Gubbins' plan had evolved and was summarised in a briefing note of 17 July. The Auxiliary Units HQ was now to become more directly involved and organise its own 'village cells' from within the LDV, to continue the task of secretly guiding army commandos through their territory and to undertake their own sabotage missions. General Paget, Chief of Staff to Home Forces, was, however, at pains to point out that these were more properly described as military actions by fighting patrols to distinguish them from the *franc-tireur* activities of the civilian HDS. Whilst recognising the time pressures, Gubbins still looked forward to a more expansive establishment: 'decentralisation therefore is initially forced upon us. If time allows, organisation, and hence control of these cells, can be more and more centralised; eventually larger units can be formed.'[55] A crucial task of the Intelligence Officers remained as laying down large weapons dumps ready for the anticipated army commandos to use behind enemy lines and to ensure coordination between the two bodies (Fig. 7). This was an interim measure while a more ambitious War Establishment was being prepared that would have superimposed the anticipated deployment of expanded Independent Companies onto the existing LDV organisation and so relieve the Intelligence Officers of administrative detail. As it became clear that the use of the putative 'MI(R)s' was increasingly unlikely, Gubbins' plan by the end of July shifted to build the Auxiliary Units so that with 'increased training, and greater efficiency, the sections can be organised into platoons, and the platoons into something in the nature of Independent Companies of Home Guards'.[56] There is nothing in this sequence of events to suggest that the link to the Home Guard was merely a cover story. An instruction to the Intelligence Officers on 27 July makes the continuing relationship to the LDV (now officially the Home Guard) clear. 'Auxiliary Units will be created within existing LDV units. Suitable men you have found not in LDV should be brought into it.'[57]

Further explanation was provided in a War Office letter of April 1941 to the local Territorial Army Associations that managed the Home Guard and who sometimes found themselves holding the supplies of weapons for the Auxiliary Units.

> Approval has been given for the enrolment of selected men into special patrols of Auxiliary Units, the personnel of which is mainly drawn from the Home Guard. Individual selection is made of the men required. They retain their Home Guard status and operate in their home localities but come under the control of Headquarters, Auxiliary Units.[58]

Fig. 6 Auxiliary Units Explosives Dumps (Small). July 1940. (*TNA CAB 120/241*)

Time fuses, Red (½ hour)	16
White (1½ hours)	11
Green (4 hours)	11
Yellow (12 hours)	11
Blue (20 hours)	11
Fuses	1 box
Adhesive tape (three quarters x 15yards)	
Detonators	35
Bickford fuse	24 ft
Instantaneous fuse	12 ft
Cordtex fuse	50 ft
Crimping tool	
Vaseline	1 tube
Large magnets	4
Magnesium incendiaries	10
Fog signals	4
Plastic explosive	83 sticks
Paraffin incendiaries	12
Medium – large incendiaries	4

Fig. 7. Auxiliary Units Explosives Dumps (Large), July 1940. (*TNA CAB 120/241*)

Time fuses, Red (½ hour)	180
White (1½ hours)	120
Green (4 hours)	120
Yellow (12 hours)	120
Blue (20 hours)	240
Fuses	31 boxes
Adhesive tape (¾ inch x 15yards)	28
Detonators	210
Large magnets	16
Magnesium incendiaries	10
Fog signals	12
Bickford fuse	95 ft
Instantaneous fuse	50 ft
Cordtex fuse	100 ft
Plastic explosive	83 sticks
Blasting gelignite	400 lb
Paraffin incendiaries	180
Small Magnesium incendiaries	150
Medium – large incendiaries	110

There was now a more aggressive mission, expanding the ill-defined harrying role of the wider Home Guard, to 'act offensively on the flanks and in the rear of any German troops . . . to harry and embarrass the enemy by all means in their power from the first day he lands, their particular targets being tanks and lorries in laager, ammunition dumps, HQs, small straggling parties and posts etc. Their object is, in co-operation with the regular forces, to prevent the invader establishing a secure foothold, and thus to facilitate his defeat.'[59] It is clear that their role was to provide support to the army during an invasion campaign rather than any longer-term 'resistance' role but Gubbins did not elaborate on how the Auxiliary Units would be able to properly undertake this harrying role without personal and support weapons. During this series of rapidly evolving changes in strategy, before the Auxiliary Units became properly established, the civilian HDS would, by necessity, continue in operation. In the summer of 1940 it was not so easy to abandon what was already a working system and the Auxiliary Units never competed as a national organisation.[60] Gubbins and the Director of Military Intelligence (Beaumont-Nesbitt) believed at this stage that the remit of the new Auxiliary Units was sufficiently distinct as a military force that it might still work alongside the hidden saboteurs of the civilian HDS.[61] But as the Auxiliary Units finally began to establish a presence on the ground, even if not satisfying Gubbins' greater ambitions, the government, with some relief, was able to reject the stop-gap solution of an SIS civilian guerrilla force in Britain. At the end of July, making the distinction between civilian and military explicit, was it was agreed that the Auxiliary Units should absorb the HDS because 'the risk of reprisals incurred by allowing civilians to engage in sabotage activities was too great'.[62] This concern clearly did not apply to encouraging resistance forces abroad!

As many village cells as possible were quickly recruited with some officers forming fifteen cells in a week.[63] The Intelligence Officers were to recruit 'key men' (a term from the HDS and quite possibly the same people), who would recruit the remaining members of their cells, and then train and supply them. The Auxiliary Units continued the recruitment policy of the HDS, often from the same business, farm or family. They were well supplied for small acts of sabotage – vehicles, dumps, sentry posts, HQs, signal communication etc. (Fig. 6), although still lacking in personal weapons to follow up any attack. This was a more opportunistic strategy than later, when the introduction of the permanent hidden Operational Bases suggests in many areas that the primary targets were fixed communication links. They would act in the crucial period where the invading forces were forming up and advancing through any bridgeheads and it was important to disrupt their supply lines and communications as quickly as possible – and at whatever cost. In the urgency of the situation, Gubbins had been obliged to abandon key elements of his 1939 booklets on guerrilla warfare, in which he had stressed not only the need for early planning prior to invasion, nomination of local leaders and provision of arms dumps but also for wireless communications and a means of liaison with HQ. Wireless communication was also a key element in the original Polish model and Thorne's deployment of army Battle Patrols but there were never the resources to deploy this across the Operational Patrols of the Auxiliary Units and only the army Scout Sections (attached from November 1940) had wireless sets through which they could be re-tasked or receive up-to-date intelligence (see below, p.114). The Home Guard patrols of the Auxiliary Units could consequently only have uncertain contact with higher authority once they had gone into action.[64] Churchill was notoriously impatient for progress on such initiatives and Gubbins, like others, reacted by producing over-optimistic reports. His progress report of 8 August, delivered by Duncan Sandys (one of Churchill's inner circle of unofficial advisors and a member of the new Ministry of Defence), claimed that 'selected units are also being provided with wireless and field telephone apparatus'. The 'wireless' probably referred to the existing Battle Patrols of XII Corps and an expectation of their expansion into the Auxiliary Units while field telephones were used to connect the Operational Bases to their Observation Posts by cable (Plate 26).[65] After the war, Gubbins admitted 'Time was [of] the essence ... wireless too was out of the question'.[66]

Virtue was eventually made of necessity and the lecture notes for the Patrol Leader's course of 1941 downplayed the need for outside communication and, abandoning any concept of strategic direction, stressed that there would be few times when the Patrol Leader would need to send a message and that trying to do so might jeopardise the security of the patrol: 'Do not, therefore, let intercommunication become your master, when it should be your slave'.[67] Wilkinson took comfort from his brutal belief that once invasion took place they would be discovered quickly and therefore any sophisticated set-up was unnecessary; this only became a problem when the organisation began to plan for a longer-term existence.[68] Like the rest of the Home Guard, the members of the Auxiliary Units were under no illusion as to their chances of survival. Long-term survival for the beach defenders, Home Guard or Auxiliary Units was not part of the agenda of GHQ in 1940; the Auxiliary Units were a short-term military expedient to hinder the invasion army. To that end, both the men of the general service battalions of the Home Guard and the Auxiliary Units patrols were only to be given a payment of £7 each upon mustering in the event of invasion to pay for just two weeks loss of earnings and/or purchase food.[69] After that time the invasion would have either been repelled by the field army – or the men would be captured or dead!

Contemporaries had a realistic appraisal of their role and consequence. Gubbins concluded that the Auxiliary Units 'were designed, trained and prepared for a particular and imminent crisis: that was their specialist role'.[70] It would have only been human nature for them to hope and plan for a longer-term role than that envisaged by GHQ. In Kent, Fleming and Calvert did organise additional dumps of hidden supplies to try to extend their operational life. In Worcestershire during 1941 the men were given vague hopes of re-supply by the new Group Commanders, although no-one was sure how this was going to be achieved.[71] The romance of their later secret hides, with their air of permanence, have given the Auxiliary Units a significance that contemporaries would not have recognised in 1940. Gubbins explained 'they were something additional . . . We were expendable. We were a bonus, that's all.'[72] His second in command, Peter Wilkinson, shared this sentiment, believing that any suggestion that Auxiliary Units could have provided a framework for long-term underground resistance was 'absurd'.[73] Sandys' August progress report also offers no suggestion of any longer-term function.[74] His careful wording may have been in response to the furious letter that he had received only a few days before (30 July) from General Paget, Chief of Staff to the new C-in-C Home Forces, General Alan Brooke, in response to the concerns expressed by Lieutenant MacLeod on 3 July about the earlier attempts of the HDS to recruit members of the Home Guard for acts of civilian sabotage in Dorset (see above, p.57). Paget begins by stressing that the new Auxiliary Units' operational wing are uniformed members of the Home Guard:

> The object of these fighting patrols is to provide within the general Home Guard organisation small units of men, specially selected and trained, whose role is to act offensively on the flanks and in the rear of any German troops who may obtain a temporary foothold in this country. Their action is to be directed particularly against tanks and lorries in laager [defensive camp], ammunition dumps, small enemy posts and stragglers, etc., and their main activities will be under cover of darkness. . . . These men, being members of the Home Guard, will of course fight in uniform.

He gets more agitated when having to stress that the role of these patrols was not 'sabotage' and neither did it imply that there was official recognition of a possibility of 'occupation'.

> Mr MacLeod refers in his letter to preparations for 'sabotage' in an 'occupied area'. The action of these units is not sabotage, but offensive action by fighting patrols against military targets. As regards the expression 'occupied area', this is an entirely wrong conception. As you know, the policy in the event of invasion is to fight the enemy on the beaches wherever he tries to land. He may, if in sufficient force, secure a temporary footing in places until counter-attacked and driven out, and it is during this phase of confused fighting that the action of these special Home Guard units will be of great value in preventing the establishment of a secure bridgehead; but there can be no question of an 'occupied area' behind the German line where civilian life will continue peacefully.

Paget finally distances Home Forces from the previous operations of the HDS in organising civilian sabotage operations and moreover states that any such organisation would be impractical and undesirable.

> This organisation [HDS] was recently transferred from the SIS and put under GOC-in-C Home Forces, but as several indiscretions immediately came to light showing the impossibility of maintaining the necessary degree of secrecy, and as in any case the military value of such an organisation, based as it was on the misconception of an 'occupied area', was insufficient to warrant the reprisals its activities would inevitably evoke, it was decided that the organisation should be closed down forthwith and its activities suspended. This has been done.[75]

For Paget, the use of the term 'occupied area' implied defeatism; something that would be fresh in the mind after the surrender of France. The fact that SIS was even contemplating planning for the failure of the army to throw the enemy back into the sea raised the blood pressure of the War Office, made worse by the fact that SIS was going to use civilians and operate outside the traditional rules of war. Paget was explicit in the wearing of uniform by the auxiliers, but a post-war desire to distance themselves from the *Dad's Army* image of the Home Guard subsequently aroused denial by some veterans and consequent confusion as to the status of the Auxiliary Units. Stuart Edmundson wrote 'There was no uniform in 1940. They were given denims to protect their clothes . . . I never trained a man in uniform and we never intended them to fight in Home Guard uniform.'[76] Likewise, Herman Kindred, an auxilier from Suffolk, said 'Our "real uniform", if you like, was just plain army denims, but they were only really to protect our ordinary clothes'. Both Edmundson and Kindred gloss over the fact that when the Auxiliary Units were founded, the only uniform for most LDV was an armband worn with civilian clothes. The Home Guard uniform for the rest of 1940 were the army-issue plain denim overalls about which Edmundson and Kindred were so dismissive; the Auxiliary Units were therefore dressed in step with the general service Home Guard and, for the War Office at least, had equal legal status. Unfortunately, at the time, the Home Guard was regarded by the Nazis as a terrorist organisation, uniform or not!

The issue of uniform in 1940 to the Auxiliary Units in order to bring the operational wing within international law was considered so serious that the late August progress report to the Prime Minister was delayed until 11 September, after the supply issue highlighted by Gubbins had been resolved. Gubbins had reported 'uniforms have been made available for the use of Auxiliary Units. A proportion of the Home Guard of Auxiliary Units already have uniforms, but it is most important that the remainder should be allotted at an early date.'[77] The official position is, therefore, absolutely clear: the fighting patrols were soldiers of the Home Guard and would wear uniform. As a concession to their anticipated night-time working, some blackened their leather gaiters and the buttons of the later battledress, although the original denims were also retained. In the detailed 1942 list of kit to be brought to the Operational Bases in the event of 'stand to' for invasion, Kent auxiliers were expected to bring both the serge and denim battledress but no civilian dress is mentioned. What the Auxiliary Units never received was the symbolic status of the camouflaged commando and airborne smock that Oxenden still craved in 1944.[78]

These early cells did not have buried Operational Bases. Samson Patrol in Broadheath, near Worcester, used the local scout hut (most of the original team were local Boy Scouts). Butcher Peter Price gave gave them weekly instruction in unarmed combat (he later became an instructor at Coleshill). They also used the army rifle range at Tyddesley Woods, Pershore, and had grenade instruction at Norton Barracks, Worcester. They continued to use the scout hut until 1941, even after their underground base was constructed in October 1940, but when obliged to move out by the local Home Guard they booby-trapped the entrance with a detonator![79] The Village Cell scheme only lasted around one month. A shortage of manpower meant it was not possible to allocate large numbers of regular troops as new Independent Companies to the scheme and Gubbins had to look towards a more self-contained model.

Phase 2. Operational Patrols
When it was realised that there were not the resources to create the home defence Independent Company/Commando units another re-think was necessary and this coincided with a move of the HQ out of London. After a bombing raid damaged the cramped HQ in Whitehall Place, Gubbins sent quartermaster Henderson to scout around the country for a more suitable HQ. Henderson focused on the area around his family estate at Buscot Park in Oxfordshire and first found temporary accommodation in Faringdon, which had good communication links. Unfortunately this HQ at Northgate House, London Street, had to be shared with the HQ of the RASC Company, 1st Armoured Brigade and was so cramped that meetings were held in The Crown public house nearby. After 20 August the Auxiliary Units were able to move to a more permanent base on the Coleshill estate at Highworth, Wiltshire, which lay four miles from Faringdon and was directly adjacent to Buscot Park. Coleshill House was owned by the Earl of Radnor and lay isolated in its own 2,500-acre parkland, hidden behind a high stone wall and protecting belts of trees. Only the Earl's two sisters were in residence at the time. Initially, the HQ staff remained in Whitehall and only came down for the weekend training courses but it eventually grew to contain HQ, a dummy Operational Base and Observation Post, firing and grenade ranges, maintenance huts for the later SDB wireless sets and a

motor transport park. A small quarry in Cuckooven quarry was used to demonstrate explosives. The students were accommodated in the stable block with some administration offices on the first floor of Coleshill House itself. Reflecting the influence of SIS, the nearby Hannington Hall initially was used as a separate HQ of the SDB. One of the popular post-war myths was that the local postmistress at Highworth, Mabel Stranks, was the 'gatekeeper' who vetted students when they arrived for a weekend course at Coleshill, with a Thompson sub-machine gun ready under her counter! There is no evidence to suggest that Highworth Post Office was anything more than a convenient, discreet postal address for the Auxiliary Units HQ and the responsibility of Mabel and her two assistants was to simply phone Coleshill House to let them know that 'I have some more of your people down here' awaiting collection.[80]

The move out of London triggered the second, more settled, phase of development that finally established the long-term character of the Auxiliary Units. Having completed the formal incorporation of the HDS, on 15 August Gubbins finally abandoned the dream of Home Guard Independent Companies and instead began to implement the 1939 model of covert Polish guerrillas as already established by Fleming in the XII Corps Observation Unit. Small patrols were now to employ 'hide-outs or secret bases' and thereby, as Gubbins confidently hoped in official reports, would secure 'undisputed advantage over any enemy troops in their area' with a longer life expectancy.[81] Wilkinson, however, later admitted that both he and Gubbins 'had to crank up the organisation as enthusiastically as we could in order to "sell" it both to the rank-and-file, and to higher authority'.[82] Initially, the auxiliers still lacked personal weapons other than privately-provided sheath knives, but they tried to make up for this with an emphasis on silent stalking in their training. Two rifles per patrol were progressively supplied from August, although some did not receive their rifles until October. They were thanks to the recent arrival of thousands of M1917 (P17) rifles from the USA for the Home Guard, even though the long and heavy weapons were poorly suited to their role. Other weapons did not begin to be distributed until September. Systematic training similarly did not get properly underway until late August/September and was by no means complete by the end of the invasion season in October. Such limitations during the period they would arguably have been most useful have tended to be glossed-over but at the time this was of no great strategic concern, as Gubbins acknowledged 'we were a bonus, that's all'.[83]

Patrols of six to eight men under a sergeant, using what became known as 'Operational Bases' as being a more positive term than the original 'hide-outs', were now formed from the Home Guard (or were newly-recruited and then enrolled in the Home Guard which, with its identifiable rank structure, ensured legal protection). It was, however, only possible to introduce army Scout Sections (which Thorne and Fleming had seen as the core 'striking force' of the concept) from November, just as Gubbins and Wilkinson left for SOE.[84] The hidden Operational Bases meant the chance of survival might now hopefully be measured in weeks rather than days. The Auxiliary Units Patrols had assumed a distinct military identity and Peter Wilkinson became disillusioned over the move away from the HDS concept to become a guerrilla branch of the Home Guard (see above, p.82). Wilkinson countered with the suggestion of an ultra-secret 'inner core' of resistance fighters, thus confirming the distinction between the two concepts. He explained: 'With Colin Gubbins' approval I made plans to recruit an inner core of "trustees" whose identity would, I hoped, remain secret and who would provide the nucleus of a British resistance movement'.[85] There is no evidence that anything on these lines was put into operation before he and Gubbins left the Auxiliary Units and Wilkinson did not believe that Gubbins' successor, the more orthodox Colonel Cyril 'Bill' Major, would have looked kindly on the scheme.

The failure to provide wireless communications to the patrols meant that the regional Intelligence Officers would not have been able to direct the patrols strategically after the latter had 'going to ground'. Major Peter Forbes, Auxiliary Units Intelligence Officer in the Scottish Borders from September 1941 – August 1943 (and later CO of the Special Duties Branch), believed he might only have been able to maintain contact with patrols in a five-mile radius and recalled: 'with hindsight, I feel my patrols would have been "blind" sitting in their OB's as to where targets were'.[86] Following invasion, the role of the Intelligence Officer and his small HQ section (which by 1942 comprised clerk, two drivers, Royal Engineers NCO and two or three NCO Instructors) was left to the discretion of the corps commanders not Auxiliary Units HQ. In the majority of cases the Intelligence Officers were left to go to ground as best they could, having already given the patrols his instructions for operations.[87] Reflecting a more dismissive attitude towards the Auxiliary Units in some Commands, others were ordered to remain with Corps HQ and one had even been tasked with acting as Police Liaison Officer after invasion! The long-standing confusion over the role of Intelligence Officers is seen in the fact that they were only provided with underground Operational Bases of their own from June 1942 when, ironically, the patrols were moving away from a hidden anti-invasion role.

The buried Operational Bases (OB) (Fig. 8) would contain beds and supplies for up to a month, together with stores of weapons and explosives. Some patrols objected to sharing their accommodation with the volatile No.76 self-igniting phosphorous grenade and so buried them a distance away – some of the crates were never found again. Although they had no wireless, the Observation Post (OP) usually had a field telephone (Type D Mk V – see Plate 26) linked by cable to an OB up to half a mile away. If necessary, the Type D phone allowed warning messages to be quietly sent by a 'ping' on the Morse key rather than giving away the position of the OB or OP by talking. If the OP was discovered, to stop the enemy simply following the cable directly to the OB, the cable entered the ground into a pipe around 5m away, which would give precious minutes warning to allow the patrol to exit along an escape tunnel, leaving a booby-trap behind them. The OBs have inspired much of the mystique of the Auxiliary Units. Until late 1940 most patrols constructed their own, following instructions at Coleshill. By the end of 1940 around 300 had been built for the patrols. The early examples could be death traps, lacking proper ventilation. Oxenden records 'The official teaching was that a pipe brought down to within a foot of the floor would provide an unfailing current of fresh air, but when the first "stay-in" exercise was held, most of the earlier OBs soon drove their occupants into the open, sicker and wiser men'.[88] The later work was usually carried out by units from the Royal Engineers or Pioneer Corps brought in from a considerable distance in order to improve security, although they might remain in the area for a year or more and be billeted in local houses. Some of the work in Northern and Southern Command was carried out by 184 Special Tunnelling Company of the 4th Special Tunnelling Engineers, whose template plan for an Operational Base has survived as well as their detailed schedule of works on building Auxiliary Units OBs during 1942 in their war diary.[89] Unfortunately, during their work in north-east England in October 1942 there was a security leak when a pegging-out plan for the local OB was left in one of their billets at Wheatley Hill, County Durham; it was found by local police and returned to Chief Engineer, IX Corps. The fall-out from this embarrassing incident is not known.

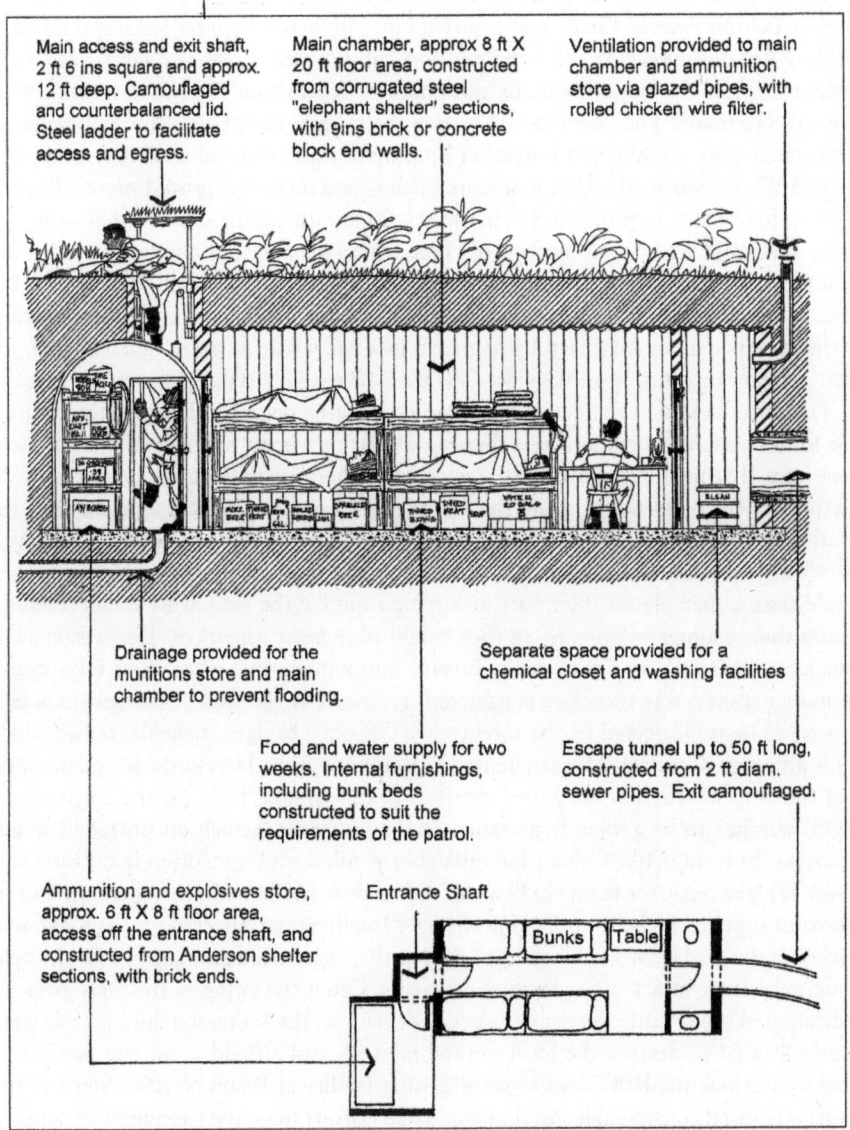

Fig. 8 Reconstruction and plan of Auxiliary Unit Operational Base, based on that at Alfrick, Worcestershire. (*Mick Wilks*)

Even with the sophistication of the later Operational Bases with hidden hatches, improved ventilation systems and escape tunnels, the chances of their survival would have been less than the permanence of their corrugated iron and brick construction now suggests. Peter Fleming feared that the OBs would be quickly discovered once undergrowth died back in winter and post-war experience suggested an even greater vulnerability. From 1957 into the 1980s, during the Cold War in North Germany, Territorial Army units of the SAS and Honourable Artillery Company together with the regular Royal Armoured Corps and Royal Artillery were all involved in the deployment of 'Stay Behind Patrols' (SBP), using buried hides for general surveillance and forward artillery fire direction.[90] In 1973 the non-too-subtly titled *Exercise Badger's Lair* was designed to test the vulnerability of hides built by 23 SAS on the Soltau training area in north Germany. They were tested by new techniques of airborne thermal imaging, false colour photography and Direction Finding of radio transmissions but it was the Second World War methods of foot search teams and dogs that proved most effective; 33 per cent of hides were discovered in the first 20 minutes of the search – mainly by the dogs, who could identify the location of a hide from a distance of 100m downwind. This weakness may explain the belated issue of 'silenced' .22 rifles, albeit only from April 1942, in an attempt to deal with tracker dogs. But once the Germans had been alerted to the presence of an Auxiliary Units patrol in a particular area through an attack on their primary target, it is unlikely the OBs would have survived any search for long.

The introduction of the patrol system in fixed bases saw a significant refinement in role towards night-time operations that would disrupt enemy supply and communications lines. The men were trained to be selective in choosing their target, both to provide maximum effect and not to waste their lives unnecessarily. Without a mechanism for strategic guidance from any higher command, the ideal was seen as one target per night for what they were told would be a three week campaign of invasion. By then, they would have either played their part in buying time for the field army to successfully mount their counter-offensive – or they would have been wiped out. Discussion as to how long the Auxiliary Units might survive into winter time when their OBs would be more exposed was therefore considered irrelevant at the time. Some obvious targets could be pre-selected by the Intelligence Officer – bridges, airfields, railway lines etc – although Geoffrey Morgan-Jones of Adam Patrol in Herefordshire maintained that the only instruction his patrol received from Captain Todd (in the spirit of the HDS) was just to be a 'bloody nuisance' to the Germans.[91] Such uncontrolled action had risks. In Kent, Mike Calvert hid milk churns filled with guncotton in culverts and under bridges ready for teams to blow up the roads *behind* an advancing enemy and so interrupt supplies to the front line but the later Intelligence Officer, Norman Field, was unclear if this had been sanctioned by GHQ as the wider strategic plan was for the field army to counter-attack along those same roads. Often the siting of the OBs gives an indication of the intended primary target, for example, the Worcestershire patrols were clearly located to destroy the local railway network and airfields, and one patrol was sited to overlook the BBC shadow broadcasting facility at Wood Norton. Some of the targets required considerable forethought. Mike Calvert filled the basements of country houses liable to be used as German HQs with explosives ready to be detonated by local volunteers if occupied by the Nazis.[92] At Clater Pitch in Herefordshire, Jacob Patrol cut slots in trees ready to receive charges which would blow them across the A44 and create an ambush for passing German staff cars on their way to what was presumed would be a requisitioned HQ. They were so thorough that the trees had to be felled post-war as being a safety hazard (the resultant gaps in the woodland bounding the road can still be seen). If the auxiliers survived the first wave of pre-ordained targets they could go on to more opportunistic ones. For this purpose, patrol members would take turns to creep out during the day on reconnoitring missions. A well-sited OP might in itself be useful in identifying local targets as well as giving some warning of an approaching enemy.

One of the most enticing supposed roles of the Operational Patrols was as deadly assassins, not just silently eliminating sentries on their sabotage missions but executing suspected collaborators or simply those that knew the location of their hidden OBs. Nigel Oxenden makes no mention of any such role in his 1944 draft official history of the Auxiliary Units and Peter Wilkinson was unimpressed by the post-war mystique that had accumulated. He was 'obviously irritated by the myth of a secret society of ninja-like assassins that was becoming an accepted part of Aux Unit folklore'.[93] Nonetheless, some veterans reported having being given sealed lists of what they assumed were details of suspected local collaborators or security risks to their existence, to liquidate upon invasion. In most cases, patrols never opened such letters and so their actual content remain a matter of speculation. Auxilier Don Handscombe from Essex recalled 'We knew of a list of people who might have collaborated with the enemy. But it was not produced to us. We were told that part of our duties may have been to deal with some of these people, but we didn't really know more than that.'[94]

There was a wider context for such supposed action. In June 1940 the Chiefs of Staff had called for the internment of all enemy aliens and members of 'subversive organisations' (primarily the Communist Party and British Union of Fascists') and suggested 'the most ruthless action should be taken to eliminate any chance of "Fifth Column" activities'.[95] Regional Army HQs repeatedly asked MI5 to release to them its lists of possible fifth columnists for arrest and on 9 June MI5's head of counter-espionage, Guy Liddell, recorded in his diary: 'The fighting services are becoming more and more restive about the 5th Column. In some cases they are taking the matter into their own hands, but generally the wrong cases.'[96] On 20 June he recorded that in Eastern Command 'The military seem to be taking the law into their own hands. . . . Some of the local units appear to have prepared a kind of Black List of their own. When the balloon goes up they intend to round up or shoot all these individuals. The position is so serious that something of very drastic kind will have to be done.'[97] The risks were obvious when Liddell recorded on 24 June:

> Maude [John Maude, MI5 officer] has discovered that the military, particularly the 55th Division in the Eastern Counties, have badgered the local police into giving them a list of people with whose bona fides they are not altogether satisfied. If and when the balloon goes up the military intend to take the law into their own hands and arrest these people. We have got hold of these lists which do not seem to have much in the way of a common-sense basis. One man's only crime appears to be that he is a dentist.[98]

It is possible that in 1940 the Auxiliary Units became caught up in this paranoia through their Intelligence Officers based at Divisional and Corps HQs. Whether any such instruction came from Auxiliary Units HQ is more doubtful. The concern of MI5 was not least because its agents had widely infiltrated potential fifth-column groups and might have been caught up in any vigilante purge. Some auxiliers reflected their ruthless HDS heritage. Jim Caws, an auxilier from the Isle of Wight, claimed they were taught to brutally deal with fifth columnists: 'We could either sort of tear them to bits to start with or shoot them first and then tear them to bits. . . . The purpose of that, I presume, was that if someone was helping the Germans and you could catch up with them we would make a mess of them and leave them on the side of the road to deter other people from doing it.'[99] Such treatment was not confined to dealing with fifth columnists. In Worcestershire, the Intelligence Officer, former SIS officer John Todd, arranged for a local butcher Peter Price (who was to become an unarmed combat instructor on the staff of Coleshill) to demonstrate the technique of evisceration, to be used against German sentries in order to unsettle their comrades.[100] John Thornton from Jacob Patrol in Herefordshire similarly remembers 'After killing the enemy we were told by Todd to cut their "knackers" off to demoralise the rest'.[101] Such barbaric suggestions were not novel but followed suggestions in SIS's 1939 D Scheme for European Resistance for dealing with captured members of the Gestapo.[102] Laurence Grand, Mike Calvert and Winston Churchill all coldly acknowledged that while such acts of terror might lead to widespread savage reprisals, the latter might stiffen the resolve to fight and also convince the Americans of the justice of joining the battle. Mike Calvert mused: 'The idea was we got these Lovat Scouts, Scotsmen, and their job was to shoot Germans in the back and that sort of thing. And then the Germans would have had retribution and shoot men of Kent and Sussex in the back and this would arouse the anger of the local population, who would then start shooting Germans.'[103] Yet even 'Mad Mike' recognised that such initial acts of provocation would be undertaken by uniformed troops rather than civilians, in order to retain the high moral ground for a US audience.

Whispers of an assassination role have been greatly exaggerated for post-war dramatic effect, illustrating the concerns that Fleming expressed in 1957 over the fallibility of oral history (see above, p.xx). Of most genuine concern was anyone who knew the location of their hidden OBs. When a patrol member asked to resign from Jehu (Alfrick) Patrol in Worcestershire because of stress, the Intelligence Officer politely shook his hand and wished him well – but then told the patrol sergeant that he would have to be killed if the invasion occurred.[104] Similarly, Charlie Mason of South Cave Patrol in Yorkshire recounted problems with a nosy gamekeeper and maintained 'That when the invasion comes, not if it comes, to get rid of him, to eliminate him, to booby trap him, certainly to eliminate him! We would eliminate anyone who threatened our existence, put our hide or existence in jeopardy.'[105] Caught up in such bravado, some auxiliers even maintained post-war that they were ready to assassinate men such as the local Chief Constable because they might know their identities. Yet checks on prospective auxiliers were carried out via requests from Home Guard Battalion COs – who therefore might also be considered security risks, and their identities were posted in Part II Orders. It has even been wildly speculated that their Intelligence Officers and Group Commanders might have been on the 'death lists'.[106] What then of cases such as at Sandown on the Isle of Wight where three members of the local patrol were recruited in July 1941 from the Hawksworth unit of the Auxiliary Fire Service? The Chief Fire Officer, Wilfred Brown, duly recorded in the Station log that these men were joining the 'Home Guard Patrol Section' and in such a small and close-knit working community it seems improbable that other colleagues were not aware of the reasons for their departure.[107] The HQ of the Worcestershire Auxiliary Units was in the Van Moppe's diamond factory at Wolverton Hall where the workers were well aware that some form of clandestine operations were based. One worker later admitted 'The Van Moppes were working for the intelligence service, we did not know officially but you would be daft if you did not realise something was going on in the cellar'.[108] Most of the patrols were based in small rural villages where it would be naïve to believe that secrets did not become known and sometimes a whole community were clearly aware of their existence. One patrol from Stobswood, near Morpeth, was remembered after the war as the 'Death or Glory Boys' who frequented a local public house. One night the locals eyes popped when a 'Glory Boy' walked in none too subtly with hand grenades dangling from his belt, .45 Colt revolvers strapped on each leg and a sub-machine gun over his shoulder.[109] Unfortunately, more OBs as well as the secret wireless stations of the SDB (see below, p.158) were discovered by the general public than the men would have liked. Harold Maryan, Intelligence Officer for the Home Guard in Hailsham, Sussex had to 'hush up' the report by a puzzled Home Guardsman who had discovered the Hellingly Patrol OB in Park Wood, Lower Dicker.[110] Rolvenden OB in Kent was discovered by two local girls who were walking through the wood. By chance, they looked across the stream and in the river bank saw a light shining from the tunnel of the emergency escape exit, opened to provide ventilation.[111] The most serious security breach occurred in the Kent Auxiliary Units where a somewhat relaxed air began to develop during 1943. On Sunday, 9 May a tour was arranged around each other's OBs, punctuated by lunch at the Fleur de Lys pub in Sandwich and afternoon refreshments at the Dog and Duck, followed by a dinner provided by the former chef of a hotel in Margate whose lobster recipes were reputed to make 'senior officers neglect their duties'.[112] In December 1943 there was a serious security breach in 'Parsnip' Patrol in Petham. The unspecified incident resulted in the patrol being disbanded and the entire membership returned to the Home Guard and their OB then sealed. The CO of the Kent Auxiliary Units wrote to his group commanders in January 1944 saying that this disbandment should be used as a warning to 'our weaker brethren'. One of those 'weaker brethren' was in Cornwall where Sergeant William Hawkey, patrol leader of the St Columb Patrol, left the Auxiliary Units in May 1943 but kept hold of 20 unused sheets of corrugated iron that had been originally supplied to build the patrol's operational base. Some of these were used to build a pigsty on his allotment but the local police became suspicious of his source, and he was arrested. In October 1943 he was fined £3 in the magistrate's court and ordered to return the sheeting.[113]

If all the tales of likely assassination victims were true then the Auxiliary Units would have caused greater disruption to the local civil and military establishment than any fifth columnist! Fortunately, when the Scottish Auxiliary Units went to ground after a false alarm in September 1940 there was no slaughter of the local population! Any scepticism over such blood-curdling post-war claims is not to deny the contemporary recognition that the consequences of invasion were likely to be brutal on both sides. If the Germans had survived being gassed on the invasion beaches then the whole British plan was to deny the enemy any chance of successfully mounting their *blitzkrieg* (lightning strike) by whatever means possible. The enemy would have faced opposition at every crossroads, village and town.[114] The *fougasse* would have blown horrific seas of burning petrol across approaching columns of vehicles; the Home Guard were publicly announcing through the press that they were going to ambush tanks with petrol bombs and home-made explosives, or kill disorientated paratroopers with scythes as they hit the ground. In their frustration, Nazi invaders were unlikely to have distinguished between an auxilier on a night-time sabotage mission and a Home Guard wearing the same denim uniform who had ignited a *fougasse* or was caught with 'dum dum' bullets. Even the use of the common Home Guard shotgun constituted a war crime in the view of the German army. Massive reprisals were likely to have followed in any case. One has only to look at the horror of war on the Eastern Front where Soviet partisans took brutal revenge on German prisoners for Nazi atrocities, followed by further Nazi retaliation against whole communities, to see how quickly guerrilla warfare could degenerate into barbarism. Bravado aside, the priority in 1940–1 was for the men to remain alive for as long as possible and this meant acting quickly, quietly and focussing on their strategic mission rather than engaging in more random violence. This was the advice given in 1940 by MI(R) and SOE to the early Polish Resistance in order to conserve their resources. By 1941, the situation in Britain was calmer and the Auxiliary Units had been more fully absorbed within the military sensibilities. The Patrol Leader's training course now cautioned them against the temptation to be bloodthirsty but the foundation of the modern legend of Auxiliary Units assassins had already been laid.[115]

Early Weapons and Explosives
Much mythology surrounds the issue of weapons to the Auxiliary Units, stemming originally from Intelligence Officers trying to boost the morale of the auxiliers and popularised in David Lampe's ground-breaking, but flawed, *The Last Ditch* (1968). The latter maintained 'GHQ having agreed that the Auxiliary Units organisation must have priority in all things, many weapons turned up at Coleshill long before the more conventional forces saw them'.[116] It has subsequently been assumed that almost any weapon issued to the Auxiliary Units came with some form of special significance. Lampe was unaware of the secret supply of foreign armies and resistance groups already undertaken by Section D during 1939 and 1940 but some of his claims must have been known to be inaccurate by his sources such as Gubbins and Beyts and were there for literary effect. Most of the weapons were received around the same time as the rest of the Home Guard or even later but in 1940, when arguably the Auxiliary Units would have been most valuable, they were treated as expendable suicide teams and the supply of personal weapons was poor.

The absolute priority until 1942 were explosives and incendiaries, which began to be supplied immediately upon the approval of the War Establishment on 2 July 1940. A great deal came from Section D and were not, therefore, subject to the same War Office budget constraints as other material. The supply of weapons from the War Office in 1940 proved more problematic. The legend has grown that money was no object in supplying the Auxiliary Units but Colin Gubbins ruefully maintained after the war that the offer of a 'blank cheque' to form the Auxiliary Units was an empty gesture: 'I had in fact been given a blank cheque but was there any money in the bank to meet it? Everything would have to be improvised.'[117] Personal weapons were of secondary importance to get them to – and hopefully safely from – their target during an expected short span of survival and were not, therefore, considered worthy of a huge investment. Gubbins admitted the Auxiliary Units would have justified their existence 'based heavily on the fact that they were costing the country nothing either in man-power or in weapons'.[118] There was even a War Office ban on the distribution of personal weapons to the Auxiliary Units during part of August, with a progress report of 4 September noting 'the distribution of arms has been held up pending decisions on policy at a high level'.[119] This situation changed from 1941 when the general supply problem had eased and Auxiliary Units could prepare for a more settled existence. COs had learned from the experience of Hopkinson with Phantom and were now able to exploit the secrecy surrounding the Auxiliary Units to requisition supplies with the minimum of scrutiny (see below, p.169).[120]

Home Guard veterans have tended to over-emphasise any delays in supplying weapons to emphasise the sacrifice they were prepared to make in the early days of the LDV/Home Guard. Conversely, there has been a tendency to overplay the equipment supplied to the Auxiliary Units as an expression of their special status and distinction from the modern comedic interpretation of the Home Guard 'broomstick army'. Decades after the event, memories had become hazy on chronology and the issue of weapons has tended to merge into a single event rather than being an evolution over a number of years. Many patrols were not actually formed until 1942 in very different circumstances to those of 1940 and the date of service of the veterans has not always been made clear. Auxilier Bob Millard claimed in 2008: 'Considering the state of the armed forces following Dunkirk, we were very quickly and very well equipped. I can't say how soon it was, but it was in a matter of a month or so, we were issued with a Smith & Wesson .38 pistol and holster, and a Fairbairn-Sykes fighting knife.' Millard's impression was coloured by his personal experience, only joining the Auxiliary Units in September 1940 or later, around the time pistols were first issued but the Fairbairn-Sykes knife did not actually arrive until mid-1941.

Until mid-1942, the Operational Patrols were focused on sabotage and for this they relied on packs of explosives, consisting of polar gelignite, blasting gelatine, the original Nobel 808 plastic or the improved PE2, and fitted with a variety of time delays produced by Section D and MI(R)c. Even in 1941 the training notes still focus on a very basic mission kit list similar to that recommended by both Tom Wintringham and John Langdon-Davies for their Home Guard guerrillas (see below, p.181):

- Revolver with 12 rounds
- Mills grenade
- demolition materials
- truncheon or fighting knife
- first-aid dressing

At the same time the notes exhorted that 'Each man should be a complete demolition unit in himself'. This could be taken literally: the explosives were often carried in pouches sewn into the inside of their battledress blouses, with a length of cordtex detonating fuze wrapped around their waist![121] If using gelignite, the advice was to ensure this was wrapped in a waterproofed paper bag so as not to cause headaches.

Lampe correctly noted that, as far as is known, the Auxiliary Units were the first British troops to receive the new plastic explosive, PE2 (although notice of its pending distribution had been given to army units as early as June 1939).[122] This was, however, only part of its story. From 1939 scientists of Section D and Woolwich Arsenal had been working on an improvement on the original Nobel 808 plastic explosive, which had been invented in 1875 and which in documentation tends to be referred to as gelignite. The PE2 was better suited for sabotage – more stable, better mouldable and easier to attach to a target, faster and even more powerful. PE2 also did not give the user a dreadful headache! When used as a primer with gelignite, the end explosion was four times more powerful and this cost-effective way of using the new explosive was used in the early years of the war when supplies were limited. Section D had first supplied its officers in Sweden with the new plastic explosive in November 1939. In May 1940, more was hidden in Norwegian caches, and left with the Dutch and French resistance. At the time, production could not match the need for bulk supplies of explosives as required by the regular forces, who continued to use Nobel 808. The threat of invasion in late May saw Section D transfer its supplies of sabotage materials from Europe to Britain and also stimulated a rapid increase in production. Most of the existing stocks of PE2 were then quickly supplied from 2 July to the Auxiliary Units. By 25 August, Section D's Technical Section at Aston House had supplied 7,200lb of plastic explosives to the Auxiliary Units but Training Officer Nigel Oxenden was adamant that by the summer of 1941 PE2 was no longer used by them and had been replaced entirely by the less efficient Nobel 808. Consequently the training notes for August 1941 do not include a section on the new plastic explosive and only say that plastic explosive is 'being introduced', suggesting there had been a hiatus in supply.[123] The use of plastic explosive is again included in the 1942 *Calendar 1938* and 1944 *Countryman's Diary 1939*, but with the proviso it was only to be used as a primer. The reduction in use of PE2 was a recognition that the explosives were increasingly unlikely to be used in action by the Auxiliary Units and the still-limited supplies could be better deployed elsewhere.

In the spirit of the urgency felt in June/July 1940, the early Auxiliary Units had been encouraged to have a gung-ho approach to using explosives. Wilkinson's manual for the Auxiliary Units (*Calendar 1937*) contained no restriction on the use of the new plastic explosive, advising that if in any doubt as to the quantity of explosive to employ, double it.[124] As the invasion crisis receded such enthusiasm was reined in. By the time of *Calendar 1938* in 1942 (compiled by two Royal Engineer Captains, Phillip Tallents and Cecil Tracy, and available for sale to auxiliaries at two shillings each), a unit charge of 1lb had been introduced.[125] The final amendment to *Calendar 1938* in late January 1944 recommended a unit charge of only 8oz (Plate 31); a covering note from HQ was careful to stress that the reduction in the size of the charge had been tested and did work.[126] If necessary, the smaller unit charges could be linked together but there was clearly a concern to avoid unnecessary expense. A Worcestershire incident illustrates concerns over the enthusiasm of the auxiliaries in using high explosives. Samson Patrol decided to help out the father of one of their members, John Boaz, by blowing up a tree in the middle of a field that needed to be ploughed, but overestimated the charge and not only scattered fragments of tree all over the field (which they had to spend the next week clearing up) but also cracked the ceilings of a nearby house. Fortunately the house belonged to the mother of a former patrol sergeant who could be appeased with minimum fuss.[127]

One advantage of plastic explosive was that it could be easily moulded to fit the target or disguised. In 1939 Section D officers in Sweden turned it into statuettes as a means of concealment and the Section D technical department soon disguised it as coal, iron ore and animal dung for booby traps. The *Brown Book* of Section D, distributed from late

1939 to its agents abroad, describes explosives concealed in pieces of coal or logs of wood. The original version of the 'doctored' coal explosive, particularly designed to sabotage trains, used real coal which had necessitated the invention of a special borer that could cut through it without splitting. The 'coal' included in the first supply packs of the Auxiliary Units was an improved version, using a bronze casting. Oxenden explained: 'The first dumps... included a hollow bronze casting of a lump of coal that could hold two ounces of H.E. and a detonator'. In 1940 the Auxiliary Units also received the new Pull and Pressure booby trap switches, designed by MI(R) for general army use. Later came the No.8 Anti-Personnel switch, also developed by MI(R) and which first entered production in January 1940 but which first appears in the Auxiliary Units' manual for 1942. This small anti-personnel mine, comprising a short hollow metal spike with a striker held back by a compression spring and a special round, was designed to be buried in paths or roads so that when pressure is applied it would fire a bullet upwards through a man's foot or groin, or into the tyre of a vehicle and was described as having 'considerable nuisance value'. As with the Home Guard, the auxiliers soon began to enthusiastically improvise their own devices, including booby-trapped water taps, igniters, 'tremble' switches and grenades hidden under objects or in beer bottles where the bottom had been cut off. Some of the improvised devices made their way into *Calendar 1938* (published 1942). Peter Fleming was scathing about what he saw as the romanticism of Gubbins and his staff 'for whom an enemy is hardly worth killing unless he can be killed with a tarantula fired from an airgun by a Bessarabian undertaker on Walpurgis night'.[128]

Section D also supplied the early Auxiliary Units with the Large and Medium Magnesium Incendiary bombs and the paraffin-filled Tyesule, as already distributed abroad and in the HDS dumps. These were, somewhat unfairly, described as 'feeble and uncertain' by Oxenden, who claimed that by the summer of 1941 the 'funny little incendiaries' were gone and replace by gelignite.[129] Although the Tyesule was now considered obsolete, improved versions of the other incendiaries were produced and the phosphorous SIP grenade remained in service. The No.76 Self-Igniting Phosphorus (SIP) grenade was invented in 1940 by Albright and Wilson Ltd of Oldbury in association with Section D as a desperate effort to satisfy the urgent need of the army for an anti-tank grenade. It was a more sophisticated Molotov cocktail, consisting of a half pint capacity glass bottle filled with a white phosphorus / benzene /water mixture and then sealed with a 'crown cap'. Also included was a short length of rubber tube that upon ignition would make the burning liquid sticky and more likely to stick to the side of a target; the grenade could be thrown by hand or later fired from the Northover Projector. The 10 June meeting of the War Cabinet were informed that one million had been ordered and were being delivered to the LDV.[130] Section D technical HQ at Aston House received a delivery of 5,000 SIP grenades in that month and were sufficiently impressed to claim in their July report to have quickly distributed 4,000 of their stock to the Auxiliary Units HQ (although a Section D inventory of the same month lists only 1,200 as being supplied). These seem not have been actually distributed to the patrols until 10 September or later, by then already having been distributed across Home Forces and Home Guard, with the priority being front-line anti-tank defences. It consequently does not appear in the 1940 manual, *Calendar 1937*. This delay was possibly due to an understakable caution to see how Home Forces would first store the volatile new grenade. The progress report to the Prime Minister on 4 September 1940 advised that

5,000 AW Bombs were finally expected to be distributed during the course of the next ten days.[131] It was vital to prevent the phosphorous from coming into contact with the air and many were buried or even kept underwater in ponds! Six million SIP grenades were produced by August 1941 but by then the army had been relieved to find better alternatives as an anti-tank weapon and the SIP grenade was now a primarily Home Guard/Auxiliary Units grenade.

The other anti-tank grenade developed (by MI(R)) during 1940 was the No.74 ST Grenade, better known as the 'Sticky Bomb'. It consisted of a glass sphere containing 1.25lb (0.57kg) of nitroglycerine and covered in a sticky stockinette, which was in turn encased in a protective sheet metal casing. When the user pulled a pin on the handle of the grenade, its casing would fall away. Pulling another pin would arm the grenade and upon being thrown, a lever was released on the handle that activated a five-second fuse. It was a short-range weapon best used from an ambush position, the idea being to smash the glass sphere against the target, squashing the explosive in order to increase the contact area for the 'poultice' effect. This would cause an inward blast to either punch a hole in the armour or at least produce deadly shrapnel from the inner face of the steel plate. It suffered from the same delays in production that plagued many of the weapons intended to be rushed into service in 1940. After pressure from Churchill to see progress, on 19 June the War Office Anti-Tank Committee decided to order one million.[132] The decision proved premature and a rushed trial on 22 June identified a somewhat fundamental problem in that the current adhesive would not stick to a wet or dirty tank![133] Some of these prototypes may have been demonstrated to the early Auxiliary Units and so it was included in *Calendar 1937* but the first production run was sent to Greece in December with large-scale production not finally underway until May 1941. This is when the Auxiliary Units appear to have received their first operational supply.[134] Between 1941 and 1943, approximately 2.5 million were produced and although the majority eventually came into Home Guard service, it continued to be used successfully in North Africa, Italy and New Guinea.

In June 1939 Section D developed the No.10 Time Pencil. The early versions comprised a 5.75in long tube made in three sections of copper, aluminium and brass, with a detonator attached over one end. A thin wire held back a spring-loaded steel striker. A glass ampoule containing an aqueous solution of copper chloride would be broken by squeezing the copper barrel and would dissolve the wire at a set rate, determined by the concentration of the acid, and release the striker which would in turn ignite a detonator and set off the main charge. To avoid failure, the advice was to use them in pairs. The first production batch of 3,700 time pencils were manufactured in September 1939. They were then sent to the Finnish army in the closing stages of the Winter War and to Section D agents across Poland, Germany, Scandinavia and the Balkans. More was left with the planned Dutch and French resistance in mid-May and were used by the Section D mission in early June to disable the Bjølvefossen power station in Norway.[135] As with plastic explosives, under the imminent threat of invasion, production increased dramatically and distribution shifted to supply forces in Britain, with 67,400 going to the Auxiliary Units by 25 August. Over a million No.10 Time Pencils had been produced by the end of 1940. The Auxiliary Units were also issued with the alternative No.9 L-Delay invented by MI(R) and designed for more general military use than the No.10 Time Pencil, being of sturdier construction. It relied on the principle that a lead alloy wire will stretch and break at a set time at a particular temperature, depending on the thickness of the wire. Once the safety pin was removed, the wire was held under tension – and would stretch and break, causing a spring to release the striker pin and thence to ignite the charge. The L-Delay was less susceptible to damp than the No.10 Time Pencil but more prone to delay variations due to temperature.

The supply of personal weapons only got properly underway from mid-August, once the system of hidden patrols under direct Auxiliary Units operational control had been finalised, settling any dispute as to whether the Auxiliary Units or Home Guard would be responsible for the cost, although there was a further delay until September when a War Office ban on the distribution of arms to the Auxiliary Units was lifted. Until then, the Auxiliary Units were not thought likely to survive long enough to make any substantial investment worthwhile. Ironically, as the risk of invasion lessened and their chances of being used in action decreased, their equipment improved! A simple fighting knife was the obvious first choice when creeping silently onto a target with the possible need to eliminate sentries. Oxenden makes much of the provision of knives as 'enhancing the reputation for toughness' as opposed to the 'church parade' activities of the Home Guard proper.[136] Nonetheless, it was for similar reasons that individuals in the Home Guard also began to quickly acquire their own knives. The British army did not have a tradition of official fighting knives, although troops in the First World War trenches had commonly made their own from discarded bayonets and this continued into the Second World War. In the 1940 publications of Wintringham, Levy and Langdon-Davies, the Home Guard were exhorted to equip themselves with a long slender fighting knife and many bought-up and converted the surplus bayonets that were still on public sale. Initially, the auxiliers also had to find their own knives: even the West Surrey 'Battle Patrol' of XII Corps Observation Unit had to make do with their large, pre-war pattern, army clasp knives.[137] One Dorset auxilier in Creech Patrol was even issued with a Stanley kitchen knife! Even later, the Essex Intelligence Officer gave his auxiliers the task of making their own fighting knife from cut-down P1888 bayonets as a test (following a precedent learned from early Commando training).

Some Intelligence Officers made their own arrangements, buying up stocks of cheap sheath knives from local retailers. The first officially-supplied knives did not arrive until the end of August and these were the cheapest commercially-available sheath knives the War Office could find. This was the Joseph Rodgers 3s 6d knife with a flimsy-looking 5.6in clipped blade, jigged bone scale handle and a cast alloy guard (Plate 20). It had reputedly already been provided to local patrols by an Intelligence Officer in the South West. The first War Office contract with Joseph Rodgers for 300 'knives, hunting' was not placed until 20 August but was followed on 14 September and 6 November 1940 with contracts for 2,100 more hunting knives specifying for 'Aux Units'.[138] Together, these were enough for the current strength of auxiliers. They were purchased at a wholesale price of 2s 10d each.[139] What the early auxiliers thought of these knives is not recorded. By contrast, the popular 4.5in Joseph Rodgers sheath knife retailed for 9s 6d and an order for 1,500 of the hefty RDB hunting knives from Wilkinson Sword on 14 November 1940 for SOE and commandos was priced at 13s 6d each.[140] It was only from mid-1941 that the Auxiliary Units began to be issued with the famous Fairbairn-Sykes fighting knife which the men proudly carried as an icon of commando forces (Plate 20). Even then, some auxiliers were asked to buy their own. The Fairbairn-Sykes knife went on public sale from

June 1942 and, unsurprisingly, many regular troops and the Home Guard soon began to equip themselves with this or one of the wide range of commercial alternatives which quickly emerged. Consequently, the discovery of a fighting knife in the attic of a deceased relative does not necessarily mean they had served in one of the elite forces.

With delays around even the supply of a simple knife it is not surprising that Gubbins was unable to implement the recommendations for weapons as described in *Art of Guerrilla Warfare*, which recommended

> Undoubtedly, therefore, the most effective weapon for the guerrilla is the sub-machine gun which can be fired either from a rest or from the shoulder – i.e. a tommy-gun or gangster gun; in addition, this gun has the qualities of being short and comparatively light. Special efforts must therefore be made to equip each band with a percentage of these guns. Carbines are suitable, being shorter and lighter than rifles, and the long range of the rifle is not necessary. After carbines come revolvers and pistols for night work and for very close-quarters, and then rifles.[141]

The Auxiliary Units were not considered a priority for the Thompson sub-machine gun, still in very short supply. Instead, the first automatic weapon issued to the Auxiliary Units patrols was the cumbersome Browning Automatic Rifle (BAR: Plate 23) which arrived on the first ships bringing the P17 rifles for the Home Guard; there were no carbines and instead each patrol had two of the standard Home Guard M1917 (P17) rifles. The patrols could not afford to get into firefights as this would only bring further enemy forces down upon them; their firearms were, therefore, not a priority and to be used only as a matter of last resort.

The M1917 rifle (known as the P17 in British service) had been the main rifle of US forces during the First World War and was still in rear-echelon service. In June 1940 an order was placed with the US government for 500,000 M1917 rifles for the Home Guard in order to relieve pressure on the limited number of British .303 calibre rifles. The first consignment of 12,000 began to be distributed to Home Guard from 8 July 1940 and by the end of that month 500,000 had been distributed. Two P17 rifles were issued to each Auxiliary Units patrol but their distribution is unlikely to have preceded the issue to the Home Guard.[142] Bob Millard recounted in around 2002 to the Bath Blitz Memorial Project that his patrol had two P17 rifles 'which we scrounged, or won, from the Home Guard. I don't know whether they knew they had disappeared or not but they turned up in the patrol.' The detail may be a romance but the sequence of issue is at least clear. To prevent delay, the first shipments to the Home Guard on 8 July were still covered in a heavy layer of protective cosmoline grease and memoirs of the Home Guard consistently refer to the effort needed to clean them ready for action; in later shipments the rifles were cleaned centrally before distribution and such references disappear. As no veteran has mentioned cleaning off the heavy cosmoline whilst in the Auxiliary Units it may be presumed the rifles first arrived in Auxiliary Units service from August or later, as indicated in the report to the Prime Minister on 8 August which states 'the men are equipped with rifles and grenades'. These reports, written by Gubbins, are littered with exaggerated claims and some patrols did not receive their rifles until October.[143] The rifle was, however, ill-suited to their current role. Training Officer Nigel Oxenden commented: 'American rifles, on a scale of two per patrol, were an early issue, nobody quite knew why, and this item was never afterwards changed.'[144] Reflecting this confusion, a March 1941 note on patrol methodology clearly stated 'rifles and bayonets are not suitable for the tasks undertaken by scout patrols'.[145] Nonetheless, the rifle was still seen as the necessary equipment of anything resembling an infantry section. They only became useful from the summer of 1942, when the Auxiliary Units had the less covert mission as a reconnaissance force against the threat of German commando raids but even now this threat was mainly met by an issue of the now readily-available Sten gun.

The progress report of 8 August 1940 also announced that 'Their activities will also include sniping'.[146] This was not necessarily meant to imply the assassination role that has become part of the Auxiliary Units legend. At the time, the patrols were just beginning to receive the P17 rifles which whilst very accurate, were not configured as specialist sniper rifles. Gubbins may have had in mind the standard British army practice for the best shot in each section (the equivalent of an Auxiliary Units Operational Patrol) to be designated as 'section sniper', whose task was to pick off individuals from the flank of an attack on an enemy position, without any expectation that they would be issued with a specialist rifle.[147] Gubbins may also have been again blurring the distinction between the Home Guard Operational Patrols and the planned army Scout Sections, who were each issued with a service rifle and eventually with four of the standard .303 sniper rifle.[148] The patrols were not officially issued with any rifle having a scope or silencer until April 1942 and then it was only a .22 rifle which in practical terms was used mainly for rabbiting (see below, p.131). The delay in any official supply of a 'silenced' .22 rifle when easily available in 1940 suggests that, despite its post-war legend as a sniper rifle, this was not considered significant during the time of greatest invasion threat. The .22 was not well-suited for such a task and it is significant that the Home Guard booklet on sniping, *Fieldcraft for the Home Guard* by A.T. Walker (1940) makes no mention of .22 rifles other than for indoor range practice, even when the P17 was still in short supply. Nonetheless, in the summer of 1940 when the Home Guard were desperate for any firearm, the .22 rifle was attractive to many volunteers if only for its relative ease of availability and it was equally natural for some Auxiliary Units patrols to also unofficially provide their own, including commercially-available telescopic sights and 'silencers' to provide at least the aura of a 'sniper' weapon, until better weapons arrived. Geoff Devereux of Samson Patrol, Worcestershire, recalled using a .22 calibre rifle that had been handed in to the police and was then given to his father (a gamekeeper) for safe-keeping. After being passed to the patrol it was fitted with scope and sound moderator.[149] Dr Barling of Jehu Patrol, Worcestershire, used his own BSA Martini underlever rifle throughout his Auxiliary Units service from 1940 to 1942. Charles Mason of the South Cave Patrol, East Yorkshire, also had a BSA Martini Model 12 with a scope and a home-made sound moderator. Such rifles do not, however, appear in the 1941 training notes as an approved weapon.

Churchill famously added a marginal note to one of Gubbins' August weekly reports that 'these men must have revolvers' – at a time they were in very short supply.[150] They had already been issued by SIS to the Home Defence Scheme but, despite the Prime Minister's intervention, handguns were not provided by the War Office until towards the end of the invasion season in 1940. The progress report on 4 September announced that 400 pistols were expected to be delivered over the next 10 days and by the end of

September a 100 per cent issue of handguns had finally been made. However, according to Training Officer Nigel Oxenden, the ammunition only followed later. They were mainly American Smith and Wesson or Colt .38 revolvers, some still in their US police surplus holsters.[151] The first handguns issued included a batch of 400 .32 Colt semi-automatic pistols, as earlier supplied to the Section D mission to Norway and their Home Defence Scheme as well as later to SOE (Plate 21). Small numbers of Beretta .32 semi-automatic pistols were also issued but such small-calibre weapons were withdrawn in 1943.[152] They initially had only 12 rounds of ammunition each, as compared to the 80 rounds issued to HDS, reflecting their use as a weapon of last resort. These were undoubtedly a huge status symbol and the men had to be dissuaded from openly toting their revolvers on the train to the Coleshill training courses as the sight of Home Guard other ranks with revolvers excited obvious curiosity. One surprising omission in their arsenal, given their emphasis on silent attack and later legend were the commercially-available 'silenced' .22 pistols such as the Colt Woodman. Neither were they later issued with the High Standard Model B, used by SOE from 1942. Together with the delay in issuing the 'silenced' .22 rifle and failure to supply the 'silenced' Sten gun or Welrod (Plate 22), this suggests that silenced weapons and assassination were never considered a priority.

The only automatic support weapon that the Auxiliary Units could obtain in 1940 was the unwieldy .300 calibre Browning Automatic Rifle (BAR: Plate 23). It had a history going back to the First World War, but only became a standard issue to US forces in 1938 as a light machine gun. It also became the standard light machine gun of the Home Guard and by 26 July, 7,400 had been issued to the Home Guard, although they may not have reached the Auxiliary Units until September. A progress report to the Prime Minister on 4 September announced that 500 BARs, with 250,000 rounds of ammunition, were expected to be delivered during the next 10 days. Although valuable in providing fire support (suggested as useful in covering a withdrawal when ambushing convoys in the March 1941 training notes), an automatic weapon was still considered a luxury and despite its limitations, weighing in at c.21lb loaded, the BAR was not replaced by the more suitable Thompson sub-machine gun (Plate 24) until after May 1941.

The Auxiliary Units did not receive the first Thompson in British service as claimed by some veterans and repeated without question thereafter. The veterans probably took their lead from the 1968 statement of Lampe that 'even the Commandos queued up behind Auxiliary Units'. One Worcestershire veteran subsequently firmly recounted in the 1990s that they received the Thompson before the Commandos – of which his brother was a member.[153] In fact, a small number of Thompsons were in use with the Phantom unit in France during January 1940, before more were issued to regimental 'fighting patrols' in the BEF and in April to the Independent Companies and Irish Guards in Norway.[154] They were also issued to the GHQ Liaison Regiment in Britain from June.[155] Some Thompsons were supplied to the XII Corps Observation Unit in 1940 but these were not to the Home Guard patrols but to the accompanying army 'Battle Patrols' (continuing the principle of issue to fighting patrols of the BEF). The Thompson began to be supplied to the Home Guard in small numbers from March–April 1941 but the Training Notes for the Auxiliary Units patrols in that month still only refer to the BAR (although the War Establishment for the HQ of the Auxiliary Units for March 1941 lists five Thompsons for its own use, probably for training).

The Auxiliary Units patrols did not receive their Thompsons until after May 1941 (by which time the Home Guard had 4,452 in service) and the subsequent issue of one to each patrol of 8 men was essentially a ratio equivalent to that established for an infantry section of 10 men. Even now, it was not considered a priority weapon: 'The tommy gun may be required to cover a withdrawal, but will not always be necessary.'[156] The Pelynt Patrol in Cornwall is even reported to have refused to accept one as it conflicted with the idea of silent conflict.[157] In Worcestershire, Samson Patrol quickly exchanged the heavy and noisy 50-round drum magazines with which it had originally been supplied with 20-round stick magazines, taped together end-to-end to allow rapid reloading. The legend of the Auxiliary Units being a priority issue may have arose out of a misinterpretation of the statement of intent in the Cabinet Conclusions of 17 June saying 'Some of these would be armed with Tommy Guns' and early reports to Churchill, on 30 July and 8 August 1940, which stated that the Auxiliary Units planned to issue Tommy Guns 'when they become available'.[158] Gubbins did receive two as a gift from a friend in the USA during 1940 and it is presumed these went into HQ stores for training purposes. As a testimony to the reluctance to cast aside established myths, despite the accumulation of published evidence from as early as 1982, the claim of the Thompson first being issued to the Auxiliary Units was still being repeated 40 years later.[159]

Training

With invasion expected in a matter of weeks, the training of men with a very mixed military background was a key priority but, as with the supply of weapons, a systematic training programme was delayed until after they established a settled HQ at Coleshill. Until then it was carried out on a hectic but ad hoc basis. One problem was the lack of instructors with relevant practical expertise (in contrast to the Asturian 'dynamiters' and Spanish Civil War veterans at the Osterley Park Home Guard Training School). With the contemporary arrogance of the War Office, Wilkinson had been sent on the MI(R) Polish Mission to advise on the training of Polish guerrillas in August 1939 but having no experience in the subject he was reduced to frantically reading Gubbins' pamphlets on the journey. Now he recounted how, in July, he was in the London office of the Auxiliary Units from 8.30am–5pm and was then driven out to meet a patrol; he would give a lecture or instruct on a night exercise, finishing around midnight, sleep in the car and then be back in the office again at 8.30am.[160] The first training manual was Section D's innocuously-titled *Home Hints*, quickly replaced during July by Wilkinson's equally innocent-sounding *Calendar 1937*. In early August, Gubbins managed to beg a small temporary training staff from Southern Command. Brigadier Richie asked for help for this from 3rd Division.

> There exists an organisation, in reality a part of the H.G.s, [Home Guard] which works under one Brigadier GUBBINS and whose role is highly secret. GUBBINS you may possibly know already as he was in Norway.
> The Chief is most anxious to help GUBBINS' show by getting hold of five good young officers, one for each of our areas, to train this personnel in intensive scouting and battle patrol training.[161]

3rd Division consequently provided five training officers, mainly from the Guards Brigade. Further support was promised from 20 August by the tank-hunting platoons of 1st and 2nd Battalions, Grenadier Guards. These were all army officers with no experience in irregular warfare.[162]

With training courses delayed, it is no surprise to find Scottish Intelligence Officer Eustace Maxwell quoted as saying he believed the training provided at the Osterley Park Training School, staffed by veterans of the Spanish Civil War, as being better than that provided for the Auxiliary Units at this time.[163] The first course was held on 22 August and Coleshill HQ then built up its own training establishment of instructors in patrolling, explosives and unarmed combat, providing weekend courses for patrol leaders. This was under Major Bill Beyts, who apart from his recent experience as a training officer with the 1st London ('Black Cat') Division, had experience in counter-insurgency work in Burma (where his unorthodox methods had included carrying out mock hangings of prisoners in order to convince their fellow villagers to reveal information). A Scottish training base was also established at Melville House in Fife. When the Scout Patrols were introduced from November, part of their role was to provide on-going local training (so avoiding the trips to Coleshill); first, however, they had to be themselves trained in the techniques of irregular warfare as the men were drawn from ordinary regimental depots. The progress report up to 1 September gives a summary of the standard of training achieved by the auxiliers during the period that they were most likely to have faced invasion.

> By the 1st September all members of the Home Guard enrolled have had preliminary instruction in the use of the special weapons. At least 50%, in some areas 90%, of them have had practical experience in using High Explosive, in pistol firing and dummy Mills Bomb throwing. 70% of the patrols have had training in field stalking and at least 50% have carried out two or more night schemes.[164]

The level of training given to the c.2,300 auxiliers recruited by the time of the invasion scare in September 1940 was therefore by no means complete. During the same period, around 4,000 members of the Home Guard had attended an intensive weekend course in explosives handling and manufacture, stalking, tank-hunting and camouflage at Osterley Park! Crucially, many of them further disseminated their knowledge by creating local training schools. However dedicated Wilkinson's efforts during July 1940 were, his theoretical approach could not compete with the recent practical experience of Hugh Slater and the Asturian 'dynamiters' at Osterley Park. The subsequent reputation of the auxiliers as highly-trained saboteurs was the result of another three and a half years of intensive training, even as the actual risk of them being called upon to exercise these skills steadily diminished.

Scout Sections
Thorne's original model of guerrilla operations in the XII Corps Observation Unit had been built around a nucleus of twenty regular army 'Battle Patrols' – what Fleming termed the 'striking force'.[165] His LDV patrols were to play a support role, trained by a further scout section, built around the contingent of Lovat Scouts. Gubbins wanted a similar system and Donald Hamilton-Hill, one of the first wave of Intelligence Officers,

remembers being told in their introductory meeting of 13 July that they should recruit two subalterns from local regiments in their areas, who would in turn each recruit the twelve best men from their regiment and form two Scout Sections.[166] Gubbins put this proposal on a formal basis in a War Establishment report of 26 July 1940 but there is no mention of them in the August report to Churchill and Scout Sections were not actually introduced until November, after the initial invasion crisis had dissipated. Battalion commanders had been reluctant to lose some of their best officers and men in the face of imminent invasion. Agreement was eventually secured only by taking soldiers from reserve units and depots rather from front-line units.[167] Gubbins was not in the position of Thorne as a corps commander to simply order the regiments under his command to comply and it may have been considered that to divert front-line troops was a waste of limited resources. Two Scout Sections drawn from men with good local knowledge were now to be allocated to each Intelligence Officer, each consisting of twelve men, including an officer and often a Royal Engineers sapper.[168] Their distribution was specifically stated to exclude the inland counties north of the Bristol Channel, i.e. Herefordshire and Worcestershire; these counties remained an anomaly throughout the whole organisation of the Auxiliary Units. Oxenden was dismissive of the quality of the early Scout Sections and particularly by the inexperience of their young officers but as they became better established so did their skills in the construction of hides and as small specialist fighting patrols, greatly increasing the strategic potential of the Operational Branch of the Auxiliary Units. Their improvement is best judged by the high percentage who joined the SAS following a targeted recruitment drive from August 1943, after the number of Scout Sections had been cut.[169]

In action, the Scout Sections would go to ground like the Home Guard patrols but they had the significant advantage that some, at least, had wireless communication, meaning they could act more strategically on behalf of the local corps commander and be re-tasked as the campaign developed. They were equipped to act as an observation unit and well-armed offensive strike force on the flanks and rear of the enemy rather than as the covert sabotage unit of the Home Guard patrols. Some had additional hidden dumps of supplies scattered around their area to extend their operational life.[170] The official War Establishment of a Scout Section in October 1940 comprised:

1 second lieutenant
1 sergeant
1 corporal
1 lance corporal
8 privates
1 batman
1 car
1 motor cycle
19 bicycles

Their weaponry was initially a basic infantry allocation and reflected the overall shortages of the time: two revolvers (twelve rounds on man) and eleven .303 rifles (fifty rounds on man). By March 1942 the weaponry for each twelve-man Scout Section had increased dramatically, including sniper rifles and Bren gun, and is listed in Fig. 9.

Fig. 9 Weapons for twelve-man Scout Section, March 1942. (*TNA WO 199/738*)

Weapon	Number	Rounds, carried	Rounds, total
Pistol, .38	12	12	576
Sniper rifle, .303	4	50	200
Thompson SMG, .45	2	200	2400
Bren Gun, .303	1	1000	1500

Threatened disbandment in 1940

By 1 September 1940, 2,300 men had been recruited to the Operational Patrols of the Auxiliary Units in over 370 patrols in the coastal counties (Figs 10 and 11).[171] In addition, although Herefordshire and Worcestershire were not included in the official list it is clear that small-scale recruiting had been started as early as late July/early August, probably on the basis of an earlier HDS network.

Once the expected invasion in June failed to materialise, the Directorate of Military Intelligence had considered the next greatest risk of invasion in 1940 lay between 8 to 10 September and on 7 September the code word *Cromwell* was issued indicating that invasion was imminent and troops should take up battle stations.[172] No invasion materialised as Hitler had concluded that his prerequisites for invasion had not been met (see Appendix 1) and Operation Sealion was abandoned on 12 October 1940. By then, the defence landscape had changed radically since the Auxiliary Units were conceived. The new C-in-C Home Forces was able to take full advantage of more troops and better equipment, better beach defences and field intelligence; the Royal Navy remained intact and the success of the RAF in the Battle of Britain boosted a confidence in survival. Churchill was already considering drawing off forces from the UK defences; on 16 September 1940 the new C-in-C Home Forces, General Alan Brooke, complained of plans to remove one-quarter of his infantry strength for service in the Middle East. Throughout the Second World War many in the General Staff regarded irregular warfare as a distasteful expedient to be discarded as soon as practicable. Having told Gubbins and Wilkinson as early as mid-September that it believed there was now little likelihood of invasion in 1940, GHQ began to re-evaluate the future of the Auxiliary Units – even as they finally began to be properly armed and were expanding. As the Operational Patrols had been set up to be self-supporting and to act independently, once they had been equipped even Wilkinson believed that there was not much more for HQ at Coleshill to do except to maintain on-going training.[173] The organisation, both on the Operational and Special Duties wings, was floundering before it had really begun to be fully operational (although the volunteers on the ground were not to know this) and the War Office considered its disbandment. Gubbins is rumoured to have ensured the survival of the Auxiliary Units only by a timely lunch with War Office staff at the Cavalry Club – but then both he and Wilkinson swiftly moved on to SOE.[174]

Despite the limitations of which Gubbins and the War Office were well aware, the Operational Patrols would still, arguably, have most proved their worth in 1940 alongside the other elements of what was considered as a suicidal holding operation to allow the field army to concentrate for a counter-attack. Writing in more relaxed post-war circumstances, the opinion of contemporaries such as Gubbins, Wilkinson and

Fleming was dismissive, yet at the time the army was desperate for any means possible to slow down the *blitzkrieg*. For Gubbins, they were a cheap, expendable, resource whose value was that they cost 'nothing in either man-power or in weapons . . . their usefulness would have been short-lived, at the longest until their stocks were exhausted, at the shortest when they were caught or wiped out. They were designed, trained and prepared for a particular and imminent crisis: that was their specialist role.'[175] They were regarded essentially as suicide bombers and the report on the progress up to 1 September 1940 concluded 'it was in fact doubtful whether many of them would have survived the first few days of invasion'.[176] In 1995 Wilkinson considered that they would have been, at best, a 'flea-bite' behind enemy lines, sowing a degree of confusion but not able to offer a decisive contribution. He even concluded 'I think that in the cold light of reason, it is at least arguable, as many senior officers held, that they were not worth the effort put into them.'[177] Of the original XII Corps Observation Unit, Fleming also wrote: 'I doubt if we should have been more than a minor and probably short-lived nuisance to the invaders.'[178] Nonetheless, even Wilkinson had to admit that they may have been able to influence operations in the early days of any bridgehead when any delay, however small, to a German breakout may have proved significant in buying time for the limited British armour to organise a counter-attack.[179] Wilkinson left the Auxiliary Units in November, believing the future lay in a return to the more covert ideas of Section D.

> I think that both Gubbins and I took a very realistic view of the limitations of Auxiliary Units and their very short-term nature. It was for this reason that before I left in November, 1940, I was, with Gubbins' knowledge and approval, planning a sort of 'inner-circle' of specially selected members of Auxiliary Units who would be really secret and who might form the nucleus of a future Resistance Organisation if they survived the first month. I saw myself as the Chief of Staff of this super-secret organisation and had planned a secret hideout for myself whilst masquerading as an engineering apprentice at Rugby . . . But this plan had not gone beyond a pipe-dream by the time Gubbins and I left Auxiliary Units and I doubt if the concept would have been acceptable to Colonel Bill Major.[180]

By November, the structure of the Operational Branch was so embedded in the Home Guard that Wilkinson's idea for an 'inner-circle' resistance organisation was no longer practicable. The strongest argument for survival was simply that the volunteers had been assured that they would not be returned to normal duty in the Home Guard and the War Office could not be certain that the threat of invasion would not return. For the next three years they were an insurance policy of diminishing value against invasion, surviving by Coleshill HQ using the argument that they were so secret that they could not tell anyone what they were doing. On the basis of subsequent developments, the deal that Gubbins negotiated for survival at the Cavalry Club is likely to have included three key elements: a) the long-awaited introduction of a regular army component to the operational structure via Scout Patrols, b) a tighter military organisation to the Operational Branch and c) a more military iteration of the Special Duties Branch that could better contribute to internal security (possibly the most important development). These changes were implemented under Gubbins' successor and with them, despite mounting scrutiny and criticism, the Operational Branch of the Auxiliary Units survived until November 1944.

Fig. 10 Contemporary tally of Operational Patrols created up to 1 September 1940 (it does not include Herefordshire and Worcestershire which by this stage had one patrol each). *(TNA CAB 120/241)*

County	Patrols	County	Patrols
Caithness and Sutherland	20	Sussex	11
East Highlands and Aberdeen	35	Isle of Wight	13
East Riding	37	East Hampshire	13
Lincolnshire	23	Dorset and West Hampshire	40
Norfolk	23	Somerset	40
Suffolk and Essex	42	Devon and Cornwall	34
Kent	25	South Wales	15

Fig. 11 Operational Patrols, Auxiliary Units by density in counties, September 1940 (A) and June 1944 (B). *(Data from TNA CAB 120/241)*

1941 Reorganisation

With the immediate fear of invasion over in October 1940, there was an opportunity to take a more considered look at the format of the Auxiliary Units than had hitherto been possible. The decision was taken to move towards a more ordered military structure and this is reflected in a major change in personnel, marking the end of the MI(R) heritage of the Auxiliary Units. Calvert went to the Mission 104 Training School in Australia and Andrew Croft joined Combined Operations. Most significantly, Gubbins, Wilkinson and Fleming left the Auxiliary Units for SOE in November 1940. The last remaining member of MI(R) was Hamish Torrance who also left the Auxiliary Units in April 1941 for SOE. This left Beyts and Henderson of the original senior management team until they too left in 1942 but the Auxiliary Units had by then taken a significant shift in direction for both the Operational and Special Duties branches.

After Colonel Cyril 'Bill' Major took over command on 20 November, the organisation moved from providing a desperate response to an immediate threat of invasion into seeking something more sustainable and more in line with orthodox military structures. Commanding Officers thereafter would have no expertise in irregular warfare and, as their military significance decreased, the post eventually appears at times to have been treated as a sinecure before retirement. 'Bill' Major of the Royal Irish Fusiliers had been commissioned from the ranks at the end of the First World War and was a long-time staff officer with no experience of irregular warfare but did have connections to Military Intelligence. After service with the Shanghai Defence Force during 1927, he had been Chief of Staff to MI2c (Military Intelligence on Japan) during 1930–3 and then remained in staff posts as a GSO(1) at the War Office. Prior to his 'official' arrival, Major joined one of the Coleshill weekend training courses in the disguise of an ordinary Home Guard auxiliary to get a better sense of the organisation from a different perspective. Having risen through the ranks this was something he could carry off better than most officers of the period. His impression is not recorded but Major then introduced a more ordered pyramid-style military hierarchy throughout the whole organisation (both Operational and Special Duties Branches). It may be that, with his connections to the DMI, the SDB now began to take on a significance that surpassed that of the Operational Branch, but a role more connected to the considerable effort to protect internal security than the anti-invasion role that has so captured post-war attention. Despite the efforts of Major and subsequent COs, the Auxiliary Units became increasingly out of step with the rapidly-changing war situation; historical inconsistencies remained, as did a continuing confusion over their purpose; together these served to confound both the contemporary War Office and modern researchers.

Under Major, the previously independent Operational Patrols were organised under a Group Commander, commissioned from the Home Guard. Oxenden notes that some of them were former members of the HDS: 'These were generally outstanding individuals, who eventually became Group Commanders'.[181] Possible examples were Edmund and Lewis Van Moppes, British-born diamond merchants of Dutch descent who had SIS connections. When they moved their diamond-processing factory from Norfolk to Worcestershire they brought with them a fit young 'gardener' who also joined the Auxiliary Units and may well have been an SIS 'minder'.[182] Lewis became Area Commander as a captain and Edmund a Group Commander as a lieutenant, with an HQ in the basement of their diamond-processing factory at Wolverton Hall. The basic principle of Major's 'group attack' philosophy was for a number of patrols to rendezvous under the Group Commander and together attack a single target. As some of the Group Commanders were in late middle age, the post was eventually relegated to one of administration. Wilkinson was appalled at this divergence from the idea of small sabotage teams working in isolation. In a 1992 interview he recorded:

> In my opinion, the greatest weakness of Auxiliary Units after we left, was that Major tried to organise it along military lines which, in my experience, is almost invariably fatal for a clandestine organisation for reasons of security.[183]

The re-organisation was, however, a new means of achieving the larger commando units that Gubbins had originally sought. Major's scheme was the product of an orthodox military mind, to partially resolve a fundamental weakness of the existing system. The early compartmentalisation of the Operational Patrols provided security but, without wireless communication, prevented patrols from acting strategically after they had destroyed their pre-determined primary target. The Group Commanders could act in lieu of the Intelligence Officers (who may, or may not, have gone to ground with the patrols) in coordinating the subsequent action of the patrols over a sub-county area. The position of the army Scout Sections in this system is not clear as it might rely on an army officer taking orders from what was likely to be a more junior Home Guard officer. It is no coincidence that this new pyramid system had a symmetry with that being put in place around the same time for the Auxiliary Units Special Duties Branch (see Chapter 8). Nonetheless, the new system still left unresolved the practical issue of how Corps HQ could communicate with the patrols or how the SDB could pass on its own local intelligence to the Operational Branch.

In January 1941 the Joint Intelligence Sub-Committee concluded that Hitler would be obliged to invade in that year to stand a chance of winning the war or at least dragging it to stalemate. If it came, the main attack was expected somewhere between the Wash and Portsmouth. Advance warning of the actual invasion might be from 24 hours up to three weeks but could only occur after the enemy had achieved air and naval superiority and in circumstances very different from the desperation felt immediately after Dunkirk.[184] The German invasion had indeed been provisionally re-scheduled for May but with the continuing failure to achieve air superiority, Hitler first turned his attention to what he thought would be a quick victory over Russia. The C-in-C Home Forces, General Alan Brooke, was able to take heart from the invasion of Russia on 22 June 1941 in removing the immediate threat to Britain, but he still considered this might be only a temporary respite, believing that Russia would only be able to resist for three or four months.[185] The speed of the initial stages of Operation Barbarossa in invading Russia only served to reinforce the sense of invincibility of the German forces and so Brooke believed that the contingency against possible invasion still had to be maintained. The survival of Russia and entry of the USA into the war in December 1941 provided considerable relief, but it was still prudent to maintain a contingency against invasion and on 16 January 1942 plans were discussed for Ulster and US forces to move into Eire in the event that German forces landed there as a preparatory stage for an invasion of Britain.

The renewed threat of invasion in the event of a rapid collapse of Soviet Russia is the context for an expansion programme of the Auxiliary Units agreed by the War Office in August 1941, which mainly concerned expansion in northern England and Scotland, reflecting concerns of a possible invasion via Norway (Fig.11).[186] The expansion into Scotland may have been encouraged by General Thorne, now C-in-C Scottish Command, to maximise his resources across the expansive coast of Scotland. It is, however, in this landscape that the lack of wireless communication would have been most apparent in reducing their strategic worth. The number of Intelligence Officers in the Operational Branch doubled, reaching its peak of twenty-two in 1941 before falling to nineteen in 1943, and finally to four in the drastic reorganisation of August 1944.[187] But the Commanding Officer no longer had the free hand given to Gubbins in building the Auxiliary Units; approval had to be obtained for each new patrol so that it fell within the total agreed establishment costs. The accountants were now in control of the war effort! Nonetheless, despite increasing grumbles from the War Office quartermaster's department, the Operational Patrols and Scout Sections continued to maintain their supplies, using the technique that Colonel Hopkinson had used to good effect on the foundation of Phantom (see Chapter 10) capitalising on the likelihood that, because the Auxiliary Units were classed as top secret, few officers in authority would feel able to ask what exactly they were up to or why they needed a particular piece of equipment.

Chapter 7

Auxiliary Units (Operations), 1942–4: A New Purpose

At the Arcadia Conference in December 1941 President Roosevelt and Churchill agreed on a strategy of 'Europe First' to defeat Nazi Germany, whilst simultaneously fighting a holding action against the Japanese in the Pacific. The global situation was still dire for the Allies but with US troops and equipment pouring into Britain from late January 1942, the chances of invasion rapidly decreased and Allied strategy became more aggressive in debating the best way to open the 'second front' for the liberation of western Europe. With conventional forces greatly improved, the operational wing of the Auxiliary Units began to lose much of its significance in the eyes of GHQ and the main issue became a political battle of survival as it increasingly had to justify its worth as anything beyond a cheap insurance policy against invasion. This tends not to be reflected in the accounts of veterans who, buoyed up by their Intelligence Officers, continued to be ready to fulfil their secret role of 1940 well into 1944.

The first reaction of Auxiliary Units HQ at Coleshill to the diminution of the invasion threat was to keep the men busy. Training was relentless and by April 1942 the organisation was expending 106,000 rounds of ammunition and 3,000 grenades per month.[1] In December 1942 the explosives supply packs were refined as 'Aux Units Mk.II' (Fig. 12) which included 20lb of explosives, the new Pocket Time Incendiary, trip and trap wire, time pencils, L-Delays, and pull and pressure switches. The Pocket Time Incendiary combined a thermite powder (magnesium mixed with metal oxide) and a time pencil-type mechanism. All of these materials could be used to create an array of booby-trap and delay devices serving to keep the men's imagination active. By now, they also had the No.8 Anti-Personnel Switch, limpet mine magnets to attach charges to metal and the 'Autumn Crocus' which was either an Auxiliary Units-specific term referring to 'planting' rows of the No.8 switch or, as used by SOE, a means of encasing the elements of a small charge (explosives, primer, detonator, igniter etc) in a waterproof bag and tying it off so that it resembled a crocus bulb.[2] Incendiary devices were now being phased out but although only the Pocket Time Incendiary was included in the 'Aux Units Mk.II' pack, *Calendar 1938* (1942) included an improved large Magnesium Incendiary (8in long) as well as the SIP grenade, and the *Calendar 1939* (1944) also included the small but crude 'Fire Pot'.

Training Officer Nigel Oxenden was not impressed and eventually complained that the increasing range of devices only encumbered the patrols and 'would never, and could never successfully be used', but instead produced a 'mental fog'. Despite all best efforts, it was difficult to prevent the men from becoming 'stale' and Oxenden came to the uncomfortable conclusion that, after an influx of new recruits, by 1942 the auxiliers knew less about explosives than in 1940.[3] This was not a view with which the veterans were likely to agree but Oxenden's opinion as their training officer cannot be easily dismissed. The Auxiliary Units were no longer a priority for officer staffing and the concept of an irregular guerrilla force was steadily being eroded. Nonetheless, bureaucratic inertia and a skill in playing up the 'too secret to question' approach finally allowed a programme of constructing Operational Bases for the Intelligence Officers and underground IN Stations for Special Duties Branch to be approved in June 1942.

Fig. 12 Contents of 'Aux. Unit Mk II' explosives pack as introduced December 1942. (*TNA WO 199/937*)

24	Copper Tube Igniters
6	Striker Boards
12	Pocket Time Incendiaries
20	1-hour Lead Delays
50	3-hour Lead Delays
50ft	Instantaneous Fuse (Orange Line)
240ft	Cordtex
100	Detonators, Nos 8 or 27
20lb	Explosive (Nobel 808, Polar Gelignite or Plastic
48ft	Safety Fuse, MkII Bickford
20	CE Primers (Two tins of 10 each)
24	Tubes, Fuse, Sealing, in those Aux. Units where the fuse is not packed in tins
1	Crimping Tool
1	Tube Vaseline
1	Spool Trip Wire .032"
3	Spools Trap Wire .014"
8	Coils Tape
1	Sandbag
6	Pull Switches
3	Pressure Switches

In February 1942 Colonel Major left to join the new RAF Regiment, whilst Captain Henderson joined the Directorate of Military Training, leaving only Major Beyts from the original senior management team. The new CO of the Auxiliary Units was Colonel, the Lord, Glanusk, aged 51. He had a distinguished service in the First World War with the Grenadier Guards but retired from the army in 1924, later becoming Lord Lieutenant of Breconshire. Having remained on the Reserve List, on 30 September 1939 Glanusk was appointed to command the training battalion of the Welsh Guards. By 1942 he was in ill health but needed a comfortable promotion to full colonel that would increase his pension before retirement. Well-connected, he was given the post in the Auxiliary Units, clearly indicating the changing attitude of the War Office towards the organisation. Glanusk brought several of his fellow Old-Etonian and Welsh Guards officers onto the staff, including Captains Lord Delamere and Marcus Wickham-Boynton. His driver and batman were also imported from the Welsh Guards. The first question Glanusk asked the then Intelligence Officer for the Scottish Borders, Peter Forbes, was 'Do you have any Gentlemen, Forbes?'.[4] Intelligence Officer Anthony Quayle in Northumberland believed the superior and patronising manner of his new commanding officer interfered with the smooth running of the patrols, and the dislike appears to have been mutual. Glanusk summoned Quayle to tell him that he had formed a 'dim view' of him; Captain Quayle told his commanding officer that he could only reciprocate his feelings; Quayle then started looking for another posting (which eventually led him into SOE).[5]

Reports indicate that the wine cellar improved enormously as the officers' mess at Coleshill became more of a social club and less a hub of clandestine warfare. The traditional military background of Glanusk is reflected in some of the changes he introduced, including parade-ground drill competitions; and during residential courses Wickham-Boynton (Camp Commandant) insisted that the kit of the participating auxiliers had to be laid out in Guards fashion. More positively, Glanusk tried to go back to basics and abandoned the system of patrol groups in favour of the original, more secure, independent patrol action, streamlining the principle of 'hit and run'. The Home Guard Group Commanders now had a purely administrative role which would increase as the number of regular army Intelligence Officers was reduced in 1944. Training Officer Nigel Oxenden was coldly analytical in his appreciation of these changes: 'From now on the patrol was self-contained and would fight alone; from now on the rank and file would not be asked to think.'[6] Oxenden believed that the widening range of booby traps and timers supplied to the patrols had only complicated their options in destroying targets and wanted to simplify their approach to sabotage. Yet their punishing training schedule, week after week and month after month, was for a role that was soon to become redundant.

In his efforts to impose order, Glanusk clarified the lines of responsibility of the Intelligence Officers should the Operational Patrols have to go to ground, which had been vague and left more or less to personal choice, with little direction from Auxiliary Units HQ. The role of the local army Corps was strengthened. A cynical mind might suggest that the Coleshill staff could thereby spend less time on tiresome operational matters about which they increasingly knew very little, especially so after Major Bill Beyts left in August 1942 (to help form SOE Force 136 in Burma). A similar devolution of operational responsibility is also evident in the organisation of the SDB where the Auxiliary Units HQ had little control over the assessment or dissemination of any military intelligence gathered. The small HQ establishment had not kept pace with its expansion in the field and in 1944 it still comprised just ten officers and eighty-seven other ranks, with the main responsibilities being in administration and training.[7] Even prior to the arrival of Lord Glanusk, Norman Field (then Intelligence Officer for Kent) had said that the Operational Patrols were expected to operate more or less independently, with only hints from Coleshill. From May 1942, however, responsibility for the patrols would formally pass from Coleshill to regional corps commanders once they prepared to go into action, giving the corps commanders a clear strategic control over the patrols that had otherwise been lacking except in the original XII Corps area.[8] Ironically, it was only from June 1942, when the Auxiliary Units were moving towards a new role of fighting more openly as reconnaissance patrols for the Home Guard that Operational Bases were built as hidden control centres for the Intelligence Officers. Even so, wireless communication remained an issue; not all Intelligence Officers had links to Divisional or Corps HQ or to the Scout Patrols. Indeed, some wireless sets had been removed from the Intelligence Officers. In May 1942 Beyts had asked for nineteen WS17 sets for the Intelligence Officers and for underground hides to be built for them. Authorisation was finally granted on 1 June for the construction of nineteen underground hides and the HQ of the Intelligence Officer was now structured to act, if necessary, as an additional operational patrol, consisting of Intelligence Officer, clerk, Royal Engineers corporal, two drivers and two or three NCO instructors. But by this time, the WS17 was out of production and the Auxiliary Units were told that they would have to source them locally.[9] Such fundamental weaknesses increased the questioning of the role and efficiency of the Auxiliary Units at Corps level and above. Thus, alongside the final decision to build hidden IN Stations for the SDB (see Chapter 8), it was only in 1942, almost two years after its formation, that the Auxiliary Units system was finally completed.

With the Auxiliary Units more directly subject to local army control, scrutiny intensified over their increasingly unlikely secret anti-invasion role and they had to find a new purpose that still made the most of the skills of the volunteers and avoided the prospect of them being returned to general service. From the early summer of 1942, the Operational Patrols were re-invented as more heavily-armed reconnaissance teams to counter the anticipated threat of German commando and parachute landings (Fig. 13). The Operational Bases were largely redundant in this role but remained useful as hidden weapons stores and discrete rendezvous points. Nonetheless, the new manuals *Calendar 1938*, first produced in 1942, and its final edition as the *Countryman's Diary 1939* (not distributed until June 1944 – Plate 30) were still firmly rooted in their sabotage heritage of 1940–1. Facing the possibility of having to become involved in a firefight – something their earlier training had tried to avoid – the new 9mm Mk II or Mk III Sten gun became the preferred weapon and its mass-production soon allowed it to be issued to a greater percentage of men (Plate 25). Some patrols came to have a 100 per cent issue. The Sten gun had first been issued to the Home Guard in March 1942 but was only later issued to the Auxiliary Units as they already had a full complement of Thompsons and the need was therefore not as urgent.[10] Replacement of the Thompsons was progressive until 1944, with those patrols still armed with the Thompson designated as Type A and those with the new Sten gun as Type B.[11] Now they also had a purpose for the otherwise superfluous long-range P17 rifles with which each patrol had been issued in 1940. In describing this new role, Oxenden displays contemporary cynicism, describing the rumours of raids as 'a gift to IOs' and 'a wonderful tonic for fading enthusiasm in the ranks'. He went on 'Sceptics wondered whether it was ever intended as anything more. The effects, with careful nursing lasted for the next two years.'[12] The anti-raiding role involved acting as scout patrols for the local Home Guard and joint exercises began to be held. Despite the repeated concerns to maintain secrecy and independence from local Home Guard control – the twin elements that assured their survival – the Operational Patrols were steadily coming out of the shadows and secrecy became a tradition rather than a necessity. Frank Soames, who joined East Devon Home Guard in 1942, took part in an exercise against what he described as the 'Special Services Home Guard'. They were 'mainly fit, strong farmers who were trained better than us. In the event of a German invasion they were meant to act like commandos, causing as much havoc as possible.' He added they 'were held a little in awe by the ordinary Home Guard'.[13] This is an acknowledgement that the auxiliers and their task was, at least by 1942, known to the local community. They were now 'accepted as an unsolved puzzle that had long ceased to arouse curiosity'.[14]

Fig. 13 List of Auxiliary Units Operational Patrol weapons, August 1942 (preceding the request for an issue of 1,416 Sten guns on 4 September 1942). (*TNA WO 199/738*)

Revolver, .38 (x7)	40 rounds total
Rifles, .300 (x2)	200 rounds total
Knives, fighting (x7)	
Knobkerries (x3)	
Grenades, Type 36M, 4 sec fuze (x48)	
No.74 S.T. Grenades (Sticky Bombs) (x 3 cases)	
No.76 SIP Grenade (x 2 cases)	
Rifle, .22 with silencer (x 1)	200 rounds
Thompson SMG, .45 (x 1)	1,000 rounds

Although the mysterious and highly-trained Operational Patrols might have engendered awe, in their new role they faced competition from the increasingly well-equipped Home Guard. Gone were the pitchfork days of 1940! Home Guardsmen were now significantly younger and 40 per cent of them were armed with the new Sten gun (Plate 25). Some battalions had even formed their own commando units, trained by regular Commandos. The new mobile columns of the local Home Guard were also equipped with backpack wireless sets meaning they could be more responsive than the Auxiliary Units. The reputation of the Home Guard had been greatly enhanced in many areas as it took over responsibilities for anti-aircraft and coastal artillery, guarding vulnerable points and even bomb disposal work. Such work was exhausting and it is perhaps not surprising that after the war Auxiliary Units veterans, who had not been able to explain their absence from such duties, were keen to stress their level of training and contribution to the war effort, glossing over the diminution of their *raison d'être* of an anti-invasion role.

As the auxiliers began to work more closely with the local Home Guard, it is ironic that it was only now that there was a belated attempt to detach them from local structures. This avoided questioning that might lead to their absorption. In an effort to improve local security, from 1 September 1942 the patrols finally ceased to be held on the strength of the local Home Guard battalion and were administered by regional, rather than local, TAAs. The Home Guard enrolment forms of new recruits were now signed by the Intelligence Officer rather than the battalion commander and were then forwarded directly to the regional TAA without further contact with the local Home Guard organisation. Nonetheless, the Malvern patrols were not taken off battalion strength until November 1942.[15] It was quickly realised that the change had produced an unforeseen problem as the civilian Identity Cards of Home Guard, which were normally stamped with the War Office stamp and name of the issuing local TAA, would now carry the name of a non-local TAA (Inverness, York or Reading) which might excite curiosity. It was therefore suggested on 21 September that the patrols should be administered as one of three 'reserve battalions' by regional TAAs, with their Identity Cards stamped simply with a new, more anonymous, battalion number.[16] Inverness became responsible for 201 Battalion covering Scotland and Northumberland, York managed 202 Battalion for Yorkshire to the Severn-Thames line, and Reading TAA managed 203 Battalion for the Southern and South-East commands.[17] This attempt at discretion was compromised by the issue of shoulder flashes bearing these numbers at the end of 1942. The visual identity of the Auxiliary Units had always caused problems but whereas in 1940 their

Home Guard uniform was generic, from 1941 new Home Guard insignia became very specific to each battalion. In March 1941 the Auxiliary Units had been forbidden to wear the new Home Guard county patches (usually the initials of the county) on their uniforms. This decision was reversed in April 1942 as an attempt to make them blend in.[18] They did not, however, wear the standard numeral patch of the battalion to which they were nominally attached (an order that was repeated twice in October).[19] Their own 201, 202 or 203 numeral patches then became distinctive in the same way that the unofficial Home Guard commando units might wear distinctive coloured lanyards. Finally came the additional distinction of the issue of webbing belts and gaiters. In an age where every small boy had become an expert in identifying unit insignia, the Auxiliary Units patrols were now clearly identifiable as an oddity.[20] This was especially ironic as Intelligence Officer Captain Todd had instructed his HDS/SDB operatives in 1940 on the important intelligence to be gained from recognising German units by their uniform distinctions. One other administrative problem that arose with this new arrangement was that, following the introduction of compulsory service in the Home Guard, new recruits who were enrolled into the Auxiliary Units by the regional TAA might find themselves subsequently summoned for enrolment in the local battalion, which then had to be explained away by the Intelligence Officer. These unplanned administrative changes meant that the Auxiliary Units had become accidentally regularised as an Independent Brigade of the Home Guard, responsible directly to GHQ but managed on its behalf by Auxiliary Units HQ, who became increasingly protective of this independence (and thereby their authority). TAA Regional HQs compiled a detailed national register of members of Auxiliary Units Operational Patrols, including their postal addresses and ID card numbers.[21] This is all in sharp contrast to the explicit policy of SIS to not list the names of its civilian Section VII operatives. Much to the relief of traditionalists, the Auxiliary Units had become a military organisation far from the original guerrilla dreams of Grand or Wilkinson.

In January 1943 the War Office carried out an analysis of the potential future use of the Auxiliary Units.[22] The study decided that the survival of the Auxiliary Units had to be judged against:

a. likelihood of invasion
b. the 'vital area' of invasion risk

The conclusion was that there was no possibility of invasion in 1943 and unlikely thereafter; and that the most vulnerable stretch of coastline was the area between Norfolk and Hampshire. Consequently it was believed that fit officers and men amongst its ranks were best employed elsewhere. Chief among the latter were the now heavily-armed Scout Sections (Fig. 9). At their height there were fifty Scout Sections in the Auxiliary Units with Fleming believing they were the strategic core of the organisation.[23] By September 1942 reductions were already being considered.[24] As compensation, an increase in the number of (cheaper) Home Guard patrols was agreed between Cornwall and The Wash – at the time the most likely area still considered for invasion or raiding.[25] By January 1943, twenty-six Scout Sections remained but this was then cut to just eight. The last were finally withdrawn in late 1943.[26] It was also suggested that eleven of the nineteen Intelligence Officers could be replaced by Home Guard officers. The precedent for this had been set as early as 1941 when in May Geoffrey Woodward, aged 41, was commissioned into the Intelligence Corps from the Home Guard and appointed as an Intelligence Officer in Norfolk. In Herefordshire, Christopher Sandford was a 39-year-old book designer and publisher and in February 1941 was commissioned as a lieutenant in the 1st Herefordshire (Leominster) Home Guard. He became Intelligence Officer for the Auxiliary Units in July and was similarly commissioned into the Intelligence Corps. Sandford continued Todd's tradition of acting as joint IO for both Operational Patrols and SDB in Herefordshire and Worcestershire, and it is possible that he had been another of Todd's HDS 'key men'. In January 1943 it was also thought possible to replace fit Signals and Royal Engineer officers by older or partially unfit officers.[27] The process continued throughout the year. In November 1943 all 'A' medical grade officers and men in the Auxiliary Units had to be listed ready for redeployment. The downgrading of officers extended to the SDB and in late 1943 civilian OUT Station operator Arthur Douglas Ingrams, of the Devon SDB, was commissioned and promoted to become IO for the county. Despite this erosion of their status, many volunteers and the Auxiliary Units HQ still held on to the 'glory days' of their initial anti-invasion role. The War Office may have concluded that the chances of invasion were now remote but Auxiliary Units HQ continued to recruit and train the men for this role as without it there was little justification for their separate existence. In December 1943 Ken Welch persuaded his father (the patrol sergeant) to let him join the Mabe Patrol in Cornwall and explained one of their tasks was to blow up the Penrhyn viaduct, carrying the railway from Falmouth to Truro.[28] Charles Stokes, aged 17 years joined the Temple Cloud patrol in Somerset on 30 June 1944. Edward Hubbard joined Titchfield Patrol in Hampshire on 3 July 1944 while Richard Ellery joined St Columb Patrol in Cornwall even later on 22 July 1944.[29] As late as September 1944 a circular to Somerset Group Commanders has a wholly unrealistic air as it describes the procedure for going out to attack the enemy after invasion 'NO night can be missed' even though this was three months *after* the decision had been taken to disband the Auxiliary Units.[30]

The men on the ground may have been oblivious to the problems increasingly affecting the Auxiliary Units at a strategic level, but they could not fail to see their special status being diminished at a personal level. As a result, both recruitment and morale suffered. During the early threat of invasion, the auxiliers had been protected from conscription and some had even been recalled after their call-up. But exemptions began to be ignored as it was increasingly difficult to keep someone in the Operational Patrols if they were itching for more immediate action. Geoff Devereux, patrol sergeant for Samson Patrol in Worcestershire, was called up and commissioned in the Grenadier Guards in August 1941. Details of resignations back into the Home Guard were also dutifully recorded on Home Guard enrolment forms and posted in Part II Orders. In the main such movement did not seem to cause problems, although when in 1941 one auxilier asked to resign from his Worcestershire patrol because of stress, the Intelligence Officer (the eccentric and ruthless John Todd) told the patrol sergeant, Tony Barling, that he would have to be killed if the invasion occurred. Barling, a medical student, himself left the patrol in December 1942 to join the Parachute Regiment as a medical officer and was captured at Arnhem. In February 1943 the Auxiliary Units' exemption from conscription was finally cancelled with a suggestion that men called up might be kept together in Royal Engineer field companies where their special training might be useful.³¹ A new horror came in June when they were ordered to return their rum rations, held in one gallon SRD jars! In some cases the War Office was too late: in Monmouthshire 'Jonah' Patrol had already extracted the rum through the sealed cork of the jar, using a veterinary hypodermic syringe and replaced the contents with cold tea, leaving no trace. The auxiliers were now in no doubt as to their falling status.

Lord Glanusk resigned his command in August 1943 due to ill health and was succeeded by his second in command, Lieutenant Colonel Frank W.R. Douglas (Plate 13) who came from the Inspectorate of the Royal Artillery, although Lampe (who interviewed him for *The Last Ditch*) claimed he had worked for DMI. Possibly taking Lampe's lead, Warwicker later maintained he had SIS connections. Douglas had been commissioned into the Royal Artillery in 1916 but after the war he became a stockbroker. Having entered the Reserve of Officers in September 1939 he was recalled as a Temporary Captain in the Inspectorate-General for Training. He joined the Auxiliary Units in 1942 probably because of this training background, replacing the expertise of Beyts.

Douglas had the difficult task of steering the Auxiliary Units through 15 months of increasing scepticism from the War Office and regional commands as to the purpose of the organisation; trying to preserve their status and independence, partly by keeping alive the urgency of preparing to resist an invasion. Not all were convinced – the Director of Staff Duties commented in August 1943 'It is doubtful whether there is any justification for the continued existence of this unit whose function is essentially of a defensive nature.'³² Although still supported by the new C-in-C, General Sir Harold Franklyn, the defence was rather desperate, with Franklyn maintaining the Operational Patrols were still useful in a raid as 'fighting patrols to cut off the withdrawal of the enemy' (without explaining how, without wireless, they would receive notification of the movements of the enemy) while, more realistically, the SDB 'are a valuable alternative means of obtaining information concerning the movements of the raiding forces'. He also argued that the return of the Home Guard members to their battalions might then suggest there was no need for the Home Guard as a whole. This was an important consideration as morale was also falling in the overworked Home Guard. At the time Franklyn states the Auxiliary Units had a staff of 62 officers and 410 other ranks 'involved in directing the 4,279 Home Guard and 2,300 civilians in the Unit'.³³ Douglas was not well-liked and did not appear to have too high an opinion of his officers as in July 1944 he personally wrote in a letter (not the sort of letter that one likes to hand to an office typist) that his remaining officers were basically unemployable elsewhere. 'Regarding officers for retention I have not suggested anything of very high grade – either mentally or physically – there are no pocket Napoleons!'³⁴

The anti-raiding role took on a new concern during the preparations for the Normandy landings and this focused minds on the practical relationship of the Auxiliary Units to the Home Guard. The Allies were intending to use the SAS to disrupt lines of communication and supply behind enemy lines and so it seemed logical to suppose that the Germans might have similar tactics in mind to disrupt the build-up and execution of Operation Overlord. Concerns were heightened by the repeated requests in 1944 from German Intelligence to their supposed agents in Britain (actually under the control of MI5) to provide the location of Eisenhower's SHAEF headquarters. On 19 May 1944 Guy Liddell of MI5 noted that the Germans had asked double-agent 'Garbo' for information on the street addresses of various HQ which would be sent to the Brandenburg

Regiment by special priority.³⁵ The Brandenburg Regiment was Hitler's English-speaking special forces unit who were trained to operate in Allied uniform. The obvious suspicion was that they were planning a series of commando raids as a spoiling tactic for D-Day. One response was to send volunteers from the Auxiliary Units to reinforce the already substantial garrison on the Isle of Wight (see below, p.137).

The Home Guard was also reorganising to meet the threat of raids and with the Home Guard and Auxiliary Units working more closely together there was a renewed fear that the patrols might be absorbed as one of the many new Home Guard commando units. On 15 May 1944 a circular letter to Auxiliary Units group commanders in Essex and Suffolk noted that 'it was decided that all patrols will be directly under the responsibility of the Home Guard Battalion Commanders with all patrols given a specific reconnaissance task upon call out, following liaison between group commanders and battalion commanders'. There followed a carefully-worded clarification of the chain of command. After completing their pre-determined task patrols would 'carry out orders that will come indirectly from the Battalion Commander' but it was nonetheless stressed that 'our patrols are in support of and <u>NOT</u> under command of the Home Guard'. Operationally, the Auxiliary Units were now the responsibility of the Home Guard battalion CO – but to protect their sense of independence the Home Guard CO would only relay their orders via the Auxiliary Group Commanders. All honour was satisfied!³⁶ The following is an extract from similar circular orders sent out a few days after D-Day regarding joint anti-raiding working.

1. In the event of Enemy Raids by Seaborne or Airborne troops, one of the operational roles to be fulfilled by troops of 201 (GHQ Reserve) Bn. will be to act as scout patrols and observers.
2. Troops of 201 (GHQ Reserve) Bn. will contact, and maintain contact with the Enemy Forces, and will pass any information they thus acquire to XXX Bn. Home Guard Sub Unit Commanders, who will be responsible for the transmission of such information to their Headquarters.
4. The command of 201 (GHQ Reserve) Bn. is entirely independent of the Home Guard, but close liaison will be maintained between the two Units on "STAND TO", and in any "STATE OF EMERGENCY" which may develop. It must be borne in mind that the Command of 201 (GHQ Reserve) Bn. troops remains under the control of the Regular Military Authorities, and that they will be acting on orders received from the Headquarters of such Authorities.
6. The secrecy regarding the formation of 201 (GHQ Reserve) Bn. H.G. will be maintained at all times, and information regarding their existence will not be divulged.³⁷

For such liaison to work there had to be joint exercises to practise recognition signals and procedures. The emphasis on the patrols not being operationally responsible to the Home Guard, even though their task was to pass their information on to them, reflected the continuing concern to protect the special status of the auxiliers at a time when they were under increasing organisational threat. In practice, because the Intelligence Officers who had the direct responsibility for the patrols were themselves responsible in action to the corps commanders, there was a unified chain of command that encompassed Home Guard, Auxiliary Units Operational Patrols and regular forces. From August 1944 Home Guard Group Commanders increasingly took on a general administrative role for the Auxiliary Units and it was even suggested that, if they survived, the Home Guard should take direct responsibility for the whole organisation.[38] The organisation was coming full circle from Gubbins' original concept of July 1940. A visual confirmation of the close relationship between Auxiliary Units patrols and their local Home Guard at this time is seen in the formal stand-down photograph of Birch and Layer Breton Home Guard in Essex which includes the local Auxiliary Units patrol, distinctive in carrying their revolvers.[39]

As a measure of the increasing confusion of purpose, it was only in April 1942, just prior to their re-tasking as a reconnaissance force, that patrols were officially issued with silenced .22 rifles, ostensibly as sniper weapons. Their issue is discussed here in some detail as it has become a core element in the mythology of the Auxiliary Units.[40] A period 'silencer' (more accurately a 'sound moderator' but the term 'silencer' was used throught the war by the War Office) on a .22 rifle could greatly reduce, if not eliminate, the sound of a bullet but would not affect the sharp click of the cocking action or cycling of the bolt (a significant consideration if shooting from short range in the dead of night). It will also eliminate the muzzle flash, hopefully making it difficult to identify the location of the shooter. The 'silencer' will also significantly reduce recoil, so improving accuracy in repeated shots. Crucially, a 'silencer' cannot hide the 'crack' of a supersonic bullet as it breaks the sound barrier in flight, limiting use to less powerful subsonic rounds.

Neither the War Office or SOE regarded the .22 rifle as a serious combat weapon during the Second World War but in the initial anti-invasion phase of 1940–1, a suppressed .22 calibre rifle could have been conceivably useful to the Auxiliary Units in observation posts against enemy tracker dogs sniffing out their hides or in quietly shooting out perimeter lights of targets prior to an assault. Yet none were issued at this time, even though at least one was issued to the HDS in 1940, in a period when any other type of rifle was scarce (see above, p.64). Some Auxiliary Units patrols acquired one unofficially, but a .22 rifle was not officially issued to the Auxiliary Units until the danger of invasion was rapidly dissipating. Although Nigel Oxenden optimistically identified their intended use as 'at first for the sniping of enemy sentries', he acknowledged that, in the absence of invasion, they were mainly used in shooting 'to fill the larder' and 'In the end they proved their value for competitive training' in the inter-patrol competitions at Coleshill.[41] Bob Millard explained: 'In my two visits to Coleshill [1941] nothing was said about sniping sentries, they were to be dealt with by the F-S knife, the garrotte . . . and a blow to the temple or carotid artery with the rubber truncheon.'[42] The legend of the Auxiliary Units as deadly assassins with .22 calibre rifles was first encouraged by Lampe's *The Last Ditch* in 1968. Assuming they had been issued from 1940, he described the rifles as 'sinister' and mistakenly claimed they had a killing range of up to a mile. In fact, their accurate range was just 100 yards and standard War Office issue .22 ammunition was considered to only have an accuracy of up to 50 yards.[43] If a .22 rifle was used as a sniper rifle to ensure a kill that gave no opportunity for a shouted warning, it was vital to engage the target at as short a range as possible with the best chance being a shot through the eye socket. But the patrols were expected to operate at night, possibly in rainy or windy conditions, against an enemy likely to be wearing a steel helmet and wrapped in a thick greatcoat, who might not be directly facing the shooter. A more useful firearm, although still only at point-blank range, would have been one of the .22 silenced pistols available commercially before the war and widely used by SOE and OSS but there is no evidence this was ever considered. Auxilier Bob Millard was realistic about their chances of success with a .22 calibre rifle.

> Two of us were rifle club members so 100 yds with target sights was standard. Rabbits at 75 yds with a scope was also a familiar shot. However, these were shots taken at leisure and under no stress. We practised in a quarry at about 100 yards and with a scope I could make a head shot in twilight conditions BUT no stress, a still target and a comfortable firing position. A sentry is not going to be standing in the open with the moon behind him.[44]

Their eventual official issue is best seen as one of a number of attempts to buoy up the morale of Auxiliary Units with a widening range of 'toys' rather than the serious issue of a covert weapon. Thousands of .22 rifles had been purchased from the USA as cheap training rifles to reduce the strain on .303 and .300 ammunition, although the War Office did not see them as a priority in the Home Guard and most went to the regular forces. Nevertheless, there may have been a glut of scoped rifles as Winchester had taken the opportunity to offload onto the British government its entire surplus stocks including Winchester/Lyman 2¾x magnification and 5x magnification scopes mounted on Model 67 and Model 69 rifles (Plate 27). The scopes served little purpose on the short training ranges where the rifles were mainly used by the army and Home Guard and the War Office was therefore searching for a use that justified their additional cost. 'Silencers' were, however, added to some of the training rifles as a standard, to reduce the noise in indoor Territorial Army Centre ranges.

Parker-Hale had begun making and selling 'silencers' from the 1920s. On 13 March 1942 they were contracted to fit them, at a cost of £641, to 600 rifles already supplied to the HQ of the Auxiliary Units and subsequently returned to the company for fitting. The contract does not specify the type of rifle and there is also no mention of fitting telescopic sights, implying these were already on the first batch of rifles.[45] Oxenden recorded that the first delivery was for 500, with the remaining 150 to follow. He described them simply as '.22 rifles of various patterns' but they were most likely Winchesters and Remingtons.[46] On 30 April at a patrol leaders meeting, patrols from East Sussex received their .22 calibre rifles with both 'silencers' and telescopic sights.[47] The issue was formally noted for the first time in the War Establishment of June 1942, with each rifle supplied with 200 rounds of ammunition. But some patrols did not receive them until October. Although some auxiliers were told by their leaders that these were 'special high velocity rifles for use by marksmen', this was clearly not the case and the variety of models highlights the absence of any serious intent to assess the range of rifles that were available as a short-range 'sniper' rifle.[48] Oxenden, writing in 1944, bemoaned that telescopic sights were included:

> The first of 500, began to arrive, but long before delivery was complete, the telescope was found to be a mistake, adding little to accuracy even when carefully zeroed, and being so easily shifted by handling that ranging shots

were always necessary. However, it was too late to stop the issue, and many rifles had no backsights, the telescopes having been fitted in their place.[49]

This implies that subsequent rifles were supplied without telescopic sights and the War Establishment equipment lists for the Auxiliary Units from May 1942 onwards simply specify a .22 calibre rifle with a 'silencer'.[50] In the 1943 patrol competitions at Coleshill, the men were tested (as in the army and Home Guard) only at ranges of 20 yards and on open sights.[51]

Among the miscellany of rifles, the most common was probably the bolt action Winchester Model 69 – the only model that was specifically documented in the official record (Plate 27).[52] Ever conscious of cost, these were half the price of accurate competition rifles.[53] Only 769 factory-scoped Model 69 rifles had been produced for commercial sale by the start of the Second World War. They had proved unpopular and were dropped from public sale in 1941 – which should have served as a warning to the War Office – but all those supplied to the British government by the enterprising Winchester came with scope bases and some with factory-fitted scopes.

One model that has acquired a particular mythology is a suppressed Winchester Model 74 semi-automatic rifle fitted with an impressive-looking No.42 telescopic sight. This derives from an illustration taken from H. Keith Melton's 1991 *OSS Special Weapons and Equipment* showing such a rifle in the style of a page from the 1944 OSS manual but also stating 'Issued by SOE'.[54] Although clearly acknowledged in the text as an artistic fabrication, the illustration soon spread across the internet as being from a genuine wartime manual. The original source of this attribution has not been verified and no evidence of its use by SOE has been confirmed. By the time of Melton's *The Ultimate Spy Book* in 1996, any reference to a SOE connection of the Winchester Model 74 had disappeared and it was now attributed to the Auxiliary Units. The assumption soon began to grow that the Winchester Model 74 must have been the standard .22 calibre sniper rifle of the Auxiliary Units.[55] Yet despite the attention it has received, it is referenced in less than a dozen patrols (and an even smaller number refer to the No.42 scope). A bolt-action rifle is still preferred as a sniper rifle over a semi-automatic but the Winchester 74 did have some features that might have made it attractive by using up stocks of a rifle that had little value elsewhere as a training rifle for bolt-action service rifles. As a semi-automatic rifle it was fed by a 14-round magazine, which it could empty in around five seconds' rapid fire. The initial sound of cocking the enclosed bolt of the Winchester 74 is far quieter than an equivalent bolt-action rifle, although when fired its blowback action makes more noise from the gas that is released at the breech.[56] Most significantly, its use with a 'silencer' might improve the lethal accuracy of a 'double tap' with a .22 round by reducing recoil between shots. The most detailed description of a Model 74 with a No.42 scope in Auxiliary Units service has come from Bob Millard. He joined the Bathampton patrol after September 1940 but left to join the Fleet Air Arm in September 1942, just five months after the issue of .22 rifles. There are discrepancies in his initial identification of the patrol .22 rifle as a Winchester Model 74, describing it as a 'five-shot', rather than noting its very distinctive 14-round tubular magazine in the butt. Nonetheless he later maintained 'we had a Winchester 74 which is a semi-automatic so two or three quick chest shots was a possibility'.[57] Any pairing of the Winchester Model 74 with the No.42 scope was, nevertheless, distinctly 'bodged up' in comparison with other innovative efforts in developing silenced weapons during the Second World War.

The No.42 scope was a simplified version of the standard x3 power No.32 sniper scope but its only documented active service use is with the co-axial BESA machine gun in the Mk VII and Mk VIII Churchill tanks, first used in 1944.[58] Here their task was not to achieve pinpoint accuracy but merely a guide to laying down a beaten zone of fire. Some No.42 scopes were experimentally used in failed 1944 trials as a potential alternative to the No.32 scope on the No.4(T) sniper rifle and, Millard's unique memory of a 1942 issue aside, this may have been the wider context for a small number finding their way to the Auxiliary Units. There was no provision for internal lateral or vertical adjustment on the No.42 scope but it had been hoped its sealed tube might avoid the problem of fogging in humid, jungle, conditions. It could only be made to work as a functional sniper scope on the No.4 rifle by using a specially-designed bracket that allowed fine adjustment for range and deflection.[59] The experiment was abandoned and no such mount was designed for use with a .22 rifle. Instead, the Parker-Hale mounts found on the surviving Winchester Model 74/No.42 scope combinations only allow a limited compensation for windage and lack the graduated 'clicks' that allow for accurate adjustment by a sniper. When attached to a Winchester 74 there is a noticeable parallax in the sight at 20m, hindering accuracy at the distance at which the Auxiliary Units trained in competition, although this is less of a problem at 50m, which is considered to be the 'sweet spot' of accuracy for the Model 74, albeit just beyond the reported accurate range of War Office .22 ammunition.[60] Immediately after the war, Parker-Hale took advantage of a surplus of the No.42 (and similar No.53) scopes and opportunistically marketed them as a telescopic sight for rifles along with their own mounts, which they admitted had only limited functionality. As Parker-Hale subsequently had War Office contracts for refurbishing and selling on to the public surplus .22 rifles this adds the complication that some supposed wartime Model 74 rifles fitted with No.42 scopes may actually be of post-war assembly.

Another 'toy' that was issued to some auxiliers in this period was the new SOE circular tyre slasher knife ('knife, pocket, circular'), produced from May 1942. This was provided to some Kent patrols but it is not, however, clear how many actually reached the Auxiliary Units as only 1,200 were produced in total.[61] The last weapon to be issued to the Auxiliary Units was the No.77 grenade (Plate 28). It was a more stable and compact alternative to the 1940 SIP grenade but was primarily a smoke grenade. It consisted of 8oz of white phosphorous in a compact metal container and was primarily designed to produce an instantaneous, but short duration, smoke screen. It did, however, also have a burning anti-personnel effect. The No.77 grenade came into general service from mid 1943 (although prototypes were used by No.4 Commando at Dieppe in August 1942). On 3 November 1943 the Auxiliary Units placed an order for 50,000 of the grenade, exceeding their issue recommendation by 2,500 per cent. At a time when they were coming under increasing pressure to justify their existence, this was an indicator of the continuing self-belief of the Auxiliary Units HQ. There then followed a bitter correspondence with the War Office (see below, p.136). They finally received 2,000 No.77 grenades for training purposes in mid-December but the rest only finally began to be distributed from 4 February 1944. Although they had won this particular battle, it may have played a part in their final downfall amidst rising criticism of other demands in the War Office, which together stimulated questions over their continued relevance.

In 1944, Nigel Oxenden, when compiling his history of the Auxiliary Units, included recommendations for any future re-embodiment of an Auxiliary Units-type organisation tasked with night-time sabotage operations. He suggested that the suppressed Welrod might be the only firearm that organisations such as the Auxiliary Units might need. He otherwise maintained 'There are strong arguments against the carrying of firearms on night operations (together with the recently-arrived No.77 grenade). One shot could betray the presence of the patrol and turn the attack into a headlong rout.'[62] The Welrod (Plate 22) was a .32 calibre bolt-action silenced pistol that had been invented as part of a joint project by SOE and the War Office to improve the options for an issue of silenced weapons to special forces. It entered service with SOE in 1943 and continued to be used by the SAS into the 1980s. The Welrod was a close-range weapon, with the advice being to place the muzzle against the target to ensure a silent kill (the expanding propellant gas might then cause more damage than the actual bullet). There is no evidence that it was ever actually issued to the Auxiliary Units, although a possible evaluation by the Scout Sections has been suggested. If a silenced pistol was the priority that Oxenden implies, it begs the question why the Welrod or one of the commercially-available suppressed Colt Woodman or the SOE Hi Standard Model B 'silenced' pistols, or even the silenced 9mm Sten gun, had not been distributed earlier. By 1944, realistically, the chance of them being used in action had passed.

Oxenden summarised the changes of fortunes in the organisation as:

- 1940 'a blaze of wild priority'
- 1941–2 a phase of organised power 'guarded by a security that nobody could get past, however much they might resent it'
- 1943–4 'a realisation that the soundest attitude was unobtrusiveness' in the hope that senior officers might forget their existence.[63]

Reflecting his cynicism, Operational Branch Intelligence Officers increasingly sought a low profile in the regions and kept away from contact with division or corps HQs in order to avoid hostile questioning on their activities and purpose. The Coleshill HQ could not so easily avoid its critics in the War Office and their case was not helped by trying to maintain their priority status over supplies. On 27 August 1943 a quartermaster complained 'I am sorry to worry you with these but they are both typical of the type of thing we get from Auxiliary Units'. One complaint was an objection to the requests for increased supplies of morphine! Another was that curse of bureaucracy – travelling expenses:

> I see no reason why Auxiliary Units should have preferential treatment. I have in the past been told more than once that their duties are so secret that their officers must go by car and not by rail. 800 miles a week does, however, seem excessive and I suggest we take this up with G/Ops, whose protegees they were in the old GHQ.[64]

On 15 September the Quartermaster's Branch (Q Branch) of the War Office probed deeper. While accepting that 'In view of the special nature of these units the purpose for which the stores are required is not revealed when the demand is made', it now sought confirmation that the Auxiliary Units were indeed essential for Home Defence and asked for details of the War Office branch where further information could be obtained.[65] On the next day, Q Branch expressed some relief that the Auxiliary Units had 'endeavoured to come down to earth and reduce their demands'.[66] Coleshill remained unperturbed. On 2 October 1943 there were complaints from GHQ that, whilst the allotment of booby-trap wire for an infantry battalion was 25yds/six months, the Auxiliary Units had requested 364,000yds/six months. GHQ commented 'This demand is quite out of proportion'.[67] In early November 1943 the Auxiliary Units were told they could only have 2,000 of the No.77 grenade for training. Undaunted they persisted with the request for 50,000 for operational needs and were told they could have them only whenever such quantities were available and there was an actual operational need. Coleshill simply repeated the request. By 10 January the dispute had reached the Director of Infantry who finally agreed that 2,000 No.77 grenades would be provided for training with a compromise over the request for 50,000 for operational needs to be made available 'over a short period and not for immediate issue'.[68] Major Hancock repeated the request for the delivery of the 50,000 on 29 January. An unhappy Q Branch still tried delaying tactics and on 31 January referred the mechanism of distribution to the Under Secretary of State.[69] On 4 February arrangements were finally made to supply 49,998 to the Auxiliary Units via the Regional Commands.[70] Meanwhile, two days earlier, the Auxiliary Units had to be firmly told that they did not have priority over field army units for .38 ammunition.[71] They were not making any new friends in the War Office and pressure for their disbandment intensified, even as some patrols were being deployed to the Isle of Wight in their first active service deployment. On 25 April the War Office wrote to GHQ Home Forces that 'There is a very strong feeling in high places in the War Office that the time must be approaching (if it has not already arrived) when Auxiliary Units will have ceased to justify their continued existence'.[72]

Despite such doubts, training courses continued to be held at Coleshill until May 1944. Many patrols were then at half strength although active recruitment continued well into June 1944. It was only around this time that the *Countryman's Diary 1939* was produced as the final Auxiliary Units training manual. By this stage it had almost a souvenir value, produced to a higher quality than earlier versions, and could afford to include some wry humour around the location of their HQ announcing on the cover '**Highworth Fertilisers** do their stuff unseen until you see **Results!**' and 'You will find the name Highworth whenever quick results are required' (bold text in original). It would not have taken much research to tie the sabotage manual into the village of Highworth and the mysterious base at Coleshill House, not least because a district meeting of the Radio Society of Great Britain was publicly advertised at around the same time by 'Cpl Bartholomew, Aux Units Signals, c/o GPO, Highworth, Swindon'! John Hartwright of Worcester was enrolled into Joshua Patrol on 27 May 1944; John Thomas from Crowle was enrolled even later on 12 June 1944. Such men were unaware that on 27 May the Director of Staff Duties at the War Office, whilst fully appreciating the 'keenness in training for their special role', had required the withdrawal by 30 June of all regular army personnel from the Auxiliary Units and for the latter to be reorganised on 'a purely Home Guard basis' or face complete disbandment.⁷³ Douglas was summoned to the War Office on 5 June, even as the D-Day invasion was preparing to get underway, to discuss the two options. By then, Douglas stated there were 'rather more than 640 patrols' comprising approximately 4,200 Home Guards of whom 4,000 had attended courses. There were also 'well above 200 R/T stations with over 3,250 civilians in SDB' (see Chapter 9). In an explicit contradiction of the post-war claims that the auxiliers were considered civilian saboteurs, Douglas pointed out 'For nearly four years auxiliers, who were hand-picked men, have had rubbed into them that they were part of the regular army and GHQ troops' expected to give two or three times the amount of training than did the rest of the Home Guard.⁷⁴

Ironically, it was at this low point that the patrols were mobilised ready for active service. During May and June 1940, some men who answered a vague appeal for volunteers to serve 'overseas' were sent to assist army guards on the Isle of Wight, at a time when all spare military capacity was needed to train for the D-Day campaign. The first inkling of the operational deployment came when on 22 April 1944 the War Office circulated a memo to the TAAs, advising them that they may receive some travel and subsistence claims from 'certain Home Guard units'!⁷⁵ The risks of enemy commando raids on the Isle of Wight had been recognised from the start of the war and by 1944 there was a garrison of over 17,000 men, a squadron of tanks, plus two Home Guard Battalions and sixteen Auxiliary Units patrols. The Auxiliary Units detachments sent to the Isle of Wight were under the command of Major Malcolm Hancock, who had served in the First World War at Gallipoli, where he won an MC. Demobilised in 1918, he established a successful career as a horse racing judge. After brief service with the LDV, on 30 June 1940 he was re-commissioned into the Coldstream Guards and later served in the Coats Mission, which was to provide protection for the Royal Family in case of evacuation to the West Midlands. He then commanded a Company in a holding battalion of the Coldstream Guards. After becoming a Staff Officer at GHQ in August 1943 he joined the Auxiliary Units in November as Deputy Assistant Quartermaster General, continuing the intake of Guards officers began by Lord Glanusk.

Without knowing their destination, volunteers including those from Scotland, Northumberland, Durham, Yorkshire, Norfolk, Suffolk, Herefordshire and Worcestershire, with several of their Group Commanders, found themselves loaded onto trains and army lorries to serve for periods of ten days to a month in relays during May to the end of June 1944. The auxiliers were to supplement the existing garrison over the invasion period, providing night-time patrols around a number of key installations needed for the success of D-Day including pumping stations for the PLUTO pipeline, a secret communications centre, radar station, airfield and munitions supply dumps as well as the defences on the Needles and Spithead approaches. Some Norfolk auxiliers were armed only with pickaxe handles.⁷⁶ Others were instructed to bring their Sten guns – but no ammunition. This rolling deployment was only a minor part of the overall defence effort but was a much-needed boost to the morale and reputation of the Auxiliary Units. Typically the patrols were used to relieve regular troops on night-time duty but at Freshwater the considerable Auxiliary Units presence from Herefordshire, Norfolk, Durham and Yorkshire patrolled a stretch of the coastal path day and night. Patrols from Norfolk arrived at Sandown approximately three weeks before the D-Day invasion to relieve regular troops guarding the pumping stations at Sandown and Shanklin, the 620,000-gallon Shanklin fuel tank and a nearby airfield.[77] They were accommodated in the Sandringham Hotel and, in a holiday atmosphere, whilst off-duty enjoyed walks along the cliffs and visits to the cinema to see *Nancy Drew Detective*, *Northern Pursuit* and the newly-released *Angels Sing*.[78] It was probably a disappointment to be relieved by Northumberland patrols who arrived just before D-Day and remained for a week following. Another building the auxiliers guarded was ostensibly a hospital, identified by Red Cross symbols, but was, in fact, a secret communication centre relaying vital information from Normandy. One Suffolk patrol was also tasked with guarding the radar station at Bembridge. The deployment to the Isle of Wight may have been intended as a final attempt to prove the worth of the Auxiliary Units; it certainly provided a 'battle honour' for men who, frustratingly, had been obliged to maintain their secret role and training but increasingly seemed to be on the sidelines of the war.

A postscript to the Isle of Wight deployment came when the northern Auxiliary Units provided a last-minute supplement to the guard of Balmoral Castle during a royal visit, to help thwart any possible German kidnap attempt. Almost inevitably, this has spawned the myth that the Auxiliary Units provided the royal bodyguard. The threat of an airborne raid on Balmoral, surrounded by the rugged and isolated landscape of the Cairngorms, was taken very seriously throughout the war and the usual guard during a royal visit consisted of a close-protection team from Special Branch, an armoured unit of the Household Cavalry, an infantry battalion and a light anti-aircraft troop. The armoured unit and one infantry company were quartered in the Balmoral Stables, with the rest of the battalion at Abergeldie Castle (2.5 miles away) and Braemar (9 miles away). Until 1944, a further infantry battalion was held in reserve at Aberdeen. Further Special Branch officers in the neighbouring village also kept a discrete watch for strangers in the area.[79] Air cover was provided by a fighter squadron deployed to the area. This was clearly no mean logistical exercise. The Royal Family were due to visit Balmoral from 11 August to late September 1944 (the Queen actually extended her stay until 16 October) but the requirements of the Normandy campaign led to a shortage of available troops for the normal guard. It was only on 18 July that it was agreed that the three-quarter strength 5th Manchester Regiment would provide the infantry component. The C-in-C Home Forces, no doubt spurred by the success of the Isle of Wight deployment then wrote to General Thorne, GOC Scottish Command, suggesting that the Auxiliary Units could help make up the shortfall.

Thorne met Colonel Douglas, the current CO of the Auxiliary Units, at the Balmoral estate on 27 July and agreed the deployment with only days before the arrival of the advance party on 6 August.[80] At extremely short notice, volunteers from several Auxiliary Units patrols from Scotland and Northumberland served in shifts to supplement the Manchester Regiment's guard of the Castle grounds. Lambert Carmichael was Group Commander of the North Northumberland Auxiliary Units and served on two occasions at Balmoral. As a farmer he did not have to justify his absence but it must have been more difficult for the miners in the contingent, without revealing their role in the Auxiliary Units. Robert Hall, a 42-year-old First World War veteran and now a bank manager, recalled taking a 12-man contingent from Bedlington. Their role was to maintain a covert guard in the grounds around the Castle to identify and intercept any intruders, but they were ordered to stay out of the way of the Royal Family, leaving

1. Sir Stewart Menzies (1890–1968). Chief of the Secret Intelligence Service 1939–52. He left much of the day-to-day operations of SIS to Dansey. *(Walter Stoneman, 1953 © National Portrait Gallery, London)*

2. Sir Claude Dansey (1876–1947). Assistant Chief of SIS during the Second World War. The strategy of SIS secret operations in Britain bear his hallmark. *(Elliott and Fry, 1947 © National Portrait Gallery, London)*

3. Laurence Grand (1898–1975). Head of sabotage section of SIS, 1938–40. Creator of the Home Defence Scheme and a major influence on the development of later irregular warfare. *(Courtesy of Lady Bessborough)*

4. Walter Samuel, 2nd Viscount Bearsted (1882–1948). SIS officer who managed the transfer of the Home Defence Scheme into the Auxiliary Units. *(Walter Stoneman, 1942 © National Portrait Gallery, London)*

5. Jo Holland (1897–1956). Head of MI(R) at the War Office. MI(R) worked with Section D, SIS but favoured the use of military special forces rather than civilian guerrillas. *(Courtesy of Elizabeth Holland)*

6. Dr Arthur Straton (1884–1943). GP, Surgeon, and Fire Guard in Newport, Isle of Wight. He was also secretly a wireless operator for a Section VII resistance cell. Killed during an air raid in April 1943 when described by MI5 as 'one of DB's people'. *(Courtesy of John Farthing)*

7. Peter Fleming (1907–71). Pre-war writer and adventurer. Tasked with investigating the potential of the LDV in guerrilla warfare in May 1940 and leader of the XII Corps Observation Unit. *(Photograph by Howard Coster, 1935 © National Portrait Gallery, London)*

8. General Andrew Thorne (1885–1970). Creator of the XII Corps Observation Unit *(Schroeder archive, Troendelag Folk Museum, Norway)*

9. 'Spuggy' Newton of SIS fitting a wireless set into a car. Newton installed wireless sets for the XII Corps Observation Unit. *(Courtesy of Geoffrey Pidgeon)*

10. Sir Colin Gubbins (1896–1976). First CO of the Auxiliary Units and later head of SOE. *(Walter Stoneman, 1944 © National Portrait Gallery, London)*

11. Colonel 'Bill' Major (1893–1977). CO of Auxiliary Units November 1940–February 1942. Formerly of the Directorate of Military Intelligence, his priority may have been in developing the Special Duties Branch. *(Photograph by A.P. Holmes, 1942; courtesy of Mick Wilks)*

12. Maurice Petherick (1894–1985). Conservative MP and SIS officer. He was one of the architects of the reformed Special Duties Branch in 1941. *(Photograph by A.P. Holmes, 1942; courtesy of Mick Wilks)*

13. Colonel Frank Douglas, last CO of the Auxiliary Units, 1943-4. *(Courtesy of Mick Wilks)*.

14. John Todd (1899–1980). SIS regional officer who was attached to the Auxiliary Units as a joint Operational and Special Duties Intelligence Officer for South Wales and the Midlands. Later head of SOE operations in SE Africa. *(Photograph by A.P. Holmes, 1941, courtesy of Mick Wilks)*

15. David Boyle (1883–1970). Lifelong intelligence officer, head of the top secret SIS Section VII network in Britain during the Second World War. From a painting by Don Pottinger. *(Courtesy of Piers Pottinger)*

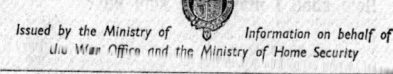

16. *Stay Where You Are* leaflet, July 1940. This advised civilians not to get involved in combat.

17. A fundamental distinction was made in 1940 between the civilian '*francs-tireurs*' of SIS who wore no recognisable uniform or badge and military guerrilla forces who were easily recognisable as combatants. The latter included the Home Guard members of the Auxiliary Units, whose Signals staff wore the circular GHQ shoulder badge, the 'battle patrols' of XII Corps Observation Unit and the reconnaissance patrols of 'Phantom'. *(© Malcolm Atkin)*

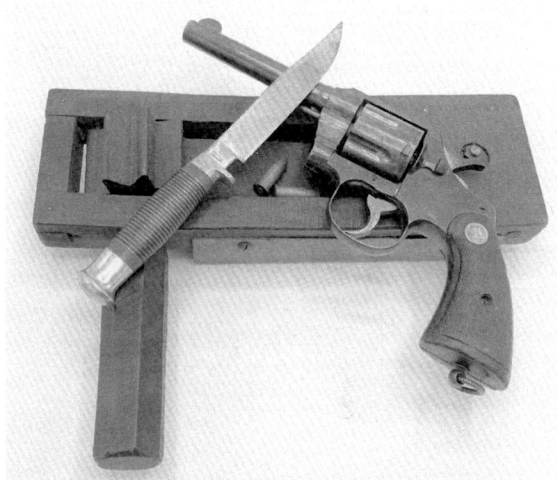

18. Personal weapons of the Home Defence Scheme (HDS) comprised an unattributable Colt.38 revolver supplied by SIS (and as later issued to the Auxiliary Units) and a commercial William Rodgers sheath knife. Cells were also supplied with a gas rattle to serve as a 'distraction weapon' – simulating a machine gun! *(© Malcolm Atkin)*

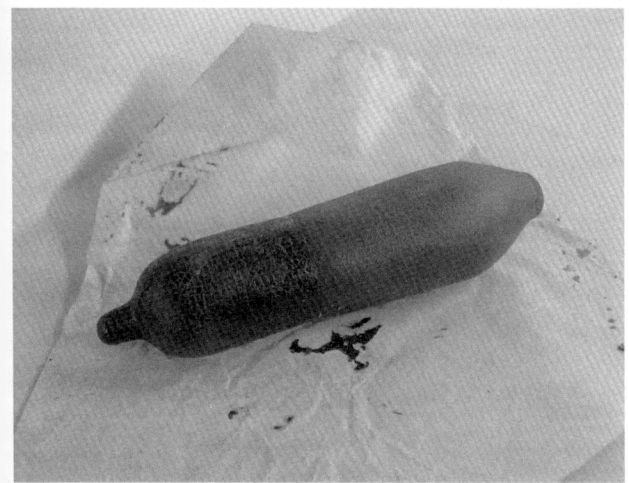

19. Tyesule paraffin incendiary, 5in long, as used by HDS and the Auxiliary Units. *(Courtesy of David Sampson)*

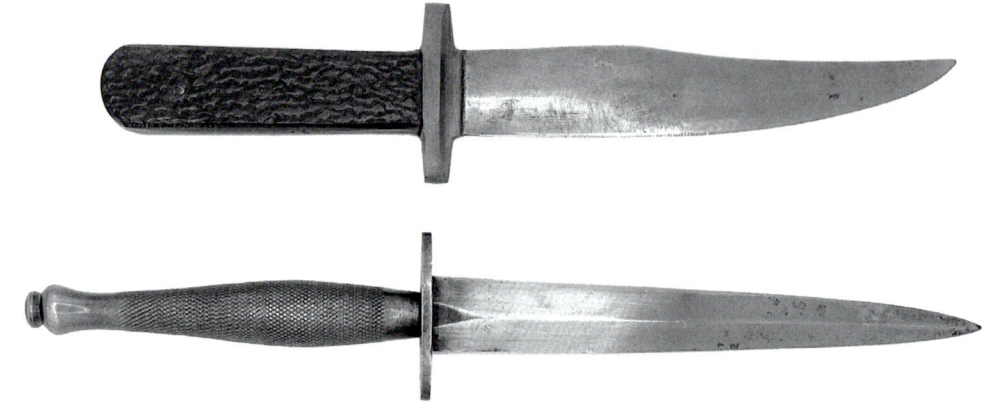

20. Rodgers sheath knife (top) and Second Pattern Fairbairn-Sykes fighting knife (bottom) as used by Auxiliary Units. *(© Malcolm Atkin)*

21. Colt.32 semi-automatic pistol and Smith and Wesson Model 10 revolver. The first 400 pistols issued to the Auxiliary Units were Colt automatics. Some weapons of this type had been bought by the War Office during the First World War. The majority were Smith and Wesson or Colt.38 revolvers, some still in surplus US police holsters.
(© Malcolm Atkin)

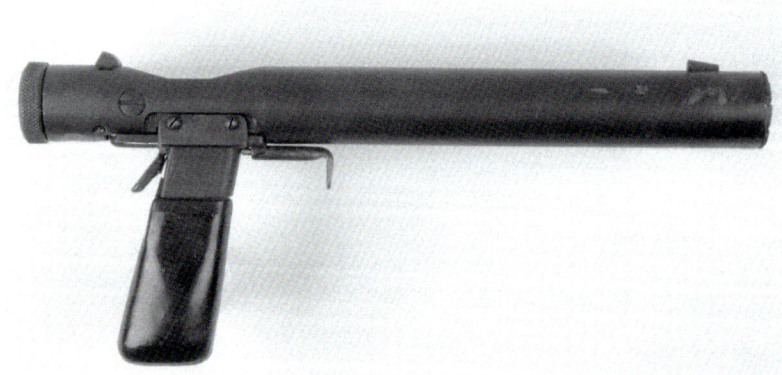

22. Welrod bolt-action silenced pistol with eight-round magazine .32 Calibre. Range point-blank to c.23m. Requires a two-handed grip to control properly. Proposed in 1944 as the only firearm an auxilier should carry, but never issued. *(© Imperial War Museums: FIR 2979)*

23. M1918 Browning Automatic Rifle (BAR), 7.27kg, .30–06 calibre. Effective range up to 1,500yds (1,370m); weight 7.27kg (15.98lb). Too cumbersome for patrol work but the earliest automatic weapon supplied to the Auxiliary Units *(© Royal Armouries: PR.5306)*

24. Thompson M1928A1 sub-machine gun .45ACP calibre. Effective range 55yds (50m); weight 4.9kg (10.8lb). This example has a simplified rear sight. Although most Thompsons were replaced in the Auxiliary Units by Sten guns during 1942, some remained in use until October 1943. The impressive-looking drum magazines contained 50 rounds but were heavy, rattled and took a long time to reload. The stick magazines containing 20 rounds were usually preferred. *(© Kate Atkin)*

25. Mk II (bottom) and Mk III (top) Sten guns, 9mm calibre. Effective range 110yds (100m); weight 3.2kg (7.1lb). Began to be issued to the Auxiliary Units in September 1942. The main virtue of the Sten gun was that it was cheap to manufacture but it had a poor reputation for reliability. It was well designed for clandestine warfare as the horizontal magazine (32 rounds) allowed it to be easily fired from the prone position. *(© Kate Atkin)*

26. Type D Mk V field telephone. Used to connect an Observation Post of the Auxiliary Units to the Operational base, allowing warnings to be given of any approaching enemy, either by the telephone or by simply tapping the morse key. *(© Malcolm Atkin)*

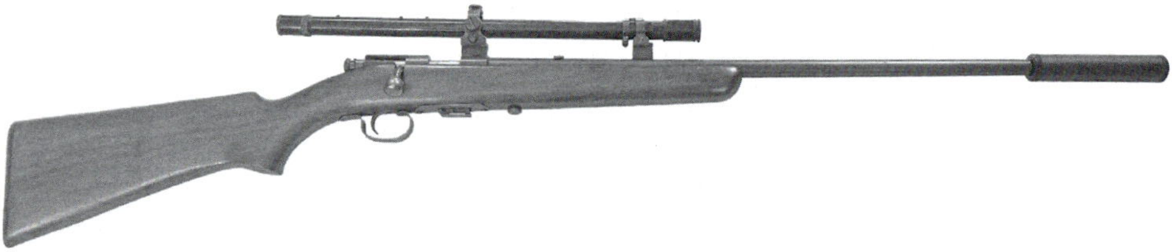

27. From April 1942 the Auxiliary Units were issued with a variety of .22 rifles, with 'silencers' and telescopic sights (although the latter were considered unnecessary). A morale-booster, they were mainly used to protect Observation Posts from sniffer dogs or simply for 'shooting for the pot'. The only documented rifle was the Winchester Model 69. As illustrated here with x5 power scope. *(© Jeff Abendshien)*

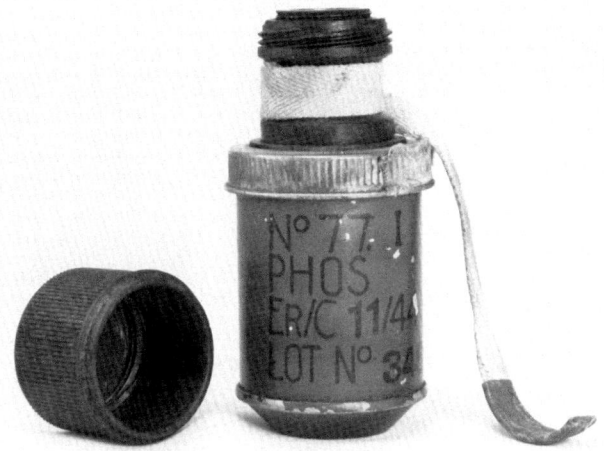

28. Type 77 phosphorous grenade. The request for 50,000 of these grenades in late 1943 over-stretched the patience of the War Office in dealing with the Auxiliary Units. Oxenden believed the 1944 Operational Patrols would only need these and the Welrod as personal weapons. *(© Kate Atkin)*

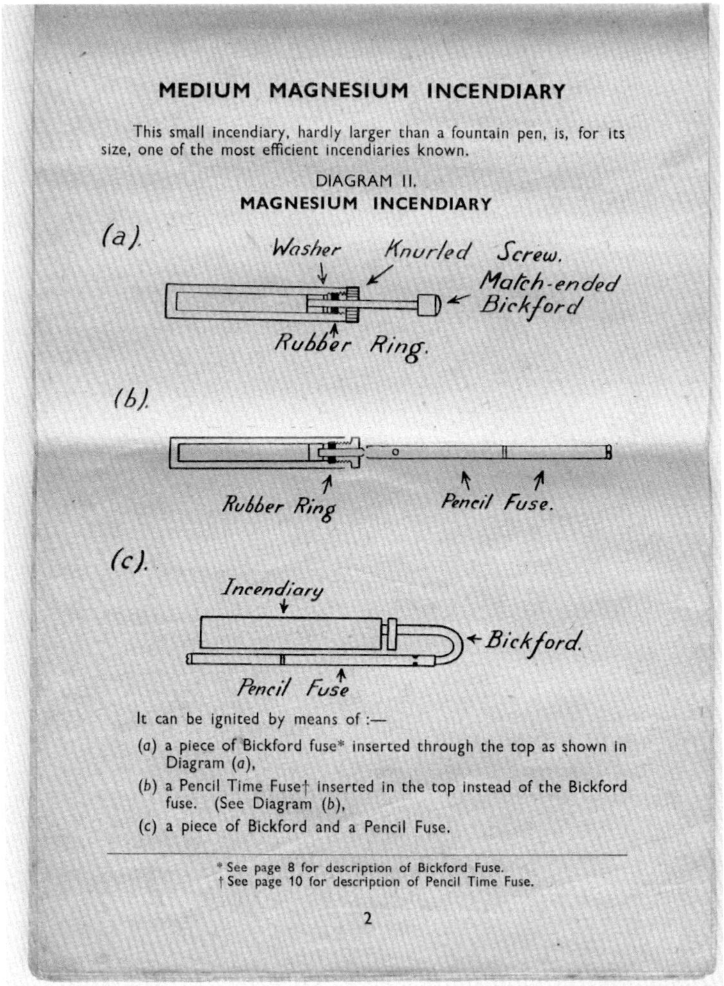

MEDIUM MAGNESIUM INCENDIARY

This small incendiary, hardly larger than a fountain pen, is, for its size, one of the most efficient incendiaries known.

DIAGRAM II.
MAGNESIUM INCENDIARY

It can be ignited by means of :—

(*a*) a piece of Bickford fuse* inserted through the top as shown in Diagram (*a*),

(*b*) a Pencil Time Fuse† inserted in the top instead of the Bickford fuse. (See Diagram (*b*),

(*c*) a piece of Bickford and a Pencil Fuse.

* See page 8 for description of Bickford Fuse.
† See page 10 for description of Pencil Time Fuse.

2

29. Page from *Calendar 1937* training manual for the Auxiliary Units. *(BRO Museum collection)*

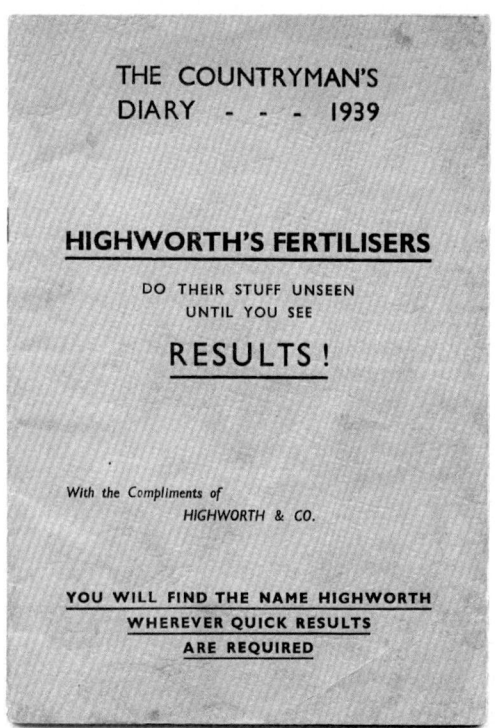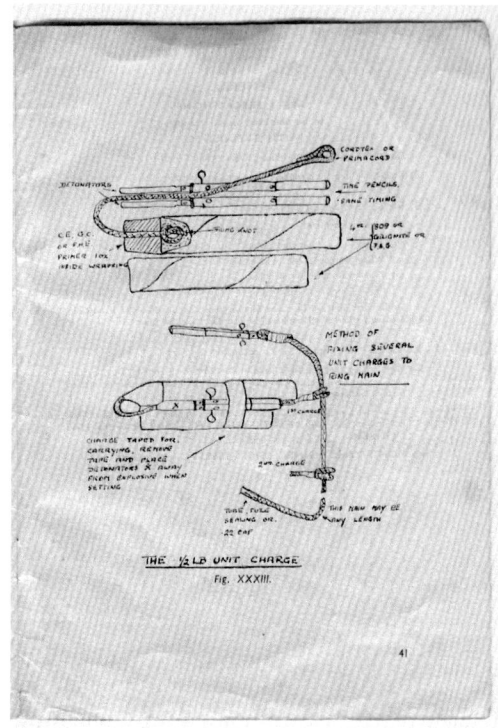

30 and 31. Auxiliary Units training manual *Countryman's Diary 1939* (June 1944). Instructions for making up a half-pound unit charge, from *Countryman's Diary*. *(BRO Museum collection)*

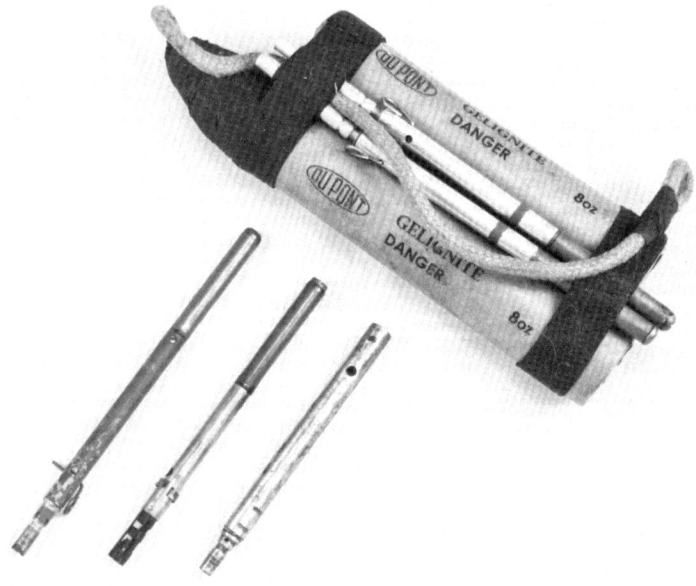

32. Time Pencils, early and late with L Delay. Shown with replica 1lb unit charge of gelignite primed with plastic explosive. *(© Kate Atkin)*

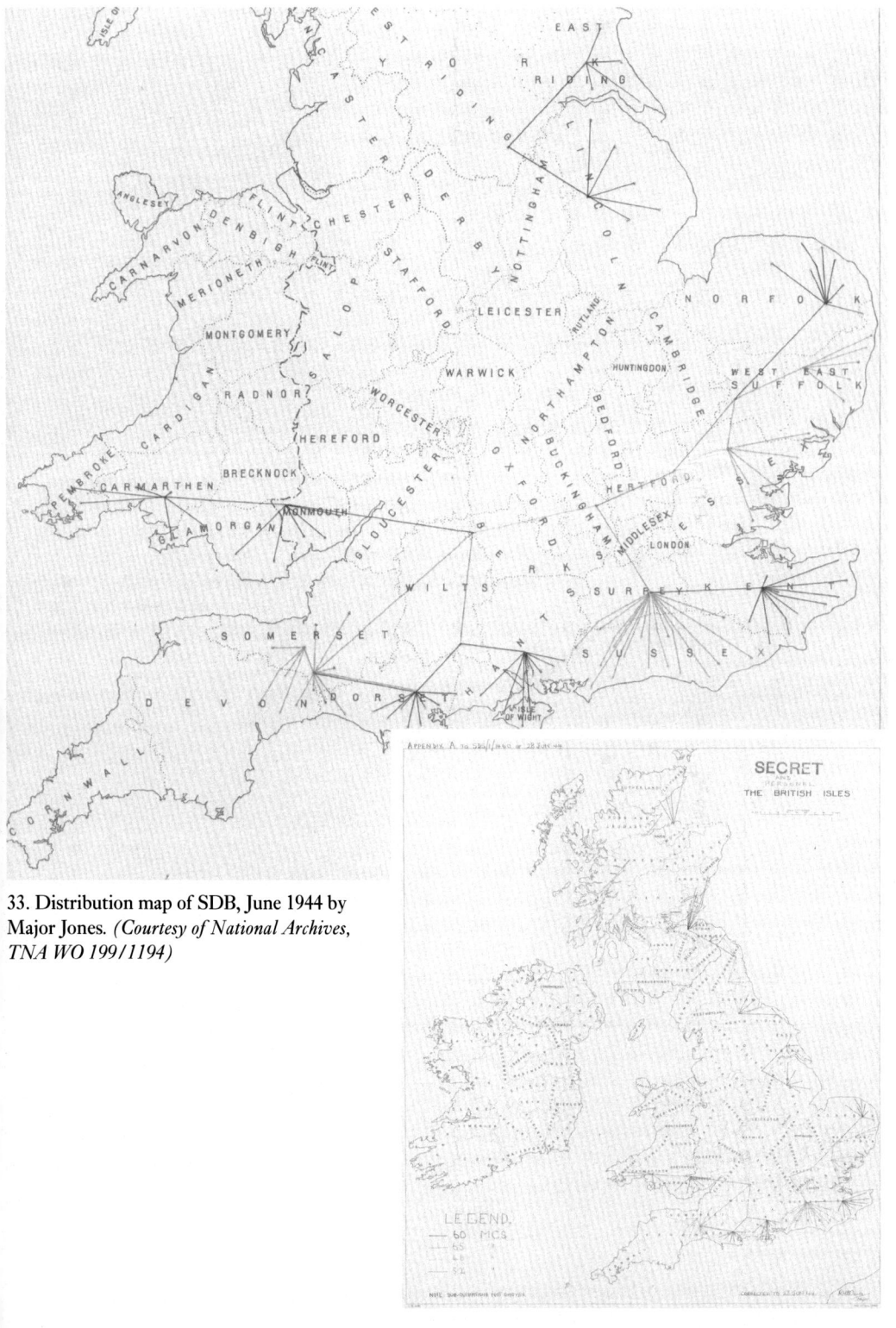

33. Distribution map of SDB, June 1944 by Major Jones. *(Courtesy of National Archives, TNA WO 199/1194)*

34. Murphy B81 portable battery-powered wireless (1939). This became a standard issue to the military, including the SDB, to receive the BEETLE emergency broadcasts.
(© Susanne Atkin)

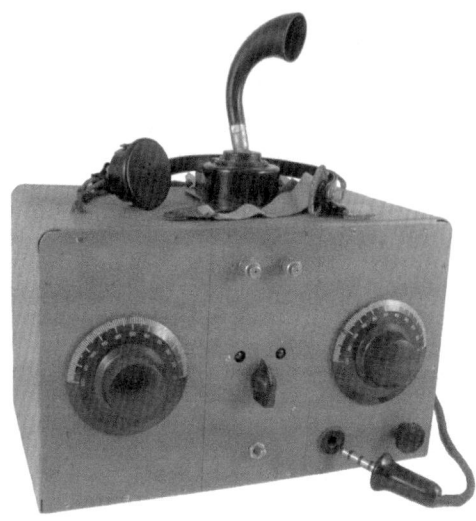

35. TRD wireless set of the Special Duties Branch, Auxiliary Units 1941–4. Designed to be easily maintained and to be used with minimal training, the controls for the IN Station sets consisted of an On/Off switch, Send/Receive switch, Receiver and Transmitter Tuning dials and Volume. This replica by Malcolm Atkin is based on contemporary accounts and research undertaken by Richard Hankins and the VMARS Witney Project.
(© Susanne Atkin)

36. WS17 Mk II wireless set as used by Auxiliary Units (Special Duties Branch). It was invented by Stanley Lewer in early 1939 for the control of balloon barrages. The WS17 Mk I operated on the 46–64 MHz frequency range and the WS17 Mk II on the 44–61 MHz frequency range. It had a range of up to 15 miles and was battery-powered in a self-contained but heavy wooden box.
(© Susanne Atkin)

37. SIS Mk VII 'Paraset'. A compact 'suitcase' set used as back-up set by SCUs and by Section VII 1941. *(© Imperial War Museum COM547)*.

38. 'Keep Mum' Poster. To test the effectiveness of the 'careless talk costs lives' campaign, the Special Duties Branch of the Auxiliary Units and Field Security Section of Military Intelligence spied on both military and civilians, sometimes acting as 'honey traps'. The internal security role of the SDB, although the least well-documented, may have been its most significant contribution to the war effort, especially in the months leading up to D-Day.

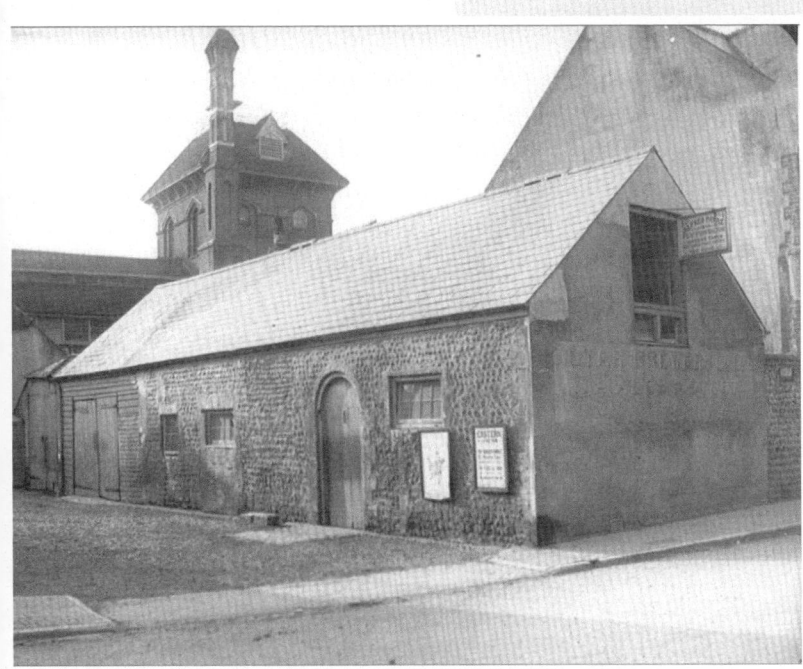

39. Star Brewery, Eastbourne, Sussex. This was the HQ of what is believed to be a Section VII sabotage and intelligence cell, operating throughout the war from March 1940. A wireless set was hidden in the brewery chimney. *(East Sussex County Council Library & Information Service)*

40. (*Left*). Section VII wireless station on Smedley Street, Matlock, Derbyshire. (*Right*) Entrance to the office of the SIS training officer at the Hydro, Matlock, seen in 2014 with former wireless operator Peter Attwater. (© *Susanne Atkin*)

41. The earliest-known published photograph of the Auxiliary Units. Aux Units (Signals) at Coleshill, just prior to final stand-down and published in the January 1945 issue of the Radio Society of Great Britain *Bulletin*. Includes a number of the inventors of the TRD. *Front Row*: George Spencer (G2K1), Jack Millie (GM8MQ), Ron Dabbs (G2RD) *Back Row*: Tom Higgins (G8JI), Bill Bartholomew (G8CK), Les Parnell (G8PP). (*Courtesy RSGB*)

42. Home Guard Part II Orders, September 1941, showing promotion of Lewis van Moppes to be Lieutenant, Auxiliary Units. Lewis and later his brother Edmund would become Group Commanders for Worcestershire Auxiliary Units. *(Courtesy of the former Army Medal Office)*

43. Home Guard Part II Orders, October 1941, identifying officers and men of the Auxiliary Unit patrols attached to 7th (Malvern) Battalion, Worcestershire Home Guard. *(Courtesy of the former Army Medal Office)*

44. The only formal recognition for the Auxiliary Units Operational Branch came in the form of simple typescript Stand-Down letters in November 1944. They even had to buy their own commemorative lapel badge (thanks to John Thornton, Herefordshire Auxiliary Units). *(© Malcolm Atkin)*

45. Tom Wintringham (1898–1949) lecturing on tank-hunting at Osterley Park Home Guard Training School, 1940. *(Zoltan Glass, Picture Post, Getty Images)*

46. Home Guard instruction in use of a remote electrical detonator at Osterley Park Home Guard Training School in 1940. *(Fox Photos, Hulton Archive, Getty Images)*

close protection to the regular forces and Special Branch. Instead, clearly enjoying themselves, they 'flitted from tree to tree with faces blackened or maintained watch in hideouts strung along the hill slopes above the castle'.[81] To later describe them as 'the Royal Family's personal bodyguard' was a typical journalistic exaggeration, but for the officers there was occasionally an opportunity to socialise with the Royal Family and Major Robert Hall even played 'Statues' with the princesses.[82] The Royal Family had a reputation for putting their guards at ease and were always punctilious in expressing their thanks. Soon after the completion of their hasty deployment, in October 1944 the Auxiliary Units members who had taken part in guard duties at Balmoral received a message of appreciation in the form of a printed letter from Colonel Douglas.

> The King has commanded me to convey an expression of his appreciation of the manner in which Auxiliary Units detachments carried out their duties whilst His Majesty was in residence at Balmoral Castle.
> This has afforded The King much gratification and He would be grateful if you would inform all concerned.[83]

The stand-down letter to the Special Duties Branch from General Franklyn was issued on 4 July 1944.[84] The disbandment of the Operational Branch was given a reprieve until November in order to bring it into the same timetable as the stand down of the rest of the Home Guard whilst the Coleshill HQ would survive until 15 January 1945 in order to manage the final close-down of the organisation (Plate 41).[85] As an interim stage, the Operational Branch was re-organised in August 1944 into four large regional areas. The number of regular army Intelligence Officers was reduced to just four and the Home Guard Group Commanders took on increased administrative and liaison duties.

As regions took on more responsibilities, the Coleshill HQ was withering and there was a threat to reduce the establishment rank of the CO from full colonel to lieutenant colonel, which was a far cry from Gubbins' initial attempt to rank the CO as a brigadier.[86] It had become difficult to maintain the Operational Bases in the face of falling numbers and the priority now was to deal with the deteriorating stockpiles of weapons and explosives. The explosives packs began to be removed from the Operational Bases in July and concerns continued to be expressed about the condition of other stored ordnance, with some No.36 grenades being declared unserviceable.[87] Security was increasingly impossible to maintain and on 26 June 1944 Major General J.G. Halstead, CO of South Wales District of Western Command, pointed out that in recent months the existence and activities of the Auxiliary Units had become known 'to those who have no responsibility in regard to these units' and blamed the 'increase in general knowledge' on the length of time they had been under training and 'partly to hidden stores of arms coming to light'.[88]

On 18 November 1944 the stand-down letter from General Franklyn for the Operational Patrols was finally issued and was distributed on 30 November (Plate 44). The morale-boosting covering letter from Colonel Douglas was understandable in the circumstances: he claimed 'It was due to you that more divisions left this country to fight the battle of France' and that their presence meant 'extra risk' could be taken 'in the defence arrangements of this country'. Such statements are difficult to fully reconcile with the facts or the more cynical opinion of the first commanders, Gubbins and Wilkinson, or Peter Fleming (see above, p.117). The protracted decline of the Auxiliary

Units Operational Branch from 1942 onwards, and the element of self-delusion that began to pervade the organisation from that time, should not, however, detract from their significance as one part of the multi-faceted, if suicidal, plans to disrupt an enemy advance in 1940, or their dedication in maintaining an intensive level of secret training over four more long years.

Chapter 8

Auxiliary Units (Special Duties Branch), 1940: Anti-Invasion Reporting

> The SPECIAL DUTIES branch of AUXILIARY UNITS is organised to provide information for military formations in the event of enemy invasion or raids in GREAT BRITAIN, from areas temporarily or permanently in enemy control.
>
> All this information would be collected as a result of direct observation by specially recruited and trained civilians, who would remain in an enemy occupied area.
>
> Major Rupert Jones, June 1944[1]

The intelligence-gathering section of the Auxiliary Units – the Special Duties Branch (SDB) – remains the most elusive element of that organisation, in no small part due to its direct links with SIS. Even within the SDB, not all members may have been aware of the full range of its responsibilities. Its history has been distorted by a focus on the physical evidence of the hidden wireless stations, and a bias in the veteran accounts towards the wireless technicians and operators. As with the Operational Branch the main attention has been in its anti-invasion role, although this was not necessarily its most significant contribution to the war effort. Despite being described as the 'eyes and ears' of the Auxiliary Units organisation, the SDB had no direct link with the Operational Branch and would have found it difficult to directly share any local intelligence gathered during an invasion other than by what seem to be some local arrangements of 'runners' and dead-letter drops. Neither would its wireless network, established in 1941, be sustainable after invasion.[2] Rather it became the 'eyes and ears' of a broader internal security operation that closely monitored the British population. The SDB functioned largely as an independent organisation – a consequence of its SIS heritage when, over the summer of 1940, Gubbins struggled to find a way of seamlessly incorporating Viscount Bearsted's rudimentary intelligence-gathering wing of the Section D Home Defence Scheme (HDS).

In the turmoil following the fall of France the War Office realised that there was an urgent need for any means of obtaining battlefield intelligence under the new threat of rapid *blitzkrieg*. One fear was that the main invasion would be preceded by the scattered landing of small parties of assault troops from fast boats and from parachute landings inland, who would then secure small bridgeheads and cut off lines of communications.[3] With the cadre of the Section VII resistance having only a limited involvement in the invasion campaign and the HDS reliant on the traditional 'runners' and grapevine telegraph, a network of observers in the coastal counties able to bypass the normal telephone communication system and immediately report the first sight of enemy activity by wireless to army commands was an urgent necessity. In the absence of such a system, the C-in-C Home Forces looked first towards the existing Coastguard Service. This was taken over by the Admiralty in late May 1940 from the Ministry of Shipping, and 4,500 Auxiliary Coastguards quickly recruited on National Service. Some were armed. On 10 June General Ironside could announce the establishment of 'A complete system of coast watching, with communications to the Headquarters of Divisions'. Details were amplified on 19 June: 'Arrangements were now complete for the watching of the whole coast by coastguards and special coast watchers, as a result of which every bit of coastline would be seen every half-hour throughout the day and night. The coast watcher posts would be in telephone communication with the nearest naval and military authorities.'[4] An additional 900 Auxiliary Coastguards were recruited from 1942, issued with army battledress, Coastguard caps and armed with rifles and Sten guns. Ironside also noted that behind the coast watching system, there was the Observer Corps, which covered most of the country. This had a dedicated field telephone system and could also fulfil the need for an anti-invasion early warning system, although the Air Ministry did not want them to lose focus on their main task of following enemy aircraft movements. Neither systems were expected to survive first contact with the enemy. After any landing, the best available method of collecting battlefield intelligence would come from the new army Phantom patrols that had proved their worth with the BEF and had been rapidly expanded to provide the most immediate battlefield intelligence (see Chapter 10). Any other means of identifying the main invasion areas would clearly be valuable.

As the Section D HDS was being absorbed into the Auxiliary Units, Gubbins had to try to find a way of incorporating its intelligence wing, modelled on traditional SIS intelligence-gathering, into a system that was more useful to the immediate needs of GHQ. Oxenden recounts that one of the weekly Wednesday Auxiliary Units progress meetings in July 1940 was attended by 'an equal number of strangers, officers and civilians, and even a woman'. Gubbins declared 'You may as well get to know each other, gentlemen; you are all in the same game'.[5] These were the operatives of the HDS and while Oxenden described them as strangers, Gubbins recognised that they were in the same 'game' – but did not acknowledge them as yet being part of the same organisation. Early references to the intelligence role of the Auxiliary Units are brief. A progress report to Churchill on 8 August 1940 stated that as well as sabotage, the second role of the Auxiliary Units was to 'provide a system of intelligence, whereby the regular forces in the field can be kept informed of what is happening behind the enemy's lines' making it very clear that the focus was on providing intelligence during an active military campaign (rather than any post-occupation resistance). The report went on to say 'In order to enable them to ... supply Home Forces with information of troops movements, etc. from behind the enemy's lines, selected units are also being provided with wireless and field telephone apparatus'.[6] This was more of the wishful thinking that peppers this report and referred more to the intended Scout Sections than the Special Duties Branch. Gubbins was driven by the overriding need to meet the anticipated invasion deadline of six to twelve weeks; the Scout Sections would offer a practical, no-fuss military mechanism for so doing, but in the event they could not be introduced until November. The progress report written by Gubbins on 4 September makes no mention of intelligence-gathering at all.[7]

Just a few days after the SDB War Establishment was agreed on 11 July, concerns were expressed about any wholesale dismantling of the HDS at this critical time in the war. SIS officer Major Maurice Petherick (Plate 12 and Appendix 2) was clearly on personal terms with Laurence Grand, if not actually employed within Section D; on 15 July he wrote a blunt letter on the subject.

> Dear Grand,
> I hate to worry you but isn't it time a halt was called before the organisation which you conceived is jettisoned to national disadvantage.
> Sincerely
> Maurice Petherick 15.7.40[8]

All the criticism of Grand's HDS by the War Office and MI5 had been directed at its sabotage organisation but no mention had been made of its intelligence-gathering arm. Lampe records that when the Special Duties Branch began it had 1,000 agents, presumably mainly those inherited from HDS – therefore comprising around one-third of the total of around 3,250 recorded by Colonel Douglas at the end of the war.[9] None of the senior officers at Auxiliary Units HQ had experience in running agent networks as this had been a clear SIS responsibility. The understanding between SIS and the War Office at the start of the war was that SIS was responsible for all agent-based activity, with the War Office, through MI(R), focused on military-based operations. Similarly, when in June 1940 the War Office was contemplating the 'Davies Plan' (see above, pp.66–69) using runners to pass through enemy lines, a handwritten note said 'SIS must run this'.[10] The War Office also lacked the technical expertise to provide a clandestine communications system over which SIS was particularly protective. SIS therefore maintained a discrete influence over the development of the early SDB and this may explain the paucity of references to the operation of any Auxiliary Units intelligence network during 1940. This is evident in Peter Wilkinson's accounts, despite the fact that at the time he seems to have been the officer within the Auxiliary Units responsible for liaising with the Special Duties Branch. In his autobiography he admits that one of his roles as GSO2 (Operations) was 'liaison with my friends in Section D' and with the other intelligence services.[11] Whilst a member of MI(R) earlier in 1940, Wilkinson had worked closely with Section D, having his own SIS identity code, and so was ideally placed for the role. Even while he was making scathing comments on HDS's inefficiency in distributing their arms dumps, he makes no comment on the existence of their intelligence network.

Despite concern over SIS involvement in the military campaign, the reality is that GHQ and Gubbins were obliged to allow the rudimentary HDS intelligence network to remain in operation and under SIS control during most of 1940 as the basis of the new SDB. Only at the very end of 1940 was it possible to begin to implement a more military version linked to Army Command HQs and even then it remained under the command of a former SIS officer (Petherick). Thus it was agreed between SIS and GHQ in July that

> While obstructive activities of the 'D' organisation are being gradually transferred to GHQ Auxiliary Units, it is considered necessary and desirable by GHQ and CSS that the Intelligence side of the activities should be maintained and developed.[12]

The agreed solution was for Section D's Viscount Bearsted to operate the existing network much as before, but under the guise of Auxiliary Units (Special Duties). From the SOE history of Section D:

> Colonel Viscount Bearsted continued his organisation en bloc under the name of 'Auxiliary Units (Special Duties)'. It was not until the danger of invasion was relatively past that the organisation as originally planned by D section was dissolved.[13]

Bearsted joined SOE in autumn 1940 and Major Petherick was then transferred from SIS into the Auxiliary Units in order to convert the 'Special Duties' into a body that GHQ could manage more directly, whilst still maintaining a discreet watching brief over SIS interests particularly, it may be argued, to ensure that the SDB did not jeopardise the continuing, deep-cover operations of Section VII. Petherick was later described by Major Beyts as the genius behind the SDB and it was probably he who devised the new pyramid structure of wireless-connected IN and OUT Stations that would feed back intelligence to army HQs. Petherick worked closely with Colonel 'Bill' Major (Plate 11), often closeted in private meetings, and the reorganisation of the SDB fits neatly into the overall pattern of highly-structured military organisation that Major favoured. From June 1941 at the latest, the SDB had a separate HQ at Hannington Hall, a few miles from Coleshill, probably reflecting an even earlier separation of the Special Duties and Operational HQs. When the Operational and SDB HQs were finally combined at Coleshill in June 1942 Hannington Hall became an 'Attery' billet for the ATS of the Aux Unit (Signals) and administration.

For Gubbins in 1940, the SDB was of secondary importance to rapidly creating an effective guerrilla force and was beyond his experience; he was content to leave Bearsted and the former HDS officers upon which it relied to their own devices. Under 'Bill' Major's reorganisation in 1941 the volunteers, like the Operational Branch, were organised under Group Leaders and 'Key Men'. Although civilian, the War Office were clear that the SDB operatives were 'organised in groups and operated under military control . . . linked through the military officer in charge of their activities to the local military command'.[14] Comparatively little is known about these men and women. A letter of October 1947 refers to a full roll having been kept of their names by the War Office but, although some local lists were compiled, this may be a contemporary confusion with the nominal roll compiled of the Operational Patrols. Any such national roll has never been released.[15] The civilian agents and wireless operators, difficult to replace, were exempted from military service and also other civil defence duties but sadly they were judged as not qualifying for the Defence

Medal, in part because SIS pointed out that their agents in Section VII had similar responsibilities but would not be put forward for any sort of public recognition.[16]

The existing civilians of the HDS who became part of the SDB may have been unaware of the change in their compartmentalised existence, never having been told precisely for whom they were working in the first place! Not a single veteran has ever directly mentioned prior service with SIS. The stories of agents being recruited by men who gave no name, wore no visible badges of rank, did not identify their organisation and carried only a copy of the Official Secrets Act and a bible as a signal of authority now seems remarkably naïve, but appears commonplace at the time. In Sussex, Intelligence Officer Robert Fraser transferred his HDS network seamlessly into the SDB with the only clue being that early cell members remember him having a wireless transmitter in his car, a feature of the HDS Intelligence Officers rather than the SDB.[17]

Although the HDS had been organised on a national basis, the distribution of the SDB network, like the Operational Branch, was predominantly coastal in order to meet the immediate threat of coast invasion.[18] Nonetheless, defence planning of 1940 and 1941 considered there was a real risk of parachute landings anywhere in the country 'with even less warning than in the case of sea-borne landings'.[19] They would be carried out 'in very different places so as to upset us and get our troops rushing about the country'.[20] The Auxiliary Units, however, had to focus their resources beside the coast, where the danger was most likely to be concentrated. The summary of duties given by Major Rupert Jones, CO from 1942 of the Auxiliary Units (Signals) section which opened this chapter, was written with both hindsight and poetic license in June 1944, when the danger of invasion had passed. In 1940 the very suggestion of permanently-occupied territory would have sent GHQ into apoplexy; it was never in the business of establishing civilian resistance organisations. Instead, the pressing need for GHQ in terms of intelligence-gathering was for a ground-based early warning system that could immediately pass on information to army commands for analysis as to the pattern of initial German landings, and thereby make the best use of the Phantom patrols that would then deploy into the area. Gubbins received authorisation to create an HQ 'Special Duties' on 11 July 1940, with the cryptic comment that the organisation had already commenced activities, a discrete way of referring to Bearsted's pre-existing intelligence-gathering wing of the HDS.[21] The agreed War Establishment for the HQ of what became the Special Duties Branch was impressive and closely mirrored that of the Operational Branch (Fig. 14).

Fig. 14 Extract from War Establishment for Special Duties Branch, 11 July 1940. (*TNA WO 260/9*)

GSO2 (major)	1
GSO3 (captain)	1
Intelligence Officers (captains)	11
Clerks, (RASC)	2
Drivers (Intelligence Corps or RASC)	12

The HQ staff would be responsible for managing the civilian agents already recruited by the HDS within the operational area of the Auxiliary Units and for tying them into a new intelligence network. There were no signallers as the SDB had no wireless communication system at this time. Twelve four-seater cars and drivers were to be provided (from Intelligence Corps and RASC); the number of cars was queried by the War Office with the explanation that 'it is the only means by which the officer can carry all his gadgets about the country'. Was it a bluff to acquire vehicles on the basis that no-one would feel able to enquire too closely as to the nature of these 'gadgets' before the introduction of wireless equipment? Or was the hope to replicate the wireless-equipped cars of the HDS? At a more personal level, Gubbins' original proposal was for the SDB to be commanded by a lieutenant colonel which would have then allowed him, as overall commander of the Auxiliary Units, to retain his temporary rank of brigadier. The head of the SDB was, however, downgraded to a GSO2 (major) and Gubbins had to revert to his substantive rank of colonel.

The volunteers of the SDB (in common with Section VII and HDS) were in the main, older, established members of the community whose absence from call-up could be explained and gave an excuse for freedom of movement across the locality. George Phillips, barrister and former High Sheriff of Carmarthenshire, was recruited in September 1941 to be Group Leader for the SDB in Carmarthenshire and continued to August 1944. He claimed the work involved 'being alone operating in the mountains by day and by night for frequent and long periods'; this extended watch-keeping may well, although possibly exaggerated, have been considered suspicious in a less well-established person. There were also younger volunteers who could not so easily explain their absence from other war work. The daughter of George Phillips, Mollie, assisted with training and was also a wireless operator but he commented 'she finds herself a subject of criticism and opprobrium, because she is locally considered to have done nothing in the war as, of necessity, her work was unknown'.[22] The best security was achieved by recruiting from family groups or close friends as illustrated by the members of the Hockley cell in Essex. The Group Leader was Kenneth Maryan-Green. Born in 1900, he had served in the North Russia campaign in 1919 as a young second lieutenant before resigning his commission. There are hints he may have previously been involved with the HDS while also an officer in the LDV, as he was known to the local commanders of the operational branch (a cross-over typical of an HDS inheritance) and had earlier worked as a London stockbroker, a prime recruiting ground for Section D. Robert Hugh Playle was a clerk for a radio company in Rochford, Essex and in 1939 a Deputy Head Observer in the Observer Corps. His brother-in-law was Charles Frederick Olley, uncle to Maryan-Green's wife Laura who was also an outstation operator. A close friend was Donald Eric Tanton, a local estate agent and auctioneer. There was also Herbert Baldwin, a retired greengrocer. Two 'cut outs' were Joyce Jay and Marjorie Drinkwater who, with blackened faces, practiced taking a message across several fields at night and leaving it in a tree stump dead-letter drop.[23]

Recruitment to the SDB HQ War Establishment proceeded in gradual stages as suitable Intelligence Officers were found to take over management of the agent networks. In the beginning there can have been few in the army who had any experience of running such networks and they relied on the existing regional officers of Section D – the men described by Grand as attached to the Auxiliary Units from his D/M group.[24] Four of the five known SDB Intelligence Officers appointed before

November 1940 had previously served with SIS. They had been commissioned onto the General List and were then promoted almost immediately: John Todd, Kenneth W. Johnson, Rupert St George Riley and Robert Fraser all received their promotions to Acting Captain on 22 July, probably marking their formal transfer to the Auxiliary Units.[25]

The career of Todd and his likely SIS connections has been discussed above (Chapter 4). Kenneth Johnson's later SOE personnel file notes 'For a short while with Lord Bearsted in MI6'. He was commissioned onto the General List but retained the common indicator of SIS service – the 'without pay and allowances' rider – on his commission until his promotion to Acting Captain. He served in the SDB until at least May 1944. Like Todd, Johnson at first was a joint Operational and Special Duties Intelligence Officer (in Glamorgan) but then became Special Duties Intelligence Officer for Glamorganshire, Herefordshire and Worcestershire. Rupert St George Riley had joined the Paris office of Section D in 1939, responsible for Switzerland. He was appointed to the Auxiliary Units Special Duties Branch in Kent on 22 July 1940 but left in December to join the Ministry of Supply department in the War Office. Robert Fraser joined Section D on 29 May 1940 to work with Walter Wren on forward planning and moved with Wren to the Home Defence Scheme. He was commissioned as Second Lieutenant on 1 July on the General List but transferred to the Intelligence Corps on 15 July, when he was attached to Bearsted alongside Riley as Intelligence Officer in Kent and Sussex. Fraser remained the SDB Intelligence Officer for the South-East Command area until at least May 1944.

The fifth in the initial round of SDB Intelligence Officers was John S. Collings, who had particularly valuable skills. He had been commissioned on 16 September 1939 into 5th (Inniskilling) Royal Dragoon Guards, but he spent little time with his regiment. In November 1939, being fluent in French and having also lived in Belgium, he became a founding member of what became the Phantom Unit (see Chapter 10) and was promoted to Acting Captain. He served a key role as head of the Intelligence section for the Phantom Unit in France and Belgium as they liaised between the forward HQs of the Allied armies. Phantom lost a number of officers in their evacuation from Ostend on 27 May but was swiftly re-organised to provide the same intelligence-gathering role in Britain. Why Collings, who had been praised for his work in the Phantom War Diary, left at this point to join the expanding SDB as Intelligence Officer for East Anglia, but without wider responsibilities, is not clear.[26] His recent practical experience in gathering intelligence in the face of *blitzkrieg* was no doubt useful, as would be his links to Phantom which was, by then, already deploying across the region. He remained as SDB Intelligence Officer for East Anglia until the spring of 1944.

Three other Intelligence Officers are known by the start of the reorganisation of the SDB in November/December. Suffolk IO Frederick Baldwin Childe was first commissioned into the Coldstream Guards in 1930, re-commissioned in April 1940 into the King's Royal Rifle Corps and on 3 November was promoted Acting Captain on 'special employment'. He transferred to the Intelligence Corps in 1941. The Yorkshire IO, Michael J. Farrer, was commissioned into the Royal Sussex Regiment in December 1939. In April he was promoted Acting Lieutenant on 'special employment' and joined the SDB on 15 July, rapidly followed by promotion to Temporary

Captain on 24 June and full Captain on 27 December. Edward Robert Ramage Fingland, the Somerset IO, was another man commissioned onto the General List followed by rapid promotion. He was commissioned on 3 August 1940 and was appointed full Captain on 14 December; he was still on the General List and only transferred to the Intelligence Corps in 1942 when he joined the HQ staff at Coleshill. The rest of the SDB Intelligence Officers were recruited from 1941 at the time that the new SDB wireless system was introduced and the network therefore needed more intensive management. Their role was borrowed from the Phantom Unit intelligence officers, who liaised between the reconnaissance patrols and forward army HQs, but details of what the SDB Intelligence Officers actually did on a day-to-day basis for four years remains vague. The role of the Intelligence Officers probably went beyond managing the wireless network into more traditional intelligence duties and field security work, perhaps in association with the Field Security Section (FSS) of the Intelligence Corps.

In 1940 the inherited system of 'runners' or couriers using dead-letter drops was a traditional and practical technique of spy networks in a period of settled occupation but would have been an uncertain and slow method of transmitting intelligence during what was expected to be a rapidly-moving invasion campaign with no defined front line. Nonetheless, at the time of Dunkirk, human couriers were still regarded by many in the military as the most reliable communication. In a *blitzkrieg*, by the time information such as 'column of tanks seen heading east from xxxx' reached an intelligence officer and was then reported to an appropriate military level who could initiate a response, the information was probably out of date. Even when the wireless network was introduced in 1941, the SDB would have had to rely almost entirely on the wireless operators to collect and then transmit the intelligence from their own observation as it is debatable whether the system of 'cut-outs' would have sufficient freedom of movement to operate in a timely manner. If one of them failed to collect the drop then the whole system failed. With hindsight, the idea of teenage couriers such as Jill Monk (née Holman) in Aylsham, Norfolk, being able to collect intelligence on German troop movements and to pass on messages to the wireless station, whilst casually pony-trekking through the middle of German invasion forces is a romantic and naïve notion: 'He [Captain Collings] thought a brat on a horse was unlikely to be suspected of anything. So I was to ride out and spot any choice targets, in terms of troops or supply dumps.' Although an oft-quoted anecdote, this related to 1942 when German invasion was becoming more unlikely; US forces were pouring into East Anglia and Allied strategists had already begun planning for the invasion of Europe.[27] Jill's father, Dr Holman, was an OUT Station operator in Aylsham and Captain Collings had become a frequent visitor; one wonders if Jill (aged 16) was primarily recruited in order to keep an overly-curious teenager occupied.

To make the SDB work more effectively, a wireless network was urgently needed. The campaign in Norway had highlighted the risks of the army relying on the civil telephone system and a meeting of the War Cabinet on 18 November 1941 continued to highlight the danger of telephone communications being cut during an airborne assault.[28] However, unlike those of SIS Section VII, whose operators had been training for months, any wireless sets had to be easily operable by untrained civilians to meet the demands of imminent invasion. Control of clandestine wireless systems was a sensitive issue and one which Gubbins, who had fallen foul of this with SIS whilst in MI(R), would have felt keenly.[29] On 15 September the head of SIS, Stewart Menzies, met with the Chief Executive Officer of the new SOE, Gladwyn Jebb, and it was agreed that Section VIII of SIS was to retain control of SOE wireless systems; it remained a major source of SOE friction with SIS until 1942. This would have reinforced Gubbins' view that the infant SDB would need to develop its own independent communication system if it was ever to come completely out of SIS control. In September, Gubbins recruited Captain John Hills, Technical Maintenance Officer at No.1 Special Wireless Group, Harpenden (the radio intercept Y Service), to build a suitable new wireless set.

Captain Hills had previously designed a receiver to intercept signals from German E-Boats operating in the English Channel and appreciated the desirability of making the new sets as hard to intercept as possible. The other criteria was that SDB needed a system that used telephony and thereby avoided the need for specialist Morse code training. Hills was able to draw upon a number of strands of earlier research. Between 1933 and 1938 a team from the Signals Experimental Unit of the OTC at Cambridge University under Professor Wilfrid Lewis and post-graduate student C.J. Milner (assisted by a number of undergraduates including future SDB officer Ken Ward) were developing, for the War Office, a duplex transceiver that could not easily be intercepted.[30] It was intended to provide secure short-range communications between artillery batteries and their forward observation posts. The work was taken over by the Signals Research Development Establishment at Bournemouth who unsuccessfully tried to turn the research into production sets.[31] Similar research was continued by Dr Edward Schröter in Section D of SIS between 1938 and 1940. By July 1940, Schröter had produced a demonstration model of a short-range, VHF duplex transceiver that used voice transmission.[32] Schröter went on to successfully oversee the development of clandestine wireless sets for SOE but there the priority was in long-range sets using Morse code and work on the duplex transceiver was shelved.[33] It is feasible that Schröter's research was handed over to Hills as part of the transfer of the HDS, for him to develop further into what became the Savage/TRD sets and this would explain why SIS claimed proprietorial rights to the TRD sets at the end of the war. In 2008, Warwicker had an unnamed source who claimed that the Section D duplex transceiver was overweight, depended on foreign components and, of seven made, only one actually worked.[34] However, any failure of the prototype does not mean that the research can be too easily dismissed as a source for the TRD. Another inspiration may have been the simple, short-range, WS17 super-regenerative set which had been invented by the notable radio ham Stanley Lewer in early 1939 to produce a short-range, low-power transceiver for the control of balloon barrages. The WS17 operated on the same frequency range as the later TRD wireless set, had a range of up to 15 miles and was battery-powered in a self-contained but heavy wooden box (Plate 36). Even if the crude WS17 was not an inspiration for John Hills, it was to prove highly significant for the operations of the SDB and by the summer of 1944 it comprised nearly 40 per cent of their wireless sets.

Gubbins left to join SOE on 18 November 1940, just as Hills was completing his first set: a VHF duplex telephony unit manufactured by Savage and Parsons Ltd of Kingsbury and therefore known as the Savage set. The set was in one box with the controls on top and already had the quench circuitry that would make the signal *undecipherable* to anyone without the same type of receiver, but not *undetectable*; a second box contained the power supply. Hills quickly established a pilot network in Kent with the new set, with five or six out-stations operated by civilians, reporting to Fleming at a base station in divisional HQ in Maidstone with ATS operators drawn from SE Command.[35] Fifty Savage sets were quickly built and the network was steadily expanded but they proved difficult to maintain. From 1 January 1941, Hills was able to assemble a small technical team at Bachelor's Hall, Hundon, Suffolk, as the core of what became the Auxiliary Units (Signals) maintenance team. It initially comprised just Lieutenant (later Captain) Ken Ward as Adjutant and Workshop Officer (see Appendix 2) who had served in the Y Intercept Service with Hills, a Royal Signals NCO and a private.[36] Ward's background as Officer-in-Charge of Operator Training at the Y Service suggests he may have been brought in specifically because of the need to create a system that relied on minimum training. He had also been an undergraduate member of the Lewis and Milner team at Cambridge, but cheerfully described himself as merely 'one of the stooges'. It was, however, Ward who had brought this work to the attention of Hills.[37] Overcoming the initial lack of electricity at Bachelors Hall, with lighting provided by pressure lanterns and in the workshops, soldering irons heated with blow lamps, 20–30 skilled former amateur radio 'hams' now in the Royal Signals were swiftly recruited (Plate 41). Together these 'hams' designed and built a replacement for the Savage set in just two weeks.[38] Jack Millie and Bill Bartholomew designed the transmitter; Tom Higgins and Ron Dabbs designed the receiver; and Les Parnell, Jimmy McNab and John Mackie designed the power supply. Mackie (a sheet metal worker by trade) also built the prototype enclosures.[39] Named TRD (Transmitter Ron Dabbs) in the contemporary tradition of SIS identifying wireless sets by their team members, it was powered from a 6v accumulator battery and operated at 48–52 MHz (similar to that of the WS17 but because of the quench circuit they were not interchangeable). The set for the IN Stations was built into a single green or black metal box 15.5in x 9.75in x 9.25in made by the Metal Box Company of North London. The controls were on the long side of the box and included two variable tuning dials for transmitting and receiving (Plate 35). Bill Bartholomew remembered the OUT Station set as being smaller, in a case about 6in wide, 9in deep and about 6in high with simpler controls sited on the short side (on/off, volume and transmit receive) with the two aerial terminals. It did not require variable tuning as the OUT Stations reported on a fixed frequency.[40] All the sets used voice transmission, the OUT Station sets having a standard GPO handset while the IN Stations had a hands-free 'Transmitter Breast No.1' as used by GPO telephone operators and RAF plotters. By June 1944 the frequencies had been rationalised with IN and OUT Stations using 60 or 65 MHz and an inner circle of Base Stations using 48 MHz or 52 MHz.[41] The normal range was 30–60 miles by line of sight but the signal could, on occasion, be picked up at much greater distances. Crucially, the fixed IN and OUT Stations relied on permanently installed and very sensitive directional aerials which imposed both a rigidity and fragility on the system. One of the Auxiliary Units (Signals) sergeants, Roy Russell, recounted how 'Communication at the high frequency we used required accurate direction for reliable reception. High winds or even branch growth could alter the delineation and lose radio contact'.[42] IN Stations might require three or four aerials so that the dipole was at the right angle for the various OUT Stations. Moving and re-establishing such stations would have been a major effort, especially during an invasion and impossible thereafter. The distance between IN and OUT Stations could be increased by the use of unmanned relay stations (with the equipment sometimes hidden up a tree) but this introduced a further rigidity in the system that required additional maintenance. The system was technologically novel but inherently flawed for its intended clandestine use. The reliance of the set on fixed frequencies, a very directional aerial and the need for regular specialist maintenance (with the Royal Signals staff having to go out and change the heavy batteries once a week as well as regularly checking the hidden aerials) meant this was a system that was likely to collapse in a matter of days after invasion. The SIS Section VII network in the UK changed its frequencies between odd and even every day; later, cautious SOE and SIS agents in Europe would frequently change the location of the wireless set to avoid detection. The question, therefore, is whether the faults in the TRD system were ignored and the network maintained under bureaucratic inertia into 1944 – or did it always have another purpose (see Chapter 9).

A legend has grown up that the TRD wireless was revolutionary in design and undetectable – a story not supported by the accounts of those involved. Ken Ward clearly stated in a 1999 interview that the design was essentially that of Hills' Savage set. The impetus for change had come from the simple desirability of rebuilding the Savage set so that it was easier for the operators to use and for the technicians to service. It was undertaken on the initiative of Dabbs, Bartholomew and the other radio 'hams' rather than from any instruction from higher authority.[43] Neither Ward nor Bartholomew mention any imperative to improve wireless security in the new design beyond what already existed in the Savage set. The TRD did use a modulated sub-carrier system that produced a type of undecipherable 'white noise' on anything other than another TRD, but the signal itself could still be detected. Ward believed that security was based not upon any radical design but more simply upon a) the relatively rare use of the VHF frequencies employed, b) the short range of the set and c) the fact that the aerials were very directional.[44] One improvement Bartholomew did make was to try to isolate the receiver from the radiation that it caused (and thereby likely to give away its position to the enemy) by the simple means of using an untuned buffer RF amplifier, but was only partially successful.[45]

By 1944 the legend of non-detectability had already been born, no doubt of some comfort to the operators. Sergeant Roy Russell of Auxiliary Units (Signals), instructed to produce spoof messages for the D-Day deception plan, expressed surprise to learn that the signals from the TRD might be intelligible to German Intelligence: 'It was the first intimation I had that the enemy could pick up our very-high-frequency; although maybe they couldn't, we'll never know.'[46] One operator in Kent, Adrian Monck-Mason, had already found a Royal Signals wireless operator looking for the signal which had been picked up locally by the army from his TRD set.[47] Barbara Culleton recorded that early versions of the TRD were prone to interference from tank radios. Presumably the problem was mutual! Bartholomew's simple fix to isolate the receiver had not worked. In August 1943 Major Kirkness advised in his 'Monthly Notes for IOs' that, on 'freak days', signals from Kent OUT Stations could be picked up at Coleshill on Strength 5, prompting fears that such signals could also be received in occupied Europe – assuming that the Germans were monitoring these little-used

VHF frequencies.[48] In May 1944 the D-Day deception planners were similarly disturbed to discover that a VHF network might be heard on the Continent (see below, p.167). Whether the enemy could actually resolve the signal without having a matching TRD is, however, more doubtful.

The legend of undetectability may have been deliberately spread during the war to reassure the operators or it may simply have been in the tradition of similar claims made by their inventors for early SIS clandestine sets. Guy Liddell refers in April 1940 to the sets sent by SIS to Norway.

> These have all been supplied by SIS since other apparatus of the kind seems singularly out of date. The sets, I gather, are designed by [XXXXXXX] and SIS have them operating from German territory and from all over the continent. Stewart [Menzies] believes that they are extremely difficult to pick up and doubts very much whether any monitoring system however widespread will be effective against them.[49]

Menzies was over-optimistic. Later experience was to show that agents could not use any wireless sets for more than 15 minutes without risking discovery by the German radio detection. The destruction of the TRDs by SIS at the end of the war (claiming proprietorial rights due to their funding) was remarkable only by its completeness and does not reflect any particular concern for the technology. In its professional paranoia over security, SIS destroyed large numbers of other clandestine wireless sets after the war and the TRD sets, being in Britain, were simply easier to locate and destroy than those in Europe.

It is useful to consider other contemporary concerns with the security of the new use of VHF. Producing a VHF transceiver was evidently not complicated: in June 1941 five youths were arrested in Nottingham after building and using VHF sets for some months – including communicating with army units. Liddell commented: 'There is of course no proper organisation for detecting VHF or for policing army traffic'.[50] Problems in the detection of VHF transmissions remained a concern for MI5 throughout the war. Interestingly, this was caused by the disinterest of the Radio Security Service (RSS), as VHF was still not considered practical for agents to use. In June 1942 Major Morton-Evans believed that 'VHF was still in the stage where it was a matter for the radio engineers and not for Intelligence'.[51] The concern of RSS was obviously in identifying long-range transmission to and from the Continent but their fears over VHF were aroused just a few days later. 'An expedition recently sent to the Isle of Wight obtained highly interesting results in this field, and the range was found to be something in the neighbourhood of 90 miles.'[52] By September 1942 the RSS did have vans dedicated to searching for VHF signals although 'the vans which handled it had to turn out on an average of once a week only'.[53] In these circumstances the IN Station operators of the SDB were able to usefully supplement the strained resources of the RSS by periodically scanning their VHF wavebands for any rogue transmissions.

Initially the workshop at Bachelors Hall was producing 7–8 sets per week as they gradually replaced the existing Savage sets (with which they were mutually compatible) in the wireless stations. The first areas to be equipped after Kent were those closest to Hundon in Norfolk, Suffolk and Essex, with their surface IN Stations at static Divisional HQs near Norwich, Halstead and Hatfield Peveril. Another early 'ham' recruit, George Spencer, was given the task of choosing suitable sites for intended underground IN Stations, although these would not actually be built until 1942 (relying until then on above ground 'Met Huts'). By the end of 1941 the team had equipped county networks from Devon to Berwick-upon-Tweed. In 1942 it was decided that the separate design and manufacturing facility at Hundon was no longer justified. Maintenance and some assembly work was transferred to Nissen hut workshops at Coleshill while the wireless section of the Inter-Services Research Board (aka SOE), now under Schröter, took over responsibility for the manufacture of new TRDs. Ken Ward became the contract manager, with an assembly contract issued to Peto Scott Ltd.[54] James McNab reported the dispersal of the 'Bachelors All' gang from Hundon in the August 1942 issue of the RSGB *Bulletin*, informing the readership that many were going to a base 'near Swindon'. In the December 1942 issue Bill Bartholomew and Les Parnell provided a further round-up of the postings, coyly describing Coleshill as 'a nice new 'all'. From June 1944, when security was clearly less of an issue, the 'hams' even began to hold meetings of the Radio Society of Great Britain in Bill Batholomew's 'digs' in Highworth. Fourteen of the Royal Signals 'hams' attended the first meeting and anyone else interested in future meetings were invited to contact 'Cpl Bartholomew, Aux Unit Signals, c/o GPO, Highworth, Swindon'.[55] The TRD continued to evolve, with a number of different versions of unknown character, called TRM and TRF, some of which were designed for loudspeaker use.[56] In 1943 it was planned to implement a major programme of replacement of the early sets:

> Several IOs have written pressing for an exchange of their old TRD sets for new ones . . . The position is that TRD sets are coming through very slowly indeed from the manufacturers, but that eventually all old sets will be replaced . . . No new ones are in stock here, and replacement will be made according to plans already made, starting with EASTCC [Eastern Command].[57]

It is not known what advantages the new versions of the TRD offered except probably to reduce interference. By June 1944 there were 250 TRD, 28 TRM and 36 TRF sets in use with the SDB, together with 200 WS17 sets, distributed amongst 30 IN Stations, 125 OUT Stations and 78 SUB-OUT Stations plus Intelligence Officer HQs.[58]

Despite the attention given to the mysterious TRD, a significant percentage of the wireless sets used by the SDB from 1943 consisted of the standard, insecure, WS17 which has implications for an understanding of the nature of the organisation, suggesting it did not now necessarily require secure communications. It is also a measure of priorities at the time that the WS17 was considered obsolete and was out of general service. The WS17 was not completely inter-operable with the TRD because of the latter's quench system and it had a different power output, but the signal from a WS17 could be received by any wireless set tuned to its frequency. Unfortunately, it also radiated a noise signal that could easily be detected within a radius of a few hundred metres. Indeed it was so noisy that it interfered with low-flying aircraft. This was clearly not a set intended for clandestine use.

Like any system, the network was subject to human error. Messages were sent by voice telephony in open speech or using simple word codes that were supposed to be regularly changed. Auxiliary Units (Signals) NCO Stan Judson described a simple sheet divided into squares, each containing an army term which could be referenced by the X and Y axis: thus square A/Y would mean '50 tanks'. As with Section VII, there were also safety phrases whereby the correct response would indicate the operator was not acting under duress. Thus 'King George for England' was to be answered with 'King's Cross for Scotland'.[59] As the modulated system was supposed to be impossible to unscramble, the fact that such codes were easy to break was not considered so important, but astonishingly, in what was described at the time as an act of stupidity, one Intelligence Officer in 1943 openly broadcast instructions for the new 'captured drill' from his IN Station to OUT Stations thus threatening the whole network.[60]

The Wireless Network

The new wireless sets needed a structure within which they could operate and this is reflected in the new War Establishment of February 1941, which included Royal Signals technicians together with Royal Signals and ATS wireless operators (Fig. 15). Colonel 'Bill' Major (Plate 11) maintained in 1968 that it was he that was responsible for creating the SDB after he took command from Gubbins on 18 November 1940.[61] Although patently untrue, Major did oversee the development of SDB into what is now seen as its classic form and extended the role of its agents. Even so, Auxiliary Units Training Officer Major Beyts is clear that it was the 'genius' of Major Petherick as the new CO of the SDB that established its character.[62] At the same time as Hills was building up his technical HQ at Bachelors Hall, Hundon, Petherick established an administrative HQ for the SDB at Hannington Hall, a few miles from Coleshill. This reinforced the separate nature of the SDB from the Operational Branch and could have been due to a continuing discreet SIS influence; SIS kept a financial hold on the SDB throughout the war, providing funds that did not need to pass through any form of War Office public accounting. When making arrangements for the disbandment of the SDB in 1944 it was noted that 'Tools and Components were to be returned to No.1 SCU [SIS Communications HQ at Whaddon] if purchased from S.D. [Special Duties] funds' together with what were described as the 'special sets' – the TRDs.[63]

Fig. 15 Extract from War Establishment for Auxiliary Units (Signals), February 1941. (*BRO Museum archive*)

		Offrs	Other Ranks						
			CQMS	Sgts	Cpls	L/Cpl	Sgmn	Drivers	Total O.R.s
MALE	R. Sigs	4	-	1	2	15	26		44
	RASC							6	6
	RE (attd)								
FEMALE	ATS	40							

One structural model for the reorganisation was the system of Observer Corps posts which had so recently demonstrated its efficiency during the Battle of Britain. The posts were organised into clusters of three to five, manned 24 hours a day, with each cluster having fixed field telephone links to an individual plotter at the local Control Centre, where the information was immediately collated and forwarded to RAF Fighter Command. The RAF strenuously made the point that the primary function of the Observer Corps was to report enemy aircraft movements, but nonetheless from the spring of 1940 each post was armed with a rifle and had flares to signal enemy landings, with instructions to keep reporting the enemy's position until overrun.[64] The new SDB was similarly organised into clusters of civilian OUT Stations linked by the TRD sets to military IN Stations. From at least 1943 there were also SUB-OUT Stations, an outer ring of manned sub-stations closer to the coast that fed into the OUT Stations.[65] At the base of the pyramid system were the observers who were to collect intelligence and pass it on to a series of couriers ('cut-outs') via dead-letter drops, who could then deliver the messages to the 'Key Man' or the wireless OUT Station. They were given leaflets on German army uniforms, insignia and weapons units to study. Ursula Pennell in Norfolk kept the leaflets in her purse or even her bra; George Vater in Monmouthshire was told they had to be memorised in a week and then burnt.[66] The crucial question was how quickly this information could be passed back to a high-enough command to make timely use of it. Even using the wireless network, this information had to be passed from the observer via a 'cut-out' to the OUT Station and then transmitted to the IN Station, typically close-by a Divisional HQ, which was staffed by Royal Signals or ATS operators and were generally around 15 miles from the coast. The IN Stations then passed it to an intelligence officer by telephone or bicycle. The IN Stations might also report to an inner circle of Base stations based at Brigade or Corps HQs (Plate 33).[67] Responsibility for acting on the collected information then passed out of the hands of the Auxiliary Units to army intelligence officers, so that anything of other than local significance would be passed from District to Regional Command and thence to GHQ. This system was likely to be too ponderous to have any significant impact during a fast-moving invasion, other than information directly noted and transmitted by the wireless operator. The whole panoply of observers and 'cut-outs' was also predicated upon the unlikely survival of the wireless connections if the IN Stations (which until 1942 did not have buried hides) were forced to move with the HQs to which they were attached. The advance of German ground troops was likely to be preceded by dive-bombing of command centres and so it is likely the SDB network would have been put out of action even before the enemy over-ran the IN Stations. The effectiveness of this system has to be judged against the contemporary collection of battlefield intelligence by Phantom reconnaissance units (see Chapter 10).

Despite the rapid improvements in clandestine wireless technology as used abroad and the opportunity to better train the operators, as well as the overall change in the strategic situation, the simple TRD network survived into mid-1944. By January 1944, the SDB was organised in ten areas, each under an Intelligence Officer reporting to the army District HQ (Fig. 16).[68] Although there had been an overall expansion in the SDB, the number of Intelligence Officers on the War Establishment had not increased significantly since its creation in July 1940 with most having served with SDB since 1941.

Fig. 16 Organisational responsibility for Special Duties Branch, June 1944. (*TNA WO 199/1194*)

	Area	Information To
Scotland	Caithness, Sutherland	North Highland District, Scottish Command
	Angus, Fife, East Lothian, Berwickshire	Scottish Command
England	Northumberland, Durham	Northumbrian District
	Yorkshire, North Riding Yorkshire,	North Riding District
	East Riding, Lincolnshire	East Riding and Lincolnshire District
	Norfolk	Norfolk and Cambridge District
	Essex, Suffolk	Essex and Suffolk District
	Kent	East Kent District, South Eastern Command
	Sussex	Sussex District, South Eastern Command
	Hampshire	Hampshire Sub-District, Southern Command
	Dorset	Dorset Sub-District, Southern Command
	Somerset, East Devon	South Western District
Wales	Pembrokeshire, Carmarthenshire	South Wales District
	Glamorgan, Monmouthshire	

The TRD system depended on the army Auxiliary Units (Signals) which provided IN Station operators and a maintenance team. The latter was small and highly qualified, but was a uniformed technical body which had received no training for operating behind enemy lines. Its history can be tracked through the detailed War Establishments. The discrepancy between the number of male and female officers is because the ATS wireless operators were given emergency commissions so as to protect discipline. There were also no mixed stations. Until April 1942 the IN Stations were almost entirely reliant on ATS operators (Fig. 17); there were usually three ATS subalterns for each wireless station, which made their operation more expensive than if they had used male Royal Signals other ranks as operators. As a consequence, with pressures on the overall costs of the Auxiliary Units increasing, the War Establishment of April 1942 (Fig. 18) cut the number of ATS officers from 136 to just 32, in favour of using male Royal Signals O/R wireless operators.[69] This, at a time when the SDB was expanding in Scotland and the South-West, was admitted to be a mistake in a letter by Lord Glanusk on 1 February 1943. The establishment was then revised back up to fifty-six ATS officers (Fig. 19).[70] The final War Establishment in June 1944 (Fig. 20) lists fifty-seven ATS officers (and three drivers). These figures do not include a small number of ATS other ranks clerks employed at the HQ of the SDB.

Fig. 17 Extract from War Establishment Auxiliary Units (Signals), March 1942. (*TNA WO 199/1194*)

		Offrs	Other Ranks					
			CQMS	Sgts	Cpls	Sgmn	Drivers	Total O.R.s
MALE	R. Sigs	4	1	7	24	-	-	32
	RASC						8	8
	RE (attd)							
FEMALE	ATS	136						

Fig. 18 Extract from War Establishment Auxiliary Units (Signals), April 1942, after decision to expand SDB. (*TNA WO 199/1194*)

		Offrs	Other Ranks						
			CQMS	Sgts	Cpls	L/Cpl	Sgmn	Drivers	Total O.R.s
MALE	R. Sigs	7	1	7	25	3	55	-	91
	RASC							12	12
	RE (attd)	4							
FEMALE	ATS	32							

Fig. 19 Extract from War Establishment Auxiliary Units (Signals), February 1943. (*TNA WO 199/1194*)

		Offrs	Other Ranks					
			CQMS	Sgts	Cpls	Sgmn	Drivers	Total O.R.s
MALE	R. Sigs	7	1	7	20	42	-	69
	RASC						12	12
	RE (attd)	4						
FEMALE	ATS	56						

Fig. 20 Extract from War Establishment of Auxiliary Units (Signals), June 1944. (*TNA WO 199/1194*)

		Offrs	Other Ranks					
			CQMS	Sgts	Cpls	Sgmn	Drivers	Total O.R.s
MALE	R. Sigs	7	1	7	20	41	-	69
	RASC						10	10
	RE (attd)	4						
FEMALE	ATS	57					3	3

Early 1941 OUT Stations would be highly vulnerable after enemy occupation: some simply consisted of wireless sets buried in a large box within a woodland and could be easily tracked. One at Donnington-on-Bain, Lincolnshire, operated by the local coal merchant and manager of the abattoir, was discovered by an RAF courting couple during a transmission. The local army unit was quickly summoned and the operators were arrested as suspected spies. Some of the soldiers were all for shooting them on the spot and one round was fired, but fortunately missed. Having been detained overnight, they were released next morning on the instructions of the Chief Constable![71] Later stations were more carefully-hidden underground beneath chicken coops, toilets etc. Unfortunately the underground station at Telscombe, Suffolk was discovered when a poacher sat on the tree stump that was cunningly set over the entrance hatch. It fell over to expose the chamber hidden beneath. Despite the dubious circumstances of discovery, the police were summoned and the station had to be moved.[72] Until early 1942 the IN Stations were sited in surface Nissen huts at static army HQs, given the cover name of 'Met Huts'. The operators were even supplied with daily weather forecasts to satisfy curious onlookers.[73] These were generally around 15 miles from the coast. If the HQ had to move because of enemy action then the IN Station was either left isolated with no secure means of quickly passing its messages to the Intelligence Officer or, if it moved with the HQ, the whole system was likely to collapse as the aerials of the OUT Stations, in territory now controlled by the enemy, could not be re-aligned. Only from early 1942 were the IN Stations provided with secure underground 'Zero' stations, with supplies with which to operate for up to three weeks.[74] Even then, if the military HQ had been obliged to retreat behind the GHQ Stop-Line then there was only a slim chance that the IN Stations would have been able to make contact with the new HQ location. Later in the war, Ken Ward pointed out that the 'Met Huts' might be sited at a distance from the Area, Divisional or Corps HQ requiring field telephones or, from 1943, the easily-detectable and short-range WS17 wireless sets used to communicate from the Met Huts to the army HQ – even bicycles were sometimes used.[75] This was hardly a secret or secure solution. Some operators maintained they had a secure telephone line in the Zero Station (although they did not know to where this reported) but the close-down report of 28 June 1944 maintains that there were no line connections.[76] The story, told decades after the event, may be a confusion with the field telephones.

The problems of maintaining the SDB wireless system during an invasion are obvious and not a system one might consider if it was seriously envisaged that the SDB would operate for any significant period during enemy occupation. As David Lampe wrote in 1968: 'The Special Duties Organisation of Auxiliary Units was beyond doubt the part of the organisation that would have collapsed most quickly after the Germans got a foothold in Britain, for underground broadcasting from fixed stations is untenable.'[77] Gubbins admitted that the Operation Branch was essentially a cheap bonus to anti-invasion planning and the same might be said of the SDB. Their main contribution might have been simply as another option for an early warning system to report initial invasion if the Auxiliary Coastguard and Observer Corps posts had been eliminated, as it was during the first few hours of landings that GHQ were most desperate to know the details of the enemy build-up in bridgehead areas. Thereafter, as it became increasingly likely that the link with the IN Stations would be broken, reconnaissance units from the GHQ Phantom Unit, already moving up and down the coast, could be deployed to provide specialist military intelligence on the enemy.

Even as the SDB became operational with their TRD sets in early 1941, both the improving military situation and the expanding panoply of intelligence sources made their anti-invasion contribution less essential. Britain would now not be so blind upon invasion as it might have been during June–August 1940 or when Hills began work on the new wireless set. Sources of advance intelligence improved steadily, notably through the later breaking of the German signal codes at Bletchley Park. After screening, such intelligence would then be quickly passed to army commands via the mobile Special Communications Units of SIS, their wireless vehicles discretely parked behind the command HQs. The Royal Navy and RAF also jointly established a chain of 'Home Defence Units' – a series of wireless stations on the east and south coasts monitoring German wireless traffic, managed by RAF Kingsdown and feeding their information direct to Fighter Command HQ and to the Royal Navy.[78] Actual landings were likely to have been reported first by the Coastguard, regular troops and Home Guard patrolling the beaches or by the anti-invasion motor boats of the naval Auxiliary Patrols. If necessary, under the terms of their agreement with MI5, agents of Section VII might also break radio silence and report the arrival and movements of the enemy. The GHQ Liaison Regiment (Phantom) had been expanded and was now dispersed across the country with its efficient high-speed communication system. In January 1941 the Reconnaissance Corps was also founded from infantry brigade reconnaissance units and distributed within corps areas ready to probe enemy lines and provide tactical information to army HQs. By now some Scout Sections of the Auxiliary Units were also in a position to be able to communicate by wireless from behind enemy lines. A renewed military significance for the SDB came only later in the war, when the limitations of the system became less critical in reporting the arrival of enemy parachute raids, especially in the run-up to D-Day.

The absence of control by the Auxiliary Units over intelligence collected by the SDB mirrors the lack of control over the actions of the Operational Patrols once they had gone to ground. One significant consequence was that there was no mechanism within the Auxiliary Units HQ by which they could re-task the Operational Patrols from information transmitted by the SDB. Oxenden records that a few joint exercises were held between the two branches of the Auxiliary Units but that the contacts seemed to lead nowhere and were allowed to die a natural death.[79] Such lack of coherence is another pointer to the rushed nature of the formation of the organisation and also to the fact that the Auxiliary Units were not intended to be an independent intelligence agency rivalling that of SIS or Military Intelligence. Its duty was to collect, not analyse or distribute intelligence. If the SDB had only served an anti-invasion role then its significance would have been short-term and limited. The stand-down letter from General Franklyn to Colonel Douglas on 4 July rightly praised the 'keenness and patriotism' of its dedicated civilian volunteers but its claim to have been able 'to furnish accurate information of raids or invasion instantly to military headquarters throughout the country' was part of a wartime hyperbole that has too often been accepted without question.[80] The real value of the SDB lay elsewhere, as will be explored in the following chapter.

Chapter 9

Auxiliary Units (Special Duties Branch), 1942–4: Internal Security and D-Day Planning

> In recent days while our own invasion forces were concentrating, an additional heavy burden was placed on those of you responsible for the maintenance of good security, to ensure that the enemy was denied foreknowledge of our plans and preparations. The Security Reports regularly provided by Special Duties have proved of invaluable assistance to our security staffs.
>
> General Franklyn 4 July 1944[1]

As the risk of invasion decreased, the SDB took on an increasing role in internal security and became part of the D-Day deception planning. Although the importance of the Operational Branch decreased during this period of the war, the role of the SDB became even more significant. After the initial transfer of men and women from the HDS 'Special Duties' during the summer of 1940 and a subsequent burst of direct recruiting in key areas, progress in expanding the SDB slowed down. It was not until a new War Establishment was presented on 4 April 1942 that the SDB expanded further:

> C-in-C has decided that the organisation of the Wireless Installation for the Intelligence side of Auxiliary Units should be expanded to, inclusive, MONTROSE, and should also include SOUTH WALES and NORTH SOMERSET areas.[2]

This was the high point in the expansion of the SDB, although it is not clear how far the plan was completed. The map of the SDB network in 1944, produced by Major Jones, shows links in Scotland that are beyond the normal range of the TRD and although it is possible that unmanned, hidden, relay stations were used, the increasingly-important internal security role of the SDB may not have relied completely on wireless communications.[3] The Auxiliary Units no longer had the free hand that they had enjoyed in the desperate days of 1940. Permission now had to be sought for every expansion and, cheap as it was to run in a national context, already some in the War Office were looking towards cuts in the organisation. As with the Operational Branch, SDB came under the same pressures to reduce the War Establishment. The difficulty in recruiting staff is illustrated in the promotion of Arthur Douglas Ingrams, a civilian OUT Station wireless operator who was appointed on his existing Territorial Reserve rank of Lieutenant in late 1943 to become SDB Intelligence Officer in Devon. Ingrams, born in 1903, had originally been commissioned into the Territorial Army Royal Garrison Artillery in 1923 but had then become a local farmer.[4] ATS commander Beatrice Temple met the 40-year-old Ingrams in late January 1944 and was not impressed, describing him as 'very ineffectual'.[5] Nonetheless, Ingrams moved as IO to Norfolk in spring 1944 with a local rank of Acting Captain, a rank he retained until the end of the war.[6]

It was only in the expansion phase of 1942 that the classic modern vision of SDB IN Station operators in buried Zero Stations where they could continue to secretly pass on messages from the OUT Stations was belatedly implemented, despite being part of the original planning in 1941. By this time the Allies were flexing their muscles for the invasion of Europe and the risk of invasion was judged by contemporaries to be diminishing, although it would have been complacent to completely discount the possibility. The underground Zero Station was more sophisticated than the Operational Bases. Stan Judson described how, in some, the hidden entrance descended into what looked like a Home Guard storage room but a hidden door opened into the transmitting room, equipped with cooking and toilet facilities, with paraffin heater, as well as bunks for sleeping. Beyond this was a generator room to provide lighting and ventilation as well as to charge the wireless batteries (as the sets were permanently switched on). Supplies were provided for up to 21 days' operation underground and a degree of comfort is suggested by the fact that the Harrietsham Zero Station in Kent was discovered when a passer-by saw an ATS operator emerge from the hatch to shake out a rug![7] Although the introduction of the Zero Stations might seem an anachronism in terms of the declining invasion threat, the original long-term plan may simply have continued through inertia. Equally, it came at a time of what was perceived as an increasing risk of airborne and commando raids that might particularly target army HQs.

Anti-Raiding Role
In August 1942 Canadian and British forces mounted a large-scale raid on the French coast at Dieppe as a sop to Stalin's demand that the Allies open a 'second front', to test tactics to be used in a later invasion and to collect intelligence. A series of smaller raids were then carried out into 1944 along the French coast and Channel Islands. Defence planners feared that the Germans might similarly use exploratory raids against Britain. The concern accelerated greatly from 1943, especially the immediate period leading up to D-Day, and had a considerable impact on the development of the Auxiliary Units as a whole. A new sense of urgency is detected in the SDB Intelligence Officers' *Monthly Notes* for August 1943 which announced that IN Stations were to be manned 'by night, as well as by day, in all raid areas'. The anti-raiding role appears to have been focused on the IN and OUT Stations rather than the more coastal SUB-OUT Stations, suggesting the main threat was seen as being inland airborne raids; there is no mention of putting OUT Stations onto 24-hour watch, which would be necessary if they were to receive immediate notice of raids from the SUB-OUT Stations.[8] The new underground Zero Stations offered better protection against the risk of an enemy attack on the associated army HQ, allowing time before detection for them to both receive information from OUT Stations and, if necessary, onwardly-report any attack on the HQ. Exercise Talbot ran from 11–13 December 1943 to test 'Key Men' and observers, and practice

communications. Devised by Major Peter Forbes, head of the SDB from August 1943, this regional exercise covered the area from the Wash down to Southend in Essex with a scenario listing a number of supposed enemy landing sites. It ran from 2pm on Saturday 11 December until 8am on Monday 13 December and involved four different networks, Ormskirk (Lincolnshire), Bowland (Norfolk), Cheviot (Suffolk) and Blidworth (Essex). The transmissions from the OUT Stations (who also received messages from the SUB-OUT Stations) were sent to the IN Station in a simple code. During the exercise, the receiving IN Stations were initially maintained continuously from midday to midnight but would then only receive messages for 10 minutes on every hour or half hour.[9]

This new role coincides with what was surely a related concern to increase the number of WS17 wireless sets (Plate 36) across the SDB. Ken Ward confirmed that the WS17 sets were used to communicate between the new Zero Stations and District, Brigade or Corps HQs if the latter was not co-located with the SDB base.[10] Whatever the claims for wireless security using the TRD, the final crucial link to army intelligence was not secure and any of the new hidden Zero Stations using the WS17 set were highly vulnerable to wireless detection.[11] Speed of communication outweighed any other concerns. Operational IOs had originally requested the WS17 in May 1942 for their own use in providing a link from their HQ unit to their Scout Sections and to army HQs, but the SDB were informed in June that the WS17 had gone out of production: they had to search for second-hand army surplus.[12] The SDB put in a request for 170 WS17 sets in 1943.

> A further 100 [WS]17 sets have now been delivered to this HQ and will be installed in accordance with recommendations already made by IOs.
>
> Fresh sites will NOT be submitted until after the completion of the current programme, which calls for some 170 of these sets.
>
> IOs will be asked for recommendations for further sites at a later date, and consideration will then be given to their installation in areas which at present are without them.[13]

Supply problems meant that the total number of WS17 sets actually supplied was still only 200 in June 1944 and there was no effort from the War Office to make up the shortfall from other types of set.[14] One other use may have been in the temporary 'Scheme' SDB wireless stations that were created for use in battle exercises during 1943. The WS17 would be ideal for such temporary use where security was not a significant issue. In one exercise at Wendover, Buckinghamshire, during September the wireless station was set up in a 3-ton truck and a tent.[15] By December 1943 the SDB had two 15cwt trucks fitted with wireless to provide a mobile capability, which would have been impossible to achieve using the TRD network.[16] (By June 1944, 40 per cent of the wireless sets used by the SDB were WS17s, which suggests that, by then, the network as a whole was not looking for any level of wireless security, beyond that provided by the rarity of VHF frequencies.) It was also in 1943, and probably for the same reason, that the IN Stations were finally brought into the BEETLE system (see above, p.41) to allow instructions from GHQ to be received and then forwarded to the network even if enemy raids caused an interruption to normal communications (see above, Chapter 3). In September 1943, thirty Murphy B81 (Plate 34) and B93 battery-powered wireless sets, the standard army BEETLE receivers, were requisitioned by Auxiliary Units (Signals).[17]

Internal Security Role

The threat of invasion or raids never materialised and in 1948 this was an argument used to disqualify the civilians of the SDB from an issue of the Defence Medal.[18] There was, however, another role that whilst being the least-well-documented, was the most sensitive and arguably their most significant contribution to the war effort. Only a handful of SDB observers and 'cut-out' couriers have ever told their story, most passed away before it was felt acceptable to recount their experiences. Perhaps not surprisingly, the few veterans who have spoken about their service have chosen to focus on their role in training to pass on intelligence on German troop movements following an invasion. That another role was to spy on one's neighbours, even acting as 'honey-traps', was very 'un-British' – especially if they still lived in the area. Yet such surveillance was an important part of the government's strategy to monitor all aspects of life in a total war and had been used in 1940 to legitimise the operation of SIS on British soil, in support of the internal security role of MI5.

The rigid wireless network had self-evident limitations in gathering battlefield intelligence and the later anti-raiding role, although providing a new *raison d'être*, still relied primarily on a rapid response from the wireless operators. This would leave the observers and 'cut-outs' without real purpose if their role was purely to feed intelligence to the OUT Stations. Although (as with the Operational Branch) the SDB might have survived partly through bureaucratic inertia, a substantial body of discreet citizens who had demonstrated their commitment and had all signed the Official Secrets Act was useful to MI5 and Military Intelligence in the same way as the Section VII network continued to assist in internal security monitoring – and cost virtually nothing to maintain. The wireless network with its inventive concealed stations has attracted attention as the most tangible aspect of the SDB and virtually all of the recorded reminiscences have been from the wireless operators or members of the Auxiliary Units (Signals) which were, however, a small percentage of the total number of volunteers. In all, by the end of the war there had been as few as 250 civilian wireless operators but around 3,500 other observers or couriers.[19] An ongoing security role also kept the SDB Intelligence Officers in what might be considered more gainful employment beyond simply arranging the regular transmission of test messages and calling up the maintenance teams of the Auxiliary Units (Signals) when required. Not all of the wireless operators may have been aware of this aspect of the SDB. As the war had progressed, it had quickly become evident that the wireless operator was most at risk from capture and so was it therefore considered desirable to only allow them only partial access to wider responsibilities of the cell?[20]

Colonel Major (Plate 11) may already have been looking to expand beyond the short-term anti-invasion role of the SDB when he and Maurice Petherick began its reorganisation in late 1940. The Auxiliary Units had already had to fight off one attempt at disbandment in September and as the threat of invasion diminished over the winter, they needed to find a new purpose for the network of civilian agents and couriers. Major was a Whitehall staff officer who had earlier worked in the Directorate of Military Intelligence (DMI) but with no background in any form of irregular warfare and his main focus in coming to the Auxiliary Units may have been the development of the spy network of the SDB, his appointment a sign that DMI wanted to better integrate this into their wider intelligence systems. This concern to prevent the SDB, with its SIS heritage, from acting in isolation can be seen later in 1942 when the then CO, Lord Glanusk, sought to expand the SDB. He was told by the War Office in September 1942 to make certain 'that we relate the increases to the general plan for collection of intelligence'.[21] Although surviving sources have skewed the balance of Auxiliary Units history towards the Operational Patrols and the wireless network, the less dramatic internal security role of the SDB may have been the critical element of the Auxiliary Units organisation. The character of the Operational Patrols begins to drift; but whilst Oxenden suggests that Operational Intelligence Officers began to avoid visiting army HQs from 1943 in order not to draw attention to their continued existence, the implication is that their SDB equivalents did not withdraw in this way, being in a stronger position.[22]

Military Intelligence had only become a separate Directorate within the War Office at the outbreak of the Second World War. There was rapid expansion thereafter which included, in May 1940, the creation of a section shared with MI5 that was responsible for military and munitions security operations. The creation of the Intelligence Corps on 19 July 1940 finally allowed military intelligence to move away from the previously ad hoc operational system within DMI. MI11 and the Field Security Section (FSS) of the new Intelligence Corps became responsible for field security, including protecting military personnel from 'fifth columnists' whilst MI14 was responsible for invasion intelligence and intelligence from 'special sources'. Over the summer of 1940, DMI had made repeated attempts to take over the running of Grand's Section D but had been out-manoeuvred by Hugh Dalton in his creation of SOE while another frustration remained in that, although under the War Office, the Auxiliary Units lay outside the remit of DMI in GHQ. The SDB became an intelligence-gathering anomaly. There were other cross-overs; the work of the Operational Patrols in testing the security of divisional HQs, airfields etc, by breaching the defences and planting dummy explosives to the embarrassment of the defenders has been well reported. Less well-known is that the Field Security Section (FSS) of the new Intelligence Corps carried out similar undercover tests of security in vital points and military bases nationwide. Another key duty of the FSS was to go undercover to eavesdrop on any dangerous 'loose talk' by off-duty troops or even plans for deliberate espionage on military installations. Stan Judson from Auxiliary Units (Signals) recorded how such monitoring in Lincolnshire led to all leave being cancelled in one divisional area because of the lack of security that was revealed. In one instance the landlord of a local pub was able to hear a conversation between RAF personnel and civilian contractors in his pub, in which details of the handover of an airfield and who would be operating from it were discussed![23] It would therefore have been logical to want to coordinate these activities, although the detail is necessarily speculative.

The FSS may have been one point of reference in Colonel Major's plans to reorganise the SDB as part of a wider military intelligence network beyond that of a short-term anti-invasion coast-watching service, one which could supplement the covert intelligence-gathering of the FSS in the vulnerable coastal areas by using local civilian observers; SDB Intelligence Officers would act as liaison officers. The coastal distribution of SDB was well-suited to this security task; from 1943 onwards it was particularly able to cover the assembly and embarkation zones of the invasion army. It would also provide the military with an independent ability to gather intelligence on suspected fifth columnists that MI5 was so reluctant to share with army commanders (see above, p.101). There is only one official mention of such a sensitive internal security role in the SDB but this clearly emphasises its importance: the C-in-C, Home Forces, General Franklyn, wrote to Douglas on 4 July 1944 'In recent days while our own invasion forces were concentrating, an additional heavy burden was placed on those of you responsible for the maintenance of good security, to ensure that the enemy was denied foreknowledge of our plans and preparations. The Security Reports regularly provided by Special Duties have proved of invaluable assistance to our security staffs.'[24] No mention of any such security reports has ever been made by local SDB operatives but the role was referred to by Major Peter Forbes, the officer in charge of the SDB from August 1943, who maintained 'it was probably the most important SD [Special Duties] work'. He explained in 2002: 'at the end of '43 the out-stations were given an important new role; that of reporting rumours circulating from East Anglia and all along the South Coast. The War Office wanted to know what was being picked up about concentrations for the invasion.' He added that once the threat of German invasion had diminished, the role of the observer was changed 'along the south coast and probably in East Anglia as well, to report on what people were talking about in pubs about where the invasion ("D" Day) was going to be and what British troops were moving into their areas, in fact anything the War Office wanted to know about leaked information about our invasion, as to where it was going to be'.[25] For the War Office, the female observers had particular attractions in such a role. Having recognised that in guerrilla warfare the 'exercise of feminine charms on occupying troops will always be worthwhile', this principle could be transferred into internal security to create 'honey traps' to catch loose-tongued troops (Plate 38).[26] Forbes devised a series of exercises across the SDB network with stories made up by the observers and passed through the network of OUT and IN Stations but as this was an internal exercise it is still not clear how the transmission of information to higher authority would work in reality. Each night, Forbes would listen to the stories coming into one of the IN Stations and then pass them on to Colonel Douglas; this is the only mention of Auxiliary Units HQ having any coordination role in intelligence work and would have been an unnecessary complication in actual operations, given that Douglas would have no means of assessing the information. In reality it might be supposed that Intelligence Officers forwarded messages to the FSS rather than funnelling everything through Douglas.

Despite Forbes' exercises, an internal security role may not have relied entirely on the wireless network. SIS had established a principle of intelligence organisations, and even parts of organisations, working in isolation from each other to increase security. SIS officer Maurice Petherick may have continued the tradition in the early SDB. Other than Forbes' exercises, no OUT or IN Station wireless operator has ever mentioned receiving such security messages and they may not have been fully aware of what was clearly regarded by GHQ as a most important task. It is possible that some of this responsibility by-passed the wireless network, with some of the dead-letter drops not feeding into the OUT Station. This would enable the Intelligence Officers to pass on information using annotated photographs, as reported by Emma, an agent from an unspecified organisation in Sussex, in a way impossible using wireless. Emma was recruited by an officer dressed as a private but wearing concealed badges of rank: 'My job was to try and get them to tell me things they shouldn't have.'[27] She worked from photos of the men supplied to her, presumably by the FSS/MI11 (which could easily acquire photographs of troops); after investigation these were placed in a dead-letter drop with either a tick or a cross, and those men with a cross against their name were quickly moved away. Emma never knew the name of the organisation for which she worked, and as she used a dead-letter drop she never knew what happened to the message thereafter. There is no other information that might identify the organisation for which she worked but it is likely that she was part of some form of joint SDB/FSS or Section VII/FSS operation. Former HDS officer, Robert Fraser, remained as SDB Intelligence Officer for Sussex until April 1944 and the theatre of an officer dressed as a private would have been typical of Section D.

In 1940-1 the presence of the Auxiliary Units Operational Branch in Herefordshire and Worcestershire, two inland counties anomalous in the Auxiliary Units structure, highlights the perceived threat of invasion coming up the Bristol Channel and SIS similarly explained to its Section VII agents in the Midlands the risk of invasion coming from that direction. Worcestershire was also at the heart of a highly important strategic area intended for the relocation of the Royal Family, government and War Office in the event of invasion. This significance was continued by the establishments of the shadow BBC transmission HQ at Wood Norton, just outside Evesham, and from 1942 the Telecommunications Research Establishment (developing radar systems) was based at Malvern. The maintenance of good internal security therefore remained an issue throughout the war. The existence of the SDB in Herefordshire and Worcestershire is confirmed by a surviving memo of 26 October 1943:

> Major Johnson will cease to be an Operational IO but will continue as IO SD in Glamorgan. Additionally he will take over from Captain Bucknall the duties of IO SD Herefordshire and Worcestershire. These changes-over will take effect as from midday on 12 November 1943.[28]

Senior Commander of the ATS within the Auxiliary Units, Beatrice Temple, visited Worcestershire a number of times with SDB staff but any evidence for a wireless network is extremely limited and no wireless network is shown as existing in these areas on the SDB map of June 1944 (Plate 33). John Todd is documented as being Intelligence Officer for the SDB in Worcestershire in 1940–1, succeeded by Captain Henry Bucknall (ex-Royal Artillery) and then Major K. Johnson; with such a specific internal security interest in the area, is it a coincidence that both Todd and Johnson are believed to have been officers of SIS? Was the intelligence operation here maintained as a particularly sensitive joint SIS/ SDB enterprise furthering the agreement made between Valentine Vivian of SIS and MI5 in 1940 (see above, p.19)? As well as accounts of a hybrid HDS/SDB network in Monmouthshire (see above, p.64) there is evidence for one SDB-type intelligence cell at Upton upon Severn, Worcestershire, based around a local coal merchant, with a series of dead-letter drops; a telephone hidden in the basement of a building at nearby Severn Stoke was said to be linked to the county Auxiliary Units HQ at Wolverton Hall (whether a telephone proper or simple OUT Station TRD is unknown). As usual, veterans have only spoken about training to identify German uniforms and units but this SDB cell also lay between the TRE base at Malvern and its secret research airfield at Defford, well placed to listen in to indiscrete conversations in local public houses.

D-Day Deception

Another late war role for the SDB connected with the preparations for D-Day was as part of the huge wireless deception planning that involved every wireless network system in Britain except the CROSSBOW signals units tracking the V1 rockets into London. The general concept for what would be known as Operation Fortitude was discussed as early as February 1943 and the wireless deception from June 1943. The latter included the invention of highly detailed radio traffic to be intercepted by German Intelligence in order to convince the enemy that troops were massing for the forthcoming invasion in East Anglia and Scotland – suggesting landings away from the actual Normandy beaches. In addition, the plan was to periodically fill the airwaves with bursts of intense wireless traffic, followed by periods of total radio silence across the whole country. By this tactic, the Germans would not be able to use periods of high or low radio traffic to predict the oncoming storm of invasion. Auxiliary Units HQ was automatically included as part of a general order to all regional commands.[29] These bursts of activity/silence occurred from autumn 1943 but especially from February 1944. Periods of wireless activity/silence could be a matter of hours or a number of days: as an example, there was to be intense activity 18–19 and 23–26 May and wireless silence from 27–30 May. This fits with the memory of Roy Russell who has recorded that in late May 1944 the SDB received orders to broadcast dummy messages in code for 24 hours a day.[30] In May 1944 there was consternation in MI5 that a possible loophole had been found in a coastal VHF network (although there is no evidence this was the SDB) that confirmed the need for this to adhere strictly to the Fortitude broadcasting schedule. Guy Liddell, head of counter-espionage in MI5, reported:

> steps had now been taken by TAR [Colonel Robertson] to get certain radio telephony circuits round the coast and in particular to the Scilly Isles, suspended. These were in VHF and it was commonly thought that they could not be picked up by the enemy. Evidence has however been produced that, in certain circumstances, they can have a range of anything up to 500 miles.[31]

The deception planners did not know if signals from the VHF TRDs and WS17 sets could be interpreted by German intelligence across the Channel or by reconnaissance aircraft – it was simply the 'noise' of the traffic that was of interest. As part of the operation, in some areas the Auxiliary Units (Signals) devised meaningless codes to transmit; in others, operators read out poetry or discussed knitting patterns as part of 'training exercises' without knowing the real reason behind the instructions. Roy Russell described how 'We made up hundreds of meaningless five-letter-coded group messages and transmitted them to our OUT Stations for their "dummy traffic" responses; round the clock'.[32] The transmission of dummy messages was a gamble as the main element of Operation Fortitude was to provide a detailed construct of a fake army moving around the country; these messages had to be consistent as otherwise it would become clear they were part of a deception. Swamping the radio waves with gibberish messages would eventually be recognised as a deception device; identifying fake from genuine code would, however, tie up the efforts of the limited number of German wireless interceptors. As German Intelligence was undoubtedly looking for some form of deception exercise perhaps it was thought best to offer up the transmission of gibberish messages as a double bluff and thereby make the main Fortitude deception exercise even more believable.

By June 1944 the SDB still had a formal War Establishment of just fourteen officers and sixteen other ranks, not much larger than the original establishment of 1940. The Auxiliary Units (Signals) had sixty-eight officers and seventy-nine other ranks engaged on signals maintenance, watch-keeping at IN Stations and training, including fifty-seven officers and three other ranks from ATS engaged in watch-keeping and training plus four Royal Engineer subalterns and thirteen drivers; twenty-one of the other ranks from the HQ establishment were carpenters and bricklayers engaged full-time on maintaining hides. This small establishment supported, according to Colonel Douglas, an unpaid civilian network of 3,250 agents, couriers and wireless operators.[33] The stand-down of the SDB was finally announced on 4 July 1944, their work in helping to protect the D-Day landings being over. The original core of the Auxiliary Units (Signals) then featured in the first published photograph of the Auxiliary Units in January 1945 (in the *Bulletin* of the Radio Society of Great Britain), to mark the final disbanding of the 'Bachelors' at Coleshill (Plate 41).[34]

We may never know the full extent of the work of the SDB whose most valuable task may have been not to spy on German invaders but to watch, listen and report on their neighbours and to protect the security of Allied forces. Unfortunately the decision was taken in 1947 that the civilians of the SDB, unlike their Home Guard colleagues in the Operational Branch, would not qualify for the Defence Medal.[35] In an argument that was both inaccurate and insulting, it was even suggested in 1948 that because no invasion had actually occurred, 'the direct contribution of these people to the defence of the UK was nil'.[36] It would be decades before their contribution to D-Day planning and internal security could be revealed.

Chapter 10

GHQ Liaison Regiment (Phantom)

For all the modern fascination with civilian spies and secret armies, their role and significance can only be properly assessed in the wider strategic context and, in the case of the HDS and SDB, by the concurrent solutions provided by more conventional intelligence-gathering. Lacking wireless communication and relying on untried observers, in 1940 the HDS and SDB were pale reflections of the Coast Watching Service, Observer Corps and the intelligence operation undertaken by the GHQ Reconnaissance Unit, code-named Phantom (GHQ Liaison Regiment from 30 January 1941). Phantom was formally classed as secret largely, it seems, because its founder Lieutenant Colonel Hopkinson perceptively realised 'it will be much easier to get equipment if we call it "secret"' although its members and vehicles were easily recognised by the white 'P' on black unit flash.[1] (This was a lesson that Gubbins quickly adopted in the Auxiliary Units.) The novel nature of Phantom may have been the reason for General Ironside, C-in-C Home Forces, to describe it to Churchill on 19 July as one of the 'Special Irregular Units' which illustrates the loose interpretation at the time of what classed as irregular warfare.[2]

The No.3 British Air Mission was created in September 1939 under Wing Commander J.M. Fairweather, with just seven officers and 22 other ranks, to furnish the commander of the RAF in France with the best information that could be supplied by the Belgian GHQ as to the disposition of both Allied and enemy troops. The tactic of *blitzkrieg* had meant that the traditional concept of a front line no longer applied and Allied troops were dispersed in 'forward defended localities' meaning it was vital for the RAF to have up to the minute intelligence to distinguish between friendly and hostile forces. The code name of this Mission was Phantom. In October 1939 an army unit (the Hopkinson Mission) command by Lieutenant Colonel Hopkinson, a staff officer in the BEF, was attached to work under the orders of Fairweather and supplement the information by ground reconnaissance. Phantom then became the code name for the combined missions. Hopkinson was a firm advocate of the value of wireless communication at a time when its reputation for reliability was poor in the army but the principle of the new unit was that it would directly transmit up to date information on the course of the campaign to the Headquarters of the RAF and BEF by wireless. Its patrols of skilled linguists, equipped with wireless in Dingo scout cars and motorcycle dispatch riders were largely drawn from the Royal Armoured Corps, Queen Victoria's Rifles (a Territorial motorcycle battalion) and Royal Signals. The next few months were spent in intensive training with wireless procedures being a priority. The W/T operators were expected to achieve consistent speeds of 20–30 words a minute and Hopkinson's mantra was 'There's no mystery about wireless. Phantom must get through'.

The experience of Phantom with the BEF is pertinent to what might be expected following an invasion of Britain. On 7 May 1940 warning was received that a German invasion of the Low Countries was imminent. The War Diary of the Hopkinson Mission for 10 May reads: 'Crack went the whip and off went the horses'. Liaison officers and patrols were immediately dispatched across the front. Their patrols negotiated the forward areas, gathering intelligence on the movements of both Allied and enemy units, enemy troop composition and listening in to German wireless traffic. The intelligence was coded and then immediately sent back to the Phantom Intelligence Section either by wireless or motorcycle dispatch rider. The Intelligence Section under Captain John Collings then quickly collated and distributed the information by wireless between the various Corps and Divisional HQs. Their patrols and the Intelligence Officers were equipped with No.11 sets with a range of over 20 miles R/T and 30–40 miles on W/T, using their own home-made code. This is roughly equivalent to the range of the TRD sets of the SDB but with the key difference being that the Phantom sets were designed for mobility. The intelligence was then transmitted to rear links whose No.9 sets had a range of 120 miles on W/T and could immediately pass on the information to RAF command and British, French and Belgian GHQs. This greatly short-circuited the normal lines of communication back from front-line units.

They immediately proved their worth and as the *blitzkrieg* progressed across the Low Countries and France, a steady flow of information was passed in to the Commander-in-Chief of the BEF who might give specific orders to collect information on particular areas of the front where intelligence was lacking. They were sometimes providing information to BEF HQ 30 hours in advance of other sources.[3] At times, theirs was the only battle intelligence reaching the HQ. By the time of its evacuation from France on 31 May 1940 the unit consisted of 15 officers and 110 other ranks. It comprised an HQ with four wireless stations, the Phantom Squadron comprising two troops of Guy armoured cars fitted with No.11 wireless sets and a motorcycle platoon, and finally John Collings' Intelligence Section mounted on motorcycles, with a Wireless Section of two No.9 and two No.11 sets.

Sadly, on 28 May 1940 Fairweather and many of the Phantom staff were lost during the Dunkirk evacuation when their ship was torpedoed by an E-Boat off Ostend. Despite this blow, within a matter of days Hopkinson had sent a formal proposal to the War Office (7 June), suggesting that they consider the possibilities of employing his reconnaissance units in Britain.[4] Their potential was stressed when Phantom officer Captain John Jackson produced a report on their activities in France to the War Office:

> It [Phantom] has continued to be not only the quickest channel, but frequently the only source of information available to the Commander-in-Chief. If this service was useful in France, it must be indispensable in the imminent battle to defend our shores.[5]

Hopkinson proposed that the organisation might consist of a headquarters located at GHQ Home Forces and four reconnaissance units, one located in South-East England, one in East Anglia, one north of the Humber and one in reserve in the Midlands. Each of the four reconnaissance units would consist of:

(i) Headquarters.
(ii) Intelligence Troop (six to ten officers mounted on motorcycle combinations, with despatch riders).
(iii) Motorcycle Squadron (six troops each of three armed motorcycle combinations, with a proportion of solo motorcyclists).
(iv) Armoured Squadron (six troops, each of three scout cars, one with a wireless set, one with a Bren gun and one with an anti-tank rifle).
(v) Signal Squadron, with four mobile No.9 sets for communication to G.H.Q. and R.A.F., five or six mobile No.11 sets for use of the Intelligence Troop and Motorcycle Squadron and a No.11 anchor set for working to the armoured troops.[6]

Hopkinson explained 'Other headquarters and units could be supplied with information under arrangements to be made locally, but the main object of getting information from the battlefield to GHQ and the RAF in the shortest possible time should not be lost sight of. The reconnaissance units therefore should be controlled by their own headquarters which would be located at GHQ and operating under the orders of the C-in-C.'[7] Hopkinson stressed the importance of the motorcycles as experience had demonstrated that they had not only speed but could also get through roads crowded with refugees. Phantom was first billeted in Lechlade, Gloucestershire, while Hopkinson drew up his plans. His intention was to provide fast and accurate information to GHQ Home Forces and the RAF regarding the points at which landings were made, their scale and their subsequent progress. In contrast to the HDS and SDB, Phantom had the advantage of a tried and tested wireless system, and skilled patrols operating with armed protection. The War Office swiftly approved and Phantom was formally reconstituted as No.1 GHQ Reconnaissance Unit on 26 June (re-named GHQ Liaison Regiment from 30 January 1941 to resolve potential confusion with the new Reconnaissance Corps).

Phantom moved briefly to a new base at Kneller Hall near Twickenham before moving the regimental HQ to the derelict Richmond Hill Hotel, Surrey, with the Royal Signals section in Wick House opposite, where an operations room was equipped with rows of powerful R107 receivers ready to monitor enemy transmissions. These buildings were adjacent to Richmond Park, whose varied terrain was used for rigorous driver training. Each man of the patrol had to be able to drive the motorcycle, armoured car and truck at speed through various obstacles and repair simple faults. Both officers and men also had to be competent wireless operators. Pembroke Lodge in the Park served as officers' mess and billet. The park was also home to the Holding Unit for new recruits and for training. Richmond, on the western outskirts of London, had good road communications to the regions in which the patrols would operate and was close to the HQ of Home Forces at St Paul's School. A Battle HQ detachment was sited in St James's Park, conveniently adjacent to the Admiralty 'Citadel'. Phantom had worked closely with the Communications Section of SIS on its return from France in order to improve the effective range of their wireless sets and it is no coincidence that they shared their St James's Park base with a mobile Special Communications Unit (SCU) of SIS. As a method of last resort, from late 1940 the patrols had carrier pigeons with a pigeon loft containing 500 pigeons installed at the James's Park HQ by Captain Sir John Wrightson. After David Niven took command of 'A' squadron in

February 1941, when it was based at Stourton House, Wiltshire, he tested the method by sending a jocular message back to St James's Park by pigeon: 'That beast Major Niven sent me away because he said I had farted in the nest.' Unfortunately the message was opened during a visit by General Paget (then GOC South Eastern Command) and a member of the Royal family. The general was apparently not amused![8] Preparing for the potential of fighting in and around London, Wrightson was also tasked with investigating the potential of using ASDIC on the pipes of the London sewage system as an alternative communications system. The unit vehicles were marked front and back with the distinctive white 'P' and Berkshire police, who used the same identifier, had to be persuaded to change their signs to 'Police'.

In France it had been found that, even with limited resources, Phantom could cover the entire forward area in a day. To meet the challenge of an invasion of Britain it doubled its size to 28 officers and 222 other ranks, divided into HQ, Intelligence Section motorcycle troop and initially three (later four) reconnaissance squadrons each of four heavily-armed patrols with an officer and six men. Half the strength was immediately deployed across the country while the other half continued training at Richmond and was ready to be deployed wherever most needed upon invasion. The patrols carried enough supplies so that each patrol was capable of operating independently for 21 hours, reporting back to a squadron HQ that could operate independently for three weeks. The messages they sent back to GHQ had high priority and would also be received by Corps and armoured division HQs.[9] Each patrol was now equipped with motorcycles and motorcycle combinations with Bren guns, a 15cwt truck (with governors illegally removed to enable speeds of 80–90mph) and a scout car equipped with a No.11 wireless set and carrying a Thompson sub-machine gun.[10] Phantom also had its own Light Aid Detachment to quickly recover and repair damaged vehicles. The squadrons immediately began detailed assessments of likely invasion beaches and harbours, aerial landing zones and potential plans of attack.

By 3 September 1940, the unit had grown to 47 officers and 455 other ranks, with four reconnaissance squadrons based in the South East, East Anglia and Yorkshire; a reserve in Gloucestershire carried out a detailed survey of the state of coastal defences in Wales in case of an invasion via Ireland.[11] Each squadron, with an HQ at the regional Corps HQ, consisted of four patrols of an officer and six men, based at divisional HQs (mirroring the SDB organisational structure). There were also three RAF observer aircraft attached to the unit, piloted by officers in the HQ group and intended to be employed purely for intercommunication purposes within the unit but not fitted with wireless. Instead, contact was to be made either by landing the aircraft or by message-dropping and ground-signalling. The Phantom Unit War Diary shows patrols moving up and down the coast from East Anglia to Dorset, in constant wireless contact with their HQ and day-by-day providing regular weather updates and visibility levels across the sea. In return they were fed the latest intelligence on German army and naval movements so they were ready to redeploy to a particular area at a moment's notice.[12] In contrast with the short-range and brittle Auxiliary Units SRD network, the Phantom network, with wireless sets now modified by SIS to extend their range, was designed so that the Reconnaissance Squadrons could operate for long periods up to a distance of 50 miles from the Patrol to the Squadron HQ and 400 miles from Squadron to the Unit HQ situated beside GHQ Home Forces. The procedure was for a Reconnaissance Squadron entering a Corps Area to send an officer to Corps Headquarters to report their proposed action and to inform the staff on which wireless frequencies and call signs the squadron would be operating. As well as transmitting directly to GHQ, a copy of the Unit cipher was also given to the Corps Staff, so that they could listen in to the Unit's wireless reports without any delay. The squadron then kept in the closest possible touch with formations and Units.

The Phantom patrols would have been at the forefront of anti-invasion intelligence-gathering, operating at considerable risk but, in the prevailing spirit of defiance, some made unofficial plans to go further. After 'A' Squadron had moved during 1941 to Montgomery's 5 Corps, David Niven maintained: 'we also made ourselves ready to go underground and a large stock of disguises was earmarked for distribution if the invasion was successful. I, personally, was ready to re-emerge dressed as a parson'.[13] Being prepared to fight on as guerrillas may just have been bravado (or even a post-war literary fantasy) but the patrols had gathered an intimate knowledge of their operating area and were well equipped to live off the land. Having worked so closely with the SCU it is also possible that they could maintain wireless contact with SIS. In acknowledgement of the contribution of Phantom, a review by GHQ on 24 October 1940 concluded that the problem of receiving speedy intelligence from the battlefield

> has been partially solved by superimposing on the normal system an independent information collecting service provided by the GHQ Reconnaissance Unit, equipped with armoured and un-armoured reconnaissance troops, liaison officers, mobile wireless sets and aircraft. The sole duty of this unit is to send to the Commander-in-Chief the very latest news of events in the more important sectors of the battle field.[14]

It was now proposed that the assessment of the received intelligence should not only be directly transmitted via wireless to higher commands by Phantom HQ but would also then be broadcast by them on a wider basis to other units via BEETLE (see above, Chapter 3). It may be noted that the SDB did not receive access to BEETLE until 1943. The number of squadrons would be expanded to six covering the West and Southwest; Hampshire, Sussex and Kent; East Anglia; Lincolnshire; Yorkshire, Durham and Northumberland; Scotland; and Ireland. By autumn 1941 the strength of Phantom was approaching 1,000 men.

The rapid development of the Phantom patrols over the summer of 1940 provided a proven means of supplying battlefield intelligence. It is not surprising that Gubbins recruited Collings to the SDB as Intelligence Officer for East Anglia, to learn any lessons from their experience, but it was evident that the HDS or SDB could offer little to compete. The SDB from 1941 could, however, use wireless communication from behind enemy lines, however briefly, to provide an additional support by providing to army commands what was likely to be only an initial impression of enemy strength and supply lines, supplementing the information gathered by the Coastguard Service and Observer Corps. Together, this might then inform the future deployment of Phantom. The SDB was a cheap option as the operatives were unpaid civilians and the support staff were small in number; their loss would be a calculated sacrifice.

Phantom went on to become one of the few success stories of the 1942 Dieppe raid and remained a key element of gathering battlefield intelligence throughout the war, including working behind enemy lines after D-Day with the SAS. Their action-packed later history means that comparatively little attention has been given to their work in Britain during 1940 and 1941 but it was an essential element in the tapestry of preparations for possible invasion.

Chapter 11

Home Guard Saboteurs, Guerrillas and 'Shock Troops'

> Part of the Home Guard's job is to carry on the struggle, if necessary, in areas temporarily overrun by the enemy. This last duty it can only carry out if it learns some of the tactics of guerrilla war.
>
> Tom Wintringham, 1941[1]

Many in the War Office originally saw the Local Defence Volunteers (LDV) only as an armed special constabulary or observation body. After a period of initial confusion as to purpose, the LDV rebranded as the Home Guard on 22 July 1940 and was firmly integrated into anti-invasion planning, albeit in what was recognised as a near-suicidal role.[2] From the outset, there was great concern to establish the LDV/Home Guard as legal combatants (also applying to the Auxiliary Units who were drawn from its ranks). Under the Local Defence Volunteers Regulations, the volunteers were 'members of the armed forces of the Crown and every such member shall ... be subject to military law as a soldier, whether on duty or not'. The legal status of the LDV/Home Guard as soldiers was repeatedly stressed during 1940 and 1941, not least to counter the Nazi accusation, broadcast over German radio on 16 May 1940, that they were armed bands of civilian *francs-tireurs* or 'murder bands'.[3]

The Home Guard, with a strength of over 1.5 million by the end of June 1940, was a huge reservoir of manpower, larger than the whole of the peacetime army. Contrary to the image of TV's *Dad's Army*, its average age was c.35 years, with the majority being in reserved occupations (with many having had previous military service), or fit young men awaiting call-up. The main role in 1940 and 1941 was one of static defence – to delay the enemy advance for as long as possible by denying free access through communication hubs. There was a secondary, less well-defined, harrying role but this became increasingly contentious as it began to be popularly labelled as guerrilla warfare.

During the First World War the predecessor of the Home Guard was the Volunteer Training Corps (later Volunteer Force). It had been explicitly trained to act as a guerrilla force, although in practice (as a precedent for the Second World War Home Guard) it was mainly used to guard vulnerable points and then to man the new anti-aircraft batteries. If necessary, the VTC were 'to take the form of bands of irregulars' and, in terms identical to the orders given to the Home Guard in 1940, were to 'constantly harass, annoy, and tire out the enemy, and to impede his progress, till a sufficient force can be assembled to smash him' (*VTC Regulations*, 1916).[4] In March 1940, the then Commander-in-Chief, Home Forces, General Walter Kirke, ordered a review of lessons from the VTC in case a similar body was needed again.⁵ Kirke established the broad outline of a plan for a local defence force which in the event of invasion would operate on a decentralised basis as small groups of guerrillas 'on the principle of the Boer Commando'.⁶ In the chaotic negotiations leading up to the approval of the LDV, on Monday 13 May the Adjutant-General's representative objected to referencing the Boer commandos, which brought back unhappy memories to the War Office and, to many, suggested anarchy.⁷ It was the beginning of a conflict of emphasis over 'guerrilla warfare' that would last for over three years. The rushed approval of the LDV without any clear idea of how it might operate has a striking parallel a month later in the formation of the Auxiliary Units.

Kirke's successor, General Ironside, initially rejected a role for the LDV in anti-invasion defence with the War Office, only regarding it as useful as an observation body for which the nickname 'Look, Duck and Vanish' was a good summary of their function. Their determination to fight and the sheer size of their potential resource soon caused a re-think. As part of Ironside's Defence Plan of 25 June 1940, the LDV took on responsibility for manning stop-lines and attempting to slow the advance of the enemy from the invasion beaches. This was just two days after the first bulk shipment of arms destined for the LDV arrived from the USA. The nationwide distribution of the LDV meant they were also likely to be the first force to make contact with airborne troops who might drop further inland. There were no illusions over their chance of survival, ordered to hold their positions to the last man and last round. The life expectancy for many Home Guard in the invasion areas was likely to be a matter of hours or days. The invasion would not have been a 'gentlemanly' war, as Ironside warned in his speech to the LDV on 5 June when he exhorted them to meet brutality with brutality.⁸ Ironside issued one million rounds of 12-bore shotgun cartridges consisting of a single large lead ball 'lethal shot'. In the First World War the Germans had declared that shotguns, as frequently used by American infantry in the trenches, were inhuman and had threatened to kill, out of hand, any soldier found with one. Now thousands of shotguns were in use by the Home Guard, using the official 'lethal shot' and home-made versions made by binding normal lead shot with candle-wax; both types of ammunition were outside the agreed conventions of ammunition to be used in war. Wintringham's Osterley Park Training School also advised the men to file their rifle ammunition into expanding 'dum dum' bullets (a practice followed in the Operational Patrols of the Auxiliary Units); the horrific wounds caused by this ammunition would make the taking of prisoners even less likely. In dealing with paratroopers appearing to want to surrender the advice from Osterley Park was 'shoot first and examine later'.⁹ The Germans would have had to rely on speed to force a British surrender before their limited supplies of fuel and ammunition were exhausted. Frustrated by a depth of defence they had not had to encounter previously, by men using methods they considered inhuman, many in the Home Guard were unlikely to have been taken prisoner, whatever their legal status.

General Alan Brooke replaced Ironside as C-in-C Home Forces on 19 July, with the advantage of increasing resources already pouring into the country from across the Empire and arms from the USA. The Home Guard, already beginning to be armed with the first of thousands of US P17 rifles as well as Lewis guns and BARs, was now given a more structured part in the plan.¹⁰ Instead of Ironside's static stop-lines there would be a greater reliance on defence in depth focused on a network of 'defended localities'. The particular task of the Home Guard was to protect communications hubs ('nodal points') as it had been pointed out that the German armour in France had largely kept to the roads. In Britain there were few roads that ran parallel and instead they tended to converge on 'nodal points' which might be towns, village crossroads or river crossings. By blocking these, even for a few hours, the enemy *blitzkrieg* could be significantly disrupted, giving time for the field army to concentrate and mount a counter-attack.[11] In 1943 the key role of the Home Guard upon any invasion was stated simply: 'The fighting task of the Home Guard is to deny rail and road communication to the enemy.'[12] Although this was still essentially a static role, Home Guard General Instruction No.10 (1 August 1940) identified the role of delaying the enemy 'by any means in their power'. It would include 'dispute, with desultory fire, every fence, ditch, wall etc, covering the approaches to their village, and, if driven in, harass the enemy from house to house as he attempts to advance through the village'.[13] Beyond such general orders, little official guidance was given on the harrying role – a gap first filled by the teachings at the unofficial Osterley Park Home Guard Training School (see below) and it was widely interpreted as including guerrilla warfare. An exception was tank-hunting, which Churchill had highlighted on 19 July 1940 among his list of specialist units needed to resist invasion. The publication of *LDV Instruction no. 8. Tanks and Tank Destruction* in July (probably written by Wintringham) put the LDV at the forefront of the crucial defence against the Panzers. It provided the basis for the expanded instructions for the army – *Tank Hunting and Destruction, Military Training Pamphlet no. 42* – not published until the end of August. Tank-hunting was treated by the volunteers as a new and deadly sport. From September 1940 Western Command organised one or more tank-hunting sections in each Home Guard battalion, comprising a minimum of a section leader and nine men. They were armed with Molotov cocktails, rifles and a Lewis gun, and equipped with an axe for tree-felling (to make road-blocks) and two crowbars. Each section would operate within a five-mile radius, tasked with stalking and destroying enemy tanks. By March 1941 there were 171 specialist tank-hunting sections in Western Command alone, with an average strength of 39 and comprising in all 7,141 men.[14]

In a complementary strategy, as the Home Guard tried to harry and slow the enemy frontal advance, the HDS and later the Auxiliary Units could hopefully attack them in the flanks and rear areas, preventing the invaders from establishing secure lines of communication and destroy fuel and stores dumps. Included in Churchill's examples of 'special irregular units' on 19 June was the proposed 1st American (Motorised) Squadron of the Home Guard, officially formed in July. Recruited from US citizens living in London, these volunteers were well-equipped from private means and were highly-regarded, especially by Churchill – not least because he recognised their propaganda value. As a measure of their status, they formed part of the guard to the HQ of C-in-C London District and took part in exercises with the Morris Detachment who were responsible for royal protection.[15]

Despite the early reluctance of the War Office to acknowledge any widespread guerrilla warfare role for the LDV, in July 1940 the shortage of equipment meant that the War Office had little choice but to accept local interpretations on how best to slow down an enemy advance. A pessimistic report to the War Cabinet on 25 May had concluded 'should the enemy succeed in establishing a force, with its vehicles, firmly ashore – the army in the United Kingdom, which is very short of equipment, has not got the offensive power to drive it out'.[16] In an attempt to restore the guerrilla function to the LDV as envisaged by Kirke, on the same day Captain Peter Fleming of MI(R) was attached to Home Forces 'for the purpose of training LDVs etc in fighting behind the German lines in case of invasion of this country'.[17] Fleming (Plate 7) did not, however, have a mechanism with which to implement his ideas until he was able to bolt-on LDV patrols to General Thorne's new XII Corps Observation Unit in Kent and Sussex. Others would not wait. For Major Gray, a company commander in Edinburgh Home Guard, the choice was in training 'second-class regular soldiers' or 'first-class guerrillas'.[18] The orders from Home Counties Command on 30 July 1940 to all Home Guard battalion commanders in that area instructed that Home Guard responsibilities would be, in order of importance 1) observation, 2) *guerrilla tactics*, 3) manning roadblocks and 4) defending centres of resistance (author's italics). The War Office belatedly tried to restrict the widening use of 'guerrilla warfare' when they realised it played into the Home Guard's predilection for independence but by then the term had become established for virtually any mobile force. It had even been validated in *Home Guard Instruction No.14: Winter Training* for 1940 which allowed for 'elementary training in guerrilla warfare'. Despite their doubts, on 30 June 1941 GHQ added a more aggressive structure to the established harrying role of the LDV by ordering them to form small permanent 'fighting patrols' or 'battle platoons' of up to 25 men, using bicycles or motor transport. They would operate 2–3 miles beyond the bounds of a defended locality and be ready to engage for the 'complete destruction of the enemy wherever and whenever he may land'.[19] In 1943 the mission of these 'fighting patrols' was summarised as being to 'observe, plan, strike, withdraw', each patrol organised as an HQ section, three rifle squads and a BAR squad together with wireless communications – resources far beyond what the Auxiliary Units could muster.[20]

Unofficial Guerrillas
The acknowledgement of a 'harrying' role formed the justification for men like Tom Wintringham to go further and promote the Home Guard as an outright guerrilla force, much to the dismay of the War Office who saw this as a distraction from their official static role but, in the summer of 1940, it had to accept any means of resisting the progress of the invasion. Wintringham's *Deadlock War* (March 1940) had challenged the convention of rigidly holding a position at all costs in favour of the principle of an 'elastic web of defence', whereby a unit would pull back or move to a flank to avoid pointless annihilation and preserving the ability for a counter-attack, while *New Ways of War* (July 1940) also stressed the need to encourage initiative in NCOs and other ranks, the necessity to be able to fight in small groups and the importance of infiltration as a tactic.[21] Such flexibility would be particularly important in a *blitzkrieg* where there was likely to be no single 'front' but rather a series of pincer attacks which might fragment defending forces. The official summary of the lectures given at the Osterley Park Training School in 1940 was published by the War Office in 1941 and openly promoted the tactics of guerrilla warfare but by 1942 the War Office was trying to provide a more consistent message and suppress any connection between the Home Guard and irregular warfare. By then local battalions had formed a range of more or less official initiatives together with ad hoc ventures sometimes difficult to distinguish from those

secretly encouraged by SIS. The absence of evidence of overall control or unified management was in line with the teaching of Section D – a decentralised resistance, both combatant and passive, created by a 'whispering' campaign of hints and suggestion that left no structure for the Gestapo to penetrate and masked the official SIS resistance, but which also might provide a reservoir of potential future recruits (see above, p.51). It should be remembered that whilst the Auxiliary Units had a clear official structure, the Operational Patrols lacked any means of easy communication to a central command once they had gone to ground and in all likelihood would then have had to act equally independently after fulfilling their initial target list.

One initiative where the distinction between official and unofficial is blurred comes from Leicestershire.[22] Beaumanor Hall in Woodhouse had been requisitioned as an intelligence school in September 1939 and also became an Y-Intercept Station in October 1941. The officer in charge of its defence, Lieutenant Dick Whitford (known as 'Two Gun Whitford' due to his habit of wearing his service revolver and a Luger on his hips), then created a number of secret 'shock sections' from 6th (Quorn) Battalion Leicestershire Home Guard, to supplement its defence. He was a former policeman in Palestine who had joined the Wireless Intercept Service in 1936 and would, therefore, have had plenty of opportunities for contact with SIS. His plan, echoing both the philosophy of Section D and the teachings of Tom Wintringham, was to recruit teams of young men aged 17–20 from the Home Guard that would operate in civilian clothes after invasion and carry out 'dirty tricks' on any occupying Germans. In the meantime, they wore normal Home Guard uniform but could not resist hinting at a special status by publicly carrying large knives on their belts. They were trained in unarmed combat and demolition, and how to use such weapons as knitting-needle knives, knuckledusters and garottes (published instructions for which could be widely found in 1940) as well as the normal range of official Home Guard weapons. Allan Hopcraft made his own single-edged knife. Hopcraft maintained 'we had rifles and Sten guns, some had Tommy guns' which means the unit continued into 1942. Hopcraft's No.3 Shock Section at Woodhouse went on to train others at Rothley and Barrow. Caches of supplies were supposedly hidden around the villages and there was at least one secret hide. Claims of an underground bunker in a copse at Bull-in-the-Hollow Farm with bunks, explosives, ammunition and medical equipment echoes both the hides of XII Corps Observation Unit and the Auxiliary Units but otherwise there is no evidence of any extraordinary supplies beyond that available to the Home Guard, or external training that might suggest they were part of a larger, more official, undertaking.[23] In language identical to that of John Todd of SIS, Whitford reportedly told his men that after an enemy occupation 'Traitors or collaborators in the village? Whitford told us to give 'em the chop'. How they would identify such persons is not stated. Hopcraft had no illusions about life expectancy but believed they were trained 'to make yourself a bloody nuisance'. In exercises, like the Auxiliary Units and FSS, they tested the defences at the Y-station and a searchlight station at Woodhouse Eaves.

The enthusiasm and resourcefulness of many in the Home Guard produced other entirely ad hoc initiatives, inspired by the teachings of Wintringham, Langdon-Davies and Levy from their books, lecture tours or the course at Osterley Park which in turn spawned local Home Guard training schools that disseminated the concepts even further. The principle behind all these units was simply to do as much damage as possible before they were destroyed, in order to divert enemy resources from attacking the field army. Like the official Auxiliary Units, they accepted that they were not expected to survive more than a few days – with no illusions about what was to befall them or how they should respond: 'Above all remember the enemy is ruthless, and similar medicine must be handed to him'.[24]

Tom Wintringham (Plate 45) and the unofficial Osterley Park Training School at Hounslow, London, had a central part to play in the popularisation of the guerrilla concept both in the Home Guard and regular army. Students were no doubt proud of the description given to them by William Joyce (Lord Haw Haw) as the 'Osterley cut-throats'.[25] The Training School was established by a curious matching of communist, aristocrat and millionaire. There was revolutionary socialist Wintringham (former commander of the British battalion of the International Brigades in Spain), the conservative publisher of *Picture Post*, Edward Hulton (who worked with Section D on propaganda schemes), and the aristocratic owner of Osterley Park, Lord Jersey. Lincolnshire-born Tom Wintringham had become the chief evangelist for the LDV/Home Guard with an international audience. He had regular columns in the *Daily Mirror*, *Tribune*, *New Statesman* and *Picture Post* and also frequently broadcast on the BBC. On 17 May Wintringham called out in the *Tribune*. 'Now Arm The People'. On 28 May he launched his stirring slogan 'An Aroused People, An Angry People, An Armed People' in the *Daily Mirror* and was never shy of telling the Commander-in-Chief and government what they ought to be doing to strengthen defences of the country. On 15 June came the first of his rousing articles in *Picture Post*, 'Against Invasion' and on 29 June 'Arm The Citizens'.

In the fraught summer of 1940 the Osterley Park Home Guard Training School offered a breath of optimism and inspiration as well as a touch of danger and rebellion in the spirit of Lawrence of Arabia, whose recent posthumously-published *Seven Pillars of Wisdom* was a best-seller. It was an intoxicating mixture. Apart from Tom Wintringham there was the exotic Canadian 'Yank' Levy with stories of guerrilla warfare from around the world; romantic Asturian 'dynamiters'; Hugh Slater, an expert in tank-hunting and street fighting; and Wilfrid Vernon who would demonstrate how to cook-up home-made explosives on a kitchen stove and make electric detonators from light bulbs. Surrealist painter Roland Penrose would demonstrate the art of camouflage using a naked Lee Miller hidden beneath camouflage netting. The 'Spanish experience' in the training at Osterley Park promoted new techniques of tank-hunting and street-fighting, as well as the importance of motivation and the ability to act in small units. It is notable, however, that neither Wintringham nor the British Battalion of the International Brigade had any practical experience of guerrilla warfare, as such. This was an expertise that 'Yank' Levy brought to Osterley Park from his experiences in South America (his Spanish experience had ended on the second day of the battle of Jarama in February 1937 when he was captured).

Despite his prominent communist background, Wintringham had not been so completely blacklisted by the War Office as is often imagined. Immediately before war broke out, Wintringham was commissioned to write articles for the new serial publication *Battle Training in Word and Picture*, which was officially approved by the War Office, its foreword written by the Chief of the Imperial General Staff. MI5 did block Wintringham's appointment to a post in the Transport, Mechanical Section of the War Office during September 1939 on the grounds that it might give him access to confidential information but even so, during June and early July 1940, he was engaged on a lecture tour on behalf of the War Office.[26] It also seems likely that Wintringham drafted the LDV instruction leaflet on *Tank Hunting*, later used as the basis of the regular army training pamphlet of August 1940. It was during the War Office tour that he refined the syllabus of the Osterley Park Training School which opened on 10 July. The course had a 'blood and thunder' approach that the students found a welcome change from the traditional parade drill being taught in many Home Guard units. But the lectures went beyond learning techniques of camouflage, making improvised explosives and ambushing tanks – and beyond the tactics described just a month before in Wintringham's *Picture Post* articles or in his book *New Ways of War*.

As the enemy advanced, the students at Osterley Park were taught how to implement the principle of 'harrying' that was an official, if secondary, role of the Home Guard: 'It is our job, when the enemy is on the march, or his foraging or scouting parties are out, to harass his flanks, to snipe every straggler. Hit and run. Hit and hold them up. Hit and scatter them.' They were also prepared for the task of working behind enemy lines in small independent groups. In *The Home Guard Can Fight* (1941), Tom Wintringham wrote: 'Part of the Home Guard's job is to carry on the struggle, if necessary, in areas temporarily overrun by the enemy. This last duty it can only carry out if it learns some of the tactics of guerrilla war'.[27] Several Home Guard units took Wintringham's teaching to heart and made plans to 'go to ground' after invasion. Wintringham asked the Home Guard:

- Are you prepared to be cut off behind the enemy's advance, and to keep on harassing him when there is no one to give you orders?
- Could you lie low, if necessary, for several days, and then seize the chance for sabotage or raiding?[28]

The course included advice on how to destroy ammunition dumps and vehicle parks, and how to prepare ambushes. This was exactly the role for which the Auxiliary Units were designed but the Osterley Park students were also being prepared to go further and fight on as a civilian resistance, following a methodology that was remarkably close to that of the HDS. It is tempting to suggest this was the result of Grand's 'hints' possibly discretely passed on by Hulton who at the time was working with Section D.[29] Wintringham preached a concept of the Home Guard as a last resort, abandoning their uniforms and fighting on in utmost secrecy as civilians in small sabotage teams hidden within the community (as applied by Lieutenant Whitford at Woodhouse). This moved the teaching from the strategy of the War Office to that of the SIS. One of the students at an Osterley Park course noted:

> Should the area be overrun by the enemy the Home Guardsman should bury his rifle and uniform and mix with civilians . . . Best results are obtained from groups of two or at most three, who should be equipped with knives and revolvers, grenades and explosives and iron rations.[30]

In 1941 Wintringham and Levy provided more advice on the methodology to be employed by suggesting that, as in the HDS, large boxes should be hidden ready to act as caches for supplies and civilian clothes.[31] Such Home Guard had to be prepared to fight without the official supplies of the Auxiliary Units. Instead, again very much in the spirit of the HDS, they were taught to improvise – to make their own explosives and grenades. They were also trained in the manufacture and use of simple electrical and chemical remote-detonating systems for ambushes (Plate 46). It is possibly no coincidence that the Osterley Park course demonstrated a Molotov cocktail using a crude delayed-action chemical ignition that was very similar to that supplied to the HDS. Also in line with Section D methodology, there was an introduction to the use of underground leaflets and newspapers, and how to sow confusion by unarmed methods (as described in *Guerrilla Warfare* by 'Yank' Levy but part written and edited by Wintringham). They were also taught how to make occupation difficult for the enemy including how to poison the water supply in occupied areas by throwing dead dogs into wells. The men were exhorted: 'Remember that the guerrilla has to work like a ghost. He has to undermine the morale of the enemy by being always unexpected and always dangerous. If the Nazis seize an English county we must make it impossible for them to send dispatches about that county without a heavy escort of armoured cars.' Security was to be everything. 'The most profound secrecy should cover the actions and plans of each group. On no account should others be taken into confidence for fear of accidental betrayal.'[32]

From 10 July to 30 September 1940 the Osterley Park courses gave direct instruction to c.5,000 potential guerrilla and resistance fighters in weapons handling, use of high explosives, camouflage and stalking. This was twice that of the Auxiliary Units volunteers, who at this time did not receive much more than the same weekend training course as organised there. It would be surprising if Gubbins, Wilkinson or Beyts had not investigated what was being taught at Osterley Park. Eustace Maxwell, one of the Auxiliary Units Intelligence Officers, did attend an Osterley course and later told his men in Aberdeen that the course on explosives was better than that provided by the Auxiliary Units.[33] At least one future member of the Auxiliary Units received his initial training in guerrilla warfare at Osterley Park – albeit probably to carry out surveillance for MI5! Norman Mackenzie joined the Sussex Auxiliary Units shortly after attending the second Osterley Park training course. Mackenzie described his time with the Auxiliary Units (before he joined the RAF) as 'the most wonderful summer of my life'.[34] Importantly, Osterley Park also inspired the creation of local training schools, armed with the lecture notes brought back by its students, extending the knowledge base even further. If Britain had been invaded during July or August, at a time when the Auxiliary Units were still in the process of initial training, it is reasonable to consider that they would have shared honours with the Osterley Park-trained guerrillas, some of whom may have gone on to be part of a British resistance.

The impact of the Osterley Park Training School went far beyond the Home Guard attendees. The innovative courses were unofficially attended by officers of the Brigade of Guards, Royal Armoured Corps and even a Naval Shore Establishment. One has to wonder if these included men of the Guards tank-hunting platoons that provided the first instructors to the Auxiliary Units, or men from General Thorne's Battle Patrols. General Thorne, CO of XII Corps and creator of the prototype Auxiliary Units system, certainly sent officers to Osterley Park. He was a long-time supporter of Wintringham's ideas on army reform (if not his politics) having met him when *How to Reform the Army* had been published in April 1939, at a high-level meeting that also included the Deputy

Chief of the Imperial General Staff and the Deputy Adjutant General.[35] They kept up a correspondence throughout the war. Thorne also became an influential patron of Hugh Slater, who he must surely have met at Osterley Park, promoting him as an instructor in a Scottish Command Training School.

The ad hoc attempt to raise guerrilla forces at Osterley Park was not welcomed by the War Office on the grounds of maintaining disciplined control of the battle front, or by MI5 for fear that the training could eventually be used to implement a socialist revolution. It was accepted in the desperate days of 1940 as a unique source of training, inspiration and good propaganda, with MI5 and the War Office obliged to tolerate the effective publicity machine of Wintringham and Hulton. The methodology disseminated from the school provided a high-profile demonstration to both the Americans and the Nazis alike that Britain was preparing to stand and fight at all costs and that a *blitzkrieg* across England was unlikely to be as easy as on the Continent. The government had allowed the press to make it plain that not only would the landscape of Britain be defended crossroads by crossroads and village by village, but also that a hidden threat might lurk in every woodland or in every dark alley. The psychological impact of the unique threat posed by the Home Guard at this point of the war, however poorly armed and whether fighting openly or as guerrillas, should not be underestimated; it was an altogether more chilling image than that presented by the comfortable, bumbling Home Guard of TV's *Dad's Army*. Wintringham was also producing instant instructional material and with no other suitable material available, the War Office distributed 100,000 copies of his 15 June *Picture Post* article 'Against Invasion: the lessons of Spain' to the LDV and employed him on a follow-up lecture tour.[36]

Given the 'communistic tendencies' of the instructors it is not surprisingly that the LDV Inspectorate asked GHQ Home Forces and MI5 to put Osterley Park under surveillance.[37] MI5 was the driving force behind the opposition to Wintringham and Slater. Their suspicions were not helped by explosives lecturer Wilfred Vernon having been identified pre-war as a Soviet spy whilst in contact with Wintringham. Slater's every attempt to officially join the war effort had been blocked by MI5 since the outbreak of war in 1939 and he remained under surveillance once he was commissioned, with every posting challenged by MI5. Slater had been active in the Communist Party since 1933 and had a string of arrests during anti-Nazi protests. Prior to becoming Chief of Operations to the International Brigades in Spain, Slater had been Political Commissar for the British Battalion and was therefore considered a hard-line communist, although he became disillusioned with the Communist Party thereafter. On 18 July, Guy Liddell of MI5 noted that: 'There is always the possibility that Wintringham might like to build up something in the nature of a future Red Army.' Despite such fears, Liddell had also reported that they had found no evidence of political indoctrination.[38] Even without clear proof of subversion, Liddell felt obliged to later warn the DMI that Wintringham was 'going round giving lectures to Western Command about guerrilla warfare' and that 'this practice is perhaps not very desirable . . .'. The fear was that his skills might conceivably be used to bring about a socialist revolution in the future, but Wintringham had few political allies at the time. The official position of the Communist Party in 1940 was to oppose the war as being an imperialist, rather than an anti-fascist, war. Both the Communist Party and the International Brigade Association (the veterans organisation) told members not to support the war effort in general and were particularly contemptuous of the Home Guard. Wintringham, Slater and Levy were considered to be renegades by their former comrades and Slater was finally expelled from the Communist Party in January 1941 specifically because 'He is actively associated with the Wintringham group'.[39]

Eventually, on 30 September, with the immediate threat of invasion passing and so mirroring the suggestion that the Auxiliary Units be disbanded, the Osterley Park School was finally taken over by the War Office. It was closed down and re-opened at Denbies, Dorking, with the same instructors and syllabus but with strict instructions to maintain a lower press profile.[40] By then, Wintringham had acquired a considerable international audience for his ideas. He was invited to the USA to advise on forming their own Home Guard. In Palestine the Irgun used Wintringham's *Picture Post* articles as the basis for one of their guerrilla manuals. Even Churchill paid Wintringham a back-handed compliment by later dismissing the Greek ELAS partisans as 'Tom Wintringhams'.[41] No doubt Wintringham was particularly proud of the fact that the Leningrad Home Guard were given exactly the same training in 1941, especially in anti-tank tactics, as that provided at Osterley Park a year earlier. The only difference, he said, was that for home-made grenades 'these proletarians use caviar tins instead of cocoa tins!'[42]

A more acceptable publicist for the Home Guard was the equally prolific John Langdon-Davies who had been a journalist and relief worker in Spain. The emphasis of his teaching was on fieldcraft but writing in the *Sunday Pictorial* in February 1941 he called for 'Home Guard Guides' that were remarkably similar to the role expected of the early Auxiliary Units. Langdon-Davies called for 100,000 Home Guard, drawn from poachers, gamekeepers, Boy Scouts and mountaineers to provide a network of hidden observers and act as guides to both direct the army towards the enemy and help the civilian population safely evacuate an area under attack. Trained to work silently at night in pairs, they would be armed with revolver, three hand grenades, knife with an 8in blade, knuckleduster and cosh – a basic inventory of weapons common to both the early recommendations of the Auxiliary Units and Wintringham at Osterley Park.[43] Although not implemented in this form, designated Home Guard guides were soon meant to be based at local post offices or on the main approach to a village, identified by a green/yellow brassard on the right arm. Langdon-Davies opened the Burwash Fieldcraft School in March 1941.[44]

By early 1941 Wintringham had become intensely frustrated by his inability to effect widespread change in the Home Guard training and policy, which came to a head in May 1941 when he learnt that his friend Hugh Slater had been conscripted as a gunner in an anti-aircraft regiment. He exploded in fury at the apparent waste of Slater's talents and resigned amidst much publicity, writing a bitter article in *Picture Post* about the continuing influence of 'blimps' in the Home Guard.[45] Wintringham was not to know that, despite the opposition of MI5, the War Office had just agreed that he should be commissioned as a Major in the Home Guard – a move which Wintringham had now made impossible. Even more ironically, Slater's conscription was merely a device of the Directorate of Military Training, necessary to allow him to be commissioned and then return as an Instructor to the Denbies Training School. MI5 was furious with what it saw as the devious Directorate of Military Training ignoring its advice. Slater, now a second lieutenant in the Border Regiment, remained under MI5 observation and to their further dismay was then posted as an Instructor at the Company Commander's Training School of Scottish Command, having been specifically requested by General

Thorne and promoted to Captain. He was then recommended for a transfer to the Intelligence Corps with the rank of major and the Director of Military Intelligence raised no objection. Slater failed the interview, although one has to wonder if some influence from MI5 was not brought to bear on the interview panel. After his resignation, Wintringham's lecture tours to the Home Guard actually increased but it is a great irony that he was never given any official recognition of the contribution that he made to the development of the Home Guard and to training in guerrilla warfare in 1940.

After the desperation of 1940, the War Office tried to reassert control over the Home Guard and repeatedly stressed in 1942, as the threat of invasion receded, that their role was not one of guerrilla warfare. In April 1942 Major G. E. Walk, of GHQ Home Forces, wrote a report reiterating that the primary role of the Home Guard was to defend their towns and villages and interrupt enemy road movements but noting that some members of the Home Guard also considered guerrilla warfare as being part of their role. Walk thought that the whole concept damaged the primary role of static defence and concluded that the Home Guard were not, and could not be, trained for a guerrilla role, and that if they tried, their presence would be likely to confuse the regular troops.[46] Major Walk's paper was formally adopted in June and an order from the GOC Home Forces decreed that guerrilla fighting by the Home Guard must not be allowed.[47] Even the term itself was banned.

> The word 'guerrilla' will not be used in future, as it is often misunderstood and if guerrilla activity is generally regarded as a possible secondary role for Home Guard there is a great risk that the obligation to fight to the last in defended localities will not be met.[48]

The Operational Orders for the East Riding and Lincolnshire Home Guards in December 1942 included the stricture on the use of detachments with a mobile harassing role;

> The role of these will be to observe, report and harass the enemy's movements, denying him the free use of the roads and destroying small parties wherever the opportunity offers. They will NOT in future be referred to as 'Guerrillas'.[49]

The Auxiliary Units waded into this debate at a time when they were feeling threatened over their special status. In early 1942 the CO, Colonel 'Bill' Major, wrote a personal letter to General Gregson-Ellis, the Deputy Chief of Staff, Home Forces, complaining that the Home Guard, especially in the Eastern Counties, had laid down a policy of guerrilla warfare for their troops saying quite openly that they were going to 'take to the woods'. He concluded:

> I cannot believe that they will be of the slightest use in this role, and will not function at all in the face of some Boche attack pressed home. In my humble opinion they will run like stink without firing a shot.[50]

One wonders what the Home Guard of 1940, who had resolutely stood-to, however poorly-armed, when the signal for invasion was mistakenly given, would have thought of such a statement. Had Major also conveniently forgotten who comprised his own Operational Patrols? The Home Guard could not, however, be so easily controlled.

Following continued pressure on the subject, Home Guard Instruction 51, issued in September 1942 was obliged to compromise by saying that guerrilla activity might be permissible in sparsely populated areas where there were no nodal points. Yorkshire Home Guard went further and recommended that small parties in towns and villages should hide in cellars, ready to emerge after the enemy had passed by and harrass headquarters and rear services.[51]

From 1942 a new term emerged to excite the imagination of the Home Guard and replace 'guerrilla'. With the media attention surrounding the exploits and image of the new commandos, the Home Guard created their own 'commando' units, sometimes to the despair of the War Office who remained suspicious about the Home Guard enthusiasm for independent action and still wanted them to focus on more static defence. Local Home Guard selected the younger and fitter men and some were trained at army commando schools or otherwise received training in unarmed combat from regular army units. Some paraded their status with distinctive lanyards and either bought a Fairbairn-Sykes fighting knife (now on public sale), purchased one of the commercial copies that had been produced, or made their own from surplus bayonets or even industrial hacksaw blades (not difficult given that many Home Guards were skilled workers in reserved occupations). The commando platoon of C Company, the 5th City of London (Press) B, wore a red lanyard and were known as 'The Red Cord Boys'. They were well-trained specialists in street fighting and in fighting underground in the London sewage system. In Northamptonshire the Sub-District Mobile Company, drawn from carefully-selected young and fit men, would form a hard-hitting mobile reserve known as 'The Green Lanyards'.

Industrial sabotage teams

The most secret responsibility of the Home Guard was to form covert industrial sabotage teams, mirroring surveys by MI5 and SIS Section D over potential threats from fifth columnists towards key infrastructure and industrial targets. Key amongst these was responsibility for sabotage in factories where they already had factory defence units and at local petrol stations. The particular duty of these 'Key Personnel' during the invasion campaign was to put factories out of action by disabling, not destroying, them if they were about to be overrun, which would allow production to be quickly restored in the event of a successful counter-attack. Only if the territory was not recovered would the HDS and its successors attempt the actual destruction of the machinery.

This plan affected factories and engineering works both large and small. In August 1941 the Air Defence Research and Development Establishment (ADRDE) at Christchurch, Dorset, carried out a review of the comprehensive plans made by their Home Guard for the immobilisation of equipment and machinery. The secrecy of the plans was stressed as was the need to delay implementation until the last possible moment. The work would entail the destruction, or removal, of essential mechanisms to a place where retrieval by the enemy would be impossible; removal or destruction of explosives or war materials that the enemy might use; concealment of valuable records or destruction of them if copies were available elsewhere; cutting off gas and electricity supplies; immobilisation of any transport left on the premises; ensuring that stocks of petrol or oil did not fall into enemy hands; and removal or concealment of any currency.[52] On a different scale, Harold Goodwin & Company Ltd, in Warley, Worcestershire, was a small garage, then working for the Ministry of Aircraft Production. When the factory Home Guard were reorganised in 1942, the Company Secretary asked for the retention of Privates Elliott, Radburn and Leslie because these three were essential to plans already made for the immobilisation of the depot. Elliott and Leslie were to be responsible for immobilising the vehicles and battery-charging equipment; Leslie would also transport vital parts to a place of safety, while Radburn was in charge of denial of access to vital spares and tyres.[53]

Conscious of the ease with which the German Panzer divisions had managed to refuel from civilian petrol pumps as they tore through the Low Countries and France, special measures were taken to protect petrol supplies. Rather than destroy the fuel stocks it was considered better to deny access to them by disabling the pumping mechanisms. Home Guard platoon commanders had a list of all petrol pumps in their area and, in a similar fashion to the Factory Unit 'Key Personnel', special 'Pump Disruption Squads' were formed to dismantle and hide the vital machinery so that only squad members would know the location.[54] A secret instruction to Home Guard of February 1941 instructed them to visit garages to ensure the security measures that they had been required to make in 1940 were still being maintained. They were to 'find out where the sack is kept into which the dismantled parts of the pump are to be placed, and how you can take possession of it if the need arises, especially if the premises are likely to be left unattended. You should also get to know how to remove the various parts from the pumps yourself, in case you may have to do the work, and where the necessary tools can be obtained on the premises.'[55] In Cumbria, a small Intelligence Section had been added to the 5th (Workington) Battalion of the Home Guard. As well as reporting any security breaches (both military and civilian) it was also charged to 'Disrupt all petroleum and crude oil supplies to prevent enemy use'. Volunteers from the battalion Transport Section formed Petrol Disruption Squads whereby all fuel containers, pumps and equipment were to be rendered inoperative. Exercises were carried out whereby all hand, mechanical and electrical fuel pumps in the Flimby, Clifton, Harrington, Seaton and Workington areas were stripped of their vital parts. Such action would have resulted in intense frustration for the enemy and severe reprisals were likely. It was, therefore, vital for the men involved to retain their anonymity. Most took their secrets to the grave.

Conclusions

> The secrecy of the British secret service starts with its official designation which nobody understands exactly. Novels, films, memoirs of agents, and articles in newspapers, often written by more or less authorised persons, produced more confusion than clarification for us.
>
> German Intelligence, 1940[1]

During the Second World War the Secret Intelligence Service (SIS) and the War Office between them constructed layers of covert anti-invasion networks in Britain as well as a more considered deep-cover resistance. They were assisted by a myriad of more unofficial efforts to resist the enemy at all costs. The complexities, which would have admirably confused the Nazis, have proved equally baffling for post-war historians. Despite their modern mystique and media appeal, the plans for guerrilla warfare as represented by the HDS and Auxiliary Units were never intended as the 'Last Ditch' of defence. They, along with the Home Guard, were part of a wider plan simply to buy time, however short and at whatever the cost, for the field army to re-group and hopefully mount a counter-attack. They were desperate expedients whose value was not in their individual significance but rather in the collective disruption they might cause to an enemy advance. Any thought of Nazi occupation was regarded as defeatist, yet in utmost secrecy SIS were prepared to think the unthinkable and had earlier made plans for a British Resistance (Section VII) that might hopefully survive and prepare the way for eventual liberation. There are many unanswered questions and in places a necessary reliance on circumstantial evidence and considered speculation which can only be tested by continuing study. This is especially true of those bodies controlled or guided by SIS, which has been an overlooked force in organising plans for clandestine warfare in Britain. In a study that has relied considerably on anecdotal evidence from the last-surviving veterans and their families, recorded decades after the event and often with limited corroboration, it is important to remain objective in assessing the evidence, whilst at the same time acknowledging the huge sacrifice that those men and women, young and old, were prepared to make.

SIS had begun a well-organised contingency plan for a British resistance (Section VII) following occupation as early as February 1940. Plans to support a military defence through guerrilla warfare only got underway during the fall of France in May 1940, when the real possibility of invasion finally broke through government complacency. This lack of foresight is all the more remarkable because the two main champions of guerrilla warfare, Section D of SIS and MI(R) of the War Office, had both been briefed in May–June 1939 by Polish Intelligence on their new guerrilla network. Section D and MI(R) had also been encouraging various opposition groups and General Staffs of neutral countries during early 1940 to put in place similar schemes before they were invaded. Fortunately, because Britain never was invaded, it had the luxury of being able to refine its plans through a number of iterations and, although none of them had to be put to the test, they remained a model into the Cold War.

Throughout the Second World War the War Office only reluctantly accepted the principles of unconventional warfare in times of crisis and were quick to discard them when improvement in resources allowed a return to more orthodox methodology. As early as the autumn of 1940 there were, therefore, efforts to disband the Auxiliary Units and better contain the guerrilla ambitions of the Home Guard. SIS Section VII absorbed that part of the HDS not taken over by the Auxiliary Units and was able to continue away from any scrutiny as an internal security mechanism and last-resort, deep-cover, resistance. The future for the Operational Branch of the Auxiliary Units, which now incorporated the XII Corps Observation Unit and part of the HDS became more problematic. As the likelihood of invasion decreased and conventional forces became stronger, it tried to find a new role as a reconnaissance unit to the Home Guard but was conflicted by its desire to remain independent. It therefore clung to its secret status to avoid scrutiny and maintained a wholly unrealistic vision of itself as an anti-invasion force into September 1944. The regular army component was steadily withdrawn but the continuance of the Home Guard patrols was tolerated because, as had been acknowledged in 1940, they were cheap to maintain and their continued existence was easier to manage as a cost-effective insurance policy against invasion than their return to general Home Guard service.

The concept of civilian saboteurs was particularly distasteful (at least operating in Britain) – British forces had been too often at the receiving end of what was considered terrorism – and the SIS Home Defence Scheme was soon absorbed into the military Auxiliary Units or withdrew deeper into the shadows as part of Section VII. What would now be lauded as 'special forces' also offended the sense of military order. Field Marshal Slim remarked, somewhat sniffily, in regard to Wingate's Chindits: 'We are always inclined in the British Army to devise private armies and scratch forces for jobs which our ordinary formations with proper training could do and do better'.[2]

Jo Holland of MI(R) tried to bring the concept which became the modern special forces into the mainstream of military thinking but in 1940 was hindered by the lack of resources. It was most obviously implemented on a small scale by General Thorne drawing his 'Battle Patrols' of XII Corps Observation Unit from battalions under his command, but it was never possible to allocate the dedicated commando units to what became the Auxiliary Units as Holland had envisaged and for which Gubbins initially planned. Gubbins' alternative of company-sized commando units of the Home Guard could only be partially realised by the Group system of patrols, but by then the means of ensuring the survival of the organisation was to withdraw into secrecy as a body that both hindered effective liaison with regular forces and created an awkward distinct entity from the rest of the Home Guard. Meanwhile, Hugh Dalton had seized ownership of the civilian-orientated methodology of Laurence Grand's Section D and created SOE outside of War Office control. Holland bemoaned in the MI(R) War Diary for 22 July: 'It looks a little as though the Army has missed the bus, so to speak, and has allowed paramilitary activities to be carried on outside its jurisdiction.'[3] Eventually the war in the Western Desert spawned 'private armies' that included the Long Range Desert Group and the Special Air Service. The latter, with the Jedburgh teams, were finally to realise Holland's vision of special forces in their campaigns behind enemy lines, liaising with local resistance forces after D-Day, until they too were temporarily disbanded.

A fundamental distinction was made at the time between short-term guerrilla action to be carried out by uniformed troops (whether regular army, Auxiliary Units or Home Guard) in support of a still-operating field army and held by the government to fall within the protection of the Hague Convention, and a longer-term civilian resistance under SIS which would be legally classed as *francs-tireurs* and was unavowable by the government. This neat division was briefly confused by Section D's HDS which was created in the turmoil of the retreat from France and with minimal consultation, on the basis of Section D's experience in Europe where the British government did not have the same qualms of using civilians in combat. At the end of July 1940 the HDS was officially turned over to the Auxiliary Units, explicitly to reject the use of civilians in a military campaign on home soil.

If the military forces were obliged to surrender then SIS would continue the fight, including organising escape lines for fugitives as well as intelligence-gathering and sabotage. Prior to invasion it was maintained only as a small cadre to ensure better security but future recruits were no doubt identified – including those in the HDS or men trained at Home Guard guerrilla schools such as Osterley Park. The plan was then to expand in preparation to support a liberation army, or fill the void on the fond expectation in 1940 that the Nazi state would soon implode. The civilian resistance organisation of Section VII left no physical remains, no insignia and very few surviving veterans to tell their story. They remained as anonymous as their leaders Boyle, Vivian, Dansey and Gambier-Parry always intended. Instead, the body that captured the public imagination was the Auxiliary Units, which has left tangible and evocative monuments in the form of its buried Operational Bases, hidden wireless stations and a relative wealth of documentation. The decision to use formed groups of the Home Guard as part of the Auxiliary Units posed unique issues of security. The army 'Battle Patrols' and 'scout sections' might attract little attention as one unit of soldiers amongst many billeted on an area, but the Home Guard patrols were expected to operate from their own small local communities. Whereas the civilian saboteurs of the SIS Home Defence Scheme or Section VII could remain anonymous by operating from within the community, the auxiliers had to perform a delicate balancing act of trying to keep their activities secret whilst wearing Home Guard uniform but not participating in local parades and drills, and periodically disappearing into the hidden operational bases. However, in 1940 the concern of GHQ was not so much the fate of those individuals but to ensure that the location of their Operational Bases and stores was not revealed. Although the risk of invasion decreased, the need to preserve the aura of secrecy increased during the war as being one of their best hopes of organisational survival. Gubbins understood the political value of the 'too secret to explain' tactic, combined with deliberately 'talking-up' the organisation but it is now clear that the Auxiliary Units were not as secret as some of the veterans had been led to believe. From the outset their details were visible on Home Guard enrolment forms and Part II Orders (Plate 42) and some volunteers did not help by openly wearing their revolvers or even drinking in local public houses alongside the rest of the Home Guard whilst wearing their mud-soaked uniforms. They were protected by the contemporary acceptance of the principle of not being overly curious over what was clearly not to be publicly-acknowledged. After a brief burst of publicity in the immediate post-war period, there was an attempt to restore the blanket of secrecy during the Cold War because the same methodology of 'stay behind' units was being employed in north Germany by the re-formed SAS against the threat of Soviet invasion. This did not stop a trickle of informative publications, but did slow the release of official documents.

In a peculiarly British way, many seem to have drifted into this secret world without asking for whom they were actually working and certainly without expecting any reward. They were compartmentalised and therefore not necessarily all told the complete role of their organisation. The most striking example is the single official reference to the key internal security role of the Special Duties Branch (SDB). Left largely to their own devices, there was also scope for the men of the Operational Branch, Auxiliary Units, to interpret their own role, as in the case of plans for assassinations. After the war, the only point of reference for veterans and media alike, was the well-known image of continental resistance groups, promoted in the hugely-influential but sometimes wildly-exaggerated account in 1968 by David Lampe. Unable to be tested at the time by the extensive documentary evidence that is now available, the post-war accounts of veterans, mainly gathered from the 1990s onwards and shaped by post-war 'received wisdom', tended to be accepted without question. This is despite the warnings by Fleming as early as 1957 over the problems of 'false memory syndrome' (see above, p.xx). Much stemmed from the understandable desire to accentuate the difference between the auxiliers and the comedic image of the *Dad's Army* Home Guard. Their reputation was enhanced by the blurring of the Home Guard patrols and the Scout Sections, whose own central role was obscured after they were dispersed, whilst the veterans from the Home Guard patrols remained in the local area and were easier to trace to tell their stories. It is frequently claimed that many men from the Auxiliary Units were recruited into the SAS, without it being made clear that the majority were regular troops from the Scout Sections (some of which joined wholesale, bored with their return to normal regimental duties) or former Intelligence Officers.[4] Some of the small number of Home Guard auxiliers that had joined had done so up to two-and-a-half years after leaving the Auxiliary Units for service elsewhere.[5]

The Auxiliary Units have latterly been given the invented tag of the 'British Resistance Organisation' (BRO), a term that became fossilised as an emotive media sound-bite and in the published record. Any concern as to how this tallied with the explicit denials by wartime leaders, their two-week life expectancy as uniformed units of Home Guard, or the TRD wireless set that was patently unsuitable for use after occupation, was glossed over in favour of the more romantic vision as a European style resistance. The exasperated original second-in-command, Peter Wilkinson, wrote in 1997 'any suggestion that Auxiliary Units could have provided a framework for long term underground resistance is, in my opinion, absurd'.[6] Historian Arthur Ward later reported 'Sir Peter told it like it was, obviously irritated by the myth of a secret society of ninja-like assassins that was becoming an accepted part of Aux Unit folklore'.[7] It was only after the publication of *Fighting Nazi Occupation* in 2015, which for the first time was able to provide a clear context for the Auxiliary Units as a military guerrilla force within the wider strategy of the War Office and the actual British Resistance of

SIS, that the popular impression slowly began to change. Even in 2022 hoary old myths continued to be repeated in print and across the internet.

The official schemes were only part of the story. The concept of guerrilla warfare had huge popular appeal in 1940–2 and there were a wide range of local initiatives. Unsurprisingly, they often shared elements in common with the official HDS and Auxiliary Units, influenced by the same popular tradition. Some may have been purely spontaneous from men who saw themselves as successors of Lawrence of Arabia or the guerrillas in Hemingway's *For Whom The Bell Tolls* but others may have been following discrete 'hints' from Section D of SIS whose basic concept was simply to create chaos amongst the invader. The most significant of these initiatives came from Tom Wintringham's Osterley Park Home Guard Training School, with a methodology that was suspiciously close to Section D's Home Defence Scheme and which taught a self-reliance that was suited to future resistance fighters, all backed up by best-selling books and articles. The methodology of the HDS and Wintringham's Home Guard guerrillas offer a chilling picture of what these *francs-tireurs* might have unleashed if Britain had been invaded in the early summer of 1940. Despite some encouragement by former Section D officers and a degree of post-war bravado, the Auxiliary Units were designed as a more respectable military alternative as a formal part of the 'Armed Forces of the Crown', operating in uniform with visible ranks, and subject to military discipline.

None of the bodies intended to fight as guerrillas during the actual invasion campaign were expected to survive into any period of occupation. Theirs was a sacrificial role to buy time for the army to regroup, characteristic of Ironside's original defence plan which even the Chiefs of Staff regarded as suicidal. If they failed then the resistance organisation of SIS Section VII would have undoubtedly proved the most significant of these unorthodox ventures in trying to prepare the way for eventual liberation. In the absence of invasion, it established an on-going internal security role in support of MI5 as one of a number of organisations (including the Special Duties Branch of the Auxiliary Units) which 'eavesdropped' on the local community, but also had a unique role in being able to use its wireless network to help locate illicit long-range broadcasts by possible enemy spies. The security around Section VII has been protected by secrecy surrounding any work of SIS but has also extended into the intelligence-gathering of all the organisations in this study, leading to a bias in attention towards the operational units and an unavoidable degree of speculation in interpreting the fragmentary evidence.

In 1940, the HDS and SDB of the Auxiliary Units tried to extend Jo Holland's original concept for local guides to pass the Independent Companies through enemy lines into establishing a more elaborate intelligence network to extend the early warning capabilities of the Coastguard Service and Observer Corps. They lacked the technical resources to do so effectively and were made largely redundant by the superior resources of Section VII and the army Phantom unit, already experienced in dealing with *blitzkrieg*. Instead, the SDB under 'Bill' Major was able to offer its observers as another internal security network around the coast that may have eventually been the most significant element of the Auxiliary Units. Like the operational branch, the SDB was cheap to maintain and a resource of up to 3,500 observers, who had all signed the Official Secrets Act, was too great to waste as the risk of invasion decreased. The irony is that their hidden TRD wireless sets and their underground bases, which have so captured the post-war imagination, may have played only a minor part in this role.

This is not a story of daring deeds conducted by fit young professional secret agents of popular fiction. British policy towards resistance groups in 1940–1 was that they avoid unnecessary violence and prepare for a time when they could support an external liberation. The policy caused some tension with the more aggressive Section D whose influence can be followed into the early Auxiliary Units. The main virtue of all those involved was to appear to be 'ordinary'. This was less successful in the Operational Branch of the Auxiliary Units whose patrol members were caught in the dichotomy of being expected to wear Home Guard uniform but not participate in normal duties. Their role might at least be suspected but the agents of HDS, SDB or Section VII had to act out their role as local coal merchant, doctor or postman both before and after occupation without apparently being involved in any recognisable war work. Young teenagers such as Peter Attwater, the young Matlock SIS wireless operator, or Jill Monk, the Norfolk SDB courier, maintained their silence for decades after the event.

Thankfully the land defences of Britain in 1940 were not put to the test. Fleming, Gubbins and Wilkinson were subsequently brutally honest about the contribution that their guerrilla units in the XII Corps Observation Unit or Auxiliary Units could have made to the conventional forces – but they were looking at their own organisations in isolation. The essential point was that they were not expected to win battles against the enemy. Together, the various irregular initiatives would have created a web of opposition across the country that the German *blitzkrieg* had not met before. Each 'flea-bite' (as Wilkinson put it), combined with the resolve of the Home Guard to defend every village and crossroads and not forgetting their vital task destroying access to fuel supplies, would cumulatively have helped grind the enemy advance to a halt and allowed the meagre regular forces a chance to counter-attack. There is no doubt it would have been a brutal campaign. War crimes may have been committed on both sides and the cold analysis at the time was that few members of the various guerrilla groups or the Home Guard in the invasion areas would have survived. As predicted by Jo Holland, European clandestine forces eventually made their most valuable military contribution when operating with regular forces at the point of external invasion. Until then, they maintained morale among activists (albeit often at a terrible cost) and after the war became a symbol of national pride that often greatly inflated the level of participation and support. Although not invaded, Britain was not immune to such tendencies and seized upon the Auxiliary Units as a British equivalent, as the only clandestine force that the media were aware of at the time.

The basic principles of the British model were revived on a European scale during the Cold War. Small anti-communist civilian 'stay behind' units were created in a number of countries; the new Territorial Army 21 and 23 SAS Regiments were specifically tasked to go to ground in North Germany, along with teams from the Royal Armoured Corps, Honourable Artillery and Royal Artillery, using underground hides on the same basic principle as those of the Auxiliary Units, whilst local resistance groups were again told to remain quiet during the military phase of any Soviet invasion. Menzies from SIS is credited with promoting this old idea in a new era. Because of their earlier expertise in this field, a number of the Continental units (later collectively known as 'Gladios') were trained by British intelligence officers in the UK. This, in itself, was reason enough in the 1970s and 1980s for the security services not to encourage interest in the organisation of such forces in the Second World War. Colonel Douglas had realised this potential as early as 1944 and noted:

> Some little while ago I know that it was considered desirable that the whole of the organisation, its functions, role and methods should remain SECRET and pigeon-holed in the War Office just in case.[8]

Unfortunately, some 'Gladios' in Italy and Belgium went 'rogue' and started a terrorism campaign to heighten the political tension and so justify a more repressive anti-communist regime. Once the story became public there was an obvious embarrassment factor in any British connection. Old secrets therefore became intertwined with new secrets. Were there plans to revive the British Auxiliary Units during the Cold War? The possibility was certainly raised but the prevailing attitude was that home defence was going to be somewhat redundant in the new age of nuclear warfare. There is no evidence that the Auxiliary Units were actually reformed and if the SAS were planning stay-behind units abroad then it is possible that they had similar plans for operations within the UK.

There were mixed fortunes for the pioneers of irregular warfare in Britain. The two principal pioneers of guerrilla warfare in Britain – Laurence Grand (Section D) and Jo Holland (MI(R)) – were soon moved out of intelligence work and, with relief to both, were able to return to regular soldiering. Both men had successful military careers and retired as major-generals. Colin Gubbins' military career was cut short by the blight of having commanded the paramilitary SOE and his long-standing antagonism towards SIS (who took control of SOE affairs after the war). Although he had reached the rank of temporary major-general he was retired on the pension of his substantive rank of colonel. Tom Wintringham was virtually written out of history and his sudden death in 1949 passed almost without comment. The later *Dad's Army* TV series presented a much more acceptable, comfortable middle-class, vision of the Home Guard than that which Wintringham and his International Brigade comrades fiercely promoted in 1940–1. The professional intelligence officers of SIS kept their secrets to their dying day and beyond. Immediately after his death, the widow of Claude Dansey loyally burnt, in their garden, what must surely have been illuminating private papers relating to his intelligence work. Most magnificently of all, David Boyle – the man who led the British resistance organisation of Section VII – managed to write a 323-page autobiography without once mentioning that he had spent most of his working life in the service of British Intelligence.[9]

The final acknowledgement must be to the ordinary men and women of all the various organisations discussed in this book, who were drawn into the plans for a secret war and accepted the risks as simply their part in the war effort. Admiration for their resolve is not diminished by the fact that there was no invasion. For that we can all be thankful.

Appendix 1

Directive 16

The Führer and Supreme Commander of the Armed Forces
Führer Headquarters,
16th July 1940.

Directive No. 16
On preparations for a landing operation against England

Since England, despite its hopeless military situation, still gives no sign of any readiness to come to terms, I have decided to prepare for invasion of that country and, if necessary, to carry it through.

The aim of this operation will be to eliminate England as a base for carrying on the war against Germany and, if necessary, completely to occupy it.

For this purpose I am issuing the following orders:-

1. The landing will be in the form of a surprise crossing on a wide front from about Ramsgate to the area west of the Isle of Wight. Some Air Force units will act as artillery, and some Naval units will act as engineers. Exercises will be carried out on the part of all units of the armed forces to ascertain whether it would be practicable before the general operation to undertake small-scale actions, such as the occupation of the Isle of Wight or Cornwall, and the results will be reported to me. The final decision I reserve for myself. Preparations for the entire operation must be completed by the middle of August.

2. These preparations include the creation of those conditions which can make invasion possible;
   a. The English Air Force must be beaten physically and morally to a point that they cannot put up any show of significant attack against the German crossing.
   b. Mine-free channels must be cleared.
   c. The Straits of Dover must be closely sealed off with minefields on both flanks; also the Western entrance to the Channel on the line from about Alderney to Portland.
   d. Strong forces of coastal artillery must command and protect the forward coastal area.
   e. It is desirable that the English Navy be tied down shortly before the crossing, both in the North Sea and in the Mediterranean (by the

Italians) and an attempt will be made to cripple naval forces based in England by air and torpedo attacks.

3. Command organisation and preparations.

Commanders-in-Chiefs will direct the forces concerned under my order and according to my general directions.

From 1 August 1940 Command HQs (Army, Navy and Air Force) will be within a radius of 50 kilometres (at the outside) from my Headquarters (Ziegenberg).

I think it would be an advantage to have the command HQ (Army and Navy) jointly stationed in Giessen.

Commander-in-Chief Army will detail one Army Group to carry out the invasion.

The invasion will be called 'Sealion'.

In preparing and carrying out the operation, units of the armed forces will have the following tasks:-

a. <u>Army:</u>

Will draw up a plan for the operation and will tabulate a ferry plan for the transport of the first wave.

AA guns detailed for the first wave will be under the command of the Army (the individual ferry groups) until they can take their share of the tasks of support and cover for the ground troops, for disembarkation harbours and for occupied air bases.

The Army will further distribute ferrying craft to the individual ferry groups and in agreement with the Navy will determine places of embarkation and landing.

b. <u>Navy:</u>

Will ensure transport craft and sail them according to the wishes of the Army, as far as they conform with the naval point of view to the individual embarkation areas. As far as possible shipping of conquered enemy states will be seized.

For every crossing point, the Navy will create the necessary HQ with escort ships and covering forces.

Besides the Air Forces employed in providing cover, the Navy will protect both flanks of the whole Channel crossing.

Orders will follow regarding the organisation of command during the crossing.

Another Naval task will be the disposition of coastal artillery, that is the unit grouping of all batteries, army and Navy, for sea targets and the organisation of the general control of fire.

The largest possible number of heavy artillery pieces will be deployed at the earliest moment to ensure the crossing and to screen the flanks from the enemy naval action.

In addition, railway artillery supplemented by all available captured guns, except those batteries (K5 and K12) intended for long-range shelling of targets in England will be brought forward and set up, using railway turntables.

Apart from this, all the available heavy coastal batteries will be built in under concrete in order to withstand the heaviest air attacks and thus, in all circumstances, command the Straits for as long as they can remain effective.

The Todt organisation will be responsible for the technical work.

  c. <u>The Task of the Air Force</u> will be:

To prevent counter-attack by the enemy air forces, to neutralise coastal fortifications which could be brought into effect against the landing positions, to eliminate initial enemy resistance on the part of ground forces, and to destroy any reserves on the march. The closest cooperation between individual Air force groups and Army transport groups is essential for this task.

Further tasks will be :-

To destroy important roads used for bringing up enemy reserves and to attack approaching enemy naval formations in areas far removed from the crossing positions.

I am requesting schemes for the employment of parachute and airborne troops. It is a question to be examined in liaison with the Army, whether it would be advantageous to keep them for the present as a reserve which could be quickly put in in case of emergency.

4. Necessary preparations for signals communication from France to England is the province of the Chief of Armed Forces Signals. The construction of the remaining eighty kilometres of the East Prussian Cable will be undertaken with the cooperation of the Navy.

5. I am requesting the Commanders-in-Chief to submit to me at the earliest moment :-
   a. the plans of the Navy and Air Force to establish the necessary conditions for crossing the Channel (see paragraph 2),
   b. the dispositions of coastal batteries in detail (Navy),
   c. a survey of the shipping tonnage to be employed and methods of getting in readiness and fitting out. Participation of civil authorities (Navy),
   d. the organisation of air cover for assembly areas of invasion troops and transport (Air Force),
   e. the operational and transport plans for the Army, organisation and equipment of the first wave,
   f. the organisation of the Navy and Air Force and the measures taken for carrying out the crossing itself, providing cover and support for the landing,

g. proposals for employment of parachute and airborne troops as well as for the deployment and control of anti-aircraft guns after sufficient ground has been gained on English soil (Air Force),
h. proposal location of Army and Navy Command HQs,
i. an appreciation from Army, Navy and Air Force as to whether and which minor operations would be considered advantageous,
j. proposals from the Army and Navy for the chain of command during the crossing.

[signed] ADOLF HITLER

Appendix 2
Key Personalities

Brief biographies of other known officers of Section D Home Defence Scheme and MI(R) can be found online at https://independent.academia.edu/MalcolmAtkin

Bearsted (Walter Samuel), 2nd Viscount (1882–1948) (Plate 4)
Educated at Eton College and New College Oxford. Bearsted served during the First World War in the Queen's Own West Kent Yeomanry, reaching the rank of Captain and being awarded the MC as well as being twice mentioned in dispatches. In 1921 he succeeded his father as Chairman of Royal Dutch Shell and became a Director of Lloyds Bank. Bearsted was also a notable art collector and philanthropist, campaigning during the 1930s for the emigration of Jews from Nazi Germany and funding a number of Jewish charities (although not a devout observer of the Jewish faith or a Zionist). In 1938 he was recruited by SIS as one of a number of wealthy international businessmen who could provide both important contacts and act as a conduit for secret funding. Bearsted had been co-opted by Section D by September 1939 and was initially expected to undertake work in China but by October he was Section D's Coordinator of Planning and became liaison officer with MI5 over their surveillance of the LEX German dissident group in England. Bearsted was involved in the planning from England of resistance networks in Scandinavia, mobilising his contacts in Shell and making available the company bank account. In late May 1940 he took charge of the Section D Home Defence Scheme in Britain and later supervised the transfer of its intelligence branch into the GHQ Auxiliary Units as Auxiliary Units (Special Duties). He joined SOE as head of HQ Advisory Section K and remained in this post until at least 1943.

David Boyle (1883–1970) (Plate 15)
Educated at Wellington School and New College Oxford. Following a pre-war career as a customs officer in Peking, a tea planter in Ceylon and a timber merchant in Bombay, during the First World War he joined the intelligence service, initially as a 'Political Officer' in Ashanti. In March 1919 he was commissioned as a reserve Second Lieutenant in the Argyll and Sutherland Highlanders. He then served as Deputy Head of Station for SIS in New York, ostensibly whilst working for the Ministry of Pensions. Whilst in New York, he was implicated in the failed attempt to kidnap De Valera and was obliged to leave the country. He was then posted by SIS to Ireland where in August he became an officer of the notorious Auxiliary Division of the Royal Irish Constabulary – a British intelligence and assassination unit. In 1921 Boyle became head of Dublin District Special Branch (D Branch) which he reorganised to more effectively counter the operations of the IRA. Later in 1921 and in 1922 he is reported as working for the Foreign Office on unspecified duties in the Far East. From 1924 to 1938 he was Head of Section N, covertly opening diplomatic mail, all the while being a director of Cunard's

and the Anchor Line. In 1938 he became personal assistant to the Chief of SIS (Admiral Sinclair). By then he was operating under the cover of being a King's Messenger. In 1939 Boyle was sent on an abortive mission to Berlin to try to make contact with dissident members of the German General Staff. From 1940 there are repeated references to his being head of the UK resistance organisation of SIS – Section VII.

In 1948 Boyle was invested as a Companion of the Order of St Michael and St George (CMG) with the citation merely saying 'attached to a department of the Foreign Office'. His 1959 autobiography is majestic in never once mentioning that he had spent much of his life in the service of British Intelligence, and he finally took his many secrets to his grave in 1970.

Mike Calvert (1913–98)
Born in India and educated at Bradfield College and the Royal Military Academy, Woolwich. After being commissioned in the Royal Engineers he entered Cambridge University and graduated with a degree in Mechanical Engineering in 1936. He commanded a detachment of Royal Engineers during the Norway campaign in 1940 and after assisting Holland with his 7 June paper on 'The operations of small forces behind enemy lines, supplied and supported by air' became Demolitions Instructor at the new commando training school at Lochailort. He was soon brought down to assist Fleming in building up the XII Corps Observation Unit and then trained the Australian Independent Companies in the Mission 104 school at Wilsons Promontory, Victoria. Calvert was then appointed to command the Mission 204 Bush Warfare School in Burma, training officers and non-commissioned officers to lead guerrilla bands in China against the Japanese. Calvert led one of the columns in Wingate's first Chindit operation in 1943 and then commanded the 77th Indian Infantry Brigade in the second Chindit operation. After being evacuated back to England following an injury, in March 1945 he took command of the Special Air Service Brigade. After the war he served as a lieutenant colonel in the Allied Military Government in Trieste but in 1950 Calvert took command of the Malayan Scouts engaged in operations against Communist insurgents, leading to the re-formation of the SAS. He lived up to his nickname 'Mad Mike' as a hard fighting, hard-drinking soldier who won a reputation as one of the outstanding leaders of irregular warfare during the Second World War but failed to settle to peacetime soldiering. On his return to the UK, in 1951 he was assigned to an administrative staff post with the British Army of the Rhine but was accused of an act of indecency and dismissed from the British Army. He struggled thereafter, trying to build a life as an engineer in Australia before returning to England.

Winston S. Churchill (1874–1965)
One of the most charismatic politicians of all time. As a young army officer he served in India, the Sudan and the Boer War. Before the First World War he was a Cabinet minister and was First Lord of the Admiralty until leaving government after the disastrous Gallipoli campaign in 1915. He then briefly served on the Western Front as CO of the 6th Royal Scots Fusiliers. He returned to government office but in the 1930s was in 'the wilderness', out of both office and favour. He led the warnings about German rearmament and appeasement and on the outbreak of the Second World War returned to government once again as First Lord of the Admiralty. He

became Prime Minister on 10 May 1940 and established a new resolve in fighting the war whatever the cost. This included proposing the use of poison gas if Britain was invaded. Churchill was, nonetheless, indecisive in some elements of defence planning, veering in his opinion of the use of civilians and women in combat and initially unsure of the role of the Home Guard. He became a legendary figure in the post-war period for leading the country through some of its most difficult years to the point where almost any wartime initiative or new weapon might be mistakenly attributed to him personally, including the Auxiliary Units. He could be infuriating to those with whom he had to work and one of the main duties of the CIGS came to be to temper his tendency to make rash decisions. Despite having an immense personal following, his Conservative Party lost the 1945 election with one of the largest defeats in British electoral history. He became Prime Minister again in 1951 before finally retiring from politics in 1955.

Claude Dansey (1876–1947) (Plate 2)

Dansey joined the Lancashire Fusiliers at the age of 20 in 1898 and in 1902, during the Boer War, was seconded as a Staff Intelligence Officer. After the Boer War he joined MI5, serving in port security during the First World War until he transferred to what became SIS. He then worked both part-time and full-time for SIS until his death in 1947. This included setting up the 'shadow' Z organisation in Europe and being appointed Assistant Chief of the Secret Service. During the Second World War he had an office on the 8th floor of Bush House where he oversaw the secret continuation of the Z organisation and probably the secret recording studios that produced material for continental radio stations. He was reputed by some to be the best intelligence agent of his generation, but at the same time he was widely hated and feared as being vindictive and short-tempered. He did not approve of the wide remit given to Section D by Admiral Sinclair and regarded Laurence Grand as being reckless. Although not named, he is likely to have been a driving force behind the creation of the British Resistance organisation of Section VII.

John Dolphin (1905–73)

Educated at Marlborough College and Loughborough Engineering College. By 1938 he had his own engineering consultancy business, as well as being a Territorial reserve officer in the Cheshire Regiment. He was recruited to Section D, SIS in 1939 and became a specialist in sabotage techniques at The Frythe, Hertfordshire (later SOE Station IX). In May 1940 it was he that first proposed the idea of the Section D HDS to Laurence Grand. After transferring to SOE, he became Commanding Officer of Station IX at Welwyn in 1943, where some of his most famous inventions were the folding 'Welbike', the 'Welman' one-man submarine and the 'Welfreighter' miniature submarine. In 1950 he became Chief Engineer at the UK Atomic Energy Authority and continued to be a prolific inventor. He finally retired from the Territorial Army Reserve in 1960 with the rank of Lieutenant Colonel.

Peter Fleming (1907–71) (Plate 7)

Educated at Eton and Christ Church, Oxford. After graduating in 1929 he was sent to the USA to learn the family business of merchant banking and returned to work in the firm of Robert Fleming and Co. After two months he joined *The Spectator* as Assistant Literary Editor and in November 1930 also joined the Grenadier Guards as an officer on the supplementary reserve. In 1931 Fleming undertook the first of his adventures in Brazil and China, reporting for *The Times*. Fleming resigned his reserve commission in March 1936 (possibly to remove suspicion about his travels) and in 1937 he toured European capitals including Prague. In May 1939 he re-joined the Grenadier Guards and after being interviewed by the Director of Military Intelligence, he was sent on a 10-day Intelligence course before returning to his regiment. On 1 August 1939 Fleming was contacted by 'a shadowy colonel' at the War Office and asked if he could go to China in a fortnight's time. He quickly wrote a paper on 'Notes on the possibilities of British military action in China' which proposed the use of British army 'advisors' to the Chinese army and also as 'fighting guerrilla leaders'. He joined MI(R) on 31 August 1939 but lack of work there meant he continued to work as a journalist until November, when he was sent for another three weeks' refresher training with the Warwickshire Yeomanry, but thereafter became central to much of the work of MI(R), flitting rapidly from one project to the next. On 25 May he was briefly attached to Home Forces, tasked with investigating the use of the new LDV in fighting behind enemy lines if Britain was invaded. Fleming then temporarily joined the Lochailort Special Training Centre as an instructor before joining XII Corps Observation Unit, pioneering the methodology of Home Guard patrols and hides that would be adopted by the Auxiliary Units. He briefly continued to serve with the XII Corps Observation Unit after it had been absorbed by the Auxiliary Units, including being responsible for the first trial of the SDB wireless network. Fleming joined SOE in mid-December 1940 and from 1942 was head of D division, which was responsible for military deception operations in South-East Asia. Peter was brother to the more famous Ian Fleming, creator of 'James Bond', whose own career in Intelligence was far more sedentary.

Richard Gambier-Parry (1894–1965)
Born at Highnam Court, Gloucester, and educated at Eton. He served in the Royal Welch Fusiliers during the First World War and was wounded three times (Mentioned in Dispatches twice). He was seconded to the Royal Flying Corps in 1918 but rejoined the Royal Welch Fusiliers in 1925 as a captain. Gambier-Parry then joined the BBC where he became interested in radio and in 1931 joined the radio manufacturer Philco becoming General Sales Manager. In 1938 he was recruited by SIS to run its new communications section (Section VIII) and brought over a number of key engineers from Philco. In 1939 he was promoted Colonel. Gambier-Parry revolutionised attitudes to radio communication within SIS and the Foreign Office. He established Station X in the tower of the SIS War Station at Bletchley Park but then relocated it to nearby Whaddon Hall, which then became the hub of SIS wireless communications and the base from which the 'Ultra' intelligence traffic was distributed worldwide. In 1941 Gambier-Parry also took charge of the Radio Security Service, monitoring the airwaves for illicit wireless stations and until 1942 his Section was also responsible for SOE communications. He was promoted Brigadier in 1942 and post-war he became Director of Government Communications at Hanslope Park until his retirement in 1955. Gambier-Parry was a man of great charm, regarded with affection by his staff (to whom he was 'Pop') but distrusted by outsiders as something of a pirate in his willingness to acquire

new responsibilities for his organisation. Gambier-Parry was one of the triumvirate (with David Boyle and Valentine Vivian) that established the secret SIS network in the UK during 1940 and in 1942 was also radio consultant for the Naval Intelligence plan of a stay-behind unit in Gibraltar (Operation Tracer).

Laurence D. Grand (1898–1975) (Plate 3)

Born in Liverpool, the son of a Canadian merchant, and educated at Rugby and the Royal Military Academy Woolwich. He was a near contemporary of Jo Holland of MI(R) at both establishments. Having been commissioned in the Royal Engineers in 1917 he then went to the School of Military Engineering at Chatham. He served at the end of the First World War in France and in North Russia during 1919. Grand went on to serve with the Indian Army in Queen Victoria's Own Madras Sappers, attached to Iraq levies in Kurdistan during 1922–3 and to the Iraq army during 1925–8. He went on to serve at the Imperial Chemical War Research department and then had a series of staff appointments. From 1935–1938 Grand served as Deputy Assistant Director of Mechanisation at the War Office. In April 1938, then a major, he was recruited to form Section D of SIS to research techniques and strategies for irregular warfare. Here, Grand displayed a passion for secrecy and cultivated an air of mystery. Never wearing uniform whilst in SIS but always elegantly-dressed with a red carnation in his button-hole and rarely without a cigarette holder in his hand, his aliases included 'Mr Graham', 'Mr Douglas' and 'Mr Francis'. Friends and foes alike described him as 'dynamic', full of enthusiasm and energy and with a sharp wit. Although he drove political enemies to distraction he was hero-worshipped by his staff.

In March 1939 Grand presented the 'D Scheme' as an active campaign of subversion and sabotage across Europe. The Foreign Office and War Office gave approval, but the plan remained a closely-guarded secret, specifically from the Chiefs of Staff. The Foreign Secretary said that he intended to forget about the matter and this lack of engagement was later to cause serious problems between Section D and government. Grand asked for a number of army officers from the War Office department researching irregular warfare, MI(R), to be attached to the scheme, including its head, Lieutenant Colonel Jo Holland. This device secured the funding of MI(R) but formed the basis of Grand's later claim that MI(R) operated under the direction of Section D. In June 1939 Sinclair and Grand promoted a unified structure for clandestine warfare under the control of SIS, but this received little attention until after Dunkirk, by which time Grand was implementing his ideas in Britain as the Home Defence Scheme. By then, Grand's ruthless approach to developing Section D had made too many political enemies and the newly-enthused War Office and Ministry of Economic Warfare both sought to take over this new field of warfare, using criticism of Grand, deserved or not, as a main plank of their argument. Admiral Sinclair had both guided and controlled Grand's enthusiasm, but his successor, Stewart Menzies, was neither as committed to the work of Section D or as strong a manager and failed to prevent Section D being absorbed into the new SOE. Even so, Grand remained in charge of what was essentially the same Section D until he was finally dismissed on 18 September 1940. Grand was then posted to India and returned to military engineering. He became Chief Engineer of 4 Corps and in 1943 was Director of Engineer Resources at GHQ India. His citation for the award of a CBE praised his organisational abilities and thereby cast doubt on earlier, politically-motivated, criticism of his skills. Grand returned to England after the war to become Chief Engineer, Home Counties District and in 1949 was promoted Major-General, becoming Director of Fortifications and Works in the War Office. He retired in 1952 and worked in the 1960s with Epar (Engineer Planning and Resources) Limited, involved with the construction of large hotels in the Levant. Grand was a staunch Conservative who unsuccessfully stood in the 1945 General Election for the Plymouth constituency of Lady Astor. Laurence Grand, much-maligned pioneer of British irregular warfare, was killed in a motorway accident in 1975.

Colin Gubbins (1896–1976) (Plate 10)

Born in Japan, the son of a British diplomat. He was educated at Cheltenham College and entered the Royal Military Academy Woolwich in 1913, commissioned part-way through his course in 1914 into the Royal Artillery. In 1916 he was awarded the Military Cross for action during the Battle of the Somme and was gassed at Arras in 1917. He was invalided home but in 1919 he became ADC to General Ironside in the North Russian campaign. From December 1919 to October 1922 he served as an artillery officer in Ireland, appointed temporary Brigade Major in November 1921.

Gubbins was then posted to India with 15th Battery, Royal Artillery and served for eight months as a GSO3 Intelligence Officer until being appointed Adjutant to 23rd Brigade, Royal Artillery on the Kyber Pass. He returned to Intelligence duties at Army HQ at Simla before enrolling at the Quetta Staff College from 1928 to 1929. Gubbins returned to Britain in January 1930 and after a year with 5th Light Brigade he transferred to the Russian section of War Office Intelligence MI3(c), serving there from 1930 to 1933. In April 1933 he returned to the Royal Artillery, responsible for training artillerymen in the Territorial Army but in 1935 joined the policy-making branch of the Military Training Directorate (MT1) in the War Office as head of the artillery section. In October 1938 Gubbins was one of the British military observers at the withdrawal of the Czech army from the Sudetenland. He joined MI(R) in April 1939, on the basis of his expertise in training, to prepare guerrilla training manuals but he became frustrated at the essentially theoretical nature of their work compared to the more actively-engaged Section D. His rivalry with, and machinations against, SIS were to have far-reaching consequences for his career.

From March to June 1940 Gubbins led the Independent Companies in Norway and there hoped to develop his ideas on guerrilla warfare but after a few days they were confined to the tasks of light infantry. On his return from Norway he found he had no job in MI(R) and he had also created suspicion within the War Office establishment over what was seen as ruthless personal ambition. On Jo Holland's recommendation, Gubbins was appointed to command the new GHQ Auxiliary Units, intended as a direct alternative to Section D's Home Defence Scheme. Gubbins left the Auxiliary Units in November for SOE, again initially chosen for his expertise in training. Gubbins finally became Executive Head of SOE in September 1943. When the war ended, SIS was given the responsibility to wind up SOE and re-allocate its resources. Gubbins was informed that there was no further role for him in the army. Although an acting major general, he was retired on the pension of his substantive rank of colonel. This treatment considerably coloured his accounts of Section D (particularly the HDS) and SIS to post-war historians. Gubbins then became managing director of a carpet and textile manufacturer.

Maurice Hankey (1st Baron Hankey) (1877–1963)

Educated at Rugby School and then joined the Royal Marine Artillery. From 1902–4 he was a coastal defence analyst in the Naval Intelligence Department – experience he frequently referred to in dealing with defence matters in the Second World War. Moving to the Civil Service, in 1912 he became Secretary to the Committee of Imperial Defence, a post he held until 1938. In 1914 he was also appointed Secretary of the War Council which led in 1919 to him becoming the first permanent Cabinet Secretary. He retired from the Civil Service in 1938 and was created Baron Hankey in 1939. Frequently called upon for security advice, Chamberlain appointed him a Minister without Portfolio and a member of the War Cabinet. During this period he conducted reviews of both MI5 and SIS. Although dropped from Churchill's War Cabinet, from May 1940 to July 1942 he was Chancellor of the Duchy of Lancaster and was a key conduit between government, the services and the intelligence services, as well as fielding all manner of suggestions from individuals keen to support the war effort. He finally left the government in 1942.

John (Jo) F.C. Holland (1897–1956) (Plate 5)

Born in India, the son of the geologist Sir Thomas Holland. Educated at Rugby and in December 1914 entered the Royal Military Academy Woolwich. He was commissioned into the Royal Engineers in July 1915 and served in Salonika as a signals officer for most of the war. He contracted amoebic dysentery in 1917, which affected his health and war service thereafter. In January 1918 he was attached to 16 Wing, RFC for training as an Observer and then joined 47 Squadron as an observer on long-range reconnaissance and combat patrols. There is no basis to the legend that he served with Lawrence of Arabia! His unit was transferred to Ireland where he re-joined the Royal Engineers, serving in a Special Signals Company. In January 1921 he was badly wounded by the IRA when shot in a Cork public house during what was either a semi-official intelligence operation or a matter of personal revenge.[1] In 1928 Holland returned to India and served with the Bengal Sappers before entering Quetta Staff College. Holland held a series of staff posts from 1934, and then joined the wide-ranging Staff Duties Directorate of the War Office. Holland should then have returned to regimental duties but was prevented by another bout of illness. Instead, in December 1938 he was appointed to lead the small think tank GS(R), which later became MI(R), on a short-term project to research the topic of irregular warfare before he was due to return to the Royal Engineers in July 1939. He worked closely with Laurence Grand of Section D, SIS and in March 1939 they together produced the 'D Scheme' which provided a blueprint for sabotage operations against Nazi Germany. He regarded MI(R) as an 'ideas factory' rather than an operational body and was focused on the use of uniformed troops instead of civilian saboteurs. In June 1940 he produced a forward-looking plan for military special forces which included the use of hides, wireless and helicopters.

In October 1940 Holland returned to regimental duties and became Deputy Chief Engineer, Northern Command. In April 1942 Holland returned to the War Office, involved in organising the priorities for Lend-Lease and later became Deputy Engineer-in-Chief, championing the concept of Assault Engineers. In September 1944 Holland finally had a chance to serve abroad, becoming Temporary Major-General, and Chief Engineer, Mediterranean, at Allied HQ in Italy but a renewed bout of illness obliged him to return to Britain after a few months. In March 1946 he was placed in charge of the administration of Western Command and in 1947 became its Chief of Staff. In July 1948 Holland became Deputy Quartermaster General at the War Office and would have been promoted to his dream of becoming Quartermaster General but was admitted to hospital in December 1948 and had to relinquish the post due to ill health in February 1949. He was then attached to the Army Council Secretariat and remained on the Secret Planning Staff 1949-50. He finally retired in December 1951 with the rank of major general.

Guy Liddell (1892–1958)

Educated at the University of Angers. Liddell served with the Royal Artillery in the First World War and was awarded the Military Cross. In 1919 he joined Scotland Yard as a civilian counter-intelligence officer. He and his section transferred to MI5 in 1931 where he became Deputy Director of the counter-espionage section, B Division. In June 1940 Liddell became Director of B Division at the time when SIS were negotiating to legalise the operation of the Section VII resistance and HDS in Britain. He established a reputation as one of the finest intelligence officers of his generation. Liddell became Deputy Director of MI5 in 1945 but his close friendship with Guy Burgess and acquaintance with the other Soviet spies Kim Philby and Anthony Blunt cast a shadow over his later career. In 1953 he took early retirement from MI5 and became a security advisor to the Atomic Energy Authority. During the Second World War Liddell kept an almost daily diary which provides a unique insight into the workings of Britain's wartime intelligence services. Although published in edited form, some of the key entries relating to the SIS intelligence network in the UK were not included. As a consequence, all references to the Diary in the present book are to the original documents in The National Archives.

Stewart Menzies (1890–1968) (Plate 1)

Educated at Eton College and then commissioned into the Grenadier Guards before transferring to the Life Guards, with whom he served in the First World War, winning the MC and DSO. After being gassed in 1915 he joined the counter-espionage section of the General Staff. After the war he joined SIS and was promoted to Lieutenant Colonel. By 1929 he was Deputy Director of SIS and head of the Military section. In 1938 Menzies was responsible for bringing Laurence Grand to the attention of Admiral Sinclair. He succeeded Admiral Sinclair as Chief in 1939 and during the Second World War he had the difficult task of building up SIS from being a small and impoverished organisation and in managing the top-secret distribution of intelligence gained from 'Ultra'. He was highly adept at political intrigue although was thought by many to be unduly under the influence of Claude Dansey and also was deemed unable to control the dynamism of Laurence Grand. Menzies was outflanked by the creation of SOE in 1940 and the two organisations had a very bumpy relationship. He retired from the Service in 1952 as a Major General.

Nigel Vernon 'Oxo' Oxenden (1885–1948)

Born in London, the son of Colonel Patrick Fitzgerald Gallwey but after his father's death, he and his mother changed their name by deed poll to Oxenden (mother's maiden name). He served in the First World War in the Welsh Regiment and Machine

Gun Corps, twice winning the MC. Oxenden relinquished his commission in 1920 but was recalled from the reserves in November 1938 and was commissioned into the Royal Northumberland Fusiliers. A year later he was promoted to Acting Captain and seconded to 341 Machine Gun Training Centre based on Alderney, Channel Islands, until their evacuation in June. Oxenden's age made a future posting unlikely. He was, however, a cousin of Gubbins and whilst staying with relatives in Sussex asked one of Colin's sisters to mention to her brother that Oxenden was looking for a post. Oxenden joined the Auxiliary Units a few weeks later on 13 July, as Intelligence Officer for Norfolk. In 1943 he became Training Officer, based at Coleshill and in 1944 was appointed to write the official history of the Auxiliary Units. It was never completed but a draft of October 1944 was discovered in 1998 and published by the British Resistance Organisation Museum. Oxenden relinquished his commission in April 1946 with the rank of Honorary Major but died in 1948 on Jersey.

Maurice Petherick (1894–1985) (Plate 12)

Educated at Marlborough College and Trinity College, Cambridge. At the start of the First World War he served with the Royal Devon Yeomanry but was wounded in 1915 and then served in the Foreign Office during 1916-17, which may have been his first contact with the intelligence services. He re-joined the Royal Scots Greys in 1917. Petherick became a successful Conservative Party MP, representing Falmouth and Penryn from 1931 to 1945. In October 1939 he was re-commissioned onto the General List, probably as a member of SIS. During part of 1940 he was a liaison officer at the Paris Embassy and was on personal terms with Laurence Grand, if not a member of Section D itself. He then became commanding officer of the Special Duties Branch of the Auxiliary Units, supervising the final integration of the HDS with the Auxiliary Units and masterminding the new wireless network.

Duncan Sandys (1908–87)

Educated at Eton and Magdalen College, Oxford. Served in the Foreign Office in London and Berlin but in 1935 entered Parliament as a Conservative MP. In that year he also became the son-in-law of Winston Churchill and thereafter became a close ally. In 1937 he was commissioned into the Territorial Army (Royal Artillery) and when war broke out he served with the BEF in Norway. On his return he appears to have spent much of summer of 1940 as one of Churchill's inner circle of unofficial advisors, based around family members. According to John Colville, Private Secretary to the Prime Minister, he spent his time 'drinking in all the most secret information'.[2] As such, he was clearly privy to knowledge of both Section D and the new Auxiliary Units and acted as a conduit between the Prime Minister and the General Staff on their development. In August he was given a formal post in the Cabinet Office under General Ismay (which became the Offices of the Minister of Defence) and as such was responsible for producing reports on the Auxiliary Units for the Prime Minister. He then returned to active service to become CO of an anti-tank regiment in Wales, although his military career was cut short by a car accident in 1941. He then became Finance Secretary to the War Office. In 1943 he became Chairman of the War Cabinet committee to investigate defence measures against the German flying bombs. He had a successful post-war political career and was given a life peerage in 1974.

Hugh Sinclair (1873–1939)
Sinclair joined the Royal Navy as a teenager, being promoted to rank of Lieutenant in 1894. He had a succession of staff posts but in January 1919 he was appointed head of the Naval Intelligence Division, promoted to Rear Admiral in 1920. He was appointed Chief of the SIS in 1923 and went onto the Naval Retired List in 1926. He was promoted to full Admiral on the Retired List in 1930. Sinclair clearly foresaw the threat of Nazi Germany, clashing with contemporary government policy of appeasement. Some of his key innovations of the late 1930s were clearly aimed to bring SIS to a war footing, including the creation of the Wireless Communication Section (Section VIII), Section D (Sabotage Section) and Dansey's shadow SIS organisation – the Z Organisation. All have a direct relevance to the present study. He died on 4 November 1939, on his deathbed recommending Stewart Menzies as his successor.

Andrew Thorne (1885–1970) (Plate 8)
Educated at Eton College and Royal Military Academy, Sandhurst. He was commissioned into the Grenadier Guards in 1904, becoming CO of 3rd Battalion in 1916. In 1932 he became Military Attaché in Berlin and whilst in Germany got the idea of stay-behind guerrilla units. In 1938 Thorne became Major General commanding London District and the Brigade of Guards. He commanded 48th (South Midland) Division as the rearguard for the Dunkirk evacuation and then was given command of XII Corps in Kent and Sussex. Here he created the XII Corps Observation Unit which was the inspiration for the Auxiliary Units. Thorne had a close connection with the Osterley Park Home Guard Training School, maintaining a correspondence with Tom Wintringham throughout the war and championed the issue of a commission to Hugh Slater. In 1941 he was appointed Commanding Officer of Scottish Command where he had a key role in the D-Day deception plan, Operation Fortitude (North). At the end of the war he was put in charge of plans for the liberation of Norway.

John Stewart Ellerman Todd (1899–1980) (Plate 14)
Born in Putney, Surrey, the son of a civil servant. He enlisted in the Honourable Artillery Company in 1917 and served as a signaller until 1919. Todd then became a successful London stockbroker but seems likely to have been recruited at some point by SIS. He was commissioned as a second lieutenant on the General List on 31 May 1940 'without pay and allowances' – a common identifier of an officer in SIS. This may have marked his appointment as a regional officer of the Section D Home Defence Scheme. Two months later he was an Acting Captain on 'special employment', marking his appointment as Intelligence Officer for the new Auxiliary Units in Monmouthshire, Herefordshire and Worcestershire. Unusually, he served as Intelligence Officer for both the Operational and Special Duties Branches of the Auxiliary Units, which, together with an absence of the usual criteria for Auxiliary Units officers, may suggest he was one of the Section D D/M Group that Laurence Grand says he loaned to the new body. If so, Todd probably remained an SIS officer, liaising with the SIS Section VII resistance network in the Midlands and North-West. He was a ruthless eccentric who recruited auxiliers on the strength of their bladders and taught the techniques of disembowelling. In August 1941 Todd was appointed a Local Lieutenant Colonel in the Intelligence

Corps, marking his transfer to SOE. Todd then led the East Africa Mission to organise espionage and the re-capture of Madagascar. He retired from the army in May 1945 as an Honorary Colonel in the Intelligence Corps but maintained contacts with the now-disbanded Auxiliary Units. In an act that belies his secret career in intelligence, he was knighted in 1963 for services as a Commissioner for the Public Works Loan Board. He died in 1980.

Valentine Vivian (1886–1969)

Joined the Indian police service in 1906 and in 1914 became Assistant Director of Criminal Intelligence. Having joined SIS, in 1925 Vivian then became head of SIS counter-espionage section (Section V). He ran the SIS 'Casuals' agent network in Britain in the late 1920s until they were taken over by MI5. In 1932 he created the SIS intelligence network in Eire and in 1940 was one of the triumvirate (with Boyle and Gambier-Parry) who established the SIS intelligence network in the UK, negotiating its presence on the mainland with MI5. He had an uncomfortable relationship with Claude Dansey, both regarding themselves as Deputy Head of SIS during the war years.

Ken Ward (1915–2011)

Enlisted with the Royal Signals aged 18. With the aid of an army scholarship, he entered Pembroke College, Cambridge, in 1933 to study Mechanical Sciences with telecommunications as an additional subject, and graduated in 1936 aged 21. As an RCS entrant, he was attached to the Signals Research Section of the Cambridge University Officers' Training Corps under Professor Milner and assisted on the duplex transceiver receiver project. He then embarked on a two-year apprenticeship with English Electric and was also commissioned into the Royal Signals Reserve. After service as an operator training instructor to the Y Service, in January 1941 he joined the new Auxiliary Units (Signals) as a lieutenant and was promoted to temporary captain in June 1941, working with a team of 'radio hams' on the development of the TRD wireless set. Following posting to SOE in early 1942 he reverted to his substantive rank of lieutenant on 'special employment'. In SOE, Ward was a procurement and contracts officer, working with John Brown who invented many of their wireless sets. He does not, however, appear to have been employed as a technical officer working directly in their development.

Tom Wintringham (1898–1949) (Plate 45)

Born in Grimsby, Lincolnshire and educated at Gresham School, Norfolk and Balliol College, Oxford. In the First World War he served as a mechanic and dispatch rider in the Royal Flying Corps. At the end of the war he was involved in a barracks mutiny and formed the British branch of the Third International. He then joined the new Communist Party of Great Britain and was imprisoned in 1925 for seditious libel. In 1930 he founded the *Daily Worker* and became the party's chief spokesperson on military matters. He was a steadfast adherent to the concept of the 'popular front' and during the Spanish Civil War was a leading proponent of the idea of the International Brigades, for a time commanding the British Battalion. His beliefs fell out of tune with

Stalinism and he was expelled from the Communist Party. At the start of the Second World War he condemned both the Communist Party for their subservience to the Hitler-Stalin Pact and the Conservatives for their policies of appeasement. He became the main publicist for the Home Guard and founded the innovative Home Guard guerrilla Training School at Osterley Park. Wintringham returned to politics in 1942 and formed the Common Wealth Party; in 1946 he joined the Labour Party. He died in 1949, already largely forgotten.

Notes

Introduction

1. Analysis of the Defence Requirements Committee, 1933, reported in Collier 1957, pp. 25–6.
2. Section D was created in April 1938 and MI(R) as a body researching irregular warfare in December 1938. See Atkin 2017, 2021 and 2023 for detailed histories of Section D and MI(R).
3. Tittenhofer 1969, p. 51.
4. Duncan Stuart, 'Of historic interest only: the origins and vicissitudes of the SOE archive', in Seaman 2006.
5. D Section Early History to September 1940: TNA HS7/3 and HS 7/4; memo of 4 December 1943 to D/CR in Samuel SOE file: TNA HS 9/1306/1.
6. Mackenzie 2000, p. 52.
7. Foot 1984, p. 17.
8. Stafford 2010, p. 122.
9. Davies 2004, p. 119.
10. C-in-C Home Forces to Under Secretary of State, 27 November 1944; GHQ to HQ, Auxiliary Units, 30 November 1944: TNA WO 199/739.
11. Oxenden 2012 reprint.
12. The newspaper for troops of South East Asia Command.
13. Collier 1957, pp. 130 and 297.
14. Fleming 1952, p. 13; 1957, pp. 270
15. Farebrother 1986, p. 19; Ward 1989, pp. 45–6; Angell 1996, p. 5.
16. Ward 2013, xii; John Warwicker '… By the Way', *Parham Airfield Museum Newsletter*, Winter 2022/23, p. 16.
17. Lampe 1968, p. 152; Chatterton 2022, p. vii.
18. Warwicker 2008, p. 82.
19. Fleming 1957, p. 9.
20. Stuart Edmundson to John Warwicker, July 1998: BRO Archive. This is an issue not unique to the Auxiliary Units but which affects many veterans, whose connections to special forces or the intelligence services is exaggerated and over-dramatised. See Gavin Mortimer, 'Who Dares … Lies' in *The Spectator*, 18 July 2015, p. 24.
21. Ward 2013, p. xii.
22. Ward to Warwicker, 28 June 2000, BRO Archive.
23. Schellenberg 2001, p. 123.

Chapter 1: Attitudes to Ungentlemanly Warfare

1. German radio broadcast upon the founding of the LDV: Graves 1943, p. 16.
2. *Official Regulations of the Volunteer Training Corps*, 1916, p. 78.
3. See Atkin 2017 for a detailed discussion of Section D.
4. Atkin 2021, p. 12.

5   Ibid., p. 106.
6   Atkin 2017, p. 112; Atkin 2021, p. 72
7   Minutes of meeting of 1 July 1940: TNA FO 1093/193; Garnett 2002, p. 30.
8   Atkin 2019, Chapter 6.
9   United Nations War Crimes Commission, *Law Reports of Trials of War Criminals*, Volume VIII, 1949.
10 On 21 November 1920 in Dublin (Bloody Sunday), the IRA assassinated twelve British undercover army officers, a policeman and a civilian informant all believed to be associated with the 'Auxiliary Division' intelligence network that was organised by Dublin Special Branch. The future leader of the British SIS resistance organisation in 1940, David Boyle, then became the commanding officer of the Auxiliary Division.
11 Langdon-Davies 1941, p. 54.
12 Pers comm Janet Hollington, with thanks.
13 *Guerrilla Warfare: Military Training Pamphlet No.54*, 1942, pp. 5–6, 8.
14 House of Commons debate for 7 May 1940, *Hansard*, vol.360, c.1120.
15 House of Lords debate for 30 July 1940, *Hansard*, vol.117, cc.26-27.
16 Graves 1943, p. 16.
17 TNA WO 199/3237.
18 Graves 1943, p. 15.
19 TNA CAB 67/7/27.
20 Minutes of the Defence Committee, War Cabinet 19 July 1940: TNA 69/1.
21 Minutes of the War Cabinet for 23 August 1940: TNA CAB 65/8/45.
22 George Orwell 1938, *Homage to Catalonia*, Chapter 3.
23 *Guerrilla Warfare: Military Training Pamphlet No.54*, 1942, p. 8.

Chapter 2: Playing the Long Game: the SIS Resistance Organisation of Section VII

1   Quoted in H.R. Trevor-Roper, *Hitler's Table Talk 1941-44: Secret Conversations*, 2013, p. 233.
2   Bennett 2009, p. 213.
3   Jeffery 2010, pp. 361–2; Davies 2004, p. 82.
4   Read and Fisher 1984, pp. 271–2.
5   Andrew 2009, p. 129.
6   Jeffery 2010, pp. 226–35.
7   Ismay 1960, p. 220.
8   *German Occupied Great Britain: Ordinances of the Military Authorities*, 1941.
9   Jeffery 2010, pp. 361–2.
10 Attwater 1999.
11 Read and Fisher 1984, p. 206.
12 Section D: Early History to September 1940, p. 4: TNA HS7/3.
13 MI5 Irish Section History: TNA KV 4/9; Jeffery 2010, p. 281.
14 Liddell Diary for 27 November 1939: TNA KV 4/185, f.186-7.
15 McMahon 2011, p. 290.
16 The Irish Intelligence Service (G-2) and IRA elements co-operated as the Irish 'Supplementary Intelligence Service' (ISIS) to carry out surveillance operations on British clandestine activity; it was also intended to form the core of a 'stay-behind' organisation in the event of German, or British, occupation. Unlike its British counterparts, members of ISIS were later formally recognised and were awarded the

'Emergency Medal' for their contribution to the Irish defence forces 1939-45; see O'Halpin 2010, pp. 74 and 131–4.
17 Ibid., p. 73.
18 TNA ADM 223/464 f.268.
19 Guy Liddell was head of MI5's B Division (counter-espionage); Liddell Diary for 8 March 1940: TNA KV 4/186, f.368.
20 Angell 1996, p. 8.
21 TNA WO 199/1194.
22 Farebrother 1986, pp. 19–20.
23 Angell 1996, pp. 74–5.
24 Farebrother 1986, pp. 19–20.
25 Ibid.
26 Angell 1996, p. 75.
27 Jeffery 2010, p. 361–2.
28 Guy Liddell Diary for 24 April 1940 in Nigel West, *The Guy Liddell Diaries*, vol.1, 2009, p. 78.
29 Pidgeon 2003, p. 90.
30 Ibid., p. 73.
31 Jeffery 2010, pp. 361–2.
32 www.staybehinds.com.
33 Thanks to David Blair for this information, 2022.
34 Memo of Philip Gregson-Ellis, BGS, 30 March 1942: TNA WO 199 738.
35 Atkin 2021, p. 77.
36 BND File Nr. 34477_OT, cited in Sinai 2021, p. 15.
37 SCU War Establishment: TNA WO 208/4697. Eventually each SCU/SLU developed into a substantial self-contained unit of up to thirty-five men, with the wireless trucks protected by a fleet of jeeps armed with 20mm cannon and twin Vickers K machine guns. See Geoffrey Pidgeon's *Secret Wireless War*, 2003, for the most comprehensive published account of the SCU/SLU organisation. TNA CAB 63/167, f.85; Memo of Director of Signals, 14 July 1941: TNA WO 208/4697.
Hankey to Menzies, 7 June 1940: TNA CAB 301/70.
38 TNA CAB 63/167, f.85.
39 TNA CAB 63/167, f.85; Memo of Director of Signals, 14 July 1941: TNA WO 208/4697.
40 Hankey to Menzies, 7 June 1940: TNA CAB 301/70.
41 *History of the Security Service 1908 – 1945, The Curry Report*: TNA KV 4/2; Jeffery 2010, p. 361.
42 Letter of Valentine Vivian to Guy Liddell, 2 July 1940: TNA KV 4/205.
43 Jeffery 2010, p. 361.
44 Liddell Diary for 18 July 1940: TNA KV 4/186, f.534.
45 Memo of the Lord President of the Council to the War Cabinet, 19 July 1940: TNA CAB 66/10/1. Swinton was the former Air Minister, appointed Chairman of the new Home Defence (Security) Executive on 28 May 1940: TNA CAB 66/8/2.
46 Director's Circular No.150, 27 July 1940: TNA KV 4/205.
47 Vivian to Liddell, 2 July 1940: TNA KV 4/205.
48 Cowgill was the former head of Special Branch in India who joined SIS in 1939; Cowgill to Comyns Carr, 28 April 1941: TNA KV 4/205.
49 Letter of Guy Liddell to Valentine Vivian, 10 October 1940: TNA KV 4/205.
50 Liddell Diary for 21 October 1943: TNA KV 4/192, f.309.
51 Report of Sir Robert Knox, Central Honours Committee: TNA WO 32/21918.

52 Interviews with Peter Attwater in 2000 by Bernard Lowry, and in 2014 by the author; Attwater 1999, *passim*.
53 Liddell Diary, 5 March 1942: TNA KV 4/189, f.398.
54 TNA KV 2/3800.
55 As confirmed by Stewart Angell, with thanks.
56 Liddell Diary for 12 April 1943: TNA KV 4/191, ff.217-18.
57 Quoted in H.R. Trevor-Roper, *Hitler's Table Talk 1941-44: Secret Conversations*, 2013, p. 233.
58 Lampe 1968, pp. 88–9.
59 Attwater 1999, p. 6.
60 *Newsletter* no.3, 1999, British Resistance Organisation Museum, Parham, p. 2.
61 Sweet-Escott 1965, p. 24.
62 Philby 2002, p. 15; in one of Section D's most successful missions, in May 1940 the 48-year-old Chidson was responsible for the smuggling of industrial diamonds out of Amsterdam – a mission that formed the basis of the film *Operation Amsterdam* (1959). He was later head of D Section's German Section.
63 Chatterton 2022, p. 168.
64 Atkin 2019, pp. 168–9, 171–7 and online Appendix 2.
65 Ruddy 2015, pp. 48-9; Chatterton 2022, pp. 166–7.
66 Letter from Eric Nussen to author, 4 October 2015.
67 Lowry and Wilks 2002, p. 113.
68 Turner 2011, Appendix A.
69 Lowry and Wilks 2002, pp. 113–15.
70 Wilks 2007, pp. 216–17.
71 Information from grandson Andrew Chatterton in 2018, with thanks.
72 TNA HS 9/1200/5.

Chapter 3: The Impact of Dunkirk: Rethinking the Military Options

1 Chiefs of Staff report to War Cabinet, *Urgent measures to meet attack*, 19 June 1940: TNA CAB 66/8/43.
2 Chiefs of Staff report to War Cabinet, *British strategy in a certain eventuality*, 25 May 1940: TNA CAB 66/7.
3 Wilkinson and Astley 1993, p. 69.
4 Fleming 1957, p. 249.
5 Liddell Diary, 3 May 1941: TNA KV 4/197.
6 GHQ to Regional Commands, 23 May 1940: TNA WO 199/1885.
7 'Points from Regions', 1 June 1940: TNA INF 1/264 published in Addison and Crang 2011, p. 64.
8 Bert Northwood interview in Whittaker 1990, p. 12.
9 General Franz Halder quoted in Fleming 1957, p. 252.
10 Vice-Chiefs of Staff Committee, 26 June 1940: TNA CAB 63/167, f.159.
11 Chiefs of Staff report to War Cabinet, *Urgent measures to meet attack*, 19 June 1940: TNA CAB 66/8/43; Joint Intelligence Sub-committee, *German Invasion of the British Isles*, 31 January 1941: TNA CAB 121/209.
12 Atkin 2019, Chapter 1.
13 TNA CAB 63/167, f.93.
14 TNA CAB 63/167, f.96.
15 TNA HS 8/259.
16 Letter of Lord Hankey to Stephen King-Hall, 9 July 1940: TNA CAB 63/92, f.101.

17 Conclusions of War Cabinet, 17 June 1940: TNA CAB 65/7/65 f.321.
18 Report to War Cabinet, 19 June 1940: TNA 69/1.
19 Ismay 1960, p. 305.
20 Royle 2010, pp. 165–7.
21 Tom Wintringham, 'Against invasion: the lessons of Spain', *Picture Post*, 15 June 1940, p. 10.
22 Purcell with Smith 2012, p. 189.
23 *Seaborne and airborne attack on the United Kingdom*, War Cabinet Chiefs of Staff Committee, 10 May 1940: TNA CAB 63/167.
24 Liddell Diary for 5 September 1939: TNA KV 4/185, f.27.
25 Fifth Column Activities in the United Kingdom, War Cabinet, Chiefs of Staff Committee, 2 May 1940: TNA CAB 63/167.
26 MI(R) War Diary, 21 May 1940: TNA HS8/263.
27 Later head of SOE Station IX at Welwyn, responsible for the development of the Welman submarine and the Welbike folding bicycle.
28 *Organisation of civil resistance in Belgium, France, UK and Ireland*, 23 May 1940. Document from unknown source provided by FCO SOE Adviser 1997, with thanks to Stephen Sutton for making it available to this author. Version as *Organisation of Civil Resistance in Belgium and France* at TNA CAB 21/1476.
29 *Mobilisation of National Resources, moral, physical and material, to deny to the enemy the advantages obtained by his methods of invasion*, ISPB, 27 May 1940: TNA CAB 63/167, f.71; TNA CAB 21/1476.
30 *Mobilisation of National Resources, moral, physical and material, to deny to the enemy the advantages obtained by his methods of invasion*, ISPB, 27 May 1940: TNA CAB 63/167, f.72.
31 *Organisation and Duties of MI(R)*, J.C.F. Holland, 3 September 1939: TNA HS 8/256.
32 TNA CAB 127/376; West and Tsarev 2009, p. 201.
33 Memo of Major General Rawson, 14 July 1941: TNA WO 208/4697.
34 Atkin 2021, pp. 107–29.
35 Ibid.
36 Minutes of ISPB meeting, 27 May 1940. Document from unknown source provided by FCO SOE Adviser 1997, with thanks to Stephen Sutton for making it available to this author; TNA CAB 21/1476.
37 Lindsay 1987, p. 109.
38 Fleming 1957, p. 269.
39 Minutes of ISPB Meeting, 27 May 1940: TNA HS 8/193.
40 Section D, Early History to September 1940, p. 14: TNA HS 7/3.
41 TNA CAB 63/167.
42 Ibid.

Chapter 4: Home Defence Scheme of Section D

1 Section D Closing Report: Great Britain's only successful experiment in total warfare, 27 August 1940, p. 8: TNA HS 8/214. According to Mackenzie, the final document contained adverse comments from CSS. These are not present in the version deposited with TNA.
2 Atkin 2017, updated as Atkin 2023.
3 Quoted in Foot 2004, from MIR files: TNA HS 8/256-61.
4 Philby 2002, p. 9.
5 TNA CAB 63/192, ff.83-4.

6   TNA HS 7/5, handwritten notes by Grand.
7   Jeffery 2010, p. 352.
8   Bennett 2009, p. 213.
9   Stirling to Goodwill, 19 August 1940: TNA HS 5/60; quote attributed to Brigadier Shearer in HS 7/4.
10 Section D: Early History to September 1940, p. 4: TNA HS 7/3.
11 Turner 2011, p. 33. When SOE took over Aston House, Langley transferred to SIS Section XIII at Whaddon.
12 Section D: Early History to September 1940: TNA HS 7/3.
13 TNA HS 8/255.
14 Ibid.
15 Mackenzie 2000, p. 37.
16 TNA HS 8/256.
17 Ibid.
18 Warwicker 2008, p. 30.
19 TNA HS 7/4; Gerald Holdsworth later ran the 'Helston Flotilla' for SOE, running agents in and out of Brittany, and had a distinguished career with them.
20 D/XE, *Pessimism*, 22 May 1940. Document provided by FCO SOE Advisor 1997, with thanks to Stephen Sutton for originally making it available to this author.
21 Minutes of ISPB Meeting, 27 May 1940: TNA HS 8/193. Nominal Roll of Auxiliary Units: TNA WO 199/3391.
22 Section D, Early History to September 1940, p. 14: TNA HS 7/3.
23 *D Organisation for Home Defence*, 1 June 1940. Document provided by FCO SOE Advisor 1997, with thanks to Stephen Sutton for making it available to this author.
24 Ibid.
25 Angell 1996, p. 77.
26 *Notes on Regional D Scheme*, 2 June 1940 and *Preliminary Notes on the Regional D Scheme*, 4 June 1940: TNA HS 8/255.
27 Jeffery 2010, pp. 352–3.
28 Atkin 2019, p. 10.
29 Mackenzie 2000, p. 52, quoting SOE Archives File 1/470/7.1.
30 'The origin of the Resistance Movement on the Isle of Wight', S.A. Watson, 1968: Isle of Wight Archives (ref. unknown) reproduced on the www.Staybehinds.com website.
31 Wilkinson and Astley 1993, p. 72.
32 Ironside report to War Cabinet, 10 June 1940: CAB 69/1.
33 Section D, Draft Notes and Lessons, section 19: TNA HS 7/5.
34 O'Brien 1955, p. 311.
35 Macleod and Kelly 1962, p. 368.
36 Wilkinson 2002, p. 103.
37 Danchev and Todman 2001, p. 173.
38 Note on First Meeting of the Secret Service Committee, 3 June 1940: TNA FO 1093/193.
39 Section D, Draft Notes and Lessons, section 19: TNA HS 7/5.
40 Ibid.
41 TNA HS 8/214.
42 Preliminary Notes on Regional D Scheme, 4 June 1940: TNA HS 8/255.
43 Maschwitz 1957, p. 136.
44 Ibid.
45 With thanks to Rev. Nathan Ward for this information.

46 Section D Closing Report: Great Britain's only successful experiment in total warfare, 27 August 1940, p. 8: TNA HS 8/214.
47 TNA HS 8/255.
48 *D Organisation for Home Defence*, 1 June 1940.
49 TNA CAB 63/89, f.43.
50 *D Organisation for Home Defence*, 1 June 1940.
51 Section D, Draft Notes and Lessons, section 19: TNA HS 7/5.
52 Oxenden 2012 (typescript 1944), p. 2.
53 Edwards 1959, p. 33.
54 Warwicker 2008, p. 178.
55 Williamson 2004, p. 13.
56 Freethy 2012, p. 51.
57 Lampe 1968, p. 105.
58 Sweet-Escott 1965, p. 38.
59 Wilkinson 2002, p. 100.
60 Pidgeon 2003, p. 125; TNA WO 208/4697.
61 Section D: Early History to September 1940, p. 8: TNA HS 7/3.
62 Section D, Early History to September 1940, p. 14: TNA HS 7/3.
63 Atkin 2017, pp. 89 and 104–05.
64 Lee Richards, 2005 and 2010, p. 18.
65 *Preliminary Notes on the Regional D Scheme*, 4 June 1940: TNA HS 8/255.
66 Section D: Early History to September 1940: TNA HS 7/3.
67 *Preliminary Notes on the Regional D Scheme*, 4 June 1940: TNA HS 8/255.
68 Section D Closing Report: Great Britain's only successful experiment in total warfare, 27 August 1940, p. 8: TNA HS 8/214.
69 TNA HS 8/255.
70 Ashley, whose family estates were in Dorset, transferred from the Wiltshire Yeomanry to be Major on the General List of the Territorial Army Reserve on 5 January 1940, possibly marking his transfer to Section D.
71 Letter of A. Gordon MacLeod to the Prime Minister, 3 July 1940: TNA CAB 120/241.
72 Letter of General Paget to Captain Sandys, 30 July 1940: TNA CAB 120/241.
73 Major General Ian Macdougall to Major General 'Pug' Ismay, 22 June 1940: TNA CAB 21/1473.
74 Letter of Ismay to Pownall, 23 June 1940: TNA CAB 21/1476; Beaumont-Nesbitt to Ismay, 24 June 1940: TNA CAB 21/1473; Gubbins, circular letter to LDV Commanders, 5 July 1940: TNA CAB 21/120; Atkin 2015, p. 69.
75 Offensive and Irregular Operations, Appendix I (paper to COS Committee): TNA HS 8/258.
76 TNA HS 8/258.
77 TNA CAB 63/192, f.108.
78 Wilkinson and Astley 1993, p. 35.
79 Meeting of 1 July 1940 to discuss the direction of sabotage: TNA FO 1093/193; MI(R), *An aide-memoire on the co-ordination of subversive activities in the conquered territories*, 6 July 1940: TNA HS 8/259.
80 TNA HS 8/258; MI(R), *An aide-memoire on the co-ordination of subversive activities in the conquered territories*, 6 July 1940: TNA HS 8/259.
81 TNA CAB 67/7/27.
82 Report VIII on the activities of D Section during July 1940, p. 1: TNA HS 8/214.
83 MI(R) War Diary for 22 July 1940: TNA HS 8/263.
84 D Section Early History to September 1940, pp. 17–18: TNA HS 7/3.

85   Mackenzie 2000, p. 52, quoting SOE Archives File 1/470/7.1.
86   Lampe 1968, p. 68.
87   Oxenden 2012, p. 2.
88   Report VIII on the activities of D Section during July 1940, p. 23: TNA HS 8/214.
89   Turner 2011, p. 96.
90   D Section Early History to September 1940, pp. 17-18: TNA HS 7/3.
91   Section D, Draft Notes and Lessons, section 19: TNA HS 7/5.
92   Ibid.
93   TNA WO 199/3391.
94   Memo of Grigson-Ellis, 30 March 1942: TNA WO 199/738.
95   Correspondence of George Vater with Mick Wilks in 2000.
96   TNA HS 7/4.
97   Interview with Geoffrey Morgan-Jones, 26 May 1999, by Bernard Lowry; Lowry and Wilks 2002, pp. 53–4.
98   TNA WO 199/3391.
99   Lampe 1968, pp. 88–9.
100 Turner 2011, pp. 22–3.
101 Turner 2011, pp. 94–5; TNA HS 7/27; Turner 2011, pp. 200–01.
102 Seaman 2006, pp. 18–19; Dalton to Grand 18 September 1940 (Dalton papers LSE/DALTON/7/3, quoted in Bennett 2009, p. 262).
103 Atkin 2021, p. 94.
104 Davies to Cornwall-Jones, 17 June 1940: TNA CAB 21/1476.
105 'Need for Organisation of Civil Resistance', F.T. Davies, 18 June 1940: TNA CAB 21/1476.
106 Ibid.
107 Hollis to Ismay, 20 June 1940: TNA CAB 21/1476.
108 TNA CAB 21/1476.
109 Letter of Hankey to Hollis, 22 June 1940: TNA CAB 21/1476.
110 Letter of Cavendish-Bentinck to Ismay, 21 June 1940: TNA CAB 21/1476.
111 Letter of Ismay to Pownall, 23 June 1940: TNA CAB 21/1476.
112 Letter of Pownall to Ismay, 25 June 1940; letter of Findlater-Stewart to Ismay, 26 June 1940: TNA CAB 21/14.
113 TNA CAB 67/7/27.
114 Dalton Diary for 25 June 1940: Pimlott 1986, p. 65.

Chapter 5: XII Corps Observation Unit

1   Fleming 1957, p. 269.
2   Wintringham 1940a, p. 279.
3   Lindsay 1987, p. 109.
4   Lovat Scouts War Diary for 19 June 1940: TNA WO 176/337.
5   XII Corps War Diary: TNA WO 166/344.
6   Lovat Scouts War Diary for 11 November 1940: TNA WO 176/337.
7   Warwicker 2008, pp. 68–9.
8   Arnold 1962, p. 53.
9   Pidgeon 2003, p. 189.
10   Calvert 1996, p. 47.
11   Hart-Davis 1987, p. 234.
12   Ibid., pp. 236–7.
13   Fleming 1952, p. 13.

14 Ibid.
15 Memories quoted on www.kentauxiliaryunits.org.uk.
16 Calvert 1964, pp. 48–9.
17 Fleming 1952, p. 13.
18 Lowry and Wilks 2002, pp. 103–06.

Chapter 6: The GHQ Auxiliary Units: Operational Wing 1940–1: Resisting the Invader

1 Section D, Early History to September 1940, pp. 17–18: TNA HS 7/3.
2 Conclusions of War Cabinet, 17 June 1940: TNA CAB 65/7/65 f.321.
3 Grand Diary mss: TNA HS 7/5.
4 Atkin 2021, p. 3.
5 *Report No.8: Investigation of the possibilities of Guerrilla Activities*: TNA HS 8/260.
6 See Atkin 2019 for a detailed history of MI(R) and its relationship to Section D.
7 Astley 2007, pp. 20–1.
8 TNA CAB 63/192, f.66.
9 TNA CAB 127/376; West and Tsarev 2009, p. 201.
10 Peter Wilkinson interviewed by Mark Seaman, 1993: IWM Audio Interview, Cat. No.13289 reel 5.
11 TNA HS 8/256.
12 Atkin 2021, pp. 54–6.
13 MI(R) War Diary, 17 June 1940: TNA HS8/263; TNA CAB 79/5/79.
14 Wilkinson and Astley 1993, p. 70.
15 *Report No.8: Investigation of the possibilities of Guerrilla Activities*: TNA HS 8/260; MI(R) War Diary, 3 June 1940: TNA HS8/263.
16 MI(R) War Diary for 17 June 1940 : TNA HS 8/263. The War Diary was compiled from notes in November 1940.
17 Peter Wilkinson interview in S. Sutton, "'Farmers or Fighters. Dissertation on the existence and function of Britain's 'secret army'. Auxiliary Units in southern England during 1940-44'". Unpublished BA dissertation 1995, Canterbury Christchurch College.
18 Wilkinson 2002, p. 104.
19 Great Britain's Only Successful Experiment In Total Warfare, by Laurence Grand, August 1940: TNA HS 8/214.
20 Report VIII, July 1940, p. 23: TNA HS 8/214; Turner 2011, p. 96.
21 Oxenden (2012), p. 2.
22 Wilkinson and Astley 1993, pp. 68 and 76.
23 TNA CAB 65/7/65.
24 Duncan Sandys to Churchill, 8 August 1940: TNA CAB 120/121.
25 Letter of 22 May 1941: TNA WO 199/3251.
26 Letter from Director General, Home Guard to county TAAs, 20 January 1941: TNA WO 199/3251.
27 TNA WO 199/2892.
28 Gubbins to LDV commanders, 5 July 1940: TNA CAB 120/241.
29 'Auxiliary Units, Home Forces: A. Organisation', Gubbins, 26 July 1940: TNA CAB 120/241 and TNA WO 199/738.
30 Wilkinson 2002, p. 104.
31 Lowry and Wilks 2002, p. 90; *Target for Tonight* lecture notes 1941: BRO Museum Archive.

32 Q Branch, GHQ to Under Secretary of State for War, 13 March 1944: TNA WO 199/737.
33 Lowry and Wilks 2002, p. 83.
34 Simak and Pye 2014, p. 194.
35 Entry for 7 April 1942, Diary of Beatrice Temple: BRO Museum Archive.
36 Formerly held by the Army Medal Office, Droitwich; Worcestershire Regiment Museum Archive.
37 Captain J. Stewart, Auxiliary Units to CO 2nd Bn Banffshire Home Guard, 3 Nov 1943: TNA WO 199 2892.
38 Warwicker 2008, p. 109.
39 Anon, *Home Guard List 1941 South Eastern Command*, p. 95, Savanah Publications 2010.
40 Director General Home Guard to TAAs, 18 October 1941: TNA WO 199/3251.
41 Director General Home Guard to TAAs, 30 March 1942: TNA WO 199/3251.
42 GHQ to Brigadier Lund, 11 July 1940: TNA WO 260/9.
43 Parham Airfield Museum Newsletter, Spring 2022, p. 12.
44 Warwicker 2002, pp. 108 and 111.
45 Lowry and Wilks 2002, p. 75.
46 Report of Colonel Gubbins, 26 July 1940: TNA WO 199/738.
47 Interview by Mick Wilks, 26 May 2000.
48 'An Appreciation of the Capabilities and Composition of a small force operating behind the enemy lines in the offensive', 7 June 1940: TNA HS 8/259 and Atkin 2021 online Appendix 2.
49 Ibid.
50 Wilkinson and Astley 1993, p. 69.
51 Astley 2007, p. 31.
52 Report in Croft Papers, courtesy of Julia Korner (daughter) and with thanks to Will Ward.
53 Gubbins to LDV Commanders, 5 July 1940: TNA CAB 120/241.
54 Letter from Gubbins to Colonel Hall, GSO1 HQ Southern Command, 20 September 1940: TNA WO 199/2151.
55 Directive to Intelligence Officers, 17 July 1940: TNA CAB 120/241.
56 'Auxiliary Units, Home Forces: Organisation', Gubbins, 26 July 1940: TNA WO 199/738 and CAB 120/241.
57 Instructions to Intelligence Officers, 27 July 1940: TNA CAB 120/241.
58 Letter of 9 April 1941 from War Office to TAAs: TNA WO 199/3251.
59 'Auxiliary Units, Home Forces: Organisation', Gubbins, 26 July 1940: TNA WO 199/738 and CAB 120/241.
60 Wilkinson and Astley 1993, p. 72.
61 DMI to Ismay, 24 June 1940: TNA CAB 21/1473; Atkin 2017, pp. 188–91.
62 D Section Early History to September 1940, pp. 17–18: TNA HS 7/3.
63 Oxenden 2012, p. 1.
64 Gubbins 1939b, *Art of Guerrilla Warfare*, paragraphs 47 and 62; Gubbins 1939a, *Partisan Leader's Handbook*, paragraph 11.
65 'Progress report of Auxiliary Units', Duncan Sandys for General Ismay to Churchill, 8 August 1940: TNA CAB 120/241. Such over-optimistic reports on the progress of supply are typical of the period.
66 Wilkinson and Astley, p. 69.
67 Precis of the lecture on 'Intercommunication, Messages and Orders', 25 October 1941: BRO Museum Archive.

68 Interview of Peter Wilkinson by Mark Seaman, 1993: IWM Audio Interview, Cat. No.13289 reel 5.
69 War Office to Berkshire TAA, 22 December 1943: TNA WO 199/3265.
70 *Gubbins Private Papers*, quoted in Wilkinson and Astley 1993, p. 74.
71 Lowry and Wilks 2002, p. 79.
72 Pryce-Jones 1975, p. 184.
73 Wilkinson 2002, p. 104.
74 Duncan Sandys to Churchill, 8 August 1940: TNA CAB 120/121.
75 Letter from General Paget to Captain Sandys, 30 July 1940: TNA CAB 120/241.
76 Stuart Edmundson, quoted in Warwicker 2004, p. 93.
77 Progress of Auxiliary Units to 1 September 1940, p. 4: TNA CAB 120/241.
78 'Stand to' exercise July 1942, Group 3 Kent, Gardner Papers via N. Bonney: www.Staybehinds.com; Oxenden 2012, p. 26. It should be noted that other Home Guard units also blackened their gaiters and so the discovery if such is not an indicator of original Auxiliary Units use.
79 Lowry and Wilks 2002, p. 84.
80 John Warwicker to Editor, *Daily Express*, 24 June 1940: BRO Archive. Eric Gray, *Daily Mail*, November 2001.
81 Progress report for period ending 1 September 1940', 4 September 1940: TNA CAB 120/241.
82 S. Sutton, 'Farmers or Fighters. Dissertation on the existence and function of Britain's "secret army". Auxiliary Units in southern England during 1940-44'. Unpublished BA dissertation 1995, Canterbury Christchurch College, p. 3.
83 Pryce-Jones 1975, p. 184.
84 Fleming 1957, p. 271.
85 Wilkinson 2002, p. 104.
86 Forbes to Warwicker, 17 January 2001: BRO Archive.
87 TNA WO 199/738.
88 Oxenden 2012, p. 6.
89 TNA WO 199/1517; TNA WO 166/8110.
90 Sinai 2021. The hides were of two types. Prefabricated, lightweight, 'T'-shaped MEXE modular shelters known as 'Ears' comprised a buried frame made up of steel pickets, spacers and arch sections, covered with a jute fabric reinforced with a wire mesh that supported an earth roof. More substantial hides incorporated 'I' beams that supported a roof made from aluminium landing mats, able to bear the weight of a tank passing overhead.
91 Lowry and Wilks 2002, p. 55.
92 Calvert 1996, pp. 48–9.
93 Ward 2013, p. xxii. See Atkin 2019, Chapter 4 for an analysis of the development of the Auxiliary Units mythology.
94 Warwicker 2008, p. 129.
95 Extract from W.P. (40) 168 in Chiefs of Staff report to War Cabinet, *Urgent measures to meet attack*, 19 June 1940: TNA CAB 66/8/43.
96 Liddell Diary for 9 June 1940: TNA KV 4/186, f.494.
97 Liddell Diary for 20 June 1940: TNA KV 4/186, f.505.
98 Liddell Diary for 24 June 1940: TNA KV 4/186, f.510.
99 Warwicker 2002, pp. 97 and 100.
100 Mick Wilks, Home Guard interview archive.
101 Lowry and Wilks 2002, p. 65.

102 *Scheme D*, 20 March 1939: TNA HS8/256.
103 Warwicker 2002, p. 104; Colville (1985), p. 192.
104 Mick Wilks Home Guard interview file with Tony Barling.
105 Williamson 2004, p. 8
106 Chatterton 2022, pp. 30 and 72.
107 https://www.facebook.com/GeoffPidgeon664
108 Betty Colebrook in *Worcester Evening News*, 6 March 1995.
109 http://www.sixtownships.org.uk/the-secret-army-page-1.html, quoted in Atkin 2019, p. 68.
110 Farebrother 1986, p. 19.
111 Staybehinds Rolvenden report.
112 Home Forces 12 April 1943: Gardner Papers, CART Archive.
113 Letter to Group Commanders, 9 January 1944: Gardner Papers, CART Archive. *Cornish Guardian*, 28 October 1943.
114 War Cabinet, 30 May 1940: 'The Prime Minister thought that we should not hesitate to contaminate our beaches with gas if this course would be to our advantage. We had the right to do what we liked with our own territory': TNA CAB 65/7/43.
115 Précis of lecture on 'Intercommunication, Messages, Orders', 25 October 1941, BRO Museum Archive.
116 Lampe 1968, p. 75.
117 Quoted in Wilkinson and Astley 1993, p. 69.
118 Wilkinson and Astley 1993, p. 74.
119 'Progress report for period ending 1 September 1940', 4 September 1940: TNA CAB 120/241.
120 See Wilkinson and Astley 1993, pp. 69 and 74; Atkin 2019, p. 67.
121 *Target for Tonight* lecture notes 1941: BRO Museum Archive.
122 Lampe 1968, p. 75.
123 Oxenden 2012 reprint (typescript 1944), p. 10; Training notes for 15-17 August 1941 course: BRO Museum Archive.
124 War Office letter 43/Engineers/1219, 22 June 1939; Auxiliary Units, *Calendar 1937*, 1940, p. 12.
125 Auxiliary Units, *Calendar 1938*, 1942, pp. 14 and 47. Cecil Tracy SOE personnel file: HS9/1480/5. Tracy had joined the Auxiliary Units in June 1942 and left for SOE in October 1942.
126 *Calendar 1937* – Amendments, 4 April 1941; *Calendar 1938* – Amendments, 31 January 1944: BRO Museum Archive.
127 Lowry and Wilks 2002, p. 85.
128 Lindsay 1987, p. 142.
129 Oxenden 2012, pp. 3 and 10.
130 Minutes of War Cabinet, 10 June 1940: TNA CAB 69/1.
131 'Progress Report for the period ending 1 September 1940', 4 September 1940: TNA CAB 120/241.
132 Minute of 19 June 1940: TNA WO 185/1.
133 Report by D of A on trial of Sticky Bomb on Hangmoor Range, 22 June 1940: TNA CAB 120/372.
134 Jefferis to Jacob, 15 December 1940: TNA CAB 120/372; Macready to Jacob, 5 February 1941: TNA CAB 120/372; Macrae 1972, p. 126.
135 Atkin 2017, pp. 173.
136 Oxenden 2012, p. 4.

137 www.staybehinds.com/thomas-edward-white. The knives were presumably the large pre-1939 issue knives with 3.5in spearpoint blades rather than the considerably smaller post 1939 knives with sheepsfoot blade having no sharpened end for stabbing.
138 Flook 2013, p. 39.
139 The thin knife made by Joseph Rodgers and William Rodgers continued in production into post-war years. Although very common at the time, the Auxiliary Units connection means that such knives now attract a premium price in the collector's market.
140 *Army and Navy Stores Catalogue 1939-40*, p. 509; Flook 2013, p. 39.
141 *Art of Guerrilla Warfare*, para.34: see Atkin 2021 online Appendix 2.
142 *Contra* Chatterton 2022, p. 61.
143 'Progress report of Auxiliary Units', Duncan Sandys to Churchill, 8 August 1940: TNA CAB 120/241; Lowry and Wilks 2002, p. 76.
144 Oxenden 2012 reprint, p. 4.
145 'Scout Patrols', 28 March 1941: BRO Archive.
146 'Progress report of Auxiliary Units', Duncan Sandys to Churchill, 8 August 1940: TNA CAB 120/241.
147 *Extracts from Army Training Memorandum No.47*, March 1944, p. 12.
148 War Establishment March 1942: TNA WO 199/738.
149 Lowry and Wilks 2002, p. 78.
150 Oxenden 2012, p. 3.
151 'Progress Report for the period ending 1 September 1940', 4 September 1940: TNA CAB 120/241. Oxenden 2012, p. 4; Letter from War Office to Eric Seal, Principal Private Secretary to Winston Churchill, 1 November 1940: TNA PREM 3/223/5.
152 Scale of Reserves for Operational Sections and Scout Patrols, 28 January 1943: TNA WO 199/936.
153 Lampe 1968, p. 75; Lowry and Wilks 2002, p. 94.
154 TNA WO 215/2; Warner 1982, p. 137. Davis 2014, p. 8; War Office UPT to Regional Commands, 20 April 1940:TNA WO 106/1889; Riley 2006, p. 47; Atkin 2021, p. 111.
155 War Office UPT to Regional Commands, 20 April 1940:TNA WO 106/1889; Riley 2006, p. 47; Atkin 2021, p. 111.
156 Memo of General Alan Brooke, C-in-C Home Forces, 19 December 1940: TNA WO 199/3249. 'Scout Patrols', 28 March 1941 and August 1941 training timetable: BROM Archive; *Target for Tonight* lecture notes 1941: BRO Museum Archive.
157 https://www.staybehinds.com/patrol/pelynt-patrol
158 Conclusions of War Cabinet, 17 June 1940: TNA CAB 65/7/65 f.321; 'Home Guard – Auxiliary Units', 8 August 1940: TNA CAB 120/241.
159 Chatterton 2022, p. 60.
160 Mark Seaman interview with Wilkinson in 1993: IWM Interview Cat. No.13289, reel 5.
161 Letter from Brigadier Richie, HQ Southern Command to Major General Gammell, 3rd Division, 1 August 1940: TNA WO 199/2151.
162 Record of a meeting between Colonel Hall, HQ Southern Command, and Major Beyts, Auxiliary Units, 9 August 1940: TNA WO 199/2151.
163 Thanks to Richard Thorpe for passing on this information.
164 Auxiliary Units, Progress report for period ending 1 September 1940: TNA CAB 120/241.
165 Lindsay 1987, pp. 141–2; Fleming 1957, p. 271.
166 Hamilton-Hill 1975, p. 17.
167 Oxenden 2012, p. 7.
168 War Establishment report of 26 July 1940, quoted in Warwicker 2004, pp. 67–8.

169 Oxenden 2012, p. 7.
170 Angell 1996, p. 15.
171 'Progress report on Auxiliary Units to 1 September 1940', p. 2: TNA CAB 120/241.
172 The German plan had actually set an original date of invasion for 15 September, pushed back to 21 September but by 11 September even Hitler was having doubts. He effectively abandoned the idea of invasion on 17 September although the plan was not finally cancelled on 12 October. Although the next suggested date for invasion was May 1941 at the earliest, by then Hitler was focused on his plans to invade Russia.
173 Mark Seaman interview with Wilkinson in 1993: IWM Interview Cat. No.13289, reel 6.
174 Oxenden 2012, p. 7.
175 Wilkinson and Astley 1993, p. 74.
176 Progress report on Auxiliary Units for period ending 1 September 1940 by Peter Wilkinson: TNA CAB 120/241.
177 S. Sutton, 'Farmers or Fighters. Dissertation on the existence and function of Britain's "secret army". Auxiliary Units in southern England during 1940-44'. Unpublished BA dissertation 1995, Canterbury Christchurch College, p. 2.
178 Hart-Davis 1987, p. 237.
179 Mark Seaman interview with Wilkinson in 1993: IWM Interview Cat. No.13289, reel 5.
180 S. Sutton, 'Farmers or Fighters. Dissertation on the existence and function of Britain's "secret army". Auxiliary Units in southern England during 1940-44'. Unpublished BA dissertation 1995, Canterbury Christchurch College.
181 Oxenden 2012, p. 2.
182 The British branch of the Van Moppes family was involved with SIS in acquiring industrial diamonds from South America and from Europe via their office in Switzerland. The family were not, however, involved in Chidson's famous removal of diamonds from Amsterdam that was immortalised in the largely fictional 1959 film *Operation Amsterdam*.
183 Quoted in S. Sutton, 'Farmers or Fighters. Dissertation on the existence and function of Britain's "secret army". Auxiliary Units in southern England during 1940-44'. Unpublished BA dissertation 1995, Canterbury Christchurch College.
184 Joint Intelligence Sub-committee, *German Invasion of the British Isles*, 31 January 1941: TNA CAB 121/209.
185 Danchev and Todman 2001, p. 166.
186 Letter of 4 April 1942, referring to agreement of 13 August 1941: TNA WO 199/738.
187 TNA WO 260/9; TNA WO 199/1194.

Chapter 7: Auxiliary Units (Operations), 1942–4: A New Purpose

1 'Revision of War Establishment – Part I', Beyts to GHQ, 4 April 1942: TNA WO 199/738.
2 See Rigden 2001, p. 326.
3 Oxenden 2012, pp. 9 and 13.
4 Letter from Forbes to Warwicker, January 2002: BRO Museum Archive.
5 Quayle 1990, p. 230.
6 Oxenden 2012, p. 13.
7 Colonel Douglas, 'Economy in Manpower', June 1944: TNA WO 199/738.
8 Warwicker 2002, pp. 107–08.
9 TNA WO 199/738.

10   Only Thompsons are referred to in the War Establishment of 20 March 1942 or in the document 'Function of IOs HQs' of 19 May 1942: TNA WO 199/738.
11   Glanusk to Grazebrook, Home Forces, 4 September 1942: TNA WO 199/738; Scale of Reserves for Operational Sections and Scout Patrols, 28 January 1943: TNA WO 199/936.
12   Oxenden 2012, pp. 14–15.
13   Elliot 2007, p. 33.
14   Oxenden 2012, p. 17.
15   Worcestershire Home Guard Part I and II Orders, formerly held by the Army Medal Office, Droitwich, until its closure in 2005; Worcestershire Regiment Museum Archive.
16   Douglas to regional TAAs, 21 September 1942: TNA WO 199/3265.
17   TNA WO 199/3251.
18   Director General, Home Guard to TAAs, 25 April 1942: TNA WO 199/3251.
19   Douglas to Regional TAAs, 2 and 8 October 1942: TNA WO 199/3265.
20   TNA WO 199/3251.
21   TNA WO 199/3389.
22   TNA WO 200/738.
23   Fleming 1957, p. 271.
24   Grigson-Ellis to Glanusk, 10 September 1942: TNA WO 199/738.
25   Ibid.
26   Colonel Douglas, 'Economy in Manpower' June 1944: TNA WO 199/738.
27   Memo of 14 January 1943: TNA WO 199/738.
28   Chatterton 2022, p. 27.
29   Data from Auxiliary Units Nominal Roll: TNA WO 199 3391.
30   Somerset County Archives, DD/SLI/12/2/26 quoted in Chatterton 2022, p. 28.
31   BGS to DAG, 4 February 1943: TNA WO 199/738.
32   Memo of Director of Staff Duties, 16 August 1943: TNA WO 199/738.
33   Letter from General Franklyn to Under-Secretary of State, War Office, 6 September 1943: TNA WO 199/738.
34   Letter from Colonel Douglas to General Franklyn, 15 July 1944: TNA WO 199/738.
35   TNA KV 4/194, f.16.
36   Captain Waugh to Group Commanders (Essex and Suffolk), 15 May 1944: BRO Archive.
37   Extract from circular memo to Home Guard Battalion Commanders, 10 June 1944: TNA WO 199/ 2892.
38   Memo of the War Office to Colonel Douglas, 17 May 1944: TNA WO 199/738.
39   Mersea Museum, Photo PBA 137 AAA. See https://www.merseamuseum.org.uk
40   The issue of .22 rifles to the Auxiliary Units is discussed in detail in Atkin (forthcoming), *passim*.
41   Oxenden 2012, pp. 11–12.
42   Information courtesy of Will Ward, CART, with thanks.
43   Lampe 1968, p. 78; Angell 1996, p. 13; *Textbook of Small Arms* (1929), p.265. The myth of the one-mile range derived from the warning on the packs of cartridges that they were 'dangerous to one mile' – this being their maximum unaimed duration in flight.
44   Information courtesy of Will Ward, CART.
45   Ministry of Supply Ledger, 1942: TNA SUPP4/101.
46   Oxenden 2012, pp. 10 and 12.
47   Recalled by Bill Webber from Firle Patrol, Sussex: Angell 1996, p. 35.

48 TNA WO 199/936 Recollection of Captain Thomas George, a Group Commander in South Wales: see Information on Letterston patrol in www.staybehinds.com.
49 Oxenden 2012, p. 10.
50 TNA WO 199/936.
51 Angell 1996, p. 13.
52 TNA WO 199/936.
53 I am grateful to Jeff Abendshien for discussion on this point.
54 Melton 1991, p. 42.
55 Angell 1996, p. 68.
56 I am grateful to Alan David from this observation from practical experience.
57 Bath Blitz Project website, 2005; quotation courtesy of Will Ward, CART. The present author sold Bob the No.42 scope that he used in his presentations on the Auxiliary Units!
58 Laidler 1993, p. 63.
59 Ibid.; Laidler and Skennerton 1993, pp. 39–41.
60 Information from Jeffery Abendshien, with thanks.
61 Flook 2022, pp. 7–9; Gardner Papers, CART archive. It should be noted that this knife is very different from the fantasy knives made from a curved blade riveted to a 1940s coin, as now widely offered for sale.
62 Oxenden 2012, p. 2
63 Ibid., pp. 17–18.
64 TNA WO 199/936.
65 Ibid.
66 Q Branch to GSD, War Office, 16 September 1943: TNA WO 199/936.
67 TNA WO 199/936.
68 Director of Infantry to Q Branch War Office, 10 January 1944: TNA WO 199/936.
69 Q Branch to Under Secretary of State, 31 January 1944: TNA WO 199/936.
70 Q Branch to HQ Regional Commands, 4 February 1944: TNA WO 199/736.
71 TNA WO 199/936.
72 War Office to Major General Callander, GHQ Home Forces, 25 April 1944: TNA WO 199/738.
73 Memo of Major General Steele, Director of Staff Duties, to Colonel Douglas, 27 May 1944: TNA WO 199/738.
74 'Economy in Manpower', Douglas, n.d.: TNA WO 199/738.
75 TNA WO 199/3251.
76 *Contra* Searle 1989, p. 112; account of Herbert Bowman of Thorpe St Andrew Patrol on CART website.
77 The PLUTO pipeline was never expected to supply the initial landings, which would rely on the shipment of four-gallon jerrycans, but the scheme was plagued by delays and it was not until 22 September that fuel began to flow from Sandown, by which time several Channel ports were in Allied hands. Despite the engineering achievement, it proved to be a costly operational failure.
78 Simak and Pye 2013, p. 59
79 The movement orders are contained within TNA WO 199/294.
80 G(Ops), GHQ Home Forces to MGGS, 21 July 1944: TNA WO 199/294.
81 *Newcastle Evening Chronicle*, 25 April 1968.
82 *Morpeth Extra*, February 2011.
83 Reproduced in Hall 2015, pl.5, p. 16.
84 TNA WO 199/738.
85 Auxiliary Units War Diary: TNA WO 166/16349.

86 TNA WO 199/738.
87 TNA W0 199/937.
88 Halsted to HQ Western Command, 26 June 1944: TNA WO 199/738.

Chapter 8: Auxiliary Units (Special Duties Branch), 1940: Anti-Invasion Reporting

1   TNA WO 199/1194 for June 1944.
2   TNA WO 32/21.
3   Hinsley et al. 1979, pp. 167–75.
4   Report to War Cabinet, 10 and 19 June 1940: CAB 69/1.
5   Oxenden 2012 (typescript 1944), p. 2.
6   Sandys/Ismay progress report to Churchill, 8 August 1940: TNA CAB 120/241.
7   TNA CAB 120/241.
8   Letter from Major Petherick to Laurence Grand, 15 July 1940, quoted in Warwicker 2008, p. 190.
9   Lampe 1968, p. 127; Douglas, 5 June 1944, records over 3,250 in the SDB and General Wemyss in 1945 refers to 3,500.
10 CAB 21/1476.
11 Wilkinson 2002, p. 100.
12 Report VIII on the activities of D Section during July 1940, p. 4: TNA HS 8/214.
13 Section D: Early History to September 1940, pp. 17–18: TNA HS 7/3.
14 Draft Memo: Application for the award of the Defence Medal to Auxiliary Units, 20 December 1948: TNA WO 32/21918.
15 Letter from War Office to Sir Robert Knox, 23 October 1947: WO 32/21918. At the time there was argument over the entitlement of the SDB to the Defence Medal but the discussion greatly confused the SDB and Operational Branch.
16 Application for the award of Defence Medal to the Auxiliary Units, 1948: WO 32/21918.
17 Angell 1996, p. 77.
18 At Matlock, Derbyshire, the site of a secret wireless station hidden in a house on Smedley Street has been signposted by the local Civic Association as a 'Ground Zero Station' of the Auxiliary Units. The wireless station operated from June 1940 and is more likely to have been part of an SIS operation.
19 Ironside Diary for 29 June 1940, p. 374.
20 Ironside Diary for 13 July 1940, p. 385.
21 TNA WO 260/9.
22 Letter from George Phillips to Winston Churchill, 31 May 1945: TNA WO 32 21918.
23 Ken Maryan-Green Papers, BRO Archive; https://www.staybehinds.com/station/hockley-outstation
24 Section D, Draft Notes and Lessons: TNA HS 8/5.
25 TNA WO 260/9; thanks to Will Ward for information on the early Intelligence Officers.
26 TNA WO 215/1.
27 Quoted in Simak and Pye 2014, p. 131.
28 TNA KV 4/188.
29 Atkin 2021, p. 82.
30 Wilfrid Lewis (1908–87) was a Cambridge academic who in 1933 was also CO of the University OTC Signals. From 1939–46 he was Senior Military Scientist at the Telecommunications Research Establishment (TRE), Malvern. He later became head

of Canada's nuclear power programme. C.J. 'Kit' Milner (1912–98) worked with Lewis whilst a PhD student of Lord Rutherford. He gained his PhD in 1936 and worked on radar-jamming devices in the UK and then the Manhattan Project in the USA during the Second World War. After the war he became Chair of Applied Physics and later Dean of Science at the University of New South Wales. The work was published as Lewis and Milner 1936.

31. Video interview with Ken Ward by John Warwicker *et al.* in 1999: IWM recording Cat. 29472, reel 1.
32. Section D, Draft Notes and Lessons, 1945, paragraph 6: TNA HS 7/5; Closing Report, August 1940, paragraph 5: TNA HS 8/214.
33. Turner 2011, p. 136; Boyce and Everett 2003, p. 206.
34. Warwicker 2008, p. 213.
35. Warwicker 2004, p. 182.
36. Video interview with Ken Ward by John Warwicker *et al.* in 1999: IWM recording 29472, reel 1.
37. Ibid.
38. TNA WO 199/1199.
39. Letter from Jack Millie to Arthur Gabbitas, 9 January 1996.
40. As described by Bill Bartholomew to Arthur Gabbitas in 1997 and to Richard Hankins, Project Witney progress report, 2003.
41. Map by Major Rupert Jones: TNA WO 199/1194.
42. Adventures of Roy Russell during World War II: BRO Museum Archive.
43. Letter from Ken Ward to John Warwicker, 24 April 1999.
44. Video interview with Ken Ward by John Warwicker *et al.* in 1999: IWM recording 29472, reel 1.
45. Letter from Bill Bartholomew to Arthur Gabbitas, 28 June 1997.
46. Adventures of Roy Russell during World War II: BRO Museum Archive.
47. Lampe 1968, pp. 125–6.
48. Monthly Notes for IOs, August 1943: BRO Museum Archive.
49. Liddell Diary for 24 April 1940 in West 2009, p. 78.
50. Liddell Diary for 2 June 1941: TNA KV 4/199 f.926.
51. Liddell Diary for 11 June 1942: TNA KV 4/190 f.642.
52. Liddell Diary for 18 June 1942: TNA KV 4/190, f.648.
53. Liddell Diary for 29 September 1942: TNA KV 4/290, f.811.
54. Notes by Ken Ward: BRO Museum Archive.
55. RSGB *Bulletin*, June 1944, p. 188.
56. TNA WO 199/1194.
57. Monthly Notes to IOs, No.5, July 1943: BRO Museum Archive.
58. Report of Major Jones, 28 June 1944: TNA WO 199/1194.
59. Stanley Judson interview with John Warwicker, IWM 29468, Reel 2.
60. Monthly Notes for IOs, No.6, August 1943: BRO Museum Archive.
61. Lampe 1968, p. 122; Gubbins was released from the Auxiliary Units on 18 November: Mackenzie 2000, p. 810.
62. Beyts 1983, p. 21.
63. TNA WO 199/1194.
64. Wood 1976, pp. 67–71.
65. TNA WO 199/738.
66. BBC interview in 1998, quoted in Simak and Pye 2014, pp. 7–8.
67. TNA WO 199/738.
68. Colonel Douglas, *Economy in Manpower*, June 1944: TNA WO 199/738.

69   TNA WO 199/738.
70   Memo of Lord Glanusk to War Office, 1 February 1943: TNA WO 199/738.
71   Memoir of Stan Judson in BRO museum.
72   Angell 1996, p. 74.
73   Video interview with Ken Ward by John Warwicker *et al.* in 1999: IWM recording 29472, reel 2.
74   Closing Report by Major Jones, 28 June 1944: TNA WO 199/1194.
75   Video interview with Ken Ward by John Warwicker *et al.* in 1999: IWM recording 29472, reel 2. It is, however, odd that no IN Station operators have mentioned using a WS17.
76   TNA WO 199/1194.
77   Lampe 1968, p. 135.
78   Hinsley *et al.* 1979, p. 180.
79   Oxenden 2012, p. 10.
80   Letter from C-in-C Home Forces, General H.E. Franklyn to Colonel Douglas on Stand Down, 4 July 1944: TNA WO 199/738

Chapter 9: Auxiliary Units (Special Duties Branch), 1940: Internal Security and D-Day Planning

1   Letter from C-in-C Home Forces, General H.E. Franklyn to Colonel Douglas on Stand Down, 4 July 1944: TNA WO 199/738.
2   Referred to in a letter from Beyts to GHQ, 4 April 1942: TNA WO 199/738, and War Establishment of 4 April 1942: TNA WO 199/738; Memo of Gregson-Ellis, 30 March 1942: TNA WO 199/738.
3   Report of Major Jones, 28 June 1944: TNA WO 199/1194.
4   *London Gazette*, April 1923.
5   Diary of Beatrice Temple, 30 January 1944: BRO Museum Archive.
6   May 2014, p. 23.
7   Edwina Burton interview by Mick Wilks, April 2000.
8   *Monthly Notes for Ios*, No.6, August 1943: BRO Museum archive.
9   Ken Maryam Green Papers, BRO Archive.
10   Video interview with Ken Ward by John Warwicker *et al.* in 1999: IWM recording 29472, reel 2.
11   Ibid.
12   Memo of War Office to Beyts, 3 June 1942: TNA WO 199/738.
13   *Monthly Notes for Ios*, No.6, August 1943: BRO Museum archive.
14   *Monthly Notes for Ios*, August 1943: BRO Museum archive; Report by Major Jones, 28 June 1944: TNA WO 199/1194.
15   Unpublished Beatrice Temple Diary: BRO Museum archive.
16   TNA WO 199/738.
17   TNA WO 199/936.
18   Minute of November 1948: TNA WO 199/21918.
19   General Wemyss to Sir Robert Knox, 15 August 1945: TNA WO199/21918.
20   Simak and Pye 2014, p. 9.
21   Gregson-Ellis to Glanusk, 10 September 1942: TNA WO 199/738.
22   Oxenden 2012, p. 18.
23   Stan Judson memoir: BRO archive.
24   Letter from C-in-C Home Forces, General H.E. Franklyn to SDS on Stand Down, 4 July 1944: TNA WO 199/738.

25 Forbes to Warwicker, 31 January 2002: BRO Archive; Parham Airfield Museum Newsletter, Spring 2022, p. 13.
26 *Guerrilla Warfare: Military Training Pamphlet No.54*, 1942, pp. 5–6, 8.
27 Ward 1997, pp. 21–2.
28 Memo from Auxiliary Units HQ, 26 October 1943: BRO Museum Archive.
29 TNA 199/1313.
30 Adventures of Roy Russell in World War II: BRO Museum Archive.
31 Liddell Diary for 11 May 1944: TNA KV 4/194, f. 394; Colonel T.A. Robertson (TAR) was a key officer in the deception plans for D-Day, being head of MI5's Section B1(a) and in charge of running the Double Cross agents.
32 Adventures of Roy Russell in World War II: BRO Museum Archive.
33 Colonel Douglas, 'Economy in Manpower', June 1944: TNA WO 199/738.
34 F.A.M. Browning (War Office) to Sir Robert Knox (Treasury), 23 October 1947: TNA WO 32 21918. At the time there was considerable confusion in the War Office in distinguishing between the Operational and Special Duties Branches in considering the claims of the Operational Branch for the Defence Medal.
35 Letter from Robert Knox (Treasury) to General Wemyss (War Office), 29 December 1945: TNA WO 32 21918.
36 Minute of November 1948: TNA WO 199/21918.

Chapter 10: GHQ Liaison Regiment (Phantom)

1 Warner 1982, p. 17.
2 Report to War Cabinet, 19 June 1940: TNA 69/1.
3 Powell 2016, p. 57.
4 Report on the work of the Mission . . . 10 May–1 June 1940, Lt Col. Hopkinson, 7 June 1940: TNA 215/1.
5 Letter from Hopkinson to DDMO, 7 June 1940; J. Jackson, *Short History of Phantom from June 1940 to March 1941*: TNA WO 215/10.
6 Report on the work of the Mission . . . 10 May–1 June 1940, Lt Col. Hopkinson, 7 June 1940: TNA 215/1.
7 Ibid.
8 Warner 1982, p. 152.
9 GHQ to Commands, 19 July 1940: TNA WO 215/5.
10 War Establishment, 26 June 1940: TNA WO 215/5.
11 Reconnaissance reports, September 1940: TNA WO 215/11.
12 TNA WO 215/9.
13 Niven 1972, p. 285.
14 'The collection and transmission of information in battle', 24 October 1940: TNA 215/10.

Chapter 11: Home Guard Saboteurs, Guerrillas and 'Shock Troops'

1 Wintringham 1941.
2 Atkin 2019, Chapter 1. The decision to rename the LDV was made on 22 July and publicly announced on the following day.
3 War Office Instructions for LDV, Wednesday 15 May 1940: TNA WO 199/1885. Radio Bremen, 16 May 1940; Burke 1940, p. 2.
4 *Official History of the VTC*, 1920; *VTC Regulations* 1916.
5 'The Volunteer Force During the Great War', March 1940: TNA WO 32/10615.

6   'Birth Pangs of the Home Guard', pp. 1–2 in IWM Carden Roe Papers DD 77/165/1.
7   Carden Roe to Walter Kirke, 21 December 1942: IWM Carden Roe Papers DD/77/165/1.
8   Local Defence Volunteers: Notes of a meeting between the Commander-in-Chief, Home Forces, and leaders of the Local Defence Volunteers held on Wednesday 5 June 1940.
9   J. Piling, *Report on Osterley Park LDV Training School*, 5–6 August 1940, p. 3 and p. 15: Wintringham Papers, King's College London Archive.
10 Home Guard General Instruction No.10, 1 August 1940, p. 1.
11 GHQ Operational Instruction No.3, 15 June 1940: TNA ADM 223/484.
12 Home Guard Instruction No.51 part IV, *Organised Home Guard Defence*, 1943, p. ii.
13 Home Guard General Instruction No.10, 1 August 1940, p. 2.
14 GOC Western Command to GHQ, 7 May 1941: TNA WO 199/360.
15 Report to War Cabinet, 19 June 1940: TNA 69/1.
16 Chiefs of Staff report to War Cabinet, British strategy in a certain eventuality, 25 May 1940: TNA CAB 66.
17 MIR War Diary: TNA HS 8/263.
18 Anon 1945b, pp. 17 and 59.
19 H.F. 301/Ops (VP), 13 June 1941 referenced in TNA WO 199/2489; HF 3010/Ops, 30 June 1941: TNA WO 199/361; Home Guard Instruction No.36. Mobile Patrols for Action Against Airborne Troops, August 1941 (referred to in 'The Role of the Home Guard', 30 April 1942): TNA WO 199/363.
20 Home Guard Instruction No.51 Part II, Battle Drill, pp. 3-4 and Part IV, The Organisation of Home Guard Defence, pp. 10 and 12.
21 Wintringham 1940a, pp. 176–83; Wintringham 1940b, p. 279.
22 Ruddy 2015, pp. 49–52.
23 Ruddy 2007, pp. 143–8.
24 J. Piling, *Report on Osterley Park LDV Training School*, 5–6 August 1940, pp. 1 and 4: Wintringham Papers, King's College London Archive.
25 William Joyce broadcast 2 August 1940.
26 Liddell Diary for 5 September 1939: TNA KV 4/185, f.21.
27 Wintringham 1941b.
28 Ibid., p. 15.
29 Section D: Early History to September 1940: TNA HS 7/3; Atkin 2017, p. 89.
30 J. Piling, *Report on Osterley Park LDV Training School*, 5–6 August, 1940: Wintringham Papers, King's College London Archive.
31 Levy 1941, p. 36.
32 Wintringham 1941, pp. 27–8.
33 Pers. comm. Richard Thorpe, with thanks.
34 Purcell with Smith 2012, p. 195. Mackenzie is not identified as a member of any of the Sussex patrols in Angell 1996, although the information is not complete.
35 Purcell with Smith 2012, pp. 181–2.
36 Minutes of Home Guard Inspectorate, 2 July 1940: TNA WO 199/62.
37 Letters of Inspectorate of LDV to MI5, July 1940: TNA WO 165/92.
38 Liddell Diary for 18 July 1940: TNA KV 4/186, f.532.
39 Circular letter of Communist Party of Great Britain, 7 January 1941, and intercepted by MI5: TNA KV 2/2325.
40 Tom Wintringham, 'The truth about guerrilla war', *The Tribune*, 19 September 1941, pp. 8–9.
41 Stafford 2000, p. 311.

42 Tom Wintringham, 'The truth about guerrilla war', *The Tribune*, 19 September 1941, pp. 8–9.
43 *Sunday Pictorial*, 16 February (1941); published in Langdon-Davies 1941, pp. 179–84.
44 Langdon-Davies 1941, pp. 179–82.
45 Tom Wintringham, 'Train the Home Guard for war', *Picture Post*, 17 May 1941, pp. 24–8.
46 TNA WO 199/363.
47 TNA WO 199/1869: GOC instructions to Corps Commanders – Operational Role of the Home Guard June 1942.
48 Southern Command order quoted in Hylton 2004, p. 52.
49 District Instruction on Operational Employment of Home Guard, GS 15/60 28 December 1942.
50 Letter from 'Bill' to Major General P.G.S. Gregson-Ellis, 1942: TNA WO 199/364. Although filed with papers of autumn 1942, the letter is most likely to have been written in early 1942 by Colonel 'Bill' Major. He had formerly been a staff intelligence officer for Eastern Command.
51 Memo of West Riding Home Guard, undated but filed after December 1942: TNA WO 199/1482.
52 Wilks 2014, pp. 40–1.
53 Ibid., p. 40: correspondence between the Harold Goodwin Company Secretary and the Warley Battalion Home Guard, dated 14 September 1942: on Home Guard files formerly held by the Army Medal Office, Droitwich.
54 Wilks 2014, p. 86; War Office letter of 13 March 1941 to the Central Midland Area HQ, found in Part 1 Orders for the 17th Battalion, Warwickshire Home Guard.
55 *Notes for the use of the Home Guard . . . appointed to deal with the immobilisation of petrol pumps in the event of emergency.* C40456-2 2/41. Private possession.

Conclusions

1 H. Schneider, A. von Ostrymiecz *et al.* (eds), *Beiträge zur Geschichte und Praxis des Englischen Geheimdienstes*, 1940.
2 Royle 2010, p. 323.
3 MI(R) War Diary for 22 July 1940: TNA HS 8/263.
4 The *Official History of Airborne Forces* quotes the figure of nearly 300 recruited from a 'special auxiliary force' that was disbanding at the time.
5 https://www.staybehinds.com/auxiliary_units_and_the_sas. Recovered 1 Dec 2022.
6 Wilkinson 2002, p. 104.
7 Ward 2013, p. xxii.
8 Colonel Douglas, 'Economy in Manpower', June 1944: TNA WO 199/738.
9 Boyle 1959.

Appendix 2:

1 Atkin 2021, p. 3.
2 Colville 1985, p. 156.

Bibliography

Andrew, Christopher (2009), *The Defence of the Realm: The Authorised History of MI5*, Middleton Press, Midhurst.

Arnold, Ralph (1962), *A Very Quiet War*, Rupert Hart-Davis, London.

Astley, Joan Bright (2007), *The Inner Circle: A View of War at the Top*, The Memoir Club, Stanhope (first publ. 1971).

Atkin, Malcolm (2015), *Fighting Nazi Occupation: British Resistance 1939–1945*, Pen & Sword, Barnsley.

Atkin, Malcolm (2017), *Section D for Destruction: forerunner of SOE*, Pen & Sword, Barnsley [revised edition published as Atkin 2023].

Atkin, Malcolm (2021), *Pioneers of Irregular Warfare: secrets of the Military Intelligence Research Department in the Second World War*, Pen & Sword, Barnsley.

Atkin, Malcolm (2023), *Section D for Destruction: forerunner of SOE and Auxiliary Units*, Pen & Sword, Barnsley [updated edition of Atkin 2017].

Atkin, Malcolm (forthcoming), *Cinderella Rifles: the .22 rifles of the Home Guard and Auxiliary Units*, MAMR Books.

Attwater, Peter (1999), *Burton House, 135 Smedley Street, Matlock: Ground Station Zero 1940-44*, Matlock Civic Association.

Bennett, Gill (2009), *Churchill's Man of Mystery: Desmond Morton and the World of Intelligence*, Routledge.

Beyts, Geoffrey (1983), *The King's Salt*, privately published, Malaga.

Boyce, Fredric and Douglas Everett (2003), *SOE: The Scientific Secrets*, Sutton Publishing, Stroud.

Boyle, David (1959), *With Ardours Manifold*, Hutchinson, London.

Brown, Anthony Cave (1988), *The Secret Servant: The Life of Sir Stewart Menzies, Churchill's Spymaster*, Michael Joseph, London.

Burke, John (1940), *Rights and Powers of the Home Guard*, Hamish Hamilton Ltd, London.

Calvert, Mike (1996), *Fighting Mad: One man's guerrilla war*, Airlife, Shrewsbury (2nd edn; first publ. 1964).

Chatterton, Andrew (2022), *Britain's Secret Defences: civilian saboteurs, spies and assassins during the Second World War*, Casement, Oxford.

Collier, Basil (1957), *The Defence of the United Kingdom*, HMSO, London.

Colville, John (1985), *The Fringes of Power: Downing Street Diaries 1939-1955*, Hodder and Stoughton, London.

Danchev, Alex and Daniel Todman (eds) (2001), *War Diaries 1939-1945: Field Marshal Lord Alanbrooke*, Weidenfeld and Nicolson, London.

Davies, Philip H.J. (2004), *MI6 and the Machinery of Spying*, Cass, Abingdon.

Davis, Tom (2014), *Great Britain: the Tommy Gun Story*, Privately published, USA.

Dilks, David (1971), *The Diaries of Sir Alexander Cadogan, OM, 1938-45*, Cassell, London.

Edwards, William B. (1959), 'Guns in our bundles for Britain', *Gun*, December 1959, pp. 32–3 and 41–3.
Elliot, Geoff (2007), *Colyon at War*, Colyon Parish History Society.
Farebrother, George (ed.), *Hailsham at War*, University of Sussex.
Fleming, Peter (1952), 'Bows and arrows', *The Spectator*, 4 April 1952, p. 13.
Fleming, Peter (1957), *Invasion 1940*, Rupert Hart-Davis, London.
Flook, Ron (2022), *Knives and Daggers of the Special Operations Executive*, Ron Flook, Bath.
Foot, M.R.D. (1984), *SOE: An Outline History of the Special Operations Executive 1940-46*, BBC.
Foot, M.R.D. (2004), *SOE in France*, Cass, Abingdon (revised edn; first publ. 1966).
Freethy, Ron (2005), *Lancashire 1939–1945: The Secret War*, Countryside Books, Newbury.
Freethy, Ron (2012), *Cheshire 1939–1945: The Secret War*, Countryside Books, Newbury.
Graves, Charles (1943), *The Home Guard of Britain*, Hutchinson, London.
Gubbins, Colin (1939a), *Partisan Leader's Handbook: Principles of Guerrilla Warfare and Sabotage*, War Office.
Gubbins, Colin (1939b), *The Art of Guerrilla Warfare*, War Office.
Hamilton-Hill, Donald (1975), *SOE Assignment*, New English Library, London (first publ. 1973).
Hart-Davis, Duff (1987), *Peter Fleming: A Biography (Oxford Lives)*, (first publ. 1974).
Hinsley, F.H. et al. (1979), *British Intelligence in the Second World War, Vol. 1*, HMSO, London.
Hinsley, F.H. and C.A.G. Simkins (1990), *British Intelligence in the Second World War, Vol. 4*, HMSO, London.
Hylton, Stuart (2004), *Kent and Sussex 1940: Britain's Front Line*, Pen & Sword Military, Barnsley.
Ismay, Lord (1960), *The Memoirs of General The Lord Ismay*, Heinemann, London.
Jebb, Gladwyn (1972), *The Memoirs of Lord Gladwyn*, Weidenfeld and Nicolson, London.
Jeffery, Keith (2010), *MI6: The History of the Secret Intelligence Service 1909-1949*, Bloomsbury, London.
Lampe, David (1968), *The Last Ditch*, Cassell, London.
Langdon-Davies, John (1941), *Home Guard Warfare*, Routledge, London.
Levy, 'Yank' (1941), *Guerrilla Warfare*, Penguin Books.
Lewer, Stanley (1996), 'On the back of an envelope... how the Wireless Set No. 17 was born', *Radio Bygones*, no. 41, June/July 1996, pp. 4–8.
Lewis, Wilfrid B. and C.J. Milner (1936), 'A portable Duplex Radio-Telephone', *The Wireless Engineer*, September 1936, pp. 475–82.
Lindsay, Donald (1987), *Forgotten General: A Life of Andrew Thorne*, Michael Russell (Publishing), Salisbury.
Lowry, Bernard and Mick Wilks (2002), *Mercian Maquis*, Logaston Press.
Macintyre, Ben (2016), *SAS: Rogue Heroes*, Viking Books.
Mackenzie, William (2000), *The Secret History of SOE*, St Ermin's Press.
Macleod, Roderick and Denis Kelly (eds) (1962), *The Ironside Diaries 1937-40*, Constable, London.

May, Hugh (2014), *Chirnside I*, Dudfield Publications.
McMahon, Paul (2011), *British Spies and Irish Rebels: British Intelligence and Ireland, 1916-1945*, Boydell Press, Woodbridge (first publ. 2008).
Niven, David (1972), *The Moon's A Balloon*, Putnam.
O'Brien, T.H. (1955), *History of the Second World War: Civil Defence*, HMSO, London.
O'Halpin, Eunan (2010), *Spying on Ireland: British Intelligence and Irish Neutrality during the Second World War*, Oxford University Press (first publ. 2008).
Otway, T.B.H. (1990), *Airborne Forces*, Imperial War Museum.
Oxenden, Nigel (2012 reprint), *Auxiliary Units: History and Achievement 1940-1944* (typescript 1944; first publ. 1998), BRO Museum, Parham.
Philby, Kim (2002), *My Silent War*, Modern Library, New York (first publ. 1968).
Pidgeon, Geoffrey (2003), *Secret Wireless War*, UPSO, East Sussex.
Pimlott, Ben (ed.) (1986), *The Second World War Diary of Hugh Dalton 1940-45*, Jonathan Cape, London.
Powell, Matthew (2016), *The Development of British Tactical Air Power, 1940-1943: A History of Army Co-operation Command*, Palgrave Macmillan.
Pryce-Jones, David (1975), 'Britain's Secret Resistance Movement', in Richard Cox (ed.) (1975), *Operation Sealion*, Thornton Cox Ltd, pp. 177–86.
Purcell, Hugh, with Phyll Smith (2012), *The Last English Revolutionary: Tom Wintringham, 1898-1949*, Sussex Academic Press (enlarged, revised and updated; first publ. 2004).
Quayle, Anthony (1990), *A Time To Speak*, Barrie & Jenkins, London.
Read, Anthony and David Fisher (1984), *Colonel Z: The Life and Times of a Master of Spies*, Hodder and Stoughton, London.
Richards, Lee (2005), 'Whispers of War – the British WW2 Rumour Campaign', *Falling Leaf*, no.183, January 2005.
Richards, Lee (2010), *Whispers of War*, Psywar.
Rigden, Denis (2001), *SOE Syllabus: Lessons in Ungentlemanly Warfare, World War II* (Public Record Office).
Riley, Jonathon (2006), *The Life & Campaigns of General Hughie Stockwell*, Pen & Sword, Barnsley.
Royle, Trevor (2010), *Orde Wingate: A Man of Genius, 1903-1944*, Frontline Books, London (first publ. 1995).
Ruddy, Austin (2015), 'Resistance Britain', *Britain at War*, March 2015.
Schellenberg, Walter (2001), *Invasion 1940: The Nazi Invasion Plan for Britain*, St Ermin's Press, in association with Little, Brown and Company (first publ. 2000).
Seaman, Mark (ed.) (2006), *Special Operations Executive: A New Instrument of War*, Routledge, London.
Simak, Evelyn and Adrian Pye (2013), *Churchill's Secret Auxiliary Units in Norfolk and Suffolk*, self-published.
Simak, Evelyn and Adrian Pye (2014), *Churchill's 'Most Secret' Special Duties Branch*, self-published.
Sinai, Tamil (2021), 'Eyes on target: "Stay-behind" forces during the Cold War', *War in History*, Vol. 28, Issue 3, July 2021, pp. 681–700.
Stafford, David (2000), *Churchill and the Secret Service*, Lume Books.

Stafford, David (2010), 'Secret Operations versus Secret Intelligence in World War', in T. Travers and C. Archer (eds) *Men at War: Politics, Technology and Innovation in the Twentieth Century* (reprint; first publ. 1982), pp. 119–36.

Sweet-Escott, Bickham (1965), *Baker Street Irregular*, Methuen, London.

Tittenhofer, Mark A. (1969), 'The Rote Drei: Getting Behind the Lucy Myth', *Studies in Intelligence*, vol. 13, No.3, pp. 51–90.

Turner, Des (2011), *SOE's Secret Weapons Centre: Station 12*, The History Press, Stroud (first publ. 2006).

Van der Bijl, Nick (2013), *Sharing the Secret: A History of the Intelligence Corps 1940-2010*, Pen & Sword Military, Barnsley.

Walker, A.T. (1940), *Fieldwork for the Home Guard*, private publication, Glasgow.

Ward, Arthur (1989), *A Nation Alone: the Battle of Britain – 1940*, Osprey, London.

Ward, Arthur (1997), *Resisting the Nazi Invader*, Constable, London.

Ward, Arthur (2013), *Churchill's Secret Defence Army*, Pen & Sword, Barnsley.

Warner, Philip (1982), *Phantom*, Pen & Sword Military, William Kimber, London.

Warwicker, John (2002), *With Britain in Mortal Danger: Britain's Most Secret Army of WWII*, Cerberus, Bristol.

Warwicker, John (2008), *Churchill's Underground Army: A History of the Auxiliary Units in World War II*, Frontline Books, London.

West, Nigel (1983), *MI6: British Secret Intelligence Service Operations 1909-45*, Weidenfeld and Nicolson, London.

West, Nigel (1992), *Secret War: The Story of SOE, Britain's Wartime Sabotage Organisation*, Hodder and Stoughton, London.

West, Nigel (ed.) (2009), *The Guy Liddell Diaries, Vol.I: 1939-1942*, Routledge (first publ. 2005).

West, Nigel and Oleg Tsarev (eds) (2009), *Triplex: Secrets from the Cambridge Spies*, Yale University Press.

Wilkinson, Peter (2002), *Foreign Fields*, I.B. Tauris Publishers, London (first publ. 1997).

Wilkinson, Peter and Joan Bright Astley (1993), *Gubbins and SOE*, Pen & Sword, London.

Wilks, Mick (2007), *The Defence of Worcestershire and the Southern Approaches to Birmingham in World War II*, Logaston Press.

Wilks, Mick (2014), *Chronicles of the Home Guard*, Logaston Press.

Williamson, Alan (2004), *East Ridings Secret Resistance*, Middleton Press, Midhurst.

Wintringham, Tom (1940a), *Deadlock War*, Faber and Faber, London.

Wintringham, Tom (1940b), *New Ways of War*, Penguin.

Wintringham, Tom (1941), *The Home Guard Can Fight*, HMSO, London.

Wood, Derek (1976), *Attack Warning Red: The Royal Observer Corps and the Defence of Britain 1925 to 1975*, Macdonald and Jane's, London.

Index

Abwehr 3, 36
Adam Patrol, Herefs Auxiliary
   Units 65, 100
ADRDE 186
Adshead, Peter 27
Air Defence of Great Britain (ADGB) 41
Airship Hole, King's Wood (Kent) 73
Alfrick Operational Base (Worcs) 99
Allin, William Neil 14
Altcar (Merseyside), Western
   Command Training Area 27
Annesley (Notts) 26
Ashdown Forest 73
Ashley, Lord (Anthony Ashley-
   Cooper) 46, 57, 85, 86, 88–9
assassination *see under* Auxiliary Units
   Operational Branch
Astley, Joan Bright 77–8
Aston House, Stevenage 45, 51, 62, 65,
   81, 106, 107
Atkin, Lord 6
Atkinson, Guy 86, 87
ATS 5, 144, 154, 155, 156–7, 161,
   166, 168
Attwater, Peter 11, 15, 16, 20–4, 25, 26,
   193; *pl. 40*
Auxiliary Coastguards 142
Auxiliary Units Operational Branch
   xv, xvi–xxi, 2, 7, 8, 27, 39, 49,
   52, 71, 75, 76–121, 122–40, 141,
   144, 145, 154, 158, 175, 177,
   179, 181, 188–94, 201, 207, 208,
   209; *pl.41*
   creation 32–5, 66, 76, 176
   anti-invasion role 126, 175, 176, 177
   anti-raiding and reconnaissance
      roles 124–5, 129–30, 161–2

arms/weapons dumps 62, 65, 74, 90,
   91, 92, 93, 115, 139
assassination role (death lists) 4, 37,
   68, 101–4, 111, 112, 131–2, 191
and Davies Plan 66–9
guiding role 57, 89, 90, 91, 184
and HDS (incl. joint working, and
   absorption by) xviii, 12, 19, 25, 44,
   45, 50, 52, 56, 58–66, 80, 81, 84–5,
   87, 88, 89, 91, 93, 97, 102, 116, 119,
   189, 191, 190, 207
hides *see below* Operational Bases
on Home Guard enrolment forms
   19–20, 190–1; *pls 42–43*
Home Guard/LDV joint-working
   with 76, 79, 82–4, 89–91, 125–6,
   129–31
HQs 84, 96–7, 144
ID cards 127
'Key Men' 16, 20, 24, 62, 93,
   144, 161
manuals 4, 25, 62, 84, 106, 107, 108,
   113, 122, 125, 136; *pls 29–31*
Observation Posts 93, 98; *pls 26–27*
Operational Bases (hides) xviii, 28,
   75, 93, 94, 96, 97, 98–103, 99, 115,
   123, 124–5, 131, 139, 161, 179,
   190, 193
Operational Patrols xv, xviii, xx, 4,
   6, 7, 11, 18, 19–20, 26–7, 35, 50,
   51, 63, 64, 65, 74, 76–121 *passim*,
   122–40 *passim*, 144, 159, 164, 168,
   175–87, 188–94, 202; *pls 17, 22, 28,
   42–43*
Scout Sections xx, 74, 81, 93, 97,
   114–16, 117, 120, 121, 127, 135,
   142–3, 159, 162, 191

and SDB 141, 160, 162, 163–6
and SIS 4, 76–7, 80–1, 88, 93, 95, 102, 119, 127
training 62, 75, 113–14, 122–3, 136–7, 181, 182, 185–6
uniforms and insignia 83, 95–6, 126–7, 193; *pl. 17*
village sabotage cells 65, 91–6
weapons and explosives (knives, grenades etc.) 27, 35, 52, 53, 62–3, 83, 88, 93, 97, 98, 100, 104–14, 115–16, 122–6, 131–6, 139; *pls 18–25, 27–8, 32*
wireless and communications (field telephone, wireless sets) 56, 73, 89, 93, 98, 115, 124–5, 144, 190; *pl. 26*
disbandment threats 128, 136, 139, 163, 184, 189
stand-down 131, 139–40, 159; *pl. 44*
see also Special Duties Branch
Auxiliary Units (Signals) 144, 145, 150, 154, 156, 162, 163, 164, 167–8, 209; *pls 17 and 41*
'Aux. Packs' or 'Aux. Units' 52, 65, 122–3

Bachelors Hall *see* Hundon
BBC 56, 88, 100, 166, 180, 202
Balmoral Castle (Scotland) 138–9
Banff (Scotland) 82, 83
Barling, Dr Tony 111, 128
Bartholomew, Cpl Bill 136, 150, 151, 153; *pl. 41*
Battle Patrols *see* XII Corps Observation Unit
Bearsted, Anthony xvii, 40
Bearsted, 2nd Viscount (Walter Samuel) xvii, 16, 38, 46, 56, 58, 59–60, 80, 141, 144, 145, 190, 199; *pl. 4*
Beaumont-Nesbitt, Gen. Frederick 44, 59, 61, 93
Beck, Alex 65
BEETLE 40–1, 162, 173
Beyts, Maj. Bill 84, 104, 114, 119, 123, 124, 129, 144, 154, 182
Bletchley Park 17

Boaz, John 83, 106
Bournemouth, Signals Research Development Establishment 149
Boyle, David ('DB') 10, 11, 13, 20, 24, 25, 45, 52, 190, 194, 199–200; *pl. 15*
Boy Scouts 7, 67, 184
Bracknell (Berks) 13
Brighton Pier 74
British Union of Fascists (BUF) 37, 101
Brooke, Gen. Alan, Viscount Alanbrooke 58, 79, 94, 116, 120, 176
Brown, John 209
Brown, Wilfred 102–3
Brown Book, Section D manual 62, 81, 84, 106–7
Bucknall, Capt. Henry Lloyd 166
Burgess, Guy 206
Burwash Fieldcraft School (Sussex) 184
Butler, Anthony 29

Cadogan, Sir Alexander 44, 61
Calendar 1937, Auxiliary Units 62, 84, 106, 107, 108, 113; *pl. 29*
Calendar 1938, Auxiliary Units 106, 107, 122, 125
Calvert, Capt. Mike 72, 73, 74, 75, 85, 94, 100, 102, 119, 200
Carmichael, Lambert 138
Carr, Comyns 19
Cavendish-Bentinck, Victor 67–8
Caws, Jim 102
Chamberlain, Neville xv, 32, 49
Channel Islands 56, 161
Chaworth-Musters, John and James 26–7
Chidson, Maj. Monty 26
Childe, Frederick Baldwin 147
children and young people 7–8, 16, 27, 28–9; *see also* Attwater, Peter; Monk, Jill
Churchill, Winston 3, 10, 32, 35, 36, 49, 61, 67, 79, 80, 93, 102, 108, 111, 113, 115, 116, 122, 142, 169, 177, 184, 200–1, 207–8
Clater Pitch (Herefs) 101
Coastguard Service xx, 41, 142, 158, 159, 192

coast watching service 12–13, 41, 142, 164–5, 169, 173
Colchester (Essex) 90
Cold War 17, 100, 189, 191, 193–4
Coleshill and Coleshill House, Highworth (Wilts) 83, 88, 96–7, 98, 102, 104, 112, 113, 114, 116, 117, 119, 122, 124, 131, 133, 135–6, 139, 144, 148, 151, 153, 168; *pl.41*
Collings, Capt. John S. 147, 148, 170, 173
Collinson, Capt. Charles 12
commandos 60, 89, 91, 112, 120, 186; *see also* Independent Companies
Communist Party (of Great Britain) 37, 101, 183–4, 210
Cornwall 33, 103, 113, 127, 128
Cornwall-Jones, Lt Col. Arthur T. 66, 67
Countryman's Diary 1939 25, 106, 125, 136; *pls 30–1*
Cowgill, Felix 19–20
Cramb, Mr 16
Crick, Alan John 86
Croft, Andrew 85, 86, 119
Cronk, Capt., leaflet 4
Culleton, Barbara 151
Curling, Brig. Gen. Bryan 90–1

'DB's organisation' *see* Boyle, David; Section VII
D-Day 37, 130, 137, 160, 161, 167–8
'D Scheme' ('Scheme D'), SIS, in Europe 3, 5, 38, 44, 45, 48, 60, 67, 77, 102, 203, 205; *see also* Norway
Dabbs, Sgt Ron 150, 151; *pl. 41*
Dalton, Hugh 3, 35, 60, 61, 66, 68, 164, 189
Dansey, Claude 10, 11–12, 25, 29, 43, 45, 60, 190, 194, 201, 207, 209; *pl. 2*
Davies, Capt. Tommy, and Davis Plan (1940) 7, 29, 66–9, 143
Delamere, Capt. Lord 123
Delmer, Sefton 24
Devereux, Geoff 111, 128; *pl. 43*
Deverill, Eric 24, 26–7
Dill, Gen. Sir John 79
Directive 16, German 195–8

Directorate of Military Intelligence (DMI) 31, 34, 38–9, 60, 61, 71, 77, 116, 163, 164, 183
D/M, D/MIR Branch 77, *and see* MI(R)
Dolphin, Capt. John 31, 38, 45, 54, 57, 201
Donnington-on-Bain (Lincs) 158
Douglas, Col. Frank W.R. 88, 129, 137, 138, 139, 143, 159, 165, 168, 194; *pl. 13*
Droitwich (Worcs) 75
Drummond, Dr 16, 24–5
Dublin 12, 199
Dunkirk, and impact of xvi, 31–41, 57, 70, 170

Eastbourne (Sussex), Star Brewery 14, 15, 26; *pl. 39*
Eden, Anthony 6–7, 17, 61, 68
Edmundson, Stuart xx, 25, 65, 86, 87, 95
Eire 12–13, 19, 40, 120, 209
Electra House 55, 61
Ellery, Richard 128
Emma (SDB agent) 25, 165–6

Fairweather, J.M. 169, 170
false memory syndrome xiii, xix, xx, 95, 112, 191
Faroe Islands 72
Farrer, Michael J. 147–8
Fenwick, Ian 85, 86
Field, Norman 75, 85, 100, 124
Field Security Section (FSS), Intelligence Corps 37, 148, 164, 165, 166, 179; *pl. 38*
fifth columnists 36–7, 43, 54, 101–2, 103, 164, 165, 186
Findlater-Stewart, Sir Samuel 68
Fingland, Edward Robert Ramage 148
Fleming, Capt. Peter xix, xx, 31, 38, 39, 40, 70–5, 80, 85, 86, 94, 97, 100, 102, 107, 114, 117, 119, 127, 150, 178, 191, 193, 202; *pl. 7*
Fleming, Richard 71, 72
Forbes, Maj. Peter 85, 98, 123, 162, 165
Ford, Frank 20–1

francs-tireurs ('free-shooters') 1–2, 3–4, 5, 6, 9, 10, 49, 60, 61, 91, 175, 190, 192; *pls* 16–17
Franklyn, Gen. Sir Harold 37, 129, 139, 159, 165
Fraser, Robert 46, 47, 145, 147, 166
Fraser, Maj. Simon, Lord Lovat 72
Fraser, William 79
Frythe, The (Herts) 201

G–2 *see* Irish Intelligence Service
Gambier-Parry, Brig. Richard 11, 13, 17–19, 24, 47, 190, 202–3
'Garbo' 129
Garth, The, Bilting (Kent) 73, 74
GHQ Liaison Regiment *and* GHQ Reconnaissance Unit *see* Phantom Unit
Gibraltar 13, 203
'Gladios' 193
Glanusk, Col., the Lord 123–4, 129, 137, 156, 164
Goodwin (Harold) & Company Ltd, Warley (Worcs) 186–7
Gort, Lord 44
Grand, Col. Laurence D. xv, xvi, 42–3, 181, 203–4, 205, 206, 207; *pl.* 3
 aliases used by (incl. 'Mr Graham') 65, 203
 Section D and HDS of SIS 3, 12, 31, 38, 40, 41, 42–53, 56–7, 59–66, 77–8, 102, 143, 181, 189, 194, 201, 203–4, 209
 ISPB meeting 35, 38, 39
 'D Scheme' in Europe devised by 18, 44, 48, 203
 SOE deputy 40, 66
 dismissal 20, 30, 66, 204
Gray, Maj. 178
Gregson-Ellis, Gen. 185
GS(R) (later D/M Branch; MI(R)) 77, 205, 207
Gubbins, Col. Colin xvii–xviii, xix, 2, 24, 34, 48, 204; *pl.* 10
 manuals (booklets) by 40, 79, 80, 93, 204
 in MI(R) 43, 60, 62, 79, 87, 204

Independent Companies (in Norway) 79, 84, 204
Auxiliary Units/SDB 43, 47, 52, 58–9, 75, 79–84, 85, 87, 89–98, 104–21 *passim*, 139, 141–6, 149, 158, 169, 173, 189, 190, 191, 193, 204
 in SOE 24, 119, 149, 194, 204–5
'Guerrilla Warfare Committee' 35
Gwynne, John 85, 86

Halesowen Home Guard 4
Halifax, E.F.L. Wood, Lord 32, 44, 61
Hall, Henry 73
Hall, Maj. Robert 138–9
Hall, Samuel 75
Hamilton-Hill, Donald 86, 114
Hancock, Maj. Malcolm 136, 137
Handscombe, Don 101
Hankey, Lord 9, 17–18, 19, 29, 34, 35, 36, 39, 43, 59, 61, 68, 78, 205
Hannington Hall (Wilts) 64, 97, 144, 154
Harker, Jasper 19
Harrietsham (Kent) 161
Harston, W.W. 86
Hartwright, John 136
Hay, Kenneth Masters 16
HDS *see* Home Defence Scheme
Hellingly Patrol, Lower Dicker (Sussex) 103
Henderson, Capt. the Hon. Michael T. 84, 90, 96, 119, 123
Herefordshire 65, 76, 88, 100, 115, 116, 128, 136, 137, 138, 166, 209; *pl.* 44
Higgins, Tom 150; *pl.* 41
Highworth (Wilts) 136; *and see* Coleshill
Hill, George 46
Hills, Capt. John 149–50, 151, 154, 159
Hogg, Dr Hector 14, 16
Holdsworth, Gerald 44–5, 46
Holland, Lt Col. Jo 2, 38–9, 43, 61, 66, 67, 72, 77–9, 80, 81, 89, 189, 192, 193, 194, 200, 203, 204, 205–6; *pl.* 5
Holland-Martin, Christopher 46, 48, 80
Holland-Martin, Thurstan 48

Hollis, Col. L.C. 7, 67–8
Holman, Dr 148
Home Defence Scheme (HDS) (*aka* Regional D Scheme of Section D), SIS xv–xviii, xx–xxi, 18, 23, 42–69, 78, 80, 169, 177, 188, 189, 190, 192, 193, 199, 201, 203, 205, 206, 209
   creation, and mobilisation 6–7, 10, 11, 31–2, 34, 35, 38–40, 42, 44–5, 190
   Auxiliary Units, joint working with and absorption of HDS *see under* Auxiliary Units Operational Branch
   and Home Guard 25, 94–5
   ISPB meeting 38–9, 40, 41, 45, 56
   'key men' 50, 62, 64, 93, 128
   opposition to 57–66, 143
   and Osterley Training School 181–2
   passive resistance 55–6
   Project D/Y 44
   recruitment 7, 15–16, 23, 25, 45, 48, 50–2, 64, 93
   sabotage 41, 52–5, 57, 63, 68, 186
   and SDB 141–6, 147
   Section VII, absorption of HDS 26, 189
   'Standfast Club' 57
   weapons, and dumps of arms and explosives 33, 39, 45, 46, 47, 49, 51–2, 53–5, 60, 61, 65, 107, 111, 112, 131, 143; *pls 18–19*
   wireless 18, 47, 56, 142, 146
   dismantled (dispersal) xvi, 12, 19, 68, 143
   see also Grand, Laurence
Home Defence Units (wireless stations) 159
Home Guard (formerly LDV) xv, xvii, xix, xx, 2, 4, 10–11, 14, 41, 43, 63, 124–33, 137, 139, 175–87, 188–94, 201, 210; *pls 42–4, 46*
   creation (LDV), and role 6, 7, 31–4, 35, 36, 48, 57, 58, 61, 68, 175–8
   LDV patrols, and Fleming 31, 38, 71, 74, 178
   harrying role (LDV/HG) 33–4, 35, 36, 38, 41, 57–8, 61, 68, 71, 76, 114, 175–8, 181, 202; *pl. 8*

1st American (Motorised) Squadron 35, 177
Auxiliary Units 76–121, *and see* Home Guard/LDV *and* Operational Patrols *under* Auxiliary Units Operational Branch
boy scouts used as messengers 7
commando units 126, 127, 130, 186, 189
enrolment forms and Part II Orders 19–20, 81, 82, 83–4, 102, 126, 128, 190–1; *pls 42–43*
guides and guiding role 57, 90, 184
hides 72, 179, 202
industrial sabotage teams xvii, 186–7
Operational Patrols 96–104, *see also under* Auxiliary Units Operational Branch
petrol supplies 186, 187, 193
sabotage 57–8, 90
tank-hunting 35, 177, 180, 181, 182, 184; *pl. 45*
training 113–14, 178, 179–84; *pls 45–46*
with XII Corps 70, 72, 74, 178
uniforms and insignia 83, 95–6, 127, 179; *pl. 17*
weapons, ammunition and explosives 27, 36, 53, 97, 104–13, 124, 125, 126, 132–3, 176, 177, 178, 182, 186, 179, 184; *pl. 25, pl. 46*
wireless sets and communications 41, 126, 178
women 5
stand-down 139
Home Guard Training School *see* Osterley Park
Home Hints, Section D manual 47, 113
Hopcraft, Allan 179
Hope, Capt. W.E. 46
Hopkinson, Lt Col. 35, 105, 121, 169–71; *see also* Phantom Unit
Horabin, Tom, MP 36
Hornby, Bob 47
Hornsea (Yorks) 54
Hubbard, Edward 128

Hundon (Suffolk), Bachelors Hall 150, 152, 153
Hulton, Edward 36, 180, 181, 183

Independent Companies 35, 39, 40, 46, 57, 70, 71, 79, 81, 89, 90, 91, 96, 97, 112, 192, 204
Ingrams, Arthur Douglas 128
IN/OUT Stations *see under* Special Duties Branch
Intelligence Corps 85, 88, 146, 164
internal security *see* MI5; Secret Intelligence Service; Section VII; Special Duties Branch
Inter-Services Project Board (ISPB) 35, 37–41, 45, 48, 50, 56, 60, 70, 76, 90
Inter-Services Research Board 153, *and see* Special Operations Executive
IRA 2, 4, 13, 25, 37, 43, 56, 77, 80, 199, 205
Ireland 2, 4, 12–13, 31, 52, 67, 68, 76, 172, 199, 204, 205
Irish Intelligence Service (G–2) 12, 13
Ironside, Gen. Edmund xv, 6, 32–3, 35, 48–9, 61, 68, 76, 78, 79, 142, 169, 176, 192, 204; *pl. 7*
Isle of Wight 24–5, 48, 85, 102, 130, 136, 137–8, 152, 195
Ismay, Gen. 'Pug' 7, 10, 35, 58–9, 67, 68, 208

Jackson, Capt. John 170
Jacob Patrol, Herefs Auxiliary Units 100–1, 102
Jebb, Gladwyn 61, 149
Jehu (Alfrick) Patrol, Worcs Auxiliary Units 99, 102, 111
Jersey, Lord 180
Johnson, Maj. Kenneth W. 147, 166
Jones, Maj., SDB distribution map 14, 16, 160, 166; *pl. 33*
Jones, Maj. Rupert 145
Joshua Patrol, Herefs Auxiliary Units 136
Judson, Stan 154, 161, 164

Kenyon, Lionel 6
Kindred, Herman 95

King-Hall, Stephen 35, 36
Kirke, Gen. Walter 175–6, 178
Kirkness, Maj. 151
Knight, Maxwell 10

Langdon-Davies, John 5, 90, 105, 109, 179, 184
Langley, Commander 43
Lawrence, Capt. William 21, 23
Levy, 'Yank' 4, 109, 179, 180, 181, 182, 184
Lewer, Stanley 149; *pl. 36*
Lewis, Prof. Wilfrid 149, 150
Liddell, Guy (Liddell Diary) 13, 15, 18, 19, 20, 24, 101, 129, 152, 167, 183, 206
Lilburn, Wilf 47
Lloyd, Lord 61
Local Defence Volunteers (LDV) *see* Home Guard
Lochailort Commando Training School, Scotland 39, 70, 72, 73, 200, 202
Lockley, Irene 26
London 33, 172
   Baker Street xvii, 88
   54 Broadway 9
   Bush House 12, 55, 201
   St James's Park 17, 171–2
   sewage system 186
   7 Whitehall Place 84, 96
Lovat Scouts 71–4, 102, 114
Lynch, Gerald Roche 29

Macdougall, Maj. Gen. Ian 58–9, 68
Mackie, John 150
Mackenzie, Norman 182
MacLeod, A. Gordon 57–8, 94-5
McNab, Jimmy 150, 153
Macpherson, Lt 71
Major, Col. Cyril 'Bill' 88, 98, 117, 119–20, 123, 144, 154, 163, 164, 185, 192; *pl. 11*
Malvern (Worcs) 83, 126, 166; *pls 42–43*
Marshall-Cornwall, Gen. 10
Maryam-Green, Kenneth 146
Maryan, Harold 103
Mason, Charles (Charlie) 102, 111

Maschwitz, Eric 46, 51
Matlock (Derbys) 14, 15, 16, 21–4, 25, 27, 28, 29, 193; *pl. 40*
Maude, John 101
Maxwell, Capt. Eustace 54, 62, 86, 114, 182
Mellor (Cheshire), Thompson found 27
Melville, Col. 71–2
Menzies, Stewart 9, 10, 11, 15, 17, 42, 43, 46, 47, 49, 59, 61, 149, 152, 193, 203–4, 205, 206–7, 208; *pl. 1*
Mew, Leonard 48
MI5 9, 10, 36–7, 38, 45, 49, 54, 101–2, 129, 143, 152, 199, 201, 206
  internal security 37, 163, 164–5, 166, 192
  and Osterley Training School 36, 180, 182, 183–5
  Section B.26 19, 24, 26
  and Section VII, SIS 18–20, 22–4, 25, 37
MI6 *see* Secret Intelligence Service (SIS)
Millard, Bob 105, 110, 131, 132, 133–4
Millie, Jack 150; *pl. 41*
Milner, Professor C.J. 149, 150, 209
Ministry of Defence 67, 93
Ministry of Economic Warfare 60, 66, 203
Ministry of Information (MOI) 26, 60
MI(R) (Military Intelligence (Research)), of the War Office xvi, xviii, 3, 17, 24, 25, 33–4, 38, 39–40, 43, 60, 61, 67, 71, 77–80, 85, 90, 104, 107, 108, 113, 143, 188, 202, 203, 204, 205
  weapons/explosives developed by 54, 105, 107, 108; *pl. 32*
  see also Independent Companies
Monck-Mason, Adrian 151
Monk (née Holman), Jill 148, 193
Monmouthshire 64, 155, 166, 209
Montague, Maj. the Hon. Lionel 46, 80
Montgomery, Gen. 74, 75
Montrose 16, 160
Morgan-Jones, Geoffrey 65, 100
Morton, Desmond 10, 61
Morton-Evans, Maj. 152

Nelson, Sir Frank 66, 68
newspapers (underground) 55, 56
Newton, 'Spuggy' 47, 73; *pl. 9*
Niven, David 171–2, 173
Norton Barracks (Worcs) 28, 75, 96
Norway xvi, 3, 38, 39, 44, 46, 53, 54, 63, 71, 79, 81, 106, 108, 112, 121, 148, 152, 204, 207, 208
Nussen, Eric 27

Observer Corps xx, 41, 142, 146, 155, 169, 173, 192
Ogilvy, Francis 46
Operation Barbarossa 120
Operation Fortitude 167, 208
Operation Overlord 129
Operation Sealion 11, 116, 196
Operation Tracer 13, 203
Operational Bases (OB) and Operational Patrols *see under* Auxiliary Units Operational Branch
Orwell, George 7
Osterley Park Home Guard Training School, Hounslow xvii, 2, 35, 36, 68, 70–1, 113, 114, 176, 177, 178, 179–84, 190, 192, 208, 210; *pls 45–46*
Oxenden, Nigel xviii, 62, 81, 86, 87, 96, 98, 101, 106, 107, 109, 111, 112, 115, 119, 122–3, 124, 125, 131, 132, 135, 142, 159, 164, 207

Paget, Gen. 58, 91, 94–5, 172
Palestine 2, 35, 36, 43, 67, 179, 184
Parnell, Les 150, 153; *pl.41*
Pearce, Charles 4
Pennell, Ursula 155
Penrose, Roland 180
Peterson, Alex 56
Petherick, Maj. Maurice 143, 144, 154, 163, 165, 207; *pl. 12*
petrol supplies 186, 187
Phantom Unit (GHQ Reconnaissance Unit; later GHQ Liaison Regiment) xv, xx–xxi, 17, 18, 35, 75, 105, 112, 121, 142, 145, 147, 148, 155, 159, 169–74, 192; *pl.17*
Philby, Kim 20, 42, 206

Phillips, George and Mollie 146
Pidgeon, Geoffrey 15
Playle, Robert Hugh 146
Pluto Pipeline 137
Pollard, Hugh 29
Pownall, Gen. Henry 43, 44, 68
Price, Peter 96, 102

Quayle, Anthony 123–4

Radio Security Service (RSS) 13, 24, 152, 202
radio stations 55–6, 73
Rainham (Kent) 51
Rawson, Maj. Gen. 18
Reconnaissance Corps 159, 171
Regional [Civil] Commissioners 40, 47, 49, 50, 51
Regional D Scheme *see* Home Defence Scheme
Richie, Brig. 113
Riley, Rupert St George 46, 147
Robertson, Col. T.A. 167
Rodgers, Joseph and William 109; *pls 18 and 20*
Rodulfo, Algernon 'Monty' 84
Rolvenden (Kent) 103
Royal Signals 151, 153, 154, 155, 156–7, 169, 171
Russell, Sgt Roy 150, 151, 167

Samson Patrol, Auxiliary Units, Broadheath (Worcs) 83, 96, 106, 111, 113, 128
Sandford, Capt. Christopher 128
Sandys, Duncan 93, 94, 207–8
SAS (Special Air Service) 39, 85, 100, 115, 129, 174, 189–90, 191, 193, 194, 200
Saunders, Douglas 46, 48, 55–6, 85, 86, 91
Schröter, Dr Edward 149, 153
Scout Sections *see under* Auxiliary Units Operational Branch; XII Corps Observation Unit
SCU *see* Special Communications Unit, of SIS

SDB *see* Special Duties Branch
Secret Intelligence Service (SIS) (*aka* MI6) xv–xvii, xxi, 5–8, 20, 35, 41, 60, 165, 188–9, 191, 192, 193, 194, 199–209
  and Auxiliary Units 4, 76–7, 80–1, 88, 93, 95, 102, 119, 127
  'Casuals' (agents) 10, 12, 209
  Communications section 171
  Davies Plan 68–9
  in Eire 12–13, 19
  francs-tireurs (civilians) 6, 190; *pls 16–17*
  and HDS 42–9, 54–5, 56–7, 58–66, 111
  internal security (covert spying) 163–4, 165–6
  ISPB meeting 38–9, 40
  Plan Y 13
  and SDB 141, 142, 143–5, 154, 163, 165, 166, 190
  Section VII and 'X Branch' 9–30 *passim*
  training 75
  'watcher' service 41
  weapons, explosives 75, 111
  wireless sets and stations 11, 12–17, 21–4, 40–1, 47, 73, 152, 172, 173, 202; *pl. 37*
  women 5
  young people 7–8
  see also Home Defence Scheme; Section D; Section VII; Section VIII; Special Communications Unit (SCU); Special Liaison Unit; 'X Branch'
Section D, sabotage section of SIS (*aka* Section IX) xv, xvi–xix, 5, 6–7, 9–10, 12, 34, 77, 146, 164, 166, 188, 189, 190, 192, 193, 199–209 *passim*
  creation 3, 42–4
  arms/weapons dumps 27–8, 46, 65, 78
  and Auxiliary Units 77–8, 80–1, 85, 90, 104–9, 117
  Brown Book training manual 62, 106–7

Home Hints manual 47, 113
ISPB meeting 38–40, 45
recruiting 146
supply base 65
women 5
disbandment 12
absorbed into SOE 61, 65, 66
see also D Scheme; Grand, Laurence;
 Home Defence Scheme
Section V of SIS (counter-espionage)
 11, 18
Section VII of SIS (resistance/
 intelligence, longer-term) xvi–
 xvii, xix, xx, 5, 9–30, 33, 38, 40,
 41, 44, 45, 51, 60, 63, 64, 66, 78, 88,
 127, 141, 144, 145, 163, 166, 188,
 190, 193, 194, 200, 201, 206, 209
 HDS absorbed by 26, 189
 internal security role 24, 37,
  166, 192
 'Key Men' 20
 Plan 333 trial 15, 19
 sabotage *see* 'X Branch'
 wireless (operators, sets) 5, 12–17,
  18, 21–4, 22, 26–7, 40, 64, 148, 151,
  159, 192; *pls 37, 39, 40*
Section VIII of SIS (wireless
 communications) 11, 73, 149,
 202, 208
Section IX of SIS *see* Section D
Severn Stoke (Worcs) 166
Sheridan, Leslie 56
Signals Research Development
 Establishment, Bournemouth 149
Sinclair, Admiral Hugh xv, 3, 9, 11, 12,
 42, 43, 44, 200, 201, 203, 206, 208
SIS (*aka* MI6) *see* Secret Intelligence
 Service
Slater, Hugh 71, 75, 114, 180,
 183–5, 208
SLU *see* Special Liaison Unit, SIS
Sluman, Revd 64
Soames, Frank 125
South Cave Patrol (Yorks) 111
Special Branch 10, 138, 139
Special Communications Unit (SCU),
 of SIS 15, 17–18, 19, 39, 73, 154,
 159, 171, 173; *pl. 41*

Special Duties Branch (SDB), of the
 Auxiliary Units xii–xiii, xiv, xvi,
 xviii, xx, xxi, 12, 29, 41, 80, 116,
 117, 119–21, 124, 127, 137, 160–8,
 169, 190, 192, 199, 207, 209
 creation 84, 143, 145
 anti-invasion reporting (1940) 41,
  119, 141–59
 anti-raiding role (1942–4) 161–8
 couriers ('cut-outs'), 'runners' and
  dead-letter drops xx, 5, 18, 21, 23,
  57, 141, 146, 148, 155, 163, 166,
  168, 193
 D-Day roles 37, 161–2, 165
 D-Day deception planning 151–2,
  160, 167–8
 Defence Medals, not awarded 20,
  144–5, 163, 168
 distribution map, by Jones (1944) 14,
  16, 160, 166; *pl. 33*
 and HDS (HDO) 47, 141–6, 149,
  160, 166
 hides underground 134, 192
 HQs 64, 97, 144
 IN/OUT Stations 5, 16, 18, 21, 73,
  123, 125, 144, 148, 150–68 *passim*
 internal security role xxi, 37, 119,
  141, 160, 163–6, 191, 192; *pl. 38*
 Isle of Wight cell 24–5
 'key men' 16, 20, 64, 155, 161
 observers 161, 163, 164–5,
  169, 184
 parachute raids/landings 125,
  145, 159
 recruitment 16
 and SIS 141, 142, 143–5, 154, 163,
  165, 166, 190
 SUB-OUT Stations 153, 155,
  161, 162
 wireless network (operators, sets,
  field telephone) 14–15, 16, 18,
  19, 41, 47, 73, 96, 103, 141, 142,
  148–59, 160–2, 163, 165, 166,
  167–8, 173, 192, 202; *pls 34–36*
 women 5
 Zero Stations 21, 158, 161, 162
 Stand-down letter xviii, 139, 159
 disbandment 154

Special Liaison Unit (SLU), of SIS 17, 18
Special Night Squads 2
Special Operations Executive (SOE) xvii–xviii, 10, 17, 40, 61, 66, 68–9, 78, 79, 81, 85, 86, 88, 104, 189, 194, 199, 201–5, 207, 209
  creation 3, 35, 164
  Station IX 201
  Station XII 87
  weapons 109, 112, 122, 131, 132, 133, 134, 135; *pl.21*
  wireless sets/communications 149, 151; *pl. 37*
Spencer, George 153
Spens, William 49
'Standfast Club', HDS 67
Star Brewery *see* Eastbourne
Station X 202
Stevens, Dr Thomas Russell 16
Stobswood (Northumberland) 103
Stokes, Charles 128
Straton, Dr Arthur 16, 24; *pl. 6*
SUB-OUT Stations *see* Special Duties Branch
Summerskill, Edith 4
Sweet-Escott, Bickham 25–6, 54
Swinton, Lord 19
Syderstone (Norfolk) 83

Tallents, Phillip 106
Temple, Beatrice 83, 166
Territorial Army Associations (TAAs) 82, 83, 91, 126–7, 137
Thomas, John 136
Thorne, Gen. Andrew 'Bulgy' xv, xvi, 32, 34, 39–40, 70–2, 74–5, 93, 97, 114, 121, 138, 178, 182–3, 185, 189, 208; *pl. 8*
Todd, John 87–8, 208–9; *pl. 14*
  alias 64
  SIS officer 28, 55, 88, 179, 208
  joint Operational and Special Duties IO 80–1, 85, 86, 87–8, 100, 102, 127, 128, 147, 166, 209
  Section D/HDS 46, 48, 64, 65, 88, 128, 209

SOE 55, 88, 209
Toon, Albert 25, 27–8, 64
Toplis, Joe 21
Torrance, Hamish 85, 86, 119
TRDs *see under* wireless sets
Tyddesley Woods (Worcs) 96

'Ultra' 202, 206
Upton upon Severn (Worcs) 65, 166
USA xvi, 11, 32, 53, 102, 120, 177
  weapons supplied by 3, 36, 97, 110–13, 132, 176; *pl.21*

Van Moppes, Edmund and Lewis 84, 103, 119–20; *pls 42–43*
Vater, George 64, 88, 155
Vernon, Wilfred 180, 183
Vivian, Valentine 11, 12–13, 19, 20, 25, 166, 190, 209
Volunteer Training Corps (VTC) 2, 175–6

Walk, Maj. G.E. 185
Walker, Capt. 34–5, 36
Warley (Worcs) 186–7
Ward, Ken (later Capt.) xx, 149, 150, 151, 153, 158, 162, 209
Warley Barracks, Brentwood 90
Wartling (Sussex) 14
Watkins, Jeffrey 54
Watson, Samuel 48
Welch, Ken 128
Welwyn (Herts), Frythe 201
Whaddon, Whaddon Hall 15, 17, 18, 154, 202
Wheatley Hill (Co. Durham) 99
White, Tom 'Chalkie' 73
White Waltham (Kent) 4
Whitford, Lt Dick 179, 181
Wickham-Boynton, Capt. Marcus 123, 124
Wilkinson, Maj. Peter 25, 32, 34, 48, 49, 54–5, 60, 62, 75, 78, 80, 81, 82–3, 84, 85, 94, 97–8, 101, 106, 113, 114, 116–17, 119, 120, 143, 182, 191, 193
Wilmington 14

Wilmott, Willie, ATS secretary 88
Wingate, Orde 2, 35–6, 189, 200
Wintringham, Tom xvii, 4, 34, 35–6, 43, 53, 68, 70, 105, 176, 177, 178–85, 192, 194, 208, 210; *pl. 45*
wireless cars 47, 55, 56, 73, 145, 146; *pl. 10*
wireless sets (types) 12, 13–15, 16, 17, 40–1, 56; *pl. 39*
  Mk II (1939) 15
  Mk III and Mk V 13, 14–15, 17, 73; *pl. 41*
  Mk VII paraset ('briefcase' sets), SIS 14–15, 17; *pl. 37*
  Murphy sets 41, 162; *pl. 34*
  No.9 and No.11 (Phantom) 170, 171, 172
  No.22 set 15, 21
  Savage 149–50
  TRD/Savage 15, 149–52, 153, 154, 155–6, 159, 160, 162, 166, 167, 170, 191, 192, 209; *pls 35 and 41*
  TRF and TRM 153
  WS17 124–5, 149, 150, 153–4, 158, 162, 167; *pl. 36*
Wolverton Hall (Worcs) 65, 103, 120, 166
women 4–5
Women's Home Defence Corps 4
Wood Norton (Worcs) 88, 100, 166
Woodhouse (Leics) 179
Woodward, G. 128
Woolwich Arsenal 105
Worcester (Worcs) 28, 29, 75, 83
Worcestershire 28, 48, 65, 75, 76, 81–2, 83, 84, 88, 94, 96, 99, 100, 102, 103, 106, 111, 112, 115, 116, 119–20, 128, 137, 166, 186–7, 194, 209; *see also* Malvern; Samson Patrol
Wren, Walter 46, 147
Wrightson, Capt. Sir John 171, 172
WS17 *see under* wireless sets

'X Branch', Section VII of SIS (sabotage) 10, 25–30
XII Corps Observation Unit xvi, xix, xx, 32, 33, 34, 39–40, 51, 70–5, 84, 97, 99, 109, 114, 117, 178, 189, 193, 200, 202, 208; *pl. 17*
  Battle Patrols 73–4, 93, 114, 182, 189
  hides 72–3, 89, 179
  wireless 13, 40, 73, 74

Y Service (Signals Interception Service) 149, 150, 179, 209

Z Organisation, SIS 11–12, 29, 201, 208
Zero Stations, SDB 21, 158, 161, 162; *see also* Matlock